Employment Department Group
Office of Population Censuses an

Standard Occupational Classification

Volume 2

First edition February 1990

Coding Index

LONDON : HMSO

First published 1990

ISBN 0 11 691285 5

British Library Cataloguing in Publication Data
Standard occupational classification.
Vol. 2, Coding index
1. Great Britain. Occupations
331.7′00941

ACKNOWLEDGEMENT

The Government Statistical Service gratefully acknowledges the major work undertaken by the Department of Applied Economics at the University of Cambridge, under the direction of Dr Kenneth Prandy; in the development and compilation of this coding index.

CONTENTS

Standard Occupational Classification Volume 2

INTRODUCTION

The Standard Occupational Classification Manual (SOC)

Volume 1 outlines the principles and concepts of the classification, approaches certain technical problems and shows the structure with descriptions of the unit groups.

Volume 2 consists of a detailed alphabetical index of job titles preceded by a description of the index and notes on coding occupations.

Volume 3 covers topics related to occupation coding including the derivation of socio-economic classifications from occupation and employment status information.

UPDATING OF SOC

Changes occur in work organisation as a result of technological developments, use of new materials, improved methods of production or delivery of services etc. New occupations arise either because tasks are enlarged, contracted or combined within and between existing occupations or because new, different tasks are introduced into the organisation of work. Such new occupations may become sufficiently important to warrant their recognition and inclusion in the classification. Additionally, new index entries for volume 2 may be required.

The Occupation Information Unit, which has been set up within the Office of Population Censuses and Surveys to support SOC, would welcome information on such changes. This will be taken into account in the periodical updating of SOC.

Please contact,

Occupation Information Unit,
Office of Population, Censuses and Surveys,
Segensworth Road,
Titchfield,
Fareham,
Hants
PO15 5RR

Telephone Titchfield (0329) 42511

CODING INDEX

Description of the index

General. Occupation titles are arranged in this index under the word most nearly describing the operation performed. These are called indexing words,

e.g. 'glass blower' is indexed under 'Blower'
'x-ray operator' is indexed under 'Operator'

For this purpose words such as 'assistant' and 'officer' are regarded as indexing words but the following terms are not:

Boy	Girl	Hand	Lad	Man
Operative	Woman	Workman	Worker	

e.g. 'office boy' is indexed under 'Office' but
'clerical officer' is indexed under 'Officer'

The index is arranged in alphabetical order of complete words. Words joined by a hyphen are treated as single words. Words joined by 'and' are indexed immediately following the single words. Occupational titles ending in any of the terms listed above are regarded for indexing purposes as two words, e.g. 'bagman' is indexed as though it were 'bag man' and therefore appears before 'bagger' in the index.
Compound words, such as 'postmaster', the final word of which may be used as an occupation title, are indexed under the final word, e.g. Master; post, Keeper; book. Some very common terms have also been indexed in their natural order.
The feminine form of an occupation title is not indexed unless it is very common or its coding differs from that of the masculine equivalent thus 'abbot' is indexed but not 'abbess'.
The two letters 'M' and 'F' appear in the index against code numbers. These relate to employment status coding. This is needed for the derivation of the social classifications which will be explained in volume 3.

Qualifying terms

(a) The indexing word is very rarely sufficient in itself to enable the occupation title to be correctly coded.
Frequently a term is made specific by the addition of a qualifying term, e.g. 'Brass turner', the indexing word 'turner' is qualified by 'brass' and then becomes codable. These qualifying terms are separated from the indexing word by a semi-colon and indented beneath it. The qualifying terms may also be used to code the indexing word that is further qualified, unless the further qualifying term is itself indexed. For example, the index entry

'Controller;
depot ... ... 142'

could be used to code 'Freight depot controller'.
The qualifying terms are indexed in reverse word order. However an occupation title may be qualified by a clause following the indexing word, for example, 'Clerk in Holy Orders'. These terms are indexed at the end of the list of qualifying terms. As these terms are usually very specific, special care is necessary in coding any such terms not actually in the index.

(b) An occupation title may depend for its coding on the branch of industry in which the person is employed. The industrial qualifiers (which relate to the activity actually engaged in and not that of the establishment as a whole) appear in the index in italics. The title so qualified is followed by a dash, or alternatively, a single qualifier may appear in brackets. These entries may be used to code occupation titles where the industry is part of the title, may be inferred from it or is provided in answer to a separate question, unless an index entry as described in (a) or (c) is relevant, e.g. the index entry 'Furnaceman-*metal trades*' can be used to code 'furnaceman'-industry 'steelworks', 'blast furnace furnaceman' or 'steel furnaceman'.

(c) In some cases the qualifier used for coding purposes is more easily stated in terms of materials worked on or dealt in, or the machinery used, or process involved and this enables a number of specific terms to be summarised in a more general word. This type of qualification appears in brackets or immediately preceding the industrial qualifiers, e.g. 'Turner-metal' (which would apply to titles 'aluminium turner' or 'lead turner'), or in a limited number of cases indented below an industrial qualifier, e.g. 'Machinist-*hosiery mfr.*-sewing'.
The general word qualifiers are also used in a few cases to differentiate coding depending on the persons professional qualifications, for an example see index entry for 'Accountant-'.

(d) Where a code number appears against an indexing word it is called a default code and that code applies to all occupation titles which include the indexing word unless they are listed specifically, generally or industrially as exceptions. An example is 'Smith;' which is used to code blacksmith or hammersmith because the words black and hammer are not listed as qualifying terms. The default codes more often appear against the entries where the indexing word is followed by a dash, see index entries for 'Loader'. Where none of the qualifying terms indented beneath 'Loader;' appear before loader in the title and none of the industry qualifiers indented beneath 'Loader-' apply then the default code on the 'Loader-' line is used.

(e) Occupation titles qualified by terms such as 'assistant', 'head', 'deputy', 'apprentice' are normally coded as though these words were not present. If, however, the coding is altered by these qualifiers the complete title is indexed.

(f) The letters n.o.s. stand for 'not otherwise specified'. When used in the index they mean that the particular index entry relates to that precise occupation title without further qualifying terms.

Industrial qualifiers. It must be noted that it is the activity in which the person is actually engaged and not that of the establishment as a whole (where this can be separately identified) which is the determining factor. Thus a person in the cardboard box making department of a food factory must be referred in the index to 'cardboard box manufacture' and not 'food products manufacture' The abbreviation 'mfr.' is used to cover manufacture, manufacturing, making, building and repairing. The following Industrial terms are used in a special sense:

Term	**Standard Industrial Classification 1980 Activity Heading**
Manufacturing	2210-2247,2410-4959
Metal trades	2210-2247,3111-3740
Clothing mfr.	4531-4536,4539
Ceramics mfr.	2410,2481,2489
Paper goods mfr.	4721-4728
Engineering	3204-3740
Food products mfr.	4115,4121-4180,4213,4221-4239
Glass mfr.	2471-2479 and the grinding of lenses and prisms from 3731-3733
Flour confectionery mfr.	4196,4197
Sugar confectionery mfr.	4214
Mine, not coal	1300,2100,2310-2396

Shipping means service afloat other than in barges, small boats, fishing vessels, launches and dredgers.

Fishing means service afloat in a vessel actually engaged in fishing, not a factory ship or tender.

Boat, barge means service afloat in a boat, barge, launch, dredger or hopper and excludes service in a fishing vessel.

Notes on coding occupations

A. General

Use of the index. Occupation titles, unless consisting of an indexing word only, are coded by first referring to the list of specific terms and then using the generalised or industrially qualified entries in the sense indicated in sub-paragraphs (b) and (c) on pages vii and ix.

Armed forces. The more usual terms for forces personnel have been included. Officers are coded 150 or 151, other ranks to 600 or 601. UK armed forces are coded 150 and 600, those belonging to foreign and Commonwealth countries to 151 and 601.

Diplomatic personnel. Members of foreign or Commonwealth diplomatic staffs are coded 100.

Coal miners. The correct coding of many occupation titles in the coal mining industry is dependent on whether the person is a face-trained coal miner. If sufficient information is given the occupation is coded according to the index; if the occupation title is vague but there is a statement indicating working at the coal face the occupation is coded to 597. Where this cannot be determined code 910 is used.

Foreman

(a) The following terms, with certain listed exceptions, may be regarded as synonymous with 'Foreman':

Boss	Gaffer	Overlooker
Charge hand	Ganger	Overseer
Charge man	Headman	Supervisor

and also assistant foreman, assistant supervisor, etc.

(b) No index entries have been made for foreman over particular groups of workers, e.g. 'foreman of labourers', or for foremen whose title included a specific occupation, e.g. 'foreman carpenter', as these are coded to the group appropriate to the people supervised or the occupation stated, i.e. as labourer and carpenter respectively.

(c) If the entry to be coded is not for a foreman, supervisor, etc. over a particular occupation the index is first referred to under the particular term, e.g. supervisor, and if not found there, is referred to 'Foreman' in the index.

(d) Works foremen, general foremen and senior foremen in manufacturing although allocated to group 110 keep the employment status of foremen.

B. Treatment of terms referred from the index

(1) **Apprentice/Graduate apprentice/Management trainee/Student apprentice/ Learner/Trainee/Trainee craftsman**

All persons in training for an occupation or profession are coded to the occupation or profession for which they are training.
Where it is not possible to determine the precise occupation for which they are in training the following conventions are applied:

unspecified apprentices or trainee craftsmen (so described)	coded 599
student apprentices ... ... graduate apprentices	coded 219
management trainees	coded 199

Improver. The term 'improver' is sometimes used as a synonym for apprentice, e.g. 'fitter's improver', for 'apprentice fitter', and is coded accordingly.

(2) **Chairman**. Apart from the industry of glass blowing a chairman is regarded as a 'company chairman' and coded as a 'Company Director' (see note (5)).

(3) **Checker**. For checkers not included in the index, if they appear to be checking articles they are coded to 861, or, if metal or electrical goods, to 860. Unspecified checkers are coded as above in manufacturing industries and to code 869 otherwise.

(4) **Clerk**. It is not practicable to list all the various chief clerks such as 'chief accounts clerk', 'chief claims clerk'. Clerks retain the code shown in the index when qualified by 'chief' but take employment status code 'Foreman' unless employed in central and local government, in which case codes 103 or 102 respectively apply.

(5) **Director/Company Director**. Directors with specific titles, e.g. sales director, are coded as shown in the index. Unspecified directors, company directors and company chairmen are coded as follows:

(a) If another occupation is stated or professional qualifications are shown they are coded to the appropriate occupation or profession. If not then:

(b) (i) If a single company is shown they are coded as a 'manager' in the appropriate industry.

(ii) If no company or more than one company is shown they are coded to group 199.

(6) **Engineer**. The term engineer presents difficulty because it is commonly used in such a variety of circumstances. The index provides for the coding of various specific engineers but even with these terms doubt often exists as to whether the person is of professional status. If the specific title is prefixed by the terms professional, chartered, administrative, advisory, chief, commissioning, consultant, consulting, design, designing, development, research, senior, superintending, or if membership of a professional institution is stated, e.g. AMIEE, it is assumed that the person is a professional engineer. In cases of doubt the person is regarded as non-professional.
Persons who state 'engineer' or 'mechanical engineer' without any indication of professional status (see preceding paragraph) are coded to group 840. There are, however, a few industries in which these terms are commonly used in a specific sense and these exceptions are listed in the index under 'Engineer; n.o.s.'. Similarly code 522 covers all electrical engineers with the exceptions listed in the index under 'Engineer; electrical; n.o.s.'.

(7) **Instructor/Lecturer/Teacher/Tutor**

(a) Teaching staff in educational establishments are coded according to the type of establishment as follows:

Universities and polytechnics	- 230
Other higher and further educational establishments (which includes colleges of education technical colleges colleges of technology)	- 231
Secondary schools (and middle schools deemed secondary)	- 233
Primary and nursery schools (and middle schools deemed primary)	- 234
Special schools	- 235

(b) Vocational and industrial trainers, teaching occupational skills are coded 391. Driving instructors giving tuition for driving private motor vehicles are coded 393.

(c) Teachers of recreational subjects at evening institutes and similar establishments, also private tutors, including private music teachers and private dancing teachers are coded 239.

(8) **Jeweller**. Jewellers engaged in manufacture or repair, are coded 518, and those wholesaling or retailing only, coded 179. If the distinction cannot be made code 179 is used.

(9) **Journeyman**. The term 'journeyman' is ignored in coding occupations except that, where doubt exists as to whether an occupation is in manufacture or distribution, as, for example, 'Confectioner', the term journeyman may be taken as implying manufacture.

(10) **Leading hand**. If another occupation is stated code to that occupation e.g. 'Plater; chrome' is used to code 'leading hand, chrome plater'. Where no other occupation is stated refer to index entries 'Leading hand-'.

(11) **Manager**. Persons managing a professional activity, such as the manager of a firm of consulting engineers or of the research department of a firm, are coded to their appropriate professions.
Managers are coded according to the branch of the establishment in which they are employed and not necessarily the industry of the establishment as a whole. For example 'Sales managers' are coded 121, 'Transport managers' are coded 140, irrespective of the main activity of the establishment.

The following terms may be regarded as synonymous with 'Manager':

Assistant Manager	Mill Manager
Under Manager	Works Manager
Departmental Manager	Factory Superintendent
Factory Manager	Works Superintendent
General Manager	Managing Director
Chairman }	
Director }	But see note (5)
Company Director }	

General managers of companies and organisations employing 500 or more persons (large establishments) are coded 101.

(12) **Quality controller**. Persons described as quality controller who hold professional qualifications are coded 218, otherwise they are coded to 861 or if quality controlling metal or electrical goods, to 860.

(13) **Farmer's wife**. Persons described as 'Farmer's wife' are coded 900 and are allocated the employment status of employees n.e.c. (which includes family workers) irrespective of any statement of employment status.

ALPHABETICAL INDEX FOR CODING OCCUPATIONS

A

	Code number
A.B.-	
armed forces-	
foreign and Common-wealth	601
U.K.	600
shipping	880
A.C.A.	250
A.C.I.S.	127
A.C.W.A.	251
A.O. (*government*)	400
A.P.A. (*power station*)	893
A.P.(T) (*local government*)-	
grade 1, 2, 3	401
grade 4, 5	102
A.R.C.O.	385
A.S.A.A.	250
Abbot	292
Above ground worker-	
coal mine	910
mine, not coal	990
Abstractor (press cuttings)	421
Accompanist	385
Accountant;	
barrack(s)	410
borough	250
certified	250
chartered	250
company	250
cost-	410
qualified	251
cost and management-	
qualified	251
district	250
financial-	250
coal mine	410
group	410
incorporated	250
management (qualified)	251
principal	250
turf	691
works-	410
qualified	251
Accountant-	410
qualified-	250
cost and works accountancy	251
management accountancy	251
government	250
Accountant and auditor	410
Accountant of Court (Scotland)	240
Accountant-secretary (*coal mine*)	250
Acetoner	999
Acid man-	820
dyestuffs mfr.	441
sugar refining	809
Acid worker-	820
ceramics mfr.	591
Acidifier	820
Acrobat	384
Actor	384
Actor-manager	M384
Actuary	252
Acupuncturist-	346
medically qualified	220
Adjudicator (national insurance regulations)	350
Adjuster;	
brake	516
claims	361
compass	517
dial (*telephone mfr.*)	860
envelope	569
lift	899
loss	361
machine-	
paper products mfr.	569
textile mfr.	516
relay	529
spring; set	516
unit-	
electricity board	540
L.R.T.	540
weight	899
Adjuster-	
gramophones	899
instruments	517
motor vehicles	540
scales	516
telephones	860
watches and clocks	517
weighing machines	516
Adjutant-	
armed forces-	
foreign and Common-wealth	M151
U.K.	M150
Adjutant-General-	
armed forces-	
foreign and Common-wealth	M151
U.K.	M150
Administrator; *see also Manager*	
contracts;	
purchasing	122
sales	121
hospital	199
office	139
pensions	139
sales	121
stores	141
transport-	
company transport	140
trust (*banking*)	120
university	191
Admiral-	
armed forces-	
foreign and Common-wealth	M151
U.K.	M150
Admiral of the Fleet-	
armed forces-	
foreign and Common-wealth	M151
U.K.	M150
Advertisement hand	959
Adviser;	
agricultural	201
art	381
beauty	661
business	364
careers	392
catering	174
cellar (*catering*)	441
Adviser; *continued*	
county planning	261
economic	252
education	232
fashion	383
financial	250
heating-	532
professional	219
home service (*gas board*)	719
horticultural	201
housing	371
insurance	361
investment	361
legal	242
literary	380
management	253
marine	399
medical	220
pension	252
poultry	201
prevention; fire	611
production	217
relations; industrial	363
safety	396
security	615
service-	719
garage	540
services; management	253
statistical	252
systems	320
taxation	362
technical-	301
accountancy	250
textile	219
traffic	399
training	124
transport	399
welfare	371
Adviser-	
agriculture	201
education	232
law	242
marketing	121
Advisor *see Adviser*	
Advocate	241
Aerialist	384
Aero-dynamicist	202
Aerographer-	596
ceramics mfr.	591
Agent;	
agricultural	719
assurance	719
bank	719
brewer's	719
brewery	719
builder's	111
buying	701
cargo (*airport*)	420
club	730
collecting	412
colliery	113
commercial	179
commission-	
farm produce	179
manufactured goods	710
raw materials	703
commission agents	703
insurance	719

Code number

- Agent; *continued*
  - commission- *continued*
    - *manufacturing* ... **710**
    - *turf accountant's* ... **691**
    - *wholesale, retail trade* ... **179**
  - company's; tug ... **719**
  - concert ... **384**
  - contractor's ... **111**
  - credit ... **730**
  - district (*insurance*) ... **719**
  - dry cleaner's ... **720**
  - dyer's ... **720**
  - election ... **190**
  - emigration ... **719**
  - engineering; civil ... **111**
  - engineer's ... **710**
  - enquiry ... **615**
  - estate ... **170**
  - estate and insurance ... **170**
  - excursion ... **177**
  - export ... **702**
  - farm ... **160**
  - film ... **384**
  - financial ... **361**
  - foreign ... **719**
  - forwarding ... **719**
  - general ... **719**
  - hiring; film ... **719**
  - house ... **170**
  - insurance ... **719**
  - land ... **170**
  - land and estate ... **170**
  - laundry ... **720**
  - law ... **242**
  - literary ... **380**
  - Lloyd's ... **719**
  - manufacturer's ... **710**
  - mercantile ... **719**
  - metal ... **703**
  - mine ... **113**
  - money ... **361**
  - mortgage ... **361**
  - naturalisation ... **719**
  - news ... **179**
  - newspaper ... **179**
  - parliamentary ... **241**
  - party (*political party*) ... **190**
  - passport ... **719**
  - patent ... **219**
  - political ... **190**
  - pools; football ... **412**
  - posting; bill ... **719**
  - press ... **380**
  - press cutting ... **F421**
  - property ... **170**
  - publicity ... **123**
  - publisher's ... **710**
  - purchasing ... **701**
  - railway ... **719**
  - receiving; laundry ... **720**
  - sales ... **710**
  - shipping- ... **140**
    - self-employed ... **719**
  - site- ... **111**
    - agricultural estate ... **170**
  - surface ... **113**
  - theatrical ... **384**
  - tourist ... **177**
  - trademark ... **399**
  - traffic (*canal*) ... **719**
  - training ... **124**
- Agent; *continued*
  - transfer; business ... **170**
  - travel ... **177**
  - underwriter's ... **719**
  - variety ... **384**
- Agent-
  - advertising ... **123**
  - agricultural estate ... **170**
  - assurance ... **719**
  - insurance ... **719**
  - manufacturer's ... **710**
  - travel ... **177**
  - *building and contracting* ... **111**
  - *mail order house* ... **730**
  - *manufacturing* ... **710**
  - *mining* ... **113**
  - *wholesale, retail trade-* ... **179**
    - *credit trade* ... **730**
    - *door to door sales* ... **730**
    - *party plan sales* ... **730**
- Agent and collector (*insurance*) **719**
- Agent and valuer; land ... **170**
- Agent-collector ... **412**
- Ager- ... **552**
  - electrical lamps ... **860**
- Ager man ... **552**
- Agricultural worker- ... **900**
  - self-employed ... **160**
  - *agricultural contracting* ... **901**
- Agriculturist ... **160**
- Agronomist ... **201**
- Agrostologist ... **201**
- Aid;
  - family ... **293**
  - laboratory ... **864**
  - nurse's ... **641**
- Aid (*hospital service*) ... **641**
- Aide-de-Camp-
  - *armed forces-*
    - *Commonwealth* ... **M151**
    - *U.K.* ... **M150**
- Airman; hot ... **830**
- Airman-
  - *armed forces-*
    - *foreign and Commonwealth* ... **601**
    - *U.K.* ... **600**
- Aircraft hand (*airport*) ... **889**
- Aircraftman-
  - *armed forces-*
    - *foreign and Commonwealth* ... **601**
    - *U.K.* ... **600**
- Aircraftwoman-
  - *armed forces-*
    - *foreign and Commonwealth* ... **601**
    - *U.K.* ... **600**
- Aircraft worker ... **912**
- Aircrew; master-
  - *armed forces-*
    - *foreign and Commonwealth* ... **601**
    - *U.K.* ... **600**
- Airport hand ... **889**
- Airwayman (*mine, not coal*) **898**
- Aligner-
  - radio and television ... **850**
  - typewriters ... **516**
- Allocator;
  - chalet ... **430**
- Allocator; *continued*
  - traffic ... **884**
- Alloyman (copper) ... **830**
- Almoner ... **293**
- Alteration hand- ... **556**
  - footwear ... **555**
- Alterer;
  - loom ... **814**
  - pattern (*carpet mfr.*) ... **814**
- Alterer (*textile mfr.*) ... **814**
- Ambassador (*Foreign and Commonwealth Office*) ... **100**
- Ambulance man ... **642**
- Ammunition worker ... **919**
- Anaesthetist ... **220**
- Analyser ... **300**
- Analyst;
  - business- ... **253**
    - *government* ... **364**
  - chief ... **200**
  - computer ... **320**
  - cost ... **420**
  - county ... **200**
  - economic ... **252**
  - financial ... **361**
  - investment ... **361**
  - methods ... **364**
  - network ... **364**
  - organisation and methods **364**
  - personnel ... **124**
  - public ... **200**
  - purchase ... **420**
  - research;
    - market ... **121**
    - operational ... **364**
  - statistical ... **252**
  - stress ... **310**
  - study; work ... **364**
  - systems; office ... **364**
  - systems- ... **320**
    - qualified ... **214**
  - tool ... **310**
  - value ... **364**
- Analyst- ... **300**
  - market research ... **121**
  - programming ... **320**
  - work study ... **364**
- Analyst-programmer ... **320**
- Anatomist ... **201**
- Anchorer ... **839**
- Ancillary worker (*hospital service*) ... **641**
- Animator (cartoon films) ... **381**
- Annealer; pot ... **823**
- Annealer- ... **833**
  - ceramics ... **823**
  - chemicals ... **820**
  - glass ... **823**
- Annealing man ... **833**
- Announcer-
  - *entertainment* ... **384**
  - *transport* ... **463**
- Anodiser ... **834**
- Anthropologist ... **291**
- Antiquary ... **291**
- Apiarist ... **902**
- Applicator; mastic ... **929**
- Appraiser ... **399**
- Appraiser and valuer ... **360**
- Apprentice; *see also notes*
  - commercial ... **430**

	Code number
Arbitragist	**361**
Arbitrator (*valuing*)	**360**
Arboriculturist	**904**
Arborist	**904**
Archman-	
brick	**500**
glass	**590**
Archaeologist	**291**
Archbishop	**292**
Archdeacon	**292**
Archer; brick	**500**
Architect;	**260**
chartered	**260**
landscape	**260**
naval	**211**
Archivist	**271**
Armourer;	**516**
cable	**899**
hose	**899**
Army worker; Church	**292**
Arranger;	
fight	**384**
floral	**791**
flower	**791**
music	**385**
Artex worker	**507**
Artexer	**507**
Artificer;	**516**
instrument	**517**
naval (*armed forces- U.K.*)	**600**
Artist;	
boot and shoe	**382**
commercial	**381**
costume	**381**
display	**381**
fashion	**381**
film	**384**
floral	**791**
graphic	**381**
hairdressing	**660**
lay-out; studio	**560**
lettering	**381**
litho	**430**
lithographic	**430**
make-up (films)	**661**
medical (*hospital services*)	**381**
paste-up	**560**
photographic	**386**
pottery	**591**
press	**381**
scenic	**381**
shoe	**382**
technical	**381**
Artist-	**381**
ceramic decorating	**591**
entertainment	**384**
glass decorating	**591**
mask mfr.	**507**
Artist and designer; fashion	**381**
Artiste	**384**
Asbestos worker	**919**
Ash and muck man	**919**
Ash man	**990**
Asphalter;	**923**
mastic	**506**
Assayer	**219**
Assayist	**219**
Assembler;	
accumulator	**850**
action;	**516**
piano	**593**

	Code number
Assembler; *continued*	
aerial	**850**
aircraft	**516**
ammeter	**859**
apparatus (*electricity board*)	**850**
armature	**850**
bakelite	**850**
battery	**850**
bedstead	**516**
belt	**850**
bench (*engineering*)	**516**
bi-focal	**859**
binocular	**859**
body (vehicle)	**851**
box	**859**
brake	**851**
brass	**851**
brush	**859**
cabinet	**859**
cable	**850**
camera	**859**
carbon block	**859**
carbon brush	**859**
card (*printing*)	**859**
case-	
electronic equipment mfr.	**859**
cell (*chemical mfr.*)	**820**
clock	**859**
clothing	**859**
coil	**850**
commutator	**850**
component-	
electrical	**850**
mechanical	**851**
computer	**850**
concrete	**923**
conveyor	**516**
cooker;	
electric	**850**
gas	**851**
core-	
electrical engineering	**850**
foundry	**531**
cosmetics	**859**
cutlery	**516**
cycle	**851**
detonator	**851**
doll	**859**
dynamo	**850**
electric fire	**850**
engine	**851**
fencing	**859**
filament	**850**
film	**569**
filter (*machinery mfr.*)	**851**
firework	**859**
flask; vacuum	**859**
footwear	**859**
frame;	
bed	**851**
spectacle	**859**
frame (*engineering*)	**516**
furniture	**859**
grocer's	**441**
gun-	**851**
hand	**516**
harness; jacquard	**814**
hood; perambulator	**859**
instrument;	**859**
electrical	**850**
optical	**859**

	Code number
Assembler; *continued*	
instrument; *continued*	
telephone	**850**
jewellery	**851**
lamp;	**851**
electric	**850**
ligature; surgical	**859**
load	**441**
lock	**851**
magnet	**850**
mattress	**554**
meter	**859**
motor-	
electric	**520**
gramophone	**850**
engineering	**851**
mould (monotype)	**560**
negative (films)	**569**
neon sign	**850**
optical	**859**
order	**441**
pad; stamp	**859**
pen	**859**
pianoforte	**593**
plastics	**859**
player	**593**
poppy	**859**
pottery	**859**
printed circuit	**850**
quartz crystal	**850**
radar	**850**
radio	**850**
record change	**850**
recorder; video	**850**
rectifier	**850**
refrigerator	**851**
relay	**850**
rifle	**851**
seat; spring	**851**
spectacle frame	**859**
spring	**851**
stator	**850**
stove-	**851**
electric	**850**
switchboard-	**850**
electrical power	**520**
switchgear	**850**
system; stereo	**850**
telephone	**850**
television	**850**
temple	**516**
toy	**859**
transformer	**850**
trim	**554**
tub	**851**
tube (*plastics goods mfr.*)	**859**
umbrella	**553**
valve-	**850**
engineer's valves	**851**
vehicle; motor	**851**
video equipment	**850**
warehouse	**441**
watch	**859**
wax (*aircraft mfr.*)	**573**
woodwork	**859**
yarn	**813**
Assembler-	
accumulators	**850**
binoculars	**859**
calculating machines	**850**
cameras	**859**

	Code number
Assembler- *continued*	
cloth hats	**553**
clothing	**859**
coach trimming	**554**
concrete	**923**
corsets	**553**
cutlery	**516**
cycles	**851**
electrical goods	**850**
electrical, electronic goods	**850**
electronic equipment	**850**
footwear	**859**
furniture	**859**
grocer's	**441**
guns	**851**
instruments	**859**
jewellery	**851**
life raft	**859**
metal goods	**851**
motor vehicles	**851**
optical instruments	**859**
paper goods	**859**
photo-lithographic plates	**560**
plastics goods	**859**
pottery	**859**
radio and television	**850**
refrigerators	**851**
rubber goods	**859**
silver goods	**518**
surgical ligatures	**859**
telephones	**850**
textile goods	**859**
toys	**859**
watches and clocks	**859**
wholesale and retail trades	**441**
window and door frames-	
metal	**851**
plastics	**859**
yarn	**813**
Assembler-fitter	**516**
Assembly hand *see Assembler*	
Assembly worker *see Assembler*	
Assessor;	**361**
bonus	**410**
claims	**361**
insurance	**361**
study; work	**364**
technical	**301**
Assistant;	
accountancy	**410**
accountant's	**410**
accounts	**410**
actuarial	**252**
administrative-	**430**
educational establishment	**191**
government	**400**
hospital service	**139**
local government-	**102**
town planning	**303**
petroleum	**139**
advertising	**719**
agent's;	
commission	**411**
estate	**719**
alteration	**556**
analyst's	**864**
anatomical	**864**
ancillary (education)	**652**
architect's	**303**
architectural	**303**
armouring	**899**

	Code number
Assistant; *continued*	
assay	**219**
assayer's	**219**
auctioneer's	**931**
audit	**410**
bakehouse	**800**
baker's	**580**
bakery	**800**
bank	**411**
banksman's (*coal mine*)	**889**
bar; snack	**953**
bar-	**622**
non-alcoholic	**953**
barker's	**919**
barrow	**732**
beaterman's	**829**
beater's	**829**
binder's	**562**
bindery	**562**
bingo	**699**
blender's (margarine)	**809**
blower's; glass	**590**
boiler's; sugar	**809**
bookbinder's	**562**
bookseller's	**720**
bookstall	**720**
borer's *(coal mine)*	**597**
bottling	**862**
brewer's (non-alcoholic)	**809**
bricklayer's	**921**
budget	**410**
building	**304**
bundler's (metal)	**863**
bureau	**430**
burner's	**913**
bursar's	**410**
butcher's	**581**
buttery	**953**
buyer's	**420**
C.S.S.D.	**641**
cafe(teria)	**953**
calender-	
paper mfr.	**821**
textile mfr.	**552**
calenderman's (*paper mfr.)*	**821**
cameraman's	**386**
canteen	**953**
canvassing (*insurance*)	**719**
care;	**644**
child	**659**
caretaker's	**672**
carpenter's	**920**
cartographic	**310**
cash and wrap	**721**
cashier's	**411**
caterer's	**953**
catering	**953**
centre;	
play	**659**
service	**720**
char house (sugar)	**809**
check-out	**721**
checker's (*metal trades*)	**869**
chemical	**864**
chemist's -	**864**
retail trade	**720**
chief-	
library	**421**
local government	**102**
churner's	**809**
circulation	**430**

	Code number
Assistant; *continued*	
civil	**430**
claims	**410**
class; nursery	**652**
classroom	**652**
clerical;	**430**
accounts	**410**
clerical-	
bank	**411**
building society	**411**
government	**400**
library	**421**
local government	**401**
police service	**401**
clerk's;	**430**
justices	**420**
clinic;	**641**
animal	**349**
clinical-	**641**
qualified	**220**
collection	**412**
collector's; rate	**401**
collier('s)	**597**
commercial	**430**
computer	**490**
confectioner and tobacconist's	**720**
confectioner's-	**720**
flour confectionery	**580**
sugar confectionery mfr.	**809**
conference	**430**
consular	**430**
contracts	**420**
control;	
air traffic	**463**
passenger *(air transport)*	**630**
production	**420**
quality	**420**
sensitometric	**569**
control-	
investment company	**410**
L.R.T.	**140**
controller *(banking)*	**411**
conveyancing	**420**
cookery	**952**
cook's	**952**
correspondence	**420**
cost	**410**
costing	**410**
counter-	**720**
bookmaker's, turf accountant's	**411**
catering	**953**
library	**421**
P.O.	**411**
take-away food shop	**720**
craft *(railways)*	**913**
crematorium	**999**
cutter's; paper	**822**
cutter's-	
clothing mfr.	**557**
paper mfr.	**822**
paper pattern mfr.	**822**
dairy *(retail trade)*	**720**
dairyman's-	
milk processing	**809**
retail trade	**720**
dealer's	**720**
dental	**643**
department; operating	**641**

	Code number
Assistant; *continued*	
depot-	
L.R.T.-	
rail	**F881**
road	**F871**
design	**310**
despatch	**441**
dip; hot	**834**
dipper's	**869**
director's; funeral	**699**
dispensary	**346**
dispenser's	**346**
dispensing	**346**
display-	
retail trade-	**381**
merchandising	**790**
shelf filling	**954**
distribution *(water board)*	**892**
diver's; sea	**929**
divisional *(insurance)*	**410**
domestic	**958**
draper's	**720**
draughtsman's	**491**
drayman's	**934**
driver's;	
crane	**932**
dumper	**889**
engine	**893**
lorry	**934**
turbine	**893**
van	**934**
driver's *(road transport)*	**934**
dryerman's (paper)	**821**
dyer's *(textile mfr.)*	**814**
economic	**252**
editorial	**380**
editor's; newspaper	**430**
educational	**652**
electrician's	**913**
electronics	**302**
electroplating	**839**
embosser's	**590**
employment	**420**
engineering;	**301**
civil	**304**
engineer's-	**301**
maintenance	**913**
establishment	**420**
estates	**412**
estimating	**410**
estimator's	**410**
etcher's	**590**
executive-	**199**
insurance	**139**
experimental;	**309**
senior	**309**
export	**420**
extrusion-	
plastics	**825**
rubber	**824**
factory	**919**
farm;	**900**
mink	**902**
film	**386**
financial	**410**
fingerprint	**420**
fireman's	**611**
fishmonger's	**582**
fitter's	**913**
flanger's	**912**
floor *(retail trade)*	**720**

	Code number
Assistant; *continued*	
florist's	**720**
forge	**839**
frier's; fish	**953**
fruiterer's	**720**
funeral	**699**
furnace *(metal trades)*	**830**
furrier's	**720**
gallery; art	**619**
galvanizer's	**912**
garage	**540**
gardener's-	**594**
market gardening	**595**
nursery	**595**
gas regulator's	**919**
general-	**430**
catering	**953**
home for the disabled	**644**
hotel	**958**
old people's home	**644**
retail trade	**720**
school meals	**953**
gilder's (electro-gilding)	**839**
glazer's	**899**
glazier's	**921**
grinder's-	**912**
plate glass	**590**
grocer's-	**720**
mobile	**731**
haberdashery	**720**
hairdresser's	**660**
hammerman's	**839**
hardener's	**912**
hatchery	**900**
heater's *(metal trades)*	**830**
horticultural	**595**
hotel	**430**
house;	
boarding	**958**
cook	**952**
dye	**814**
green-	**595**
ceramics mfr.	**869**
test *(steelworks)*	**864**
household	**958**
housing	**401**
hydropulper	**821**
income	**410**
information	**430**
inspector's-	
banking	**411**
local government	**401**
metal trades	**869**
insurance	**410**
iron checker's	**912**
jeweller's	**720**
joiner's	**920**
jointer's	**913**
keeper('s);	
hall *(local government)*	**672**
school	**672**
store	**441**
kiln	**829**
kitchen	**952**
laboratory	**864**
ladler's (glass)	**590**
laminating *(paper mfr.)*	**821**
language	**239**
launderette	**673**
laundry	**673**
legal	**350**

	Code number
Assistant; *continued*	
letterpress	**891**
lettings *(local government)*	**401**
library	**421**
licensee's	**622**
lifter's	**913**
lighting; street	**699**
linesman's	**913**
linotype	**919**
lithographer's	**869**
lithographic	**560**
litigation	**420**
loader's	**919**
machine *see Machinist*	
machine man's *(paper mfr.)*	**821**
mains *(water company)*	**990**
maintenance-	**899**
machinery, plant	**894**
maker's;	
boiler	**913**
book	**699**
cheese	**809**
coach	**913**
crucible	**591**
dress	**559**
rope	**814**
shoe	**555**
taper	**899**
tool	**912**
management; housing	**430**
manager's	**430**
market	**732**
marketing;	**420**
sales	**411**
mason's	**921**
matcher's; colour	**814**
matron's	**958**
meals; school	**953**
measurement; work	**364**
mechanic's	**913**
medical *(hospital)*	**641**
melting pot (electric cable)	**829**
mercer's	**720**
merchant's	**720**
metallurgical	**309**
meteorological	**202**
meter	**913**
methods	**364**
midday *(school)*	**659**
mill;	**990**
offal *(tobacco mfr.)*	**802**
rolling	**839**
miller's (food)	**809**
milliner's	**557**
millwright's	**913**
minder's; machine *(printing)*	**891**
minder's *(cotton mfr.)*	**814**
mixer's; colour	**829**
mortuary	**699**
moulder's *(abrasive mfr.)*	**591**
museum	**271**
N.A.A.F.I.	**720**
newsagent's	**720**
non-teaching *(schools)*	**652**
nursery-	**650**
agriculture	**595**
nursing	**640**
off-licence	**720**
office;	**420**
drawing	**491**
receiving	**720**

Code number

Assistant; *continued*
- onsetter's **889**
- operations (freight handling) **889**
- oven (*bakery*) **800**
- painter's **869**
- passenger *(railways)* ... **140**
- pawnbroker's **720**
- perfumer's **720**
- personal; manager's ... **459**
- personal- **459**
  - managerial **459**
- personnel **363**
- pharmacy **720**
- photographer's **386**
- photographic **386**
- physiotherapy **343**
- pickler's (galvanized sheet) **839**
- planning; town **303**
- planning- **399**
  - *local government* ... **303**
- plant; pilot **913**
- plasterer's **921**
- plater's **913**
- plating *(electroplating)* ... **839**
- play leader's **659**
- playgroup **659**
- plumber's **913**
- polisher's; glass **590**
- postal (*P.O.)* **411**
- post office- **411**
  - sub-post office **720**
- potter's **590**
- poulterer's **720**
- poultry **900**
- presentation *(printing)* ... **569**
- press *(printing)* **891**
- principal-
  - *building society* **131**
  - *local government* ... **102**
  - *public utilities* **113**
- printer's **891**
- printing **891**
- process *(printing)* **569**
- producer's *(entertainment)* **384**
- production- **420**
  - *broadcasting* **384**
- professional *(local government-surveyor's dept.)* ... **262**
- programme *(broadcasting)* **384**
- progress **420**
- provision **720**
- publicity **123**
- publisher's **441**
- purchasing- **420**
  - *wholesale trade* **701**
- rate fixing **401**
- rating **401**
- reader's **430**
- records **420**
- reelerman's *(paper mfr.)* ... **821**
- refectory **953**
- refiner's **820**
- registrar's **420**
- relations;
  - customer **430**
  - employee **420**
  - public **420**
- remover's; furniture ... **931**
- repairer's; wagon **913**
- repairer's *(coal mine)* ... **910**
- reprographic **490**

Code number

Assistant; *continued*
- research; marketing ... **420**
- research- **300**
  - agricultural **201**
  - biochemical **201**
  - biological **201**
  - botanical **201**
  - chemical **200**
  - engineering;
    - electrical **212**
    - electronic **213**
    - mechanical **211**
  - geological **202**
  - historical **399**
  - horticultural **201**
  - medical **300**
  - meteorological **202**
  - physical science **202**
  - zoological **201**
  - *broadcasting* **399**
  - *government* **399**
  - *journalism* **399**
  - *printing and publishing* **399**
  - *university* **230**
- reshearer's **913**
- restaurant **953**
- roller's **839**
- room;
  - blowing **811**
  - control-
    - *fire service* **420**
    - *L.R.T.* **893**
  - cutting *(clothing mfr.)* ... **557**
  - dark **569**
  - dining **953**
  - engine **893**
  - grey **441**
  - linen **441**
  - pattern *(textile mfr.)* ... **441**
  - print *(engineering)* ... **490**
  - publishing **420**
  - receiving *(tailoring)* ... **889**
  - retort *(food products mfr.)* **809**
  - sale-
    - *auctioneer's* **931**
    - *retail, wholesale trade* **720**
  - sample **441**
  - show **720**
  - still **953**
  - stock **441**
  - test (electrical) **869**
- rotary *(printing)* **891**
- safety **396**
- salaries **410**
- sales *see Assistant; shop-*
- sample (*chocolate confectionery mfr*). ... **809**
- sawyer's **920**
- school; nursery **652**
- scientific **300**
- sculptor's **381**
- secretarial **459**
- secretary's **430**
- seedsman's **720**
- senior- **F430**
  - *C.S.S.D.* **401**
  - *local government* ... **401**
  - *retail trade* **F720**
- service;
  - customer **430**
  - passenger **630**

Code number

Assistant; *continued*
- shipping **420**
- shipwright's **913**
- shop;
  - machine **912**
  - paint **869**
  - spreading (cables) ... **899**
  - work *(education establishments)* **699**
- shop- **720**
  - *take-away food shop* ... **720**
- shotfirer's *(coal mine)* ... **597**
- showman's **384**
- silverer's **834**
- sinker's **898**
- slitter's (film) **822**
- smith's; **839**
  - boiler **913**
  - copper **913**
  - gold **518**
  - silver **518**
- sorting (*P.O.)* **940**
- sound **386**
- spinner's-
  - *textile mfr.* **814**
  - *tobacco mfr.* **802**
- spreader's; colour **919**
- staff- **420**
  - *railways* **363**
- stall; **732**
  - book **720**
- stamper's *(drop forging)*... **839**
- standards; trading **401**
- station (*electricity board)* **893**
- stationer's **720**
- statistical **252**
- stenter **814**
- stenterer's **814**
- stereotyper's **560**
- stevedore **930**
- steward's **630**
- stock **441**
- stoker's **893**
- stores- **441**
  - *retail trade* **720**
- stretcher **814**
- studio **386**
- study; work... ... ... **420**
- sub-post office **720**
- sub-station **893**
- supervisory (school meals) **659**
- supplies **441**
- surgery; dental **643**
- surgery- **641**
  - *general medical service* **460**
  - *hospital* **641**
- survey; hydrographic ... **889**
- survey-
  - *government* **929**
  - *local government* ... **401**
- surveying **929**
- surveyor's; **929**
  - quantity **312**
- T.S.S.U. **641**
- tailor's **556**
- taster's; tea **863**
- taxation **401**
- teacher's **652**
- teaser **919**
- technical- **309**
  - quantity surveyor's ... **312**

Code number

- Assistant; *continued*
  - technical- *continued*
    - veterinarian's ... **349**
    - *civil engineering* ... **304**
  - temperer's ... **912**
  - tender's; machine; paste-board ... **821**
  - terminals *(transport)* ... **889**
  - test ... **309**
  - tester's; meter ... **869**
  - theatre; operating ... **641**
  - therapy; occupational ... **347**
  - thrower's ... **590**
  - timberman('s) *(coal mine)* **597**
  - time study ... **420**
  - timekeeper's ... **410**
  - tool grinder's ... **912**
  - trade(s) *(shipbuilding)* ... **913**
  - trader's;
    - market ... **732**
    - street ... **732**
  - tradesman's *(metal trades)* **913**
  - traffic; passenger *(air transport)* ... **630**
  - traffic *(telecoms)* ... **462**
  - treasurer's ... **410**
  - trek (*equestrian trekking centre*) ... **902**
  - trimmer's *(upholstering)* ... **559**
  - undertaker's ... **699**
  - underwriter's ... **410**
  - upholsterer's ... **553**
  - valuation ... **410**
  - valveman's ... **999**
  - veterinary ... **349**
  - veterinary surgeon's ... **349**
  - ward ... **641**
  - wardrobe ... **699**
  - warehouse; ... **441**
    - printing ... **569**
  - warehouseman's ... **441**
  - weaver's ... **814**
  - welder's ... **537**
  - welfare; ... **371**
    - school ... **652**
  - wireman's ... **913**
  - work; social ... **371**
  - worker's; butter ... **919**
  - x-ray ... **342**
  - yard ... **990**
- Assistant-
  - *catering* ... **953**
  - *dressmaking* ... **559**
  - *dry cleaners* ... **673**
  - *investigation branch (P.O.)* **615**
  - *library* ... **421**
  - *retail trade see Assistant; shop-*
  - *tailoring* ... **556**
  - *take-away food shop see Assistant; shop-*
- Associate;
  - research- ... **209**
    - agricultural ... **201**
    - biochemical ... **201**
    - biological ... **201**
    - botanical ... **201**
    - chemical ... **200**
    - economic ... **252**
    - engineering;
      - electrical ... **212**
      - electronic ... **213**

Code number

- Associate; *continued*
  - research- *continued*
    - engineering; *continued*
      - mechanical ... **211**
    - geological ... **202**
    - historical ... **399**
    - horticultural ... **201**
    - medical ... **300**
    - meteorological ... **202**
    - mining ... **210**
    - physical science ... **202**
    - zoological ... **201**
    - *broadcasting* ... **399**
    - *government* ... **399**
    - *journalism* ... **399**
    - *polytechnic* ... **230**
    - *printing and publishing* **399**
    - *university* ... **230**
  - sales (*insurance*) ... **719**
- Assorter-
  - galvanized sheet ... **860**
  - tinplate ... **860**
- Astrologer ... **699**
- Astronomer ... **202**
- Astrophysicist ... **202**
- Athlete ... **387**
- Attache ... **399**
- Attacher ... **859**
- Attendant;
  - aerial *(mine, above ground)* **889**
  - aerodrome ... **889**
  - aid; first ... **641**
  - alternator ... **893**
  - ambulance ... **642**
  - amenity ... **959**
  - amusement ... **699**
  - animal ... **902**
  - anode ... **834**
  - aquarium ... **902**
  - arcade ... **699**
  - ash ... **889**
  - auto(matic) ... **841**
  - backwash ... **814**
  - bar; snack ... **953**
  - bar- ... **622**
    - non-alcoholic ... **953**
  - basin; outflow ... **809**
  - bath(s); ... **699**
    - copper (*glass mfr.*) ... **834**
    - salt ... **833**
  - battery- ... **899**
    - *mine, not coal* ... **990**
  - bay;
    - lubrication ... **540**
    - sick ... **641**
    - wash ... **999**
  - bed;
    - bacteria ... **990**
    - filter *(water works)* ... **892**
  - belt; ... **889**
    - casting ... **590**
  - bingo ... **699**
  - block; amenity ... **959**
  - board;
    - control ... **893**
    - spread ... **811**
    - switch- ... **893**
      - telephones ... **462**
  - boat ... **880**
  - boiler; ... **893**
    - temper (margarine) ... **809**

Code number

- Attendant; *continued*
  - boiler; *continued*
    - vacuum (margarine) ... **809**
  - booster ... **893**
  - box;
    - dod ... **590**
    - drawing ... **811**
    - gill ... **811**
  - bridge; ... **889**
    - sluice ... **889**
    - swing ... **889**
    - weigh ... **863**
  - buffet ... **953**
  - bunker- ... **889**
    - *coal mine* ... **889**
  - burner (coalite) ... **829**
  - bus; school ... **630**
  - cab ... **959**
  - cabin; weigh ... **863**
  - cage ... **886**
  - calender-
    - linoleum ... **829**
    - paper ... **821**
    - rubber ... **824**
    - textiles ... **552**
  - camp ... **959**
  - canteen ... **953**
  - car;
    - dining ... **621**
    - mine ... **889**
    - restaurant ... **621**
    - sleeping ... **630**
  - car-
    - *airport* ... **955**
    - *steel mfr.* ... **889**
  - card *(textle mfr.)* ... **811**
  - care ... **644**
  - carriage *(railways)* ... **630**
  - caster; monotype ... **560**
  - cemetery ... **990**
  - centre; sports ... **699**
  - centrifugal-
    - *chemical mfr.* ... **820**
    - *food products mfr.* ... **809**
    - *textile mfr.* ... **814**
  - chair ... **959**
  - charge ... **644**
  - children's ... **652**
  - chlorination ... **820**
  - cinema ... **699**
  - class ... **652**
  - cleaning ... **958**
  - cleansing ... **958**
  - clinic ... **641**
  - club ... **699**
  - coach ... **959**
  - coal ... **889**
  - cock; wash-off ... **809**
  - composition (matches) ... **820**
  - compression; air ... **893**
  - compressor ... **893**
  - condenser- ... **820**
    - *blast furnace* ... **999**
    - *power station* ... **893**
  - conditioner-
    - *paper mfr.* ... **821**
    - *tobacco mfr.* ... **802**
  - converter; tow-to-top ... **811**
  - conveyor ... **889**
  - cooler ... **809**
  - craft (*electricity board*) ... **913**

	Code number
Attendant; *continued*	
crane	**932**
creche	**650**
creel; sisal	**821**
creeper *(coal mine)*	**889**
crematorium	**999**
crossing-	
railway	**883**
road	**619**
crusher	**890**
cupola	**830**
customs	**441**
cylinder (*tobacco mfr.*)	**802**
dental	**643**
depot *(coal mine)*	**910**
diffuser	**809**
dipper's	**869**
diver's	**929**
dock	**889**
donor; blood	**641**
door	**699**
dormitory *(college)*	**958**
dryer-	
macadam	**829**
plasterboard	**829**
dynamo	**893**
earth; fuller's (margarine)	**809**
electrolytic	**834**
elevator;	
goods	**441**
wet char	**919**
engine; winding	**886**
engine-	**893**
shipping	**880**
engineer's *(D.O.E.)*	**990**
equipment; automatic *(food products mfr.)*	**809**
evaporator; steepwater	**809**
evaporator-	**820**
food products mfr.	**809**
exhaust(er)	**999**
expeller; oil (maize)	**809**
explosive(s) *(coal mine)*	**441**
fair; fun	**699**
fan	**999**
felt *(paper mfr.)*	**821**
field; playing	**699**
filter-	
starch mfr.	**809**
water works	**892**
filtration	**820**
flight	**630**
forecourt *(garage)*	**722**
frame; twist	**812**
frame-	
mine, not coal	**890**
textile mfr.	**811**
furnace;	
blast	**830**
crematorium	**999**
furnace-	
chemical mfr.	**820**
glass mfr.	**823**
metal trades- annealing	**833**
metal trades-	**830**
games	**699**
garage	**540**
gas *(steelworks)*	**893**
gate;	**615**
flood	**889**
toll	**412**

	Code number
Attendant; *continued*	
gear; extractor *(gas works)*	**820**
gear *(coal mine)*	**893**
gearhead	**889**
generator	**893**
governor *(gas works)*	**999**
grainer *(paper mfr.)*	**821**
granary	**441**
green; bowling	**699**
grinder (cement)	**829**
ground;	**594**
fair	**699**
play	**659**
gun	**912**
gymnasium	**699**
hall;	
billiard	**699**
bingo	**699**
dance	**699**
dining	**953**
town	**672**
health; animal	**349**
health *(local government)*	**401**
heat(s)	**820**
heating	**893**
hoist	**886**
holder; gas	**894**
hopper-	
coal mine	**910**
mine, not coal	**990**
refuse destruction	**990**
hospital	**641**
hostel	**959**
hotel	**699**
house;	
bath	**699**
blower	**999**
boiler	**893**
boiling	**820**
booster	**893**
compressor	**893**
engine	**999**
exhaust	**999**
filter-	**829**
mine, not coal	**890**
water works	**892**
meter *(gas works)*	**430**
powder	**441**
power	**893**
press	**892**
pump	**999**
retort	**820**
screen	**990**
shift	**959**
slip	**829**
wash	**673**
humidifier	**821**
hut; beach	**959**
hydro *(laundry)*	**673**
hydrotherapy	**699**
incinerator *(hospital services)*	**999**
instrument-	
chemical mfr.	**820**
steelworks	**830**
invalid	**644**
inversion	**809**
jigger *(asbestos opening)*	**811**
journey *(coal mine)*	**889**
kennel	**902**
kiln-	
glass	**823**

	Code number
Attendant; *continued*	
kiln- *continued*	
brick mfr.	**823**
cement mfr.	**829**
ceramics mfr.	**823**
glaze and colour mfr.	**829**
kiosk	**720**
kitchen	**952**
laboratory	**990**
lamp-	**959**
coal mine	**441**
railways	**990**
landing *(coal mine)*	**889**
landsale	**889**
lathe;	**840**
rubber	**824**
launderette	**673**
laundry	**673**
lavatory	**959**
leg; marine	**880**
lehr	**823**
leisure	**699**
library	**421**
lid; carbonising	**516**
lift	**955**
light(ing)	**699**
light and bell	**521**
light and power	**521**
loader *(coal mine)*	**889**
loading; barge	**930**
lobby	**699**
locomotive	**912**
lodge	**615**
loom	**552**
lorry	**934**
lubrication-	**894**
motor vehicles	**540**
luggage; left	**959**
machine *see Machinist*	
machinery;	**893**
lift	**894**
magazine;	**441**
plasterboard	**829**
main; hydraulic	**919**
market	**990**
mayor's	**619**
meals; school	**953**
medical	**641**
mess	**953**
meter; parking	**614**
midday (school meals)	**659**
mill;	
mortar	**829**
rod	**516**
saw	**897**
wash	**820**
wood	**821**
mill-	
cement mfr.	**829**
metal goods mfr.	**516**
rolling mill	**516**
mixer; concrete	**829**
mixer-	
ceramics mfr.	**829**
food products mfr.	**809**
molasses	**809**
montejuice	**809**
mortuary	**699**
motor	**893**
mouth; drift *(coal mine)*	**886**
multiplex (margarine)	**809**

	Code number
Attendant; *continued*	
museum	**619**
neutraliser	**809**
night-	
home for the disabled	**644**
hospital service	**641**
old people's home	**644**
nursery	**650**
nursing	**641**
outfall works	**990**
oven;	
core	**839**
drying; cylinder	**820**
gas	**820**
oven-	
bakery	**800**
ceramics mfr.	**823**
chemical mfr.	**820**
coke ovens	**820**
food products mfr.	**809**
paddy *(coal mine)*	**889**
pan *(food products mfr.)*	**809**
paraffin	**820**
park;	**615**
amusement	**699**
car	**955**
parking	**955**
petrol	**722**
picker; waste	**811**
pier-	**889**
entertainment	**699**
pig	**900**
plan	**441**
plant;	
acid	**820**
ammonia	**820**
ash	**999**
auxiliary	**893**
boiler	**893**
breeze	**829**
chlorination	**820**
cleaning; air	**999**
coal	**890**
coke	**889**
conditioning; air	**999**
cooling; dry	**820**
crushing; ore	**890**
drainage *(mining)*	**999**
electric	**893**
fume *(lead mfr.)*	**899**
gas	**820**
grading; coke	**829**
lime	**890**
purifying; water	**892**
refrigerating	**999**
retort	**820**
sewage	**892**
shot blast	**841**
softening; water	**892**
sulphate	**820**
tar	**820**
treatment; water	**892**
washing; vehicles	**999**
water	**820**
welding	**537**
plant-	**893**
chemical mfr.	**820**
gas works	**820**
quarry	**890**
plodder (margarine)	**809**
Attendant; *continued*	
point;	
transfer; conveyor	**889**
polisher's; glass	**591**
pool; swimming	**699**
potter's	**590**
poultry	**900**
press-	
ceramics mfr.	**590**
chemical mfr.	**820**
sugar refining	**809**
producer; gas	**820**
property; lost	**959**
pump;	
air-	**893**
sugar refining	**809**
petrol	**722**
pump-	**999**
garage	**722**
sewage works	**892**
pumping	**999**
punch	**841**
purifier	**820**
pyrometer *(metal mfr.)*	**830**
quencher; coke	**919**
refrigerator	**999**
reservoir	**929**
retort *(coal gas, coke ovens)*	**820**
river	**929**
roll;	
cold	**839**
milling (asbestos)	**829**
roller; edge	**590**
room;	
ambulance	**642**
ball	**699**
bath	**699**
battery	**999**
blowing	**811**
boiler	**893**
changing	**959**
cloak	**959**
cold *(brewery)*	**801**
compressor	**893**
dining	**953**
dressing	**959**
engine-	**999**
shipping	**880**
first aid	**641**
grey	**441**
ice	**809**
ladies'	**959**
lamp	**441**
linen	**441**
locker	**959**
luggage	**959**
medical	**641**
mess	**953**
plan	**441**
power	**893**
print	**891**
pump	**999**
refreshment	**953**
rest	**959**
sample *(food products mfr.)*	**861**
show	**720**
sick	**641**
still	**953**
stock	**441**
tool	**441**
waiting	**959**
Attendant; *continued*	
room; *continued*	
ward	**621**
wash	**959**
rope *(coal mine)*	**889**
rotary (asbestos)	**811**
safety *(chemical works)*	**396**
saloon	**622**
sanitary	**958**
scale;	**863**
green	**919**
school	**959**
screen-	
ceramics mfr.	**829**
gas works	**829**
mine	**890**
scrubber *(coke ovens)*	**999**
scutcher	**811**
seat	**959**
sewage	**892**
sewerage	**892**
shed *(transport)*	**990**
shunter	**884**
sieve; rotary (*tobacco mfr.*)	**802**
silo	**441**
sluice	**889**
softener; water	**892**
sprinkler	**892**
stall;	
coffee	**953**
market	**732**
stall *(amusements)*	**699**
stand *(L.R.T.)*	**990**
station;	
ambulance	**642**
filling	**722**
petrol	**722**
power	**893**
pumping	**999**
service	**722**
sub *(electricity board)*	**893**
station *(gas works)*	**999**
statutory	**934**
sterilizer-	
distillery	**801**
medical services	**641**
still	**820**
storage; liquor	**820**
store;	**441**
liquor	**801**
stores-	**441**
retail trade	**720**
stove;	
core	**839**
starch	**809**
studio	**959**
sub-station	**893**
surgery	**641**
switch *(coal mine)*	**884**
synagogue	**672**
syphon	**999**
tank-	
cable mfr.	**599**
local government	**990**
sugar refining	**809**
tar and liquor	**820**
teaser	**811**
telephone	**462**
theatre-	**699**
hospital	**641**
thickener	**821**

	Code number
Attendant; *continued*	
thrower's	**590**
tip	**990**
tipper *(coal mine)*- ...	**597**
above ground	**889**
tippler *(coal mine)* ...	**889**
toilet	**959**
traffic *(coal mine)*... ...	**883**
train-	**630**
coal mine	**881**
transformer	**893**
travel	**630**
treatment; water	**892**
tumbler	**673**
turbine	**893**
turnstile	**411**
unit; cracker	**890**
valve	**999**
van	**934**
vat *(textile dyeing)* ...	**552**
ventilation	**999**
wagon	**889**
ward	**641**
washer;	**820**
beet	**809**
washer's	**809**
washery *(coal mine)* ...	**890**
water	**999**
welfare	**371**
wharf; oil	**930**
winch	**886**
Attendant-	
agricultural machinery ...	**901**
public conveniences ...	**959**
road goods vehicles ...	**934**
ambulance service... ...	**642**
art gallery	**619**
baths	**699**
catering	**953**
cinema	**699**
domestic service	**670**
entertainment	**699**
gas works	**820**
government	**941**
home for the disabled ...	**644**
hospital service	**641**
local government	**959**
museum	**619**
old people's home ...	**644**
racing stables	**902**
sewage farm	**892**
water works	**892**
Attender *(tinplate mfr.)* ...	**839**
Attorney	**241**
Au pair	**659**
Auctioneer	**719**
Audiologist	**346**
Audiometrician	**346**
Auditor;	
chief *(coal mine)*	**250**
internal	**410**
stock	**420**
Auditor-	**410**
qualified	**250**
government	**250**
insurance	**410**
local government	**250**
Auditor of Court (Scotland)	**240**
Author-	**380**
technical	**380**
Autoclave worker	
(aluminium refining) ...	**820**
Autolysis man	**809**
Auto-setter *(metal trades)* ...	**519**
Auto-weigher...	**863**
Auxiliary;	
craft *(D.O.E.)*	**919**
dental	**346**
nursing;	**640**
animal	**349**
Aviator	**331**
Axeman	**904**

B

	Code number
B.Ch.	**220**
Babbitter	**839**
Back end man *(textile mfr.)*	**552**
Back hand *(leather cloth mfr.)*	**814**
Back man *(textile mfr.)*	**552**
Back room man *(distillery)*	**801**
Back-end man *(cement mfr.)*	**829**
Backer;	
carpet	**550**
mirror	**834**
saw	**899**
spindle *(rolling mill)*	**839**
stencil paper	**821**
Backer-	
clothing mfr.	**553**
fustian mfr.	**552**
linoleum mfr.	**829**
paper mfr.	**821**
rolling mill	**839**
Backer-up-	
sawmilling	**920**
steelworks	**839**
Backwasher	**814**
Bacon hand	**720**
Bacteriologist	**201**
Badge worker	**553**
Badger	**591**
Bag hand-	**559**
paper products mfr.	**569**
Bagman *(cement mfr.)*	**862**
Baggage man	**931**
Bagger;	
cake	**862**
coal	**862**
fibre *(asbestos mfr.)*	**862**
Bagger-	**862**
footwear mfr.	**555**
Bagger-off *(starch mfr.)*	**862**
Bagger-out	**553**
Bailer *see Baler*	
Bailiff;	
estate	**160**
farm	**160**
land	**160**
rent	**619**
reservoir	**929**
river	**395**
water	**395**
Bailiff-	
certificated	**619**
county, high courts	**619**
level, sewer commissioners	**F929**
local government	**619**
property owning	**619**
Baister *see Baster*	
Bakehouse worker	**800**
Baker;	
hand oven	**800**
master	**580**
Baker-	
bakery	**580**
flour confectionery mfr.	**580**
food products mfr.	**809**
retail trade-	**179**
employee	**580**
shipping	**580**
textile mfr.	**552**

	Code number
Baker and confectioner-	
bakery	**580**
retail trade-	**179**
employee	**580**
Bakery hand	**800**
Bakery worker	**800**
Baking powder operative	**809**
Balancer;	
armature	**520**
dynamic(s)	**860**
flyer	**516**
shaft; crank	**860**
sound	**386**
wheel-	
abrasive mfr.	**599**
railway workshops	**860**
Balancer-	
abrasive mfr.	**599**
engineering	**860**
Balcony man	**590**
Baler;	
hay	**901**
paper	**862**
salle	**862**
scrap	**899**
Baler-	**862**
oil wells	**999**
Ballast man	**930**
Baller;	
cross	**813**
wool	**813**
Baller-	
twine	**813**
yarn	**813**
ceramics mfr.	**829**
iron works	**830**
wool combing	**811**
Ballerina	**384**
Ballistician	**202**
Band master	**385**
Bander;	
armature	**850**
cigar	**862**
clay	**591**
coil	**862**
glass	**591**
wash	**591**
Bander-	
boot polish mfr.	**862**
cardboard box mfr.	**569**
ceramics mfr.	**591**
iron and steelworks	**862**
rubber tyre mfr.	**824**
textile mfr.-	**894**
textile bleaching, dyeing	**552**
Bandsman	**385**
Bandyman *(provender milling)*	**809**
Bank hand-	
coal mine	**886**
rope mfr.	**814**
Bankman; rail	**889**
Bankman *(rolling mill)*	**912**
Banker; merchant	**120**
Banker-	
stone working	**500**
finance-	**131**
self-employed	**361**
merchant banking	**120**
mine, not coal	**886**
yarn warping	**812**

	Code number
Banker hand	**500**
Banksman;	
crane	**932**
staple pit	**886**
Banksman-	
blast furnace	**912**
canal contractors	**929**
civil engineers	**932**
coal mine	**886**
manufacturing	**932**
mine, not coal	**886**
opencast coal mining	**863**
salt works	**886**
Bar-cellarman	**622**
Barber	**660**
Bargain man-	
mine, not coal-	
above ground	**990**
below ground	**898**
Barge hand	**880**
Bargeman	**880**
Bargee	**880**
Bark worker	**897**
Barker *(rope mfr.)*	**552**
Barmaid	**622**
Barman;	
coffee	**953**
head	**F622**
tea	**953**
Barman-	
catering, hotels, public houses, etc.	**622**
railway shed	**516**
Barrelman (rice starch)	**809**
Barreller	**842**
Barrer *(footwear mfr.)*	**555**
Barrister	**241**
Barrow boy *(retail trade)*	**732**
Barrow man-	**889**
retail trade	**732**
Basket man *(retail trade)*	**990**
Basket worker	**599**
Bassoonist	**385**
Baster	**556**
Batman (civilian)	**670**
Batcher; concrete	**829**
Batcher *(textile finishing)*	**811**
Batchman *(glass mfr.)*	**829**
Bater	**810**
Bathman-	
bacon curing	**809**
baths	**699**
Batter; felt	**814**
Batter *(pottery mfr.)*	**590**
Batterer	**841**
Battery man-	
coke ovens	**889**
food products mfr.	**809**
iron and steelworks	**899**
mine, not coal	**990**
Battery worker	**990**
Bayman; service	**540**
Bayman *(steelworks)*	**912**
Beader-	
coach building	**541**
embroidering	**553**
footwear mfr.	**555**
tin box mfr.	**841**
Beamer-	
shipbuilding	**534**
textile mfr.-	**552**

	Code number
Beamer- *continued*	
textile mfr.- continued	
textile finishing	**814**
wire weaving	**899**
Bearer; mace	**699**
Bearer *(funeral direction)* ...	**699**
Beater;	
carpet	**673**
feather	**814**
fire	**893**
gold	**518**
leaf	**839**
panel-	
motor vehicle repair ...	**542**
metal trades	**533**
silver	**518**
Beater-	
feather dressing	**814**
footwear mfr.	**555**
metal trades	**533**
paper mill	**821**
textile finishing	**552**
Beater and sprayer; paint ...	**542**
Beaterman-	
asbestos-cement mfr. ...	**829**
celluloid mfr.	**820**
paper mfr.	**821**
Beater-up *(tobacco mfr.)* ...	**802**
Beautician;	**661**
canine	**902**
Bedman-	
asphalt mfr....	**829**
blast furnace	**830**
Bedder-	
ceramics mfr.	**829**
college	**958**
Beekeeper	**902**
Beetler	**552**
Behinder	**839**
Bell man-	
blast furnace	**830**
mining	**521**
Bellows man *(shipbuilding)*	**912**
Bellyman; piano	**579**
Belt hand	**889**
Belt worker;	**889**
conveyor	**889**
Beltman; machine	**555**
Beltman-	
coal mine-	**889**
above ground	**890**
engineering	**555**
patent fuel mfr.	**919**
Belter (forks and spades) ...	**842**
Bench hand; saw	**899**
Bench hand-	
cabinet making	**571**
cardboard box mfr. ...	**859**
chemical mfr.	**820**
coach trimming	**554**
footwear mfr.-	**555**
bespoke	**555**
joinery mfr....	**570**
leather goods mfr. ...	**555**
metal trades-	**899**
brass foundry	**839**
electrical engineering ...	**520**
instrument mfr.	**517**
plastics goods mfr. ...	**825**
printing-	**919**
newspaper printing ...	**862**

	Code number
Bench hand- *continued*	
rubber flooring mfr. ...	**824**
rubber footwear	**555**
stationers	**862**
sugar confectionery mfr. ...	**809**
Bench man; laboratory ...	**864**
Bench man-	
cabinet making	**571**
chemical mfr.	**820**
coke ovens	**919**
footwear mfr.-	**555**
bespoke	**555**
joinery mfr....	**570**
rolling mill	**912**
Bench worker-	
cabinet making	**571**
engineering	**899**
footwear mfr.	**555**
glass mfr.	**590**
instrument mfr.	**517**
laminated plastics mfr. ...	**825**
leather goods mfr. ...	**555**
newspaper printing ...	**862**
Bender;	
arch	**839**
bar;	**536**
handle	**839**
copper (generators) ...	**850**
element	**850**
fish hook	**899**
frame (shipyard)	**899**
glass	**590**
iron	**530**
knife	**899**
pipe	**899**
plate	**534**
spoke *(cycle mfr.)*	**839**
spring *(spring mfr.)* ...	**530**
steel	**536**
timber	**579**
tube-	**899**
glass	**590**
wire	**899**
Bender-	
cardboard box mfr. ...	**569**
glass mfr.	**590**
rolling mill	**839**
stick making	**579**
wood products mfr. ...	**579**
Bender and fixer; bar ...	**536**
Bender and slotter (cardboard)	**569**
Berthing man...	**889**
Beveller-	
footwear mfr.	**555**
glass mfr.	**591**
printing	**569**
Bhandary	**620**
Bibliographer...	**380**
Billet man	**912**
Billeter *(rolling mill)* ...	**839**
Bin man; tempering... ...	**809**
Binman-	
local government-	**990**
cleansing dept.	**933**
Binder;	
armature	**850**
blanket	**553**
book	**562**
carpet	**553**
chair	**559**
iron	**912**

	Code number
Binder; *continued*	
leather;	**562**
hat	**553**
printer's	**562**
publisher's	**562**
slipper	**555**
stationer's	**562**
straw	**901**
umbrella	**559**
vellum	**562**
Binder-	
blanket mfr.	**553**
bookbinding	**562**
brush mfr.	**599**
canvas goods mfr. ...	**553**
cardboard box mfr. ...	**569**
fabric glove mfr.	**553**
footwear mfr.-	**555**
rubber footwear	**859**
hat mfr.	**553**
hosiery mfr.	**553**
printing	**562**
Bindery worker	**562**
Bingo operative	**699**
Biochemist	**201**
Biographer	**380**
Biologist	**201**
Biophysicist	**202**
Bishop	**292**
Bitter *(cardboard box mfr.)*	**569**
Bitumen worker	**820**
Blacker-	**869**
ceramics mfr.	**591**
Blacker-in (enamelled slate)	**869**
Blacksmith	**530**
Blacksmith-engineer... ...	**530**
Blader (turbines)	**516**
Blancher (fruit, vegetables)	**809**
Blaster;	
sand-	**844**
briar pipe mfr.	**579**
ceramics mfr.	**591**
shot	**844**
vapour	**844**
Blaster-	
furnace	**830**
mine, not coal	**898**
Bleach hand *(textile mfr.)* ...	**552**
Bleach worker *(textile mfr.)*	**552**
Bleacher; yarn	**552**
Bleacher-	
feather	**552**
flour	**809**
oil	**820**
paper	**821**
textiles	**552**
wood pulp	**821**
Bleacher and dyer	**552**
Blender;	
batch	**820**
butter	**809**
coal-	
coke ovens	**820**
steel mfr.	**829**
cocoa	**809**
coffee	**809**
colour-	
chemical mfr.	**820**
textile spinning	**811**
flour	**809**
grease (mineral oil) ...	**820**

	Code number
Blender; *continued*	
liquor	**829**
oil	**820**
pigment (chemicals)	**820**
rag	**811**
shade (wool)	**811**
spice	**809**
tea	**809**
varnish	**820**
whisky	**801**
Blender-	**820**
margarine	**809**
spirits	**801**
wines	**801**
wool	**F811**
arc welding electrode mfr.	**820**
asbestos composition goods mfr.	**811**
candle mfr.	**829**
cast stone products mfr.	**829**
chemical mfr.	**820**
explosives mfr.	**820**
food products mfr.	**809**
fur fibre mfr.	**814**
linoleum mfr.	**829**
man-made fibre mfr.	**829**
mineral oil refining	**820**
mineral water mfr.	**809**
oilskin mfr.	**814**
petroleum storage and distribution	**820**
plastics goods mfr.	**829**
tobacco mfr.	**802**
wool blending	**F811**
Blockman-	
butchers	**581**
fishmongers	**582**
metal trades	**912**
mine, not coal	**500**
Block worker; concrete	**599**
Blocker;	
fur	**557**
gold	**569**
hat	**559**
lens	**590**
Blocker-	
bookbinding	**562**
brick mfr.	**590**
footwear mfr.	**555**
hat mfr.	**559**
laundry	**673**
leather goods mfr.	**555**
lens mfr.	**590**
lifting tackle mfr.	**516**
textile mfr.	**814**
wood heel mfr.	**897**
Blouse hand	**556**
Blower;	
bottle	**590**
bulb (lamp, valve)	**590**
core	**531**
dry	**552**
fur	**814**
glass	**590**
glaze	**591**
sand	**844**
shot	**844**
soot *(power station)*	**893**
steam	**825**
thermometer	**590**
Blower-	
ceramics mfr.	**591**
chemical mfr.	**893**
cotton mfr.	**552**
glass mfr.	**590**
plastics goods mfr.	**825**
steelworks	**830**
textile finishing	**552**
Blower-up *(textile mfr.)*	**811**
Blowing room hand	**811**
Blowing room operative	**811**
Blowlamp worker *(shipbuilding)*	**534**
Blowpipe worker (quartz glass)	**590**
Blue coat *(holiday camp)*	**699**
Bluer-	
laundry	**673**
textile mfr.	**552**
Boardman-	
bakery	**580**
bookmakers	**699**
Boarder *(hosiery mfr.)*	**552**
Boat hand	**880**
Boatman;	**880**
foy	**880**
Boatswain-	**F880**
fishing	**F903**
Boatwright	**534**
Bobber;	
emery	**842**
fish	**930**
Bobber-	
metal goods	**842**
wood products	**579**
arc welding electrode mfr.	**842**
embroidery mfr.	**919**
fish dock	**930**
Bobber and polisher; spur	**842**
Bobbin and carriage hand	**516**
Bobbin worker; bottle	**813**
Bobbiner	**813**
Bodyguard	**615**
Boiler;	
acid	**829**
biscuit	**800**
fat	**829**
fruit	**809**
glue	**820**
grease	**820**
gum-	
sugar confectionery mfr.	**809**
textile dyeing	**552**
jelly	**809**
liquorice	**809**
oil-	**820**
oilskin mfr.	**814**
pan *(sugar refinery)*	**809**
rag	**821**
salt	**820**
sauce	**809**
size	**820**
soap	**820**
starch	**820**
steam	**893**
sugar	**809**
tar-	
building and contracting	**929**
gas works	**820**
woodpulp	**821**
Boiler-	
chemicals	**820**
Boiler- *continued*	
flax	**552**
food products	**809**
sugar confectionery	**809**
paper mfr.	**821**
textile finishing	**552**
Boilerman-	**893**
food products mfr.	**809**
gelatine, glue, size mfr.	**820**
paper mfr.	**821**
textile waste merchants	**814**
Boiling hand; soap	**820**
Boiling man; tar *(cable mfr.)*	**829**
Boiling-off man	**552**
Bolter; roof *(coal mine)*	**597**
Bolter-	
metal trades	**534**
textile dyeing	**862**
Bolter-down *(metal trades)*	**839**
Bolter-up *(metal trades)*	**851**
Bombadier-	
armed forces-	
foreign and Commonwealth	**601**
U.K.	**600**
Bonder; garment; rainproof	**559**
Bonder (electrical)	**850**
Bonderiser	**834**
Boner-	
corsets	**859**
fish	**582**
meat	**581**
Bookbinder	**562**
Bookkeeper-cashier	**410**
Bookkeeper-typist	**410**
Booster; gas *(steelworks)*	**893**
Boot and shoe operative	**555**
Boot and shoe worker	**555**
Borer;	
artesian	**898**
brush	**599**
cylinder	**511**
fine; barrel	**511**
horizontal	**511**
iron	**511**
ironstone	**898**
jig	**511**
methane *(coal mine)*	**597**
scissors	**511**
shot	**898**
spill (barrel, small arms)	**511**
tong (tubes)	**511**
tool room	**511**
tunnel	**509**
tyre	**511**
universal	**511**
vertical	**511**
well	**898**
wheel	**511**
wide (tobacco pipes)	**579**
wood	**897**
Borer-	
brush mfr.	**599**
coal mine-	**597**
above ground	**599**
fancy comb, slide mfr.	**899**
metal trades	**511**
mine, not coal	**898**
shipbuilding	**534**
wood wind instruments mfr.	**897**
Borer and cutter; cross	**897**

	Code number
Boss; *see also Foreman*	
mine	**113**
shift	**F898**
Bo'sun-	**F880**
fishing	**F903**
Botanist	**201**
Bottle hand	**590**
Bottler	**862**
Bottom hand *(coal mine)*	**886**
Bottom man *(coke ovens)*	**889**
Bottomer-	
cardboard box mfr.	**569**
metal goods mfr.	**841**
surgical footwear mfr.	**555**
Bouker	**552**
Boule de table	**699**
Bowker	**552**
Bowler; tyre	**912**
Bowler-	
entertainment	**387**
steelworks	**912**
Bowyer	**579**
Box hand-	**862**
printing	**560**
sugar refining	**889**
Box worker;	
cardboard	**569**
metal	**841**
Boxman *(steel mfr.)*	**830**
Boxer-	**862**
carpet mfr.	**569**
entertainment	**387**
Boxer-in	**517**
Boxer-up *(ceramics mfr.)*	**862**
Braider;	
asbestos	**814**
net	**814**
twine *(fishing net mfr.)*	**814**
whip	**599**
wire	**899**
Braider-	
basket mfr.	**599**
cable mfr.	**899**
clothing mfr.	**553**
cordage mfr.	**814**
fishing net mfr.	**814**
flexible tubing mfr.	**899**
rubber hose mfr.	**824**
telephone mfr.	**899**
textile smallwares mfr.	**814**
vehicle building	**559**
Brake hand *(printing)*	**891**
Brakeman *see Brakesman*	
Brakeman and steersman	**872**
Braker; wagon	**889**
Braker-	
mine, not coal	**889**
Brakesman; engine	**889**
Brakesman-	
biscuit mfr.	**800**
blast furnace	**889**
coal mine	**889**
mine, not coal	**889**
printing	**891**
transport-	**872**
railways	**881**
Brander	**569**
Brass worker	**899**
Brazer	**537**
Brazier	**537**

	Code number
Breaker;	
bear	**839**
billet	**899**
boiler	**899**
cake	**809**
can	**811**
car	**899**
coal	**890**
cotton	**811**
egg	**809**
engine	**899**
horse	**902**
iron	**911**
ore *(blast furnace)*	**829**
rail	**899**
rock-	**890**
construction	**929**
scrap	**899**
ship	**899**
skull	**839**
slag	**829**
stone-	**829**
mine, not coal	**890**
wagon	**889**
waste	**811**
woodpulp	**821**
Breaker-	
blast or puddling furnace	**912**
mine, not coal	**890**
paper mfr.	**821**
rolling mill	**839**
scrap merchant	**899**
textile finishing	**814**
textile spinning	**811**
Breaker and filler	**890**
Breakerman; rag	**821**
Breakerman-	
foundry	**911**
paper mfr.	**821**
Breaker-down *(rolling mill)*	**839**
Breaker-off-	
foundry	**843**
glass mfr.	**590**
type foundry	**899**
Breaker-up	**912**
Breaksman *see Brakesman*	
Breaster; heel-	**555**
wood	**897**
Breeder; plant *(research estab.)*	**201**
Breeder-	
dog	**169**
fish	**903**
horse	**169**
maggot	**902**
mealworm	**902**
stock	**160**
fishing net mfr.	**814**
Breeze man	**889**
Brewer;	
ginger beer	**809**
head	**219**
technical	**219**
under	**219**
vinegar	**219**
working	**219**
Brewer-	
qualified	**219**
brewery	**219**
distillery	**219**
mineral water mfr.	**809**
vinegar mfr.	**219**

	Code number
Brewery worker	**801**
Brick hand	**590**
Brick worker	**590**
Bricker;	
ladles *(iron works)*	**500**
mould	**500**
Bricklayer	**500**
Bricky	**500**
Bridgeman;	**889**
sluice	**889**
weigh	**863**
Bridgemaster	**889**
Brigadier-	
armed forces-	
foreign and Common-wealth	**M151**
U.K.	**M150**
Brightener;	**842**
oil	**820**
Brineman	**809**
Brineller	**860**
Briner	**809**
Broacher	**840**
Broadcaster	**384**
Broker;	
air	**703**
bill	**361**
bullion	**703**
commodity	**703**
diamond	**703**
discount	**361**
exchange	**361**
financial	**361**
foreign exchange	**361**
insurance	**361**
investment	**361**
jewel	**703**
licensed	**361**
marine	**703**
money	**361**
mortgage	**361**
pawn	**179**
printer's	**719**
produce	**703**
scrap	**733**
share	**361**
ship	**703**
stock	**361**
stock and share	**361**
tea	**703**
yacht	**703**
Broker-	
finance	**361**
insurance	**361**
transport	**703**
wholesale, retail trade	**703**
Bronze worker;	
architectural	**899**
ornamental	**899**
Bronzer;	
metal	**834**
printer's	**569**
Bronzer-	**834**
printing	**569**
Brother	**292**
Brow hand *(mining)*	**889**
Browner	**834**
Bruiser-	
enamel sign mfr.	**533**
leather dressing	**810**
Brush hand-	**507**

	Code number
Brush hand- *continued*	
brush mfr.	599
coach painting	869
Brush worker	599
Brusher;	
cloth *(textile finishing)*	552
enamel	869
flannelette	552
flour	809
glaze	591
glove	810
paint	869
pigment	821
roller	552
sanitary	591
scratch	842
tube *(railways)*	899
wire	842
Brusher-	
carpet mfr.	552
ceramics mfr.	591
clothing mfr.	919
coal mine	597
dyeing and cleaning	673
file mfr.	912
footwear mfr.	555
foundry	843
hosiery mfr.	552
leather finishing	810
needle mfr.	899
paper mfr.	821
scissors mfr.	842
textile mfr.	552
wallpaper mfr.	821
wool spinning	552
Brusher-in; scratch	842
Brusher-off-	
clothing mfr.	919
metal trades	869
Brusher-up *(footwear mfr.)*	555
Buckler	859
Buddler	890
Buffer;	
band	824
blacksmith's	842
blade	842
brass	842
comb-	825
metal	842
cutlery	842
hollow-ware	842
lime	842
sand	842
slate	500
spoon and fork	842
wheel; emery	810
Buffer-	
bone, etc.	599
flax processing	811
footwear mfr.	555
furniture mfr.	869
glass mfr.	591
leather dressing	810
metal trades	842
rubber goods mfr.	824
Buffer and polisher	842
Builder;	
ambulance	541
arch; brick	500
armature	520
barge	534

	Code number
Builder; *continued*	
barrow	579
bead (tyre)	824
belt *(rubber goods mfr.)*	824
boat	570
body (vehicle)	541
box *(P.O.)*	500
caravan	541
carriage	541
cart	579
chassis	537
chimney	500
coach	541
commutator	520
condenser	850
conveyor	516
core	850
cupola	500
cycle	516
drum (cables)	572
fireplace	506
fork (cycles)	516
frame-	
cycle mfr.	516
vehicle mfr.	541
furnace	500
garage	509
harness *(textile mfr.)*	814
heel	859
hose	824
house	504
jobbing	509
kiln; brick	500
lathe	516
loom	516
machine	516
maintenance	509
manhole	500
master	504
micanite	829
millstone	500
mop *(steelworks)*	839
motor	516
organ	593
oven	500
plate (mica, micanite)	829
radiator; car	533
retort	500
roller	824
rubber	824
sewer	500
ship	534
staircase	570
stove	500
table (sewing machine)	516
tank (rubber lining)	824
tool; machine	516
transformer	520
tread	824
tyre	824
vat	572
vehicle	541
wagon	541
wheel-	
perambulators	851
rubber	824
vehicles	851
wood	579
Builder-	
building and contracting	504
plastics goods mfr.	825

	Code number
Builder and contractor	504
Builder and decorator	504
Builder and repairer; boat	570
Builder-up; last	555
Building operative	509
Building worker	509
Bulb worker *(horticulture)*	595
Bulker *(tobacco mfr.)*	802
Bummaree	931
Bumper-	
ceramics mfr.	590
coal mine	889
hat mfr.	814
textile mfr.	814
tin box mfr.	841
Buncher;	
hank	814
watercress	862
Buncher-	
cigar mfr.	802
textile mfr.	814
Bundler;	
bag	862
flax	814
scrap	863
sheet (metal)	863
waste *(textile mfr.)*	862
Bundler-	862
brush mfr.	863
clothing mfr.	859
metal trades	863
Bundler and wrapper (cigarettes)	862
Bunker-	
coal mine	889
docks	930
Bunkerman; kiln-	
chemical mfr.	820
lime burning	820
Bunkerman-	
blast furnace	889
chemical mfr.	820
coal gas, coke ovens	889
coal mine	889
power station	990
Burden man	552
Burler	553
Burler and mender	553
Burner;	
acetylene	537
brick	823
chalk	820
gas-	
building and contracting	537
coal gas, coke ovens	820
gypsum	820
head *(ceramics mfr.)*	823
kiln-	
carbon goods mfr.	829
cement mfr.	829
ceramics mfr.	823
glass mfr.	823
lead	537
lime	829
mould *(rubber tyre mfr.)*	829
oxy-acetylene	537
profile	537
rotary furnace *(aluminium refining)*	820
sand	823
scrap *(steelworks)*	537

	Code number
Burner; *continued*	
tile	823
Burner-	
scrap metal	537
cement mfr.	829
ceramics mfr.	823
charcoal mfr.	829
chemical mfr.	820
coal mine	537
demolition	537
glass mfr.	823
lime burning	829
metal trades-	537
sinter plant	839
railways	537
Burnerman;	820
acid	820
Burner-off-	
incandescent mantles ...	829
glass mfr.	591
Burnisher;	
gold (*ceramics mfr.*) ...	591
Burnisher-	
ceramics mfr.	591
footwear mfr.	555
metal trades	842
Burr man	814
Burrer	810
Bursar;	M191
domestic	173
Burster	597
Busman	873
Busher; lead	839
Butcher; master	581
Butcher-	581
fish, poultry	582
Butcher-driver	581
Butcher-manager	178
Butler;	F670
wine	621
Butterman	990
Butter worker	809
Butter and tacker; welt ...	555
Button man;	
colliery	889
haulage	889
Button worker	899
Buttoner-	
clothing mfr.	559
rolling mill	839
Buttoner-up (bolts and nuts)	899
Buttonhole hand	553
Buttonhole worker	553
Buyer;	
advertising	701
job	719
media	701
print	701
space	701
store	179
Buyer-	701
retail trade	700
wholesale trade	701
Byeworker (*coal mine*) ...	910

C

	Code number
Cabman	**889**
Cabin boy (*shipping*)	**630**
Cabin man (*mine, not coal*)	**958**
Cabinet worker	**571**
Cable hand-	**913**
L.R.T.	**524**
tramways	**524**
Cable man	**913**
Cable tank man	**599**
Cable worker (*cable mfr.*)	**899**
Caddie	**699**
Cadet; officer-	
armed forces-	
foreign and Commonwealth	**M151**
U.K.	**M150**
Cadet-	
nursing	**340**
police	**610**
shipping	**332**
Café worker	**953**
Cafeteria hand	**953**
Cage hand (*coal mine*)	**886**
Cageman (*mine, not coal*)	**886**
Cager	**810**
Cake man; linseed	**809**
Caker (liquorice)	**809**
Calciner; dextrin	**809**
Calciner-	**820**
mine, not coal	**829**
Calculator;	
colour	**814**
sensitometric	**569**
Calender hand; fabric	**552**
Calender hand-	
laundry	**673**
leathercloth mfr.	**552**
linoleum mfr.	**829**
plastics goods mfr.	**825**
rubber mfr.	**824**
Calenderman; super	**821**
Calenderman-	
asbestos-cement goods mfr.	**829**
linoleum mfr.	**829**
paper mfr.	**821**
rubber mfr.	**824**
textile mfr.	**552**
Calenderer;	
asbestos	**829**
rubber	**824**
Calenderer-	
canvas hosepipe mfr.	**552**
laundry	**673**
paper mfr.	**821**
rubber mfr.	**824**
textile mfr.	**552**
Calibrator (instruments)	**517**
Call boy-	
entertainment	**699**
railways	**631**
Caller; bingo	**699**
Caller-over (*glass mfr.*)	**441**
Calligrapher	**381**
Cameraman;	**386**
chief (films)	**M384**
Campanologist	**385**
Canal worker	**929**
Canchman (*coal mine*)	**597**
Candler; egg	**861**
Cane worker	**599**
Caner-	**599**
corset mfr.	**859**
Canner	**862**
Cannery worker	**862**
Canon	**292**
Canteen hand	**952**
Canteen worker	**952**
Canvasser;	
advertisement	**719**
advertising	**719**
freight	**719**
insurance	**719**
political	**190**
tele-ad	**792**
telephone	**792**
traffic	**719**
Canvasser-	**730**
advertising	**719**
clothing mfr.	**553**
insurance	**719**
transport	**719**
Canvasser and collector	**730**
Capper;	
bobbin	**851**
bottle	**862**
paper	**862**
Capper-	**850**
cartridge mfr.	**599**
lamp, valve mfr.	**850**
polish mfr.	**862**
Capper and sealer; end	**899**
Capstan hand; brass	**840**
Capstan hand (*railways*)	**886**
Capstan man	**886**
Capsuler	**862**
Captain;	
barge	**332**
dredger	**332**
ferry	**332**
fire	**M153**
lighter	**332**
port	**140**
underground	**F898**
Captain-	
hovercraft	**M332**
airline	**M331**
armed forces-	
foreign and Commonwealth	**M151**
U.K.	**M150**
boat, barge	**332**
Church Army	**292**
fishing	**169**
mine, not coal	**F898**
Salvation Army	**292**
shipping	**332**
Captain-superintendent	**110**
Car worker	**851**
Carbide worker	**820**
Carbon worker	**599**
Carbonating hand	**809**
Carbonation hand (sugar)	**809**
Carbonation man (sugar)	**809**
Carbonator man	**820**
Carbonator (*brewery*)	**801**
Carboniser;	
cloth	**814**
nickel (*valve mfr.*)	**590**
piece	**814**
rag	**814**
Carboniser; *continued*	
wool	**814**
Carboniser-	
ball bearing mfr.	**833**
gas works	**820**
textile mfr.	**814**
Carburizer	**833**
Card and drawing hand (jute)	**811**
Card hand (flax, hemp)	**811**
Card room hand	**811**
Card room man	**811**
Card room operative	**811**
Card room worker	**811**
Carder;	
asbestos	**811**
comb	**862**
cotton	**811**
fibre	**811**
hair	**811**
head	**F811**
speed	**811**
under	**F811**
Carder-	
button mfr.	**862**
hook mfr.	**862**
pencil mfr.	**862**
textile mfr.-	**811**
lace finishing	**552**
Carding operative (textile)	**811**
Carding room man	**811**
Cardiographer	**346**
Cardiologist	**220**
Caretaker-	**672**
reservoir	**929**
Cargo worker	**930**
Carman-	**872**
blast furnace	**889**
coal merchants	**872**
coke ovens	**887**
Carpenter	**570**
Carpenter and joiner	**570**
Carpenter-diver	**599**
Carpet worker	**550**
Carrier;	
bag-	**889**
docks	**931**
bar	**839**
coal	**872**
deal-	**889**
docks	**930**
dust	**889**
fish box	**930**
general	**872**
glass (*glass mfr.*)	**889**
hod	**921**
lap	**889**
piece	**889**
pitwood	**930**
prop	**930**
railway	**872**
rivet	**899**
roller	**990**
set	**441**
timber (*docks*)	**930**
ware	**889**
Carrier-	**889**
docks	**930**
mine, not coal-	**872**
below ground	**889**
n.o.s.	**872**
transport	**872**

	Code number
Carrier-away	889
Carrier-in (*glass mfr.*)	823
Carrier-off	889
Carrotter	810
Cartman	889
Carter; coal	872
Carter-	
farming	902
mine, not coal	889
transport	889
Cartographer	310
Cartographer-draughtsman	310
Cartoner	862
Cartoonist	381
Carver;	
architectural	500
frame	579
gold	599
ivory	599
letter-	
brass	599
wood	579
monumental	500
stock (gun)	579
stone	500
wood	579
Carver-	
food	699
furniture	579
wood	579
Case worker;	
family	293
social (general)	293
Case worker-	
piano organ mfr.	571
welfare services	293
Casein worker (*food products mfr.*)	809
Caser; die	899
Caser-	
metal	833
packing	862
Cashier;	
bank	411
building society	411
chief-	F411
government	103
school	411
Cashier-	411
café	721
canteen	721
restaurant	721
garage	721
local government	401
retail trade	721
Caster;	
brass	839
china	590
cold (rubber)	824
concrete	599
die	531
furnace; blast	839
hollow-ware (*ceramics mfr.*)	590
ingot	839
iron	839
lead (*battery mfr.*)	839
metal	839
monotype	560
needle	839
parchester	501
roller (printer's)	824
Caster; *continued*	
sanitary	590
shot	839
slab	599
statue	590
stone	599
strip	839
tile	599
type	839
at machine	531
Caster-	
plaster	590
cast stone products mfr.	599
ceramics mfr.	590
footwear mfr.	824
glassware mfr.	590
metal trades	839
printing	560
Casting man (*blast furnace*)	839
Castrator-	902
farm livestock	900
Cataloguer	420
Catalyst man	820
Catcher;	
bar	839
bird	902
chicken	902
cigarette	869
finishing	839
machine	869
mill; sheet	839
mole	699
pole (linoleum)	829
rabbit	902
rat	699
rivet	899
roll; cold	839
sheet (paper)	821
Catcher-	
paper mfr.	821
steelworks	839
Catcher and sticker (wire)	839
Caterer	174
Catering worker	952
Cattleman	900
Caulker	534
Caulker-burner	534
Causticizer	820
Cellar boy *see Cellarman*	
Cellarer	801
Cellarman;	
bar	441
oil	441
Cellarman-	
bacon, meat curing	919
brewery	801
catering	441
hotel	441
rubber mfr.	829
steelworks	830
textile mfr.	441
wine mfr.	441
wine merchants	441
Cellist	385
Cellophaner	862
Cellroom man	820
Cement worker	829
Cementer;	
envelope	859
outsole	859
paper	821
Cementer; *continued*	
rubber	859
ship	506
upper	859
Cementer-	
ceramics mfr.	591
electrical insulator mfr.	850
footwear mfr.	859
lens mfr.	859
metal capsule mfr.	851
plastics goods mfr.	859
rubber goods mfr.	859
Cemetery worker	990
Centerer (*lens mfr.*)	591
Centerer and edger (*lens mfr.*)	591
Centrer *see Centerer*	
Ceramicist	219
Ceramist	219
Certifier; money order	861
Chain boy	929
Chainman-	929
docks	441
mine, not coal	889
Chairman; company (*large establishment*)	101
Chairman- *see also notes*	
appeals tribunal, inquiry, etc.	M350
glass mfr.	590
large establishment	101
Chalkman	552
Chamberman-	
acids	820
chemical mfr.	820
cold storage	441
Chamberlain;	
burgh	120
city	120
Chambermaid	958
Chambermaster	110
Chamferer	841
Chandler	179
Changer;	
card	814
drill	898
frame (carpets)	814
gold	834
mould (*rubber mfr.*)	824
roll	839
roller	569
rope (*coal mine*)	889
Changer-	
flax mfr.	811
textile printing	569
Channeller-	
footwear mfr.	555
metal trades	841
mine, not coal	898
Chaplain-	292
armed forces-	
foreign and Commonwealth	M151
U.K.	M150
Char house man	820
Char kiln man	820
Charman; wet	919
Charman (*sugar refining*)	919
Charwoman	958
Chargehand *see Foreman*	
Chargeman;	
battery	899

	Code number
Chargeman; *continued*	
track (*railways*)	**F922**
Chargeman- *see also Foreman*	
coal mine	**597**
copper, zinc refining	**887**
Charger;	
accumulator	**899**
battery	**899**
blunger	**829**
cartridge	**599**
coal	**887**
cordite	**599**
cupola	**889**
drill	**898**
flux dust	**889**
furnace (*metal mfr.*)	**889**
kiln	**820**
ore	**887**
oven	**887**
retort (*gas works*)	**887**
spare (*blast furnace*)	**889**
tube (*brass tube mfr.*)	**912**
Charger-	
coke ovens	**887**
firework mfr.	**599**
gas works	**887**
linoleum mfr.	**829**
metal mfr.-	**889**
tinplate mfr.	**839**
mine, not coal	**887**
slag wool mfr.	**829**
Chargerman	**887**
Charging hand; battery	**899**
Charlady	**958**
Chartist	**420**
Chaser;	
gold	**518**
platework	**518**
production	**420**
progress	**420**
silver	**518**
stock	**420**
Chaser-	
metal-	**899**
precious metal	**518**
manufacturing-	**420**
jewellery, plate mfr.	**518**
Chauffeur	**874**
Chauffeur-gardener	**874**
Chauffeur-handyman	**874**
Chauffeur-mechanic	**874**
Chauffeur-valet	**874**
Checker;	
bank-note	**861**
coupon (competitions)	**420**
dipper	**863**
dock	**420**
drawing	**310**
gate	**615**
gauge	**860**
goods	**420**
ingot (*steelworks*)	**860**
invoice	**410**
iron	**860**
linen (*hotel, etc.*)	**441**
machine (*engineering*)	**860**
map	**310**
meter	**412**
mica	**869**
milk	**861**
moulding	**861**

	Code number
Checker; *continued*	
paper (*paper mfr.*)	**861**
photographic (*printed circuit board mfr.*)	**569**
progress	**420**
steel (*coal mine*)	**441**
stock	**440**
stores	**440**
supports	**441**
ticket (*entertainment*)	**699**
timber	**441**
time	**410**
Checker- see also notes	
drawing office	**310**
electrical, electronic equipment	**860**
bakery	**861**
Bank of England	**861**
bingo hall	**699**
brewery	**861**
building and contracting	**420**
ceramics mfr.	**869**
chemical mfr.	**864**
clothing mfr.	**861**
coal mine	**441**
dairy	**F731**
docks	**420**
drug mfr.	**869**
electrical, electronic engineering	**860**
food products mfr.	**861**
metal trades	**860**
oil refining	**420**
paint mfr.	**869**
petroleum distribution	**420**
piano mfr.	**593**
plastics goods mfr.	**861**
printing	**861**
rubber goods mfr.	**861**
textile products mfr.	**861**
transport	**420**
warehousing	**441**
wholesale, retail trade	**420**
wood products mfr.	**861**
Checker and packer	**862**
Checker and weigher	**441**
Checker-loader	**420**
Checker-out	**721**
Checkweighman	**863**
Checkweigher	**863**
Cheese worker	**809**
Cheesemonger	**179**
Cheeser-	**813**
biscuit mfr.	**800**
Chef;	
head	**F620**
pastry	**F620**
Chef-	**620**
food products mfr.	**809**
Chef de cuisine	**F620**
Chemical worker	**820**
Chemist;	
agricultural	**201**
analytical	**200**
biological	**201**
chief	**200**
consulting	**200**
development	**200**
electroplating	**200**
government	**200**
homeopathic	**221**

	Code number
Chemist; *continued*	
industrial	**200**
inorganic	**200**
laboratory	**200**
managing	**200**
manufacturing	**200**
metallurgical	**200**
nuclear	**200**
organic	**200**
pharmaceutical	**221**
photographic	**221**
physical	**200**
polymer	**200**
research	**200**
research and development	**200**
shift	**200**
soil	**201**
superintending	**200**
technical	**200**
textile	**200**
wholesale	**179**
works	**200**
Chemist-	**200**
pharmaceutical	**221**
n.o.s.	**221**
retail trade	**221**
Chemist and druggist (*retail trade*)	**221**
Chequerer	**590**
Chick-sexer	**902**
Child care worker	**370**
Chiller man (*brewery*)	**801**
Chimney hand (*building and contracting*)	**509**
Chipper;	
pneumatic	**899**
steel (*steelworks*)	**899**
tyre	**843**
Chipper-	
ceramics mfr.	**591**
chipboard mfr.	**821**
metal trades-	**899**
fish hook mfr.	**841**
shipbuilding	**534**
painting	**869**
road surfacing	**923**
Chipper and painter	**507**
Chipper and scaler	**912**
Chipper and scraper	**534**
Chipper-in (*rolling mill*)	**839**
Chiropodist	**344**
Chiropractor	**347**
Chlorate of soda man	**820**
Chlorinator (*water works*)	**892**
Chlorine worker; electrolytic	**820**
Chocker (*coal mine*)	**597**
Chocolate hand	**809**
Chocolate worker	**809**
Chocolatier	**809**
Chopper;	
firewood	**990**
sugar	**809**
wood (*sawmilling*)	**897**
Chopperman (*paper mfr.*)	**811**
Choreographer	**384**
Chorister	**384**
Chorus girl	**384**
Chromer-	**552**
metal trades	**834**
Chummer-in (*ceramics mfr.*)	**590**
Church Army worker	**292**

	Code number
Church worker	**292**
Cider worker	**801**
Cinema worker	**699**
Cinematographer	**386**
Circuit man; electric light ...	**521**
Circular hand...	**551**
Circus hand	**990**
Civil servant (n.o.s.) ...	**400**
Civil servant-	
assistant secretary and above-	
government	**100**
grade 5 and above-	
government	**100**
Cladder	**501**
Clammer (*roller engraving*)	**569**
Clampman (*fire brick mfr.*)	**829**
Clamper-	
pencil mfr.	**859**
roller engraving	**569**
textile finishing	**552**
Clapper boy	**386**
Clapper-loader	**386**
Clarifier man	**809**
Clarinettist	**385**
Classer	**863**
Classifier;	**863**
livestock	**902**
Clatter (*celluloid*)	**825**
Clay boy (*metal mfr.*) ...	**912**
Clay man-	
ceramics mfr.	**829**
clay pit	**898**
Clay worker-	
ceramics mfr.	**590**
clay pit	**898**
Cleaner;	
aircraft	**958**
bag	**999**
bank	**958**
bar (*catering*)	**958**
barrel	**999**
belt (*coal mine*)	**889**
berth	**958**
blende	**890**
boat	**958**
bobbin	**814**
bogie	**990**
boiler	**899**
bone	**829**
book	**990**
boot	**555**
bottle	**999**
box (*textile printing*) ...	**919**
brass	**919**
bristle	**811**
buddle	**990**
building	**896**
bus	**958**
button	**825**
cab	**958**
canteen	**958**
car	**958**
card	**899**
cardroom	**814**
carpet	**673**
carriage	**958**
cask	**999**
casting	**843**
chimney	**957**
church	**958**
clock	**517**
Cleaner; *continued*	
closet	**958**
cloth	**552**
clothes	**673**
coal	**890**
core	**839**
crane	**894**
cycle	**912**
decomposer (*nickel mfr.*)	**912**
domestic	**958**
drain	**958**
drum	**919**
dry	**673**
dye vat (straw plait) ...	**919**
engine; carding	**899**
engine-	
coal mine	**894**
railways	**894**
shipping	**880**
water works	**894**
equipment	**990**
factory	**958**
feather	**814**
fish	**582**
floor	**958**
flue	**957**
frame (cycles, motors) ...	**912**
fruit	**809**
fur	**673**
garment	**673**
general	**958**
glass (dry plates)	**569**
gulley	**990**
gut	**829**
hat	**559**
heald	**899**
heddle	**899**
hide	**810**
hospital	**958**
house;	**958**
boiler	**899**
power	**958**
hydraulic	**894**
hygiene	**959**
iron	**843**
jet	**919**
key (locks)	**899**
kiosk; telephone	**958**
kitchen	**958**
laboratory	**958**
lace	**814**
lamp-	**990**
coal mine	**910**
lens	**919**
library...	**958**
line	**889**
loco	**894**
locomotive	**894**
loom	**814**
machine-	**990**
textile mfr.	**814**
maintenance	**990**
meat	**581**
metal	**843**
meter	**517**
motor (*garage*)	**958**
mould	**919**
night	**958**
office	**958**
omnibus	**958**
picture	**381**
Cleaner; *continued*	
piece	**552**
pipe	**899**
pirn	**814**
pit (*railways*)	**990**
plant	**990**
plate-	
catering	**952**
printing	**569**
press (*rolling mill*) ...	**839**
printer's	**889**
rag	**811**
ramie	**552**
rice	**809**
ring	**843**
river	**929**
road-	**957**
mine, not coal	**990**
road and yard (*railways*)	**958**
roller	**814**
room;	
mess...	**958**
show	**958**
sack	**999**
school...	**958**
scrap-	**912**
tobacco mfr.	**802**
seed	**809**
sheet (*plastics mfr.*) ...	**919**
ship's	**958**
shop	**958**
silver-	**899**
catering, hotels, etc. ...	**952**
domestic service	**952**
skin; sausage	**809**
spillage	**910**
sponge	**829**
station (*railways*)	**958**
steam (*building and contracting*)	**896**
steel (*foundry*)	**843**
still	**919**
stone-	**896**
iron	**890**
street	**957**
table (*textile mfr.*)	**814**
tank	**990**
tape; magnetic	**999**
telephone	**958**
tin-	
bakery	**919**
food canning	**919**
mine, not coal	**890**
toilet	**959**
tray (*bakery*)	**919**
tripe	**809**
tube; boiler	**899**
tube-	
blast furnace	**912**
lamp, valve mfr.	**999**
railways	**899**
upholstery	**958**
vacuum	**673**
vat	**990**
wagon (*coal mine*) ...	**910**
ware	**869**
warehouse	**958**
warp (*textile mfr.*)	**814**
waste	**811**
watch	**517**
window	**956**

	Code number
Cleaner; *continued*	
wire (*wire mfr.*)	**839**
wood	**821**
works	**958**
workshop	**958**
yard	**958**
Cleaner-	**958**
educational establishments	**958**
food products	**809**
industrial premises	**958**
institutional premises	**958**
machinery-	**990**
textile machinery	**814**
metal goods	**899**
office premises	**958**
residential premises	**958**
vehicles	**958**
asbestos-cement mfr.	**599**
cartridge mfr.	**839**
catering, hotels, etc.	**958**
ceramics mfr.	**591**
clothing mfr.	**559**
coal mine	**910**
domestic service	**958**
dyeing and cleaning	**673**
electroplating	**839**
enamelling	**839**
entertainment	**958**
fellmongery	**810**
footwear mfr.	**555**
foundry	**843**
fur goods mfr.	**673**
galvanized sheet mfr.	**834**
government	**958**
lamp, valve mfr.	**893**
local government	**958**
musical instruments (brass mfr.)	**899**
needle mfr.	**899**
optical instrument mfr.	**919**
P.O.	**958**
piano mfr.	**869**
printing	**919**
railways	**958**
retail trade	**958**
silk throwing	**813**
textile finishing	**814**
Cleaner and balancer (weighing machine)	**516**
Cleaner and greaser	**894**
Cleaner-doorman	**958**
Cleaner-engineer	**894**
Cleaner-stoker	**958**
Cleanser-	
local government	**933**
soap mfr.	**820**
Clearer;	
credit	**412**
oven (*bakery*)	**800**
table	**959**
tuyere bottom	**912**
warp	**552**
Clearer-	
cotton doubling	**812**
embroidering	**559**
textile finishing	**552**
Cleaver;	
diamond	**518**
lath	**579**
wood	**579**

	Code number
Cleaver-	
precious stones	**518**
cricket bat mfr.	**579**
Clergyman	**292**
Clerical worker-	**430**
local government	**401**
Clerk; *see also notes*	**430**
accountancy	**410**
accountant's	**410**
accounts	**410**
actuarial	**420**
administration	**430**
advertising	**420**
allocator	**420**
articled-	
accountancy	**250**
legal services	**242**
assurance	**410**
audit-	**410**
qualified	**250**
average adjuster's	**410**
bank	**411**
barrister's	**350**
bill(ing)	**410**
bonus	**410**
booking;	
stores	**440**
warehouse	**440**
booking (travel agency)	**420**
bookmaker's	**411**
building society	**411**
cargo	**420**
cash	**411**
charge	**420**
chartering (*sea transport*)	**420**
chief-	**F430**
banking	**F411**
building society	**F411**
courts of justice	**240**
government	**103**
insurance	**F410**
local government	**102**
P.O.	**F430**
claims-	**411**
insurance	**410**
clearance	**420**
cloakroom	**959**
coding	**420**
committee	**399**
community charge	**401**
compilation	**420**
computer	**420**
confidential	**459**
continuity (*film making*)	**430**
control;	
air traffic	**463**
credit	**410**
data	**420**
load (*aircraft*)	**420**
material	**440**
production	**420**
quality	**420**
stock	**440**
control (*local government*)	**401**
conveyancing	**420**
correspondence	**420**
cost	**410**
costing	**410**
counter	**411**
course (*betting*)	**420**
data entry	**490**

	Code number
Clerk; *continued*	
deputy (*local government*)	**102**
despatch	**440**
estimating (*insurance*)	**410**
export	**420**
filing	**420**
fingerprint	**420**
forwarding	**420**
freight	**420**
head	**F430**
higher grade	**400**
hire	**420**
import	**420**
information; travel	**420**
insurance	**410**
intake	**420**
invoice(ing)	**410**
judge's	**350**
junior	**430**
law-	**420**
articled	**242**
ledger	**410**
left luggage	**959**
library	**421**
litigation	**420**
machine; weigh (*coal mine*)	**863**
managing-	**M350**
qualified solicitor	**242**
accountancy	**M399**
manifest	**420**
office;	**430**
booking	**411**
box	**411**
buying	**420**
personnel	**420**
post	**411**
sales	**410**
officer's; sheriff	**412**
order;	**410**
mail	**440**
sales	**440**
pay-	**410**
totalisator	**411**
planning	**420**
poll-tax	**401**
press cuttings	**421**
principal-	
government	**103**
local government	**102**
P.L.A.	**140**
processing; data	**420**
progress	**420**
property	**401**
purchasing	**420**
quarter sessions	**240**
query; sales	**440**
rating	**401**
receiving office	**720**
records;	**420**
stock	**440**
stores	**440**
reservations (*travel*)	**420**
routeing	**420**
sales; telephone	**792**
schedule	**420**
schedules (*transport services*)	**420**
secretarial	**430**
security	**411**
senior (*local government*)	**401**
sheriff (Scotland)	**240**
shipping	**420**

	Code number
Clerk; *continued*	
solicitor's-	**420**
articled	**242**
sorting (*P.O.*)	**940**
staff-	**420**
local government	**102**
statistical	**420**
statistics	**420**
stock	**440**
stockbroker's	**410**
stockroom	**440**
storekeeper's	**440**
stores	**440**
supervising	**F430**
tally;	**420**
timber	**441**
technical	**420**
tele-ad	**792**
time	**410**
town	**102**
transport	**420**
travel agency	**420**
travel enquiry	**420**
turf accountant's	**411**
valuation;	**410**
higher grade (*Inland Revenue*)	**132**
voyages	**420**
wages	**410**
warehouse	**440**
weigh	**863**
weighbridge	**863**
weighing	**863**
in holy orders	**292**
of arraigns	**240**
of the council	**102**
of the course	**176**
of the court	**240**
of the executive council	**M399**
of the peace	**240**
of the scales	**863**
of works	**112**
to the assessments committee	**M399**
to the board (*local government*)	**102**
to the commissioners (*Inland Revenue*)	**100**
to the council	**102**
to the county council	**102**
to the district council	**102**
to the executive council	**M399**
to the justices	**240**
to the parish council	**102**
to the rural district council	**102**
to the urban district council	**102**
Clerk-	
advertising, publicity	**420**
assurance company	**410**
bank	**411**
building society	**411**
college	**420**
credit card company	**410**
government	**400**
health authority	**401**
insurance company	**410**
law courts	**400**
library	**421**
local government	**401**
police service	**401**
Post Office	**411**

	Code number
Clerk- *continued*	
prison service	**400**
school	**420**
stockbrokers	**410**
university	**420**
Clerk and steward	**176**
Clerk and telegraphist; sorting	**940**
Clerk-in-charge	**F430**
Clerk-bookkeeper	**410**
Clerk-buyer	**420**
Clerk-messenger	**430**
Clerk-packer	**430**
Clerk-receptionist	**430**
Clerk-storekeeper	**440**
Clerk-storeman	**440**
Clerk-telephonist	**430**
Clerk-typist-	**430**
college	**420**
government	**400**
health authority	**401**
local government	**401**
police service	**401**
school	**420**
university	**420**
Clerk-warehouseman	**440**
Clicker;	
machine	**555**
press	**555**
Clicker-	
footwear mfr.	**555**
leather goods mfr.	**555**
printing	**F560**
Climber (*constructional engineers*)	**535**
Clinker man	**919**
Clipper;	
card top	**899**
cloth	**552**
horse	**902**
knot	**552**
poodle	**902**
press (*press cutting agency*)	**421**
veneer	**897**
Clipper-	
coal mine	**889**
hosiery mfr.	**859**
metal trades	**839**
rope mfr.	**552**
tannery	**810**
textile finishing	**552**
Clock hand (*ball bearing mfr.*)	**860**
Clocker	**553**
Clogger	**555**
Closer;	
channel	**859**
repairs	**555**
Closer-	
clothing mfr.	**553**
footwear mfr.	**555**
foundry	**839**
toy mfr.	**555**
wire rope mfr.	**899**
Cloth man (*clothing mfr.*)	**861**
Cloth worker (*textile finishing*)	**552**
Clothier;	
boiler	**929**
card	**899**
Clothier (*retail trade*)	**179**
Clothier and outfitter	**179**
Clown	**384**

	Code number
Coach (sports)	**387**
Coachman	**889**
Coal man-	**990**
coal merchants	**872**
Coaler	**990**
Coastguard	**619**
Coat and skirt hand	**556**
Coat hand	**556**
Coater;	
cathode	**899**
celluloid (*film mfr.*)	**829**
ceramics	**591**
chocolate	**809**
colour	**834**
dry plate	**829**
emulsion	**829**
filament	**899**
hand (*oilskin mfr.*)	**814**
paper-	**821**
photographic	**829**
prime	**507**
sugar-	
confectionery mfr.	**809**
pharmaceutical mfr.	**820**
tablet	**820**
tar (*coal gas, coke ovens*)	**829**
Coater-	
linoleum mfr.	**829**
photographic film mfr.	**829**
stencil paper mfr.	**821**
tinplate mfr.	**834**
wire mfr.	**834**
Coating man (*roofing felt mfr.*)	**814**
Cobberer	**809**
Cobbleman	**880**
Cobbler	**555**
Coder-	**420**
manufacturing	**862**
Cogger (*rolling mill*)	**832**
Coiffeur	**660**
Coiler;	
copper	**839**
rope	**814**
tape	**814**
Coiler-	
cable mfr.	**899**
electrical goods mfr.	**850**
rope mfr.	**814**
rubber tubing mfr.	**824**
spring mfr.	**899**
steel mfr.	**839**
wire mfr.	**839**
wire rod mfr.	**839**
wire rope mfr.	**899**
Coiner	**841**
Coke man (*coke ovens*)	**919**
Coke worker (*coke ovens*)	**820**
Coker (*coal gas, coke ovens*)	**820**
Collar hand (*clothing mfr.*)	**553**
Collator (*printing*)	**562**
Collector;	
ash	**889**
ash pit	**889**
assistant (*Inland Revenue*)	**400**
blood	**581**
car	**874**
cash	**412**
chief (*Inland Revenue*)	**103**
cloth	**889**
club	**412**

	Code number
Collector; *continued*	
cop	**889**
credit	**412**
debt	**412**
dust (*local government*)	**933**
egg-	**872**
poultry farm	**900**
excess luggage	**631**
fee; parking	**412**
fern	**902**
glass (dry plates)	**889**
higher grade (*Inland Revenue*)	**103**
insurance	**719**
kelp	**903**
metal; scrap	**733**
meter	**412**
milk	**872**
moss	**902**
mutuality	**412**
pools	**412**
rate;	**401**
chief	**102**
reed	**902**
refuse	**933**
regional	**103**
rent	**412**
sack	**872**
salvage-	**889**
local government-	
cleansing dept.	**933**
scaleboard	**889**
scrap-	**889**
self-employed	**733**
seaweed	**903**
senior-	
gas board	**F412**
government	**103**
local government	**401**
subscription	**412**
superintendent (*local government*)	**102**
tax; assistant	**400**
ticket-	**959**
L.R.T.	**631**
railways	**631**
toll	**412**
tow (flax)	**811**
waste (works)	**889**
of parts	**441**
of taxes;	**132**
assistant	**400**
Collector-	
credit trade	**412**
Customs and Excise	**103**
electricity board	**412**
entertainment	**411**
finance company	**412**
football pools	**412**
gas board	**412**
Inland Revenue	**132**
insurance	**719**
local authority	**401**
photographic films mfr.	**889**
retail trade	**412**
textile mfr.	**889**
Collector and salesman	**730**
Collector-agent-	**412**
insurance	**719**
Collector-driver; refuse	**872**
Collector-driver (*local government*)	**401**
Collector-salesman	**730**
Collier-	
barge	**930**
coal mine	**597**
Colliery worker	**910**
Colonel-	
armed forces-	
foreign and Commonwealth	**M151**
U.K.	**M150**
Colonel-Commandant-	
armed forces-	
foreign and Commonwealth	**M151**
U.K.	**M150**
Colourman;	**829**
artist	**179**
Colour worker-	
paint mfr.	**829**
printing	**569**
Colourer;	
hand (picture postcard)	**569**
print	**569**
Colourer-	
artificial flowers	**869**
carpets	**814**
metal	**833**
steel pens	**833**
wallpaper printing	**569**
Colourist;	**814**
copy	**430**
photographic	**569**
postcard	**569**
Columnist	**380**
Comber-	
fur dressing	**810**
textile mfr.	**811**
Combiner-	
canvas goods mfr.	**814**
paper mfr.	**821**
Combing operative (*textile mfr.*)	**811**
Comedian	**384**
Commandant-	
airport	**140**
armed forces-	
foreign and Commonwealth	**M151**
U.K.	**M150**
fire service	**M153**
Commander-	
hovercraft	**M332**
armed forces-	
foreign and Commonwealth	**M151**
U.K.	**M150**
shipping	**332**
Commentator	**380**
Commissionaire	**699**
Commissioner;	
land	**262**
of oaths	**242**
Commissioner-	
government	**100**
legal service	**240**
police	**M152**
Commodore-	
armed forces-	
foreign and Commonwealth	**M151**
U.K.	**M150**
shipping	**332**
Community worker	**371**
Commutator hand	**520**
Companion	**670**
Companion-help	**670**
Companion-housekeeper	**670**
Companion-nurse	**340**
Companyman (*coal mine*)	**597**
Compiler;	
catalogue	**420**
crossword	**380**
directory	**420**
index	**420**
order	**441**
technical	**380**
Compo man	**899**
Composer (music)	**385**
Compositor	**560**
Compounder-	**829**
chemical mfr.	**820**
food products mfr.	**809**
mineral water mfr.	**809**
plastics goods mfr.	**829**
rubber mfr.	**824**
Compressor;	
engineer's	**893**
gas	**893**
heel	**555**
tablet	**820**
Compressor hand	**893**
Compressor man	**893**
Concaver (*footwear mfr.*)	**897**
Concentrator	**820**
Concentratorman (*paper mfr.*)	**821**
Conche man	**809**
Concher	**809**
Conchologist	**201**
Concrete worker; pre-cast	**599**
Concrete worker-	**923**
concrete products mfr.	**599**
Concreter;	**923**
granolithic	**506**
Condenser-	
milk processing	**809**
textile mfr.	**811**
Condenser hand	**850**
Condenser man-	**820**
blast furnace	**830**
Conditioner;	
air	**999**
leaf	**802**
paper	**821**
yarn	**552**
Conditioner-	
food products mfr.	**809**
paper mfr.	**821**
tannery	**810**
textile mfr.	**552**
Conductor;	
bus	**875**
floating bridge	**889**
music	**385**
musical	**385**
omnibus	**875**
P.S.V.	**875**
paddy	**889**

(Co)

	Code number
Conductor; *continued*	
trolleybus	875
Conductor-	
entertainment	385
railways	881
road transport	875
Coner; wood (silk)	814
Coner-	
felt hood mfr.	559
textile mfr.	814
Confectioner; flour	580
Confectioner-	179
employee-	580
sugar confectionery mfr.	809
Confectioner and tobacconist	179
Confectionery hand	800
Confectionery worker (*sugar confectionery mfr.*)	809
Conjurer	384
Connector;	
armature	850
cable	524
coupling	532
Connector (rubber boots and shoes)	859
Constable;	
chief;	M152
assistant	M152
deputy	M152
market	615
police *see Constable-*	
private	615
Constable-	
non-statutory	615
airport	610
docks	610
government	610
Kew gardens	615
Min. of Defence	610
police service	610
railways	610
Royal parks	610
Construction worker	929
Constructor;	
naval	211
permanent way	922
road	923
roof (*building*)	570
roofing	501
steel	535
switchboard	520
Consul	103
Consultant;	
actuarial	252
advertising	123
agricultural	201
aid; hearing	346
architectural	260
beauty-	661
retail trade-	720
door to door sales	730
bridal	383
business	364
catering	174
ceramics	219
chemical	200
colour (*paint mfr.*)	219
computer	214
corsetry	559
cosmetics	720
cost (qualified)	251

	Code number
Consultant; *continued*	
dental	223
design (*engineering*)	216
ear piercing	661
economic	252
editorial	380
educational	239
engineering;	211
chemical	215
civil	210
fashion	383
financial	361
forestry	201
heating-	532
professional	219
industrial	218
insurance	719
investment	361
legal	241
management	253
marketing	121
medical	220
metallurgical	219
mortgage	361
organisation and methods	364
patent	219
pension	252
perfumery	720
personnel	124
production	217
property	170
recruitment	124
relations; public	123
research; operational	364
resource; human	253
sales	121
scheme-	
community industries	124
training	124
scientific	219
security	615
services; management	253
shipping	719
software; computer	214
statistical	252
study; works	364
systems	320
tax	362
technical *see Engineer-prof.-*	
training	124
travel	420
wig	661
Contract worker (*coal mine*)	597
Contractor;	
advertisement	123
advertising	123
agricultural	160
bill posting	719
bricklaying	500
builder's	504
building	504
cartage	872
catering	174
civil engineer's	896
cleaning (self-employed)	958
clothing	179
coal	179
decorating	507
demolition	896
drainage	929
electrical	521

	Code number
Contractor; *continued*	
fencing	929
flooring	506
forestry	904
gardening	594
general	896
haulage	872
hire; plant	719
landscape	594
office cleaning	719
painting	507
penning	929
plastering	502
ploughing	160
plumbing	532
public works	896
removal	931
road	896
roofing	501
stone (*coal mine*)	597
timber	179
transport (road)	872
Contractor-	
bricklaying	500
agricultural contracting	160
building and contracting	896
coal mine	929
mine, not coal	898
painting, decorating	507
pipe lagging	895
plastering	502
transport	872
Contractor's man (*coal mine*)	597
Controlman; bunker	889
Controlman-	820
blast furnace	830
margarine mfr.	809
Controller;	
account	410
ambulance	199
apron	889
area-	
fire service	153
retail trade	179
assistant (*prison service*)	154
budget	410
cash	411
catering	174
charge (*metal mfr.*)	889
chief (*railways*);	140
deputy	F881
coal (*metal mfr.*)	889
computer	126
contract	420
converter	F830
conveyer (*coal mine*)	889
cost	410
credit	130
data; computer	490
depot-	142
distribution	142
despatch	142
display	381
divisional	199
economics	252
electrical-	521
railways	F893
export-	121
export agency	702
financial	120
freight-(*railways*)	142

	Code number
Controller; *continued*	
furnace-	
metal goods mfr.	**830**
metal mfr.	**F830**
sherardizing	**830**
gas (*steelworks*)	**301**
goods (*railways*)	**142**
humidity	**552**
inventory	**141**
load (*aircraft*)	**420**
locomotive	**883**
maintenance;	
planned-	**516**
coal mine	**110**
plant	**516**
marketing	**121**
materials	**141**
merchandise	**121**
mortgage	**411**
movement; ground (*airport*)	**330**
network (*telecoms*)	**821**
office	**139**
operations (*transport*)	**140**
oxygen	**399**
pest	**699**
plant	**516**
power (*railways*)	**F893**
price	**430**
production-	**110**
building and contracting	**111**
progress	**420**
project (*metal trades*)	**110**
proof; newspaper	**430**
purchasing	**122**
quality *see notes*	
radar; area	**330**
radio	**463**
regional (*government*)	**103**
reservation (*airline*)	**420**
sales	**121**
schedule	**420**
school meals	**174**
section (*railways*)	**883**
senior (*fire service*)	**153**
services; management	**253**
shift	**110**
shipping	**140**
shop (*metal trades*)	**110**
signals	**140**
site	**111**
sound	**386**
spares	**441**
staff	**363**
statistical	**252**
stock	**141**
stores	**141**
sub-contracts-	
production	**110**
building and contracting	**111**
supplies	**141**
technical *see Manager*	
telecommunications	**139**
temperature (*tobacco mfr.*)	**802**
traffic;	**140**
air	**330**
train	**883**
trainsman's relief	**883**
transport	**140**
treatment; water	**892**
wages	**139**
waste	**420**

	Code number
Controller; *continued*	
works	**110**
of aircraft	**330**
of distribution	**142**
of factories (*P.O.*)	**110**
of typists	**F452**
Controller-	
water treatment	**892**
banking	**120**
fire service	**153**
government	**103**
insurance	**361**
prison service	**154**
railways	**883**
Controller hand (*printing*)	**891**
Convenor; works	**190**
Converter;	
paper-	**821**
paper products mfr.	**569**
polythene	**820**
steel	**830**
timber	**897**
Converter-	
gas board	**532**
metal mfr.	**830**
Converter man-	
chemical mfr.	**820**
glucose mfr.	**809**
metal mfr.	**830**
Conveyancer	**350**
Conveyor	**889**
Conveyor hand	**889**
Conveyor man	**889**
Cook;	
chief	**F620**
head	**F620**
mastic (*asphalt mfr.*)	**829**
pastry-	**620**
bakery	**580**
Cook-	**620**
bakery	**800**
food products mfr.	**809**
tripe dressing	**809**
Cook in charge	**F620**
Cook-cleaner	**620**
Cook-companion	**620**
Cook-general	**620**
Cook-housekeeper	**670**
Cook-manager	**174**
Cook-steward	**620**
Cook-supervisor	**F620**
Cooker; potato crisp	**809**
Cooker (*food products mfr.*)	**809**
Cookerman (*cereal food mfr.*)	**809**
Cooler-	
brewery	**801**
chemical mfr.	**820**
food products mfr.	**809**
Cooler hand (*sugar refining*)	**809**
Cooler man *see Cooler*	
Cooper; wine	**862**
Cooper-	**572**
tobacco mfr.	**572**
Co-ordinator;	
computer	**126**
legal	**242**
marketing	**121**
placement	**392**
production	**399**
sales	**121**
training	**124**

	Code number
Copier;	
design	**430**
pattern; paper	**822**
Copper	**813**
Copperman (*textile mfr.*)	**813**
Copperworker; electro (*textile printing*)	**569**
Copper worker (*refining*)	**912**
Copperas heap man	**919**
Copperer (carbon brushes)	**839**
Copperhead worker	**801**
Coppersidesman	**801**
Coppice worker	**904**
Copyholder	**430**
Copyist;	
braille	**569**
design	**430**
designer's	**430**
milliner's	**557**
music	**385**
photo	**490**
Copyist-	
millinery mfr.	**557**
textile printing	**430**
Corder-	
footwear mfr.	**555**
printing	**859**
tobacco mfr.	**802**
upholstering	**559**
Cordite worker	**820**
Cordwinder	**555**
Corer; hard	**599**
Corer (*foundry*)	**531**
Corker-	**862**
fishing rod mfr.	**859**
Cornetist	**385**
Coroner	**350**
Corporal; underground	**F886**
Corporal-	
armed forces-	
foreign and Commonwealth	**601**
U.K.	**600**
Corporation employee	**990**
Corporation worker	**990**
Corrector;	
chart (*Trinity House*)	**310**
die	**515**
press	**430**
proof; newspaper	**430**
spring (*vehicle mfr.*)	**516**
Corrector (*hosiery mfr.*)	**814**
Correspondent;	
banking	**420**
claims	**410**
foreign	**380**
newspaper	**380**
sales	**420**
technical	**380**
turf	**380**
Corrugator-	
asbestos-cement products mfr.	**829**
galvanized sheet mfr.	**841**
paper mfr.	**821**
Corsetiere	**559**
Coster	**732**
Costermonger	**732**
Costume hand	**556**
Costumier	**556**
Cotton operative	**919**
Cotton room man	**441**

	Code number
Cotton room worker	**441**
Cotton worker	**919**
Coucher	**821**
Council employee	**990**
Council worker	**990**
Counsel; Queen's	**241**
Counsellor;	
investment	**361**
school	**392**
student	**392**
Counsellor-	
government	**103**
welfare services	**371**
Counter;	
bank-note	**863**
bobbin	**441**
paper	**861**
Counter-	
bolt mfr.	**862**
mine, not coal	**863**
paper mfr.	**861**
printing	**441**
textile mfr.	**441**
Counterhand	**953**
Counterman-	
chemicals	**441**
drugs	**441**
catering	**953**
hosiery mfr.	**862**
retail trade	**720**
take-away food shop	**720**
turf accountants	**411**
wool warehouse	**441**
Counter-off	**441**
Coupler (*hose pipe mfr.*)	**859**
Courier-	**941**
tour operator	**630**
Couturier	**383**
Coverer;	
bar; metal	**899**
biscuit	**800**
boiler	**929**
box (wooden fixture boxes)	**859**
buckle	**859**
button	**859**
cabinet (*furniture mfr.*)	**859**
case	**859**
chocolate	**809**
elastic (*textile mfr.*)	**814**
fireworks	**859**
hat	**859**
heel	**859**
helmet	**859**
hood (cars, perambulators)	**553**
lead	**839**
pipe	**929**
rexine	**554**
roller-	
printing	**824**
textile mfr.	**555**
roof	**501**
rubber-	
cable mfr.	**824**
surgical bandage mfr.	**814**
textile mfr.	**824**
tennis ball	**859**
umbrella	**553**
wheel (rubber)	**824**
wire (*insulated wire mfr.*)	**824**
Coverer-	
bookbinding	**562**
Coverer- *continued*	
cardboard box mfr.	**859**
coat hanger mfr.	**559**
corset mfr.	**851**
insulated wire, cable mfr.	**899**
leather goods mfr.	**859**
piano mfr.	**859**
rubber goods mfr.	**824**
Coverer and liner; case	**859**
Cowman	**900**
Coxswain	**332**
Crabber;	
french	**552**
yorkshire	**552**
Crabber-	
fishing	**903**
textile mfr.	**552**
Cracker; egg	**809**
Cracker hand (*paper goods mfr.*)	**859**
Cracker-off	**591**
Craftsman;	
assistant-	
L.R.T.	**913**
metal trades	**913**
distribution (*gas board*)	**516**
engineering	**516**
general (*building*)	**509**
leaded light	**503**
museum	**571**
research and development	**599**
underground (*coal mine*)	**516**
Craftsman-	
government	**599**
instrument mfr.	**517**
L.R.T.	**516**
Cramper (nails, needles)	**841**
Crane man	**886**
Cranker (*ceramics mfr.*)	**829**
Cranker-up (*ceramics mfr.*)	**829**
Crater-	
manufacturing-	**862**
printing	**891**
Cream hand (liquorice)	**809**
Creamer (*biscuit mfr.*)	**800**
Creamery hand	**809**
Creamery worker	**809**
Creaser; vamp	**555**
Creaser-	
footwear mfr.	**555**
textile mfr.	**814**
Creaser and lapper	**814**
Creeler	**814**
Creosoter; timber	**821**
Creper;	**552**
silk	**812**
Crewman	**930**
Cricketer	**387**
Criminologist	**291**
Crimper;	
detonator	**851**
vamp	**555**
Crimper-	
cable mfr.	**899**
flax mfr.	**812**
footwear mfr.	**555**
textile mfr.-	**552**
textile spinning	**812**
Critic	**380**
Crochet worker	**551**
Croft hand	**552**
Crofter-	
farming	**160**
textile mfr.	**552**
Cropper-	
agriculture	**900**
metal trades	**899**
textile mfr.	**552**
Crossing man; level	**883**
Croupier	**699**
Crowder	**823**
Crowner	**555**
Crozier	**814**
Crucible man (metal)	**830**
Crucible worker	**590**
Crusher;	
bone	**829**
burr	**552**
calamine	**820**
coal-	**829**
coal mine	**890**
malt	**801**
seed	**809**
slag	**890**
Crusher-	
abrasives	**890**
chemicals	**820**
minerals-	**829**
mines and quarries	**890**
rock (*mine, not coal*)	**890**
ceramics mfr.	**829**
seed crushing	**809**
Crusherman-	
rock (*mine, not coal*)	**890**
Crystal worker; quartz	**518**
Crystalliser (*sugar confectionery mfr.*)	**809**
Crystallographer	**202**
Cuber (*seed crushing*)	**809**
Cultivator;	
shellfish	**903**
watercress-	**160**
employee	**595**
Cupel man	**830**
Cupola hand (*metal mfr.*)	**830**
Cupola man	**830**
Cupper; shell	**841**
Curate	**292**
Curator;	**271**
picture	**271**
Cureman	**829**
Curer-	
food products	**809**
rubber	**829**
skins	**810**
Curler;	
feather	**814**
soft	**813**
yarn	**813**
Curler (*hat mfr.*)	**559**
Currier	**810**
Custodian; castle	**672**
Custodian-	**619**
security services	**615**
Cutler;	**899**
cloth	**814**
silver	**518**
Cutlery worker	**899**
Cut-off man-	
corrugated paper mfr.	**821**
glass mfr.	**590**

	Code number
Cutter;	
acetylene	**537**
alteration	**557**
asbestos (*mattress mfr.*)	**559**
bacon	**581**
bag-	**555**
canvas	**559**
band; rubber	**824**
bandage	**559**
bar	**899**
bass	**811**
belt-	**555**
abrasives mfr.	**822**
bias	**559**
billet (*steelworks*)	**899**
biscuit	**800**
blank (*spoon, fork mfr.*)	**841**
block-	
linoleum mfr.	**899**
wallpaper mfr.	**899**
blouse	**557**
bobbin	**814**
bottom	**898**
box (cardboard)	**822**
box maker's	**897**
brace	**555**
bread (*bakery*)	**800**
brick	**590**
bridle	**555**
brilliant (*glass mfr.*)	**591**
butcher's	**581**
button;	**825**
pearl	**899**
cable	**899**
cap	**557**
card-	
paper products mfr.	**822**
textile mfr.	**814**
carpet	**506**
cheese	**720**
circle	**841**
clay	**898**
cloth-	
bookbinding	**562**
clothing mfr.	**557**
made-up textiles mfr.	**557**
textile mfr.	**552**
clothier's	**557**
clothing	**557**
coal (*coal mine*)	**597**
collar-	**557**
rubber	**824**
copse	**904**
cork	**599**
corset	**559**
costume	**557**
cotton	**599**
design-	
clothing mfr.	**559**
printing	**899**
designer	**559**
diamond-	**518**
glass mfr.	**590**
die-	
engraving	**569**
footwear mfr.	**555**
disc (*rubber mfr.*)	**824**
dress (fibre)	**811**
felt (*textile mfr.*)	**559**
fibre	**811**
file	**899**
Cutter; *continued*	
film-	
cine film processing	**822**
photographic film mfr.	**822**
fittings	**555**
flag	**559**
flame	**537**
flyer	**513**
frock	**557**
fur	**557**
fustian	**552**
gas	**537**
gear	**513**
gimson (*brake lining mfr.*)	**829**
glass;	**590**
optical	**591**
glass lustre	**591**
glove;	**557**
boxing	**555**
gold	**899**
grass	**594**
guillotine-	
asbestos-cement goods mfr.	**599**
leather goods mfr.	**555**
metal trades	**899**
paper goods mfr.	**822**
wood products mfr.	**897**
hand (*clothing mfr.*)	**557**
hat	**557**
hay (*farming*)	**902**
heath	**902**
hedge	**902**
hemp	**811**
hosiery	**557**
insulation	**899**
key	**840**
knife;	
band	**557**
hand	**557**
machine-	**557**
metal trades	**899**
knife (*leather glove mfr.*)	**557**
laces	**559**
leaf-	
precious metals	**518**
tobacco	**802**
leather-	**555**
bookbinding	**562**
clothing mfr.	**557**
tannery	**810**
lemon	**809**
lens	**591**
letter; glass	**591**
letter-	
die sinking	**569**
monumental masons	**500**
linen (*button mfr.*)	**557**
lingerie	**557**
lining-	
clothing mfr.	**557**
footwear mfr.	**555**
litho (*ceramics mfr.*)	**869**
lozenge	**809**
machine; punching (*metal trades*)	**841**
machine-	
coal mine	**597**
clothing mfr.	**557**
leather goods mfr.	**555**
mine, not coal	**898**
manilla	**811**
Cutter; *continued*	
mantle	**557**
material	**557**
measure	**557**
meat	**581**
metal;	**899**
scrap	**537**
mica	**829**
mould	**515**
mushroom	**902**
negative	**822**
nut	**839**
oxy-acetylene	**537**
panel-	
metal	**899**
wood	**897**
paper	**822**
pattern;	
iron (*footwear mfr.*)	**555**
metal	**515**
paper	**822**
pattern-	
clothing mfr.	**557**
footwear mfr.	**555**
fur goods mfr.	**559**
jacquard card cutting	**814**
leather goods mfr.	**555**
textile mfr.	**430**
peat	**902**
peel	**809**
pile	**552**
pin;	**899**
vice	**513**
plastics	**825**
plate-	
engraving	**599**
photographic film mfr.	**590**
press-	
footwear mfr.	**555**
leather goods mfr.	**555**
made-up textiles mfr.	**557**
paper goods mfr.	**822**
textile mfr.	**559**
print	**822**
profile-	**513**
footwear mfr.	**555**
puff	**555**
punch	**569**
rag	**811**
rail	**899**
rasp	**899**
reed	**902**
rib (*hosiery mfr.*)	**559**
ribbon (typewriter ribbons)	**559**
ring	**590**
roll	**559**
roller	**569**
rotary-	
metal trades	**899**
paper products mfr.	**822**
rubber	**824**
sack	**559**
saddle	**555**
sample (*footwear mfr.*)	**555**
scallop	**552**
scrap	**537**
screw	**513**
seal	**569**
sett	**500**
sheet; asbestos	**829**
shell; pearl	**899**

	Code number
Cutter; *continued*	
shirt	**557**
shoe	**555**
shopman (butcher's) ...	**581**
silver	**899**
skin-	
clothing mfr.	**557**
tannery	**810**
slate	**500**
slipper	**555**
soap	**829**
sole-	**555**
clog	**897**
sponge	**829**
steel	**537**
stencil-	
metal trades	**533**
printing	**822**
stiffening	**555**
stilt	**590**
stock	**557**
stone	**500**
strap (*leather goods mfr.*)	**555**
straw (*farming*)	**902**
sugar	**809**
sweet	**809**
table (*glove mfr.*)	**557**
tailor's	**557**
test (*rolling mill*)	**899**
thread	**559**
thrum	**811**
tie	**557**
timber...	**897**
tip (*cemented carbide goods mfr.*)...	**899**
tobacco	**802**
tool (*metal trades*) ...	**515**
top	**898**
transferrer's	**869**
tread	**824**
trimming	**557**
tube-	
glass...	**590**
metal	**899**
paper	**822**
turf	**594**
tyre	**824**
umbrella cloth	**559**
under	**557**
upholstery	**559**
velvet	**552**
veneer	**897**
wafer	**800**
waste (*textile mfr.*) ...	**814**
watercress	**902**
willow	**904**
wiper	**811**
wire	**899**
wood (*forestry*)	**904**
worm	**513**
Cutter-	
bone, etc.	**599**
clothing	**557**
precious stones	**518**
abrasive paper, cloth mfr.	**822**
artificial flower mfr. ...	**559**
bakery	**800**
bookbinding	**562**
butcher's shop	**581**
candle mfr.	**599**
canvas goods mfr.... ...	**559**

	Code number
Cutter- *continued*	
ceramics mfr.	**590**
clothing mfr.	**557**
coach trimming	**559**
coal mine	**597**
embroidering	**557**
fancy goods mfr.	**599**
flour confectionery mfr. ...	**800**
food products mfr. ...	**809**
footwear mfr.	**555**
furniture mfr.	**897**
glass mfr.	**590**
glove mfr.	**557**
glue mfr.	**829**
haberdashery mfr.... ...	**557**
hat mfr.	**557**
hosiery and knitwear mfr.	**557**
leather goods mfr. ...	**555**
lens mfr.	**591**
linoleum mfr.	**829**
metal trades-	**899**
boiler mfr.	**537**
cable mfr....	**899**
cutlery mfr.	**841**
nail mfr.	**841**
perambulator mfr. ...	**841**
shipbuilding	**537**
steel pen mfr.	**841**
mine, not coal	**898**
packing case (wood) mfr.	**897**
paper mfr.	**822**
paper pattern mfr. ...	**822**
paper products mfr. ...	**822**
plastics goods mfr. ...	**825**
powder puff mfr.	**555**
printing	**822**
rubber goods mfr.... ...	**824**
soft toy mfr.	**559**
sugar confectionery mfr....	**809**
tannery	**810**
textile mfr.-	**814**
textile finishing	**552**
woollen, worsted mfr. ...	**552**
tobacco mfr.	**802**
upholstering	**559**
woodworking	**897**
Cutter and booker	**518**
Cutter and caulker (*shipbuilding*)	**534**
Cutter and fitter	**557**
Cutter and grinder; tool ...	**512**
Cutterman; coal	**597**
Cutterman-	
coal mine	**597**
paper mfr.	**822**
Cutter down (*rolling mill*)...	**839**
Cutter-grinder (*metal trades*)	**513**
Cutter-off-	
metal trades-	**899**
iron pipe mfr.	**843**
Cutter-out (*cutlery mfr.*) ...	**839**
Cutter-through (*steelworks*)	**834**
Cutter-up; scrap	**899**
Cycle hand	**851**
Cycle worker...	**851**
Cyclist	**387**
Cylinderman (*paper mfr.*) ...	**821**
Cytologist	**201**
Cytotaxonomist	**201**

D

	Code number
Dairy hand-	
farming	**900**
milk processing	**809**
Dairyman-	
farming	**900**
margarine mfr.	**809**
milk processing	**809**
retail trade-	**720**
delivery round	**731**
Dairy worker- *see Dairyman*	
margarine	**809**
milk processing	**809**
Damper (*textile mfr.*)	**552**
Damperman (*paper mfr.*)	**821**
Dancer	**384**
Darner-	
hotel, etc.	**553**
textile mfr.-	**553**
sack repairing	**559**
Datal hand-	
coal mine	**910**
mine, not coal	**990**
Datal man *see Datal hand*	
Datal worker *see Datal hand*	
Dataller *see Datal hand*	
Dateler *see Datal hand*	
Dateller *see Datal hand*	
Dauber; ladle (*iron and steel-works*)	**912**
Dauber (*coal gas, coke ovens*)	**919**
Dayman-	
mining see Datal hand	
theatre	**990**
Day wage man *see Datal hand*	
Day worker *see Datal hand*	
Deacon	**292**
Dealer;	
accessories; motor	**179**
antiques	**179**
car	**179**
cattle	**179**
chipped potato	**174**
estate	**719**
exchange; foreign (*banking*)	**361**
firewood	**732**
fish	**178**
fish and chip	**174**
game	**179**
general	**733**
investment	**361**
log; fire	**732**
metal; scrap	**733**
money	**361**
paper; waste	**733**
pig	**179**
poultry	**179**
property	**719**
rag	**733**
rag and bone	**733**
scrap	**733**
share	**361**
stock and share	**361**
store; marine	**179**
tyre	**179**
Dealer-	
finance	**361**
wholesale, retail trade-	**179**
market trading	**732**
party plan sales	**730**

	Code number
Dean-	**292**
university	**230**
Deburrer	**843**
Decatiser	**552**
Deck hand-	
fishing	**903**
milk processing	**809**
shipping	**880**
Deckie (*fishing*)	**903**
Decorator;	
aerograph	**596**
aerographing (*ceramics mfr.*)	**591**
art	**869**
cake	**580**
card (greeting, etc. cards)	**859**
display	**381**
floral	**791**
glass-	**591**
painting	**591**
house	**507**
interior-	**381**
building and contracting	**507**
slip	**591**
tin plate	**891**
Decorator-	**507**
ceramics	**591**
flour confectionery	**580**
leather cloth	**552**
sugar confectionery	**809**
building and contracting	**507**
metal trades	**507**
wallpaper mfr.	**569**
Decoy man	**902**
Degger	**552**
Degreaser-	
metal trades	**839**
tannery	**810**
Dehairer; pig	**581**
Dehydrator man; tar	**820**
Delegate; union; trade	**190**
Delicatessen	**179**
Delimer	**810**
Delinter	**890**
Deliverer;	
allowance	**940**
book	**941**
car	**874**
coal	**872**
milk	**731**
newspaper	**941**
parcel	**941**
Deliverer (*textile mfr.*)	**889**
Delivery boy-	**941**
bakery	**731**
dairy	**731**
Deliveryman;	
baker's	**731**
coal	**872**
Deliveryman-	**872**
laundry	**731**
newsagents	**941**
retail milk trade	**731**
retail trade-	
delivery round	**731**
textile mfr.	**889**
Delver (*mine, not coal*)	**898**
Demographer	**252**
Demolisher	**896**
Demolition worker	**896**
Demonstrator;	**719**
technical	**719**

	Code number
Demonstrator-consultant	**719**
Demonstrator-salesman	**719**
Denierer (*man-made fibre mfr.*)	**826**
Dentist	**223**
Depositor-	
electroplating	**834**
welding	**839**
Depository hand (*sugar confectionery mfr.*)	**809**
Depotman-	**931**
blast furnace	**889**
Depot worker	**931**
Deputy-	
coal mine	**F597**
lodging house	**F670**
mine, not coal	**F898**
Dermatologist	**220**
Derrick floor man (*oil wells*)	**898**
Derrickman-	**886**
oil wells	**898**
De-ruster	**839**
Descaler (*steelworks*)	**839**
Deseamer (*steelworks*)	**537**
Designer;	
aircraft	**211**
applications	**382**
architectural	**260**
art	**381**
body (*vehicle mfr.*)	**382**
book	**382**
C.A.D.	**310**
chief	**F310**
circuit (*telecommunications*)	**216**
cloth	**382**
clothing	**383**
commercial	**382**
computer	**216**
concrete; reinforced	**260**
costume	**383**
design; aided; computer	**310**
display	**381**
dress	**383**
electrical	**216**
electronics	**216**
embroidery	**382**
exhibition	**381**
fashion	**383**
formwork	**260**
furniture	**382**
garden	**594**
gem	**382**
graphic	**381**
handbag	**382**
industrial	**382**
interior	**381**
jewellery	**382**
kitchen	**381**
lighting	**386**
lithographic	**382**
machinery; electrical	**216**
mechanical	**310**
nautical	**211**
naval	**211**
packaging	**382**
pattern (*textile printing*)	**382**
pottery	**382**
printer's	**382**
project *see Engineer-prof.-*	
set	**381**
shopfitting	**382**

Code number

Designer; *continued*
- stage **381**
- structural **260**
- systems- **320**
  - qualified **214**
  - *railway signalling* **216**
- textile **382**
- tool **310**
- toy **382**
- typographical **560**

Designer-
- ceramics **382**
- clothing **383**
- footwear **382**
- glassware **382**
- leather goods **382**
- plastics goods **382**
- scenery **381**
- wallpaper **382**
- wood products **382**
- *advertising* **381**
- *broadcasting* **381**
- *flour confectionery mfr.* **580**
- *fur goods mfr.* **383**
- *metal trades* **216**
- *millinery mfr.* **383**
- *rubber goods mfr.* **382**
- *soft toy mfr.* **382**
- *textile mfr.* **382**

Designer-cutter-
- *clothing mfr.* **559**
- *paper products mfr.* **822**

Designer-detailer **310**

Designer-draughtsman **310**

Desilveriser **830**

Desizer **814**

Despatch; goods **441**

Despatch hand **441**

Despatch man-
- *bakery* **441**
- *catering* **953**

Despatch worker **441**

Despatcher; **441**
- flight **330**
- goods **441**
- radio **463**
- rail **863**
- road **863**
- traffic (*aircraft*) **420**

Destroyer (pest) **699**

Destructor man; refuse **999**

Detective;
- hotel **615**
- private **615**
- store **615**

Detective-
- *airport* **610**
- *docks* **610**
- *government* **610**
- *police service* **610**
- *private detective agency* **615**
- *railways* **610**
- *retail trade* **615**

Detector; crack (*metal mfr.*) **860**

Detonator worker (*chemical mfr.*) **599**

Developer;
- estate **719**
- film **569**
- property **719**

Code number

Developer-
- *coal mine* **597**
- *photographic processing* **569**
- *textile mfr.* **552**

Development worker (*coal mine*) **597**

Devil (*printing*) **919**

Devilman (*paper mfr.*) **811**

Deviller **811**

Devulcaniser man (*rubber reclamation*) **829**

Dewer **552**

Diagnostician (*H.M. Dockyard*)-
- electrical **529**

Diarist **380**

Die man (*plastics goods mfr.*) **825**

Dietician **347**

Digester **820**

Digester worker **820**

Digger;
- bait **903**
- coal (*coal mine*) **597**
- grave **929**
- peat **902**
- trench **929**
- turf **594**

Digger (*mine, not coal*) **898**

Digger man **885**

Dingman **533**

Dinker (*coal mine*) **597**

Diplomat **100**

Dipper;
- acid **839**
- automatic (*ceramics mfr.*) **591**
- brass **839**
- cellulose **869**
- chocolate **809**
- core **839**
- enamel **869**
- fondant **809**
- galvanizing **834**
- glove **824**
- machine (*ceramics mfr.*) **591**
- metal **834**
- paint **869**
- rubber **824**
- tank (*petroleum distribution*) **863**
- toffee **809**
- wire **834**

Dipper-
- *ceramics mfr.* **591**
- *leather dressing* **810**
- *match mfr.* **899**
- *metal trades-* **869**
  - *arc welding electrode mfr.* **834**
  - *galvanizing* **834**
  - *precious metal, plate mfr.* **834**
- *oil refining* **863**
- *paper mfr.* **821**
- *rubber mfr.* **824**
- *sugar confectionery mfr.* **809**
- *textile mfr.* **552**

Dipper and stripper **839**

Director; *see also notes*
- airport **140**
- art **381**
- casting (*entertainment*) **M384**
- commercial **121**
- company (*large establishment*) **101**
- contracts (*construction*) **111**

Code number

Director; *continued*
- divisional (*Red Cross*) **M371**
- film **M384**
- financial **120**
- funeral **690**
- housing **M371**
- managing- *see Manager-*
  - *large establishment* **101**
- marketing **121**
- media **123**
- museum **271**
- musical **385**
- operations (*transport*) **140**
- personnel **124**
- purchasing **122**
- regional (*government*) **103**
- sales **121**
- sales and export **121**
- stage **M384**
- technical **110**
- traffic (*transport*) **140**
- zoo **271**
- of contracts (*government*) **122**
- of education **232**
- of music (*entertainment*) **M385**
- of photography **M384**
- of production (*entertainment*) **M384**
- of programmes **M384**
- of research-
  - biological science **201**
  - chemistry **200**
  - physical science **202**
- of social services **M102**

Director-
- *large establishment* **101**
- *W.R.N.S.* **M150**

Director and Secretary **127**

Dis hand **569**

Disc man **591**

Discharger-
- *coal gas, coke ovens* **889**
- *docks* **930**

Disinfector **699**

Disintegrator-
- *asbestos composition goods mfr.* **811**
- *food products mfr.* **809**

Dismantler;
- engine; aircraft **516**
- furnace **921**
- machinery **899**
- ship **899**

Dismantler-
- *building and contracting* **896**
- *coal mine* **597**
- *scrap merchant, breakers* **899**

Dispatch; goods **441**

Dispatch hand **441**

Dispatch man-
- *bakery* **441**
- *catering* **953**

Dispatch worker **441**

Dispatcher; **441**
- flight **330**
- goods **441**
- radio **463**
- rail **863**
- road **863**
- traffic (*aircraft*) **420**

Dispenser; drink **622**

	Code number
Dispenser-	346
food and beverages	953
bakery	863
licensed trade	622
Display hand-	
firework mfr.	699
retail trade-	381
shelf filling	954
Displayman; window	791
Displayman-	
printing	560
retail trade-	381
shelf filling	954
Distiller-	820
lead, zinc refining	830
Distributor;	
circular	941
film	719
leaflet	941
paste (*aluminium*)	839
weft	889
work	889
Distributor-	
manufacturing	889
wholesale, retail trade	179
Ditcher;	929
stone	500
Diver	599
Divider;	
hand-	517
bakery	800
mathematical instrument	517
thermometer	517
Divider-	
clothing mfr.	859
type foundry	863
Divider hand (*bakery*)	800
Diviner; water	699
Dock crew	930
Dock man-	930
ship repairing	912
Dock worker-	930
dry dock	912
Docker; cork	599
Docker (*docks*)	930
Dockside worker	930
Dockyard worker	912
Doctor;	220
saw	899
Dodger; can	811
Dodger (*textile finishing*)	811
Doffer;	814
ring	812
Doffer and setter	814
Dogger	839
Dogger-on	839
Dogger-up (tubes)	839
Dollier-	
silversmiths	842
textile mfr.	552
Dolly hand	552
Dollyer	552
Dolomite man (*iron, steelworks*)	829
Domestic-	958
hospital	958
Domestic worker	958
Donkeyman-	886
shipping	F880
Door boy-	
catering, hotels, etc.	699
Door boy- *continued*	
iron, steelworks	912
Doorman; furnace	839
Doorman-	699
coke ovens	919
forging	839
Doper-	
aircraft mfr.	869
leather dressing	810
Doubler;	
asbestos	812
cloth	814
ring	812
warp	814
Doubler-	
metal rolling	839
textile mfr.-	812
textile bleaching	814
textile dyeing	814
Dough man	800
Draffman (whisky)	801
Drafter;	
fibre	811
slipper	811
stone	500
Drafter (*brush mfr.*)	811
Draftsman;	
costs; law	410
parliamentary	241
Dragger;	
bar	830
pipe (*brickworks*)	889
set	889
skip	889
Dragger-down	839
Drainman	990
Drainage worker	929
Drainer-	929
brewery	919
Dramatist	380
Draper;	179
credit	730
Draughter *see Drafter*	
Draughtsman;	310
cartographical	310
chief	F310
lithographic	560
printer's	560
Draughtsman-engineer	310
Draughtsman-surveyor	310
Drawer;	
bar	831
brick	889
brush	599
card	811
chock (*coal mine*)	597
cloth-	861
textile finishing	552
coke (*coke ovens*)	889
cotton	811
fine	553
fork	839
hair	811
kiln-	
ceramics mfr.	889
chemical mfr.	820
lime-	
lime burning	829
mine, not coal	889
oven (*ceramics mfr.*)	889
pick	530
Drawer; *continued*	
plate (wire)	839
prop-	898
coal mine	597
rod (metal)	831
salvage (*coal mine*)	597
steel-	831
coal mine	597
strip (metal)	831
tape (metal)	831
timber-	
coal mine	597
mine, not coal	898
tube (metal)	831
waste (*coal mine*)	597
wire	831
wool	811
worsted	811
yarn	811
Drawer-	
glass	590
metal	831
ceramics mfr.	889
coal mine	889
glass mfr.	590
metal trades-	831
forging	530
puddling	830
zinc refining	830
mine, not coal	889
paper mfr.	889
textile mfr.-	811
jute mfr.	552
lace mfr.	861
textile finishing	552
textile weaving	552
Drawer and marker (*assay office*)	839
Drawer and setter (*brick mfr.*)	823
Drawer-in (*textile mfr.*)	552
Drawer-off-	
coal mine	889
textile mfr.	814
Drawing hand (*textile mfr.*)	811
Drawtwist operative; nylon	812
Drayman	872
Dredgeman-	885
shell fish	903
Dredger-	885
shell fish	903
Dredgerman	885
Dredgermaster	F885
Dreep man (*by-products mfr.*)	820
Drencher	810
Dresser;	
bag	552
bass	811
bow	899
box;	862
axle	843
brick (*brick mfr.*)	591
bristle	811
card	899
casting	843
cloth	552
concrete	599
core	843
diamond	518
doll	599
fibre	811

	Code number
Dresser; *continued*	
flame (*rolling mill*)	**537**
flour	**809**
fly	**599**
fur	**810**
gypsum	**829**
hair-	
broom, brush mfr.	**811**
hairdressing	**660**
heald	**899**
iron	**843**
kerb	**500**
leather	**810**
lime	**829**
meat	**581**
metal	**843**
pipe	**843**
plate	**843**
potato	**902**
poultry	**582**
sack	**552**
scissors	**899**
seed	**809**
sett	**500**
silk	**811**
skin-	**810**
sausage mfr.	**809**
slate	**500**
steel	**843**
stick	**579**
stone-	**500**
concrete products mfr.	**599**
tin	**890**
tripe	**809**
tube	**843**
wallstone	**500**
warp	**552**
weld	**899**
wheel	**843**
wig	**661**
window	**791**
wire	**839**
wood	**579**
woollen	**552**
yarn	**552**
Dresser-	
entertainment	**699**
footwear mfr.	**555**
fur dressing	**810**
leather dressing	**810**
metal trades-	**843**
bolt, nut mfr.	**839**
typefounding	**899**
mine, not coal	**500**
stone dressing	**500**
textile mfr.-	**811**
felt mfr.	**552**
rope, cord, twine mfr.	**552**
textile finishing	**552**
textile weaving	**552**
Dressmaker	**556**
Drier *see Dryer*	
Driftman (*coal mine*)	**597**
Drifter-	
coal mine	**597**
mine, not coal	**898**
Drill man (*mine, not coal*)	**898**
Driller;	
air	**511**
asbestos	**599**
axle box	**511**
Driller; *continued*	
barrel	**511**
brush	**599**
button	**825**
casement (metal)	**511**
ceramic	**591**
circle (*textile machinery mfr.*)	**511**
diamond (*well sinking*)	**898**
die; diamond	**518**
faller	**511**
frame	**511**
gas burner	**511**
gas ring	**511**
glass	**590**
hackle	**511**
hand	**534**
hydraulic	**534**
machine-	
metal trades	**511**
mine, not coal	**898**
mica	**899**
micanite	**899**
pin	**511**
plate	**534**
porcelain	**591**
portable	**534**
pottery	**591**
radial	**511**
radial arm	**511**
rail	**511**
rim	**511**
sample-	
mine, not coal	**898**
steelworks	**534**
shipwright's	**534**
test (steel)	**534**
tip	**511**
tool room	**511**
vertical	**511**
well-	**898**
offshore	**F898**
wheel	**511**
wire; diamond	**518**
wood	**897**
Driller-	
asbestos composition goods mfr.	**599**
asbestos goods mfr.	**599**
civil engineering contracting	**898**
coal mine-	**597**
workshops	**511**
metal trades-	**511**
boiler mfr.	**534**
constructional engineering	**534**
shipbuilding	**534**
mine, not coal	**898**
plastics goods mfr.	**825**
well sinking	**898**
Driver;	
ambulance	**642**
angle dozer	**885**
articulator	**872**
assistant-	
iron and steelworks	**830**
textile spinning	**812**
belt	**889**
bogie	**887**
bridge;	**889**
swing	**889**
bulldozer	**885**
Driver; *continued*	
bus	**873**
cab	**874**
calender (*insulated wire, cable mfr.*)	**899**
car;	
auto	**882**
charger	**887**
coke (*gas ovens*)	**887**
electric (*steelworks*)	**889**
furnace; blast	**889**
lorry	**887**
motor	**874**
rail	**882**
scale	**887**
shuttle	**882**
weigh	**887**
carriage	**874**
carrier; straddle	**886**
cart	**889**
caster	**839**
charge	**887**
charger-	
coal gas, coke ovens	**887**
steelworks	**889**
closer (*wire rope mfr.*)	**899**
coach	**873**
compressor	**893**
control (*steelworks*)	**830**
controller (*steelworks*)	**889**
conveyor	**889**
crane	**886**
crawler	**885**
crusher (*mine, not coal*)	**890**
delivery-	**872**
car delivery service	**874**
derrick	**886**
diesel-	
coal mine	**882**
railways	**882**
digger	**885**
dredger	**885**
drill (*mine, not coal*)	**898**
drott	**885**
drum (*steelworks*)	**886**
dumper	**887**
elevator	**886**
engine;	
cable	**886**
diesel (*coal mine*)	**882**
haulage	**886**
locomotive	**882**
shunting	**882**
traction	**872**
winding	**886**
engine-	**893**
agriculture	**901**
mining	**893**
railways	**882**
shipping	**880**
euclid	**887**
excavator	**885**
exhauster (*gas works*)	**999**
extruding	**825**
fan	**999**
gantry	**886**
gear (*rolling mill*)	**832**
gearhead (*coal mine*)	**887**
gig	**552**
goods	**872**
grab	**886**

	Code number
Driver; *continued*	
grader	**885**
guide; coke	**889**
H.G.V.	**872**
hammer	**839**
haulage; motor	**872**
haulage-	
mining	**886**
road transport	**872**
hauler (*coal mine*)	**886**
hearse	**874**
hoist	**886**
horse	**889**
house; power	**893**
hyster	**887**
incline	**886**
internal	**887**
J.C.B.	**885**
launch	**880**
library; mobile	**872**
lift;	**886**
fork	**887**
lister	**889**
loader-	**872**
airport	**931**
building and contracting	**885**
loco	**882**
locomotive	**882**
lorry	**872**
machine;	
armouring	**899**
cable	**899**
cabling	**899**
insulating	**899**
lapping	**899**
layer-up	**899**
spreading (asphalt, concrete)	**885**
stoking	**887**
tubing	**899**
machine-	
agriculture	**901**
asbestos-cement goods mfr.	**829**
civil engineering	**885**
gas works	**887**
magnet (*steelworks*)	**886**
mail;	
motor	**872**
paddy (*coal mine*)	**886**
manipulator (*steelworks*)	**889**
minibus	**873**
mini cab	**874**
mixer; concrete	**829**
motor;	
dumpy	**887**
electric	**889**
railway	**872**
telpher	**886**
motor-	**872**
coal mine	**893**
funeral direction	**874**
navvy	**885**
omnibus	**873**
P.S.V.	**873**
paddy (*coal mine*)	**886**
pile	**885**
plant (*building and contracting*)	**885**
police; civilian	**874**
press	**839**
printer's	**891**
pump	**999**

	Code number
Driver; *continued*	
racing	**387**
rack (*rolling mill*)	**839**
ram	**889**
ransom	**889**
refuse	**872**
rest (*rolling mill*)	**839**
roll	**832**
roller-	**885**
oil wells	**898**
steelworks	**832**
rolley	**872**
rolly	**872**
saw (*metal trades*)	**899**
scammell	**872**
scoop	**885**
scraper	**885**
sentinel	**885**
shear(s) (*metal trades*)	**899**
shearer (*coal mine*)	**597**
shovel	**885**
shunter	**882**
skid (*rolling mill*)	**839**
skip (*blast furnace*)	**886**
spray; water (*rolling mill*)	**839**
stacker	**887**
stenter	**552**
surface (*coal mine*)	**882**
sweeper;	**874**
road; mechanical	**874**
table (*rolling mill*)	**839**
tandem (*coal mine*)	**886**
tanker	**872**
taxi	**874**
test (*motor vehicle mfr.*)	**516**
tilter	**830**
tip	**886**
tipper	**872**
tool; mechanical	**885**
tractor-	
agriculture	**901**
building and contracting	**872**
forestry	**904**
local government	**872**
manufacturing	**872**
mining	**872**
opencast coal mining	**872**
road transport	**872**
train	**882**
tram	**873**
transport-	**872**
internal transport	**887**
traverser	**889**
trolley	**887**
trolleybus	**873**
truck;	
bogy	**887**
clamp	**887**
electric	**887**
fork	**887**
fork lift	**887**
lister	**889**
power	**887**
ransom	**887**
stacker	**887**
works	**887**
truck-	**887**
road transport	**872**
tug	**880**
turbine	**893**
turbo-blower	**893**

	Code number
Driver; *continued*	
van	**872**
vehicle;	
articulated	**872**
motor	**872**
wagon	**872**
winch	**886**
Driver-	
agricultural machinery	**901**
vehicles-	
goods transport	**872**
passenger transport-	**874**
bus, coach	**873**
works trucks	**887**
coal mine-	
above ground	**882**
below ground-	
pony	**889**
train	**882**
L.R.T.	**873**
mine, not coal-	
above ground	**887**
below ground	**898**
railways	**882**
shipping	**880**
Driver and collector-	**412**
car delivery service	**874**
coal mine	**874**
laundry	**731**
Driver-attendant; ambulance	**642**
Driver-conductor	**873**
Driver-fitter-	**872**
public service vehicle	**873**
Driver-handyman	**874**
Driver-instructor-	**393**
public transport	**391**
Driver-loader (*airport*)	**931**
Driver-mechanic-	**872**
agricultural machinery	**901**
bus, coach	**873**
passenger transport vehicles	**874**
Driver-postman	**940**
Driver-salesman	**731**
Driver-storeman	**441**
Driver-warehouseman	**441**
Drop man (*blast furnace*)	**830**
Dropper; fire (*railways*)	**990**
Dropper-	
bacon and meat curing	**809**
oil refining	**820**
sugar confectionery mfr.	**809**
sugar refining	**809**
Dropperman	**821**
Drosser	**830**
Drossman	**830**
Drover	**902**
Drowner	**929**
Drug room man	**441**
Druggist-	**221**
wholesale trade	**179**
Drum and cagehand (*tannery*)	**810**
Drumhand	**810**
Drum man (*tannery*)	**810**
Drummer; glycerine	**862**
Drummer-	
entertainment	**385**
tannery	**810**
Dry dock worker	**912**
Dry man-	
china clay	**829**
mine, not coal	**958**

	Code number
Dry worker (*paper mfr.*)	**821**
Dryer;	
bacon	**809**
can (*textile mfr.*)	**814**
clay	**829**
clip (*textile mfr.*)	**814**
cloth	**814**
colour (*dyestuff mfr.*)	**820**
core (*foundry*)	**839**
cylinder (*textile mfr.*)	**814**
dyed (*textile mfr.*)	**814**
felt	**814**
gelatine	**820**
glue	**820**
grain (*malting*)	**801**
hair	**814**
kiln (wood)	**821**
machine (*textile mfr.*)	**814**
ore	**829**
pearl	**829**
pulp	**809**
rag	**814**
salt	**829**
sand	**829**
tobacco	**802**
veneer	**821**
warp	**814**
wool	**814**
yarn	**814**
Dryer-	
abrasive paper mfr.	**821**
cereal foods mfr.	**809**
chemical mfr.	**820**
laundry	**673**
metal trades	**829**
paper mfr.	**821**
photographic film mfr.	**569**
photographic film processing	**569**
refractory goods mfr.	**823**
soap mfr.	**820**
tannery	**810**
textile mfr.	**814**
vulcanised fibre mfr.	**821**
Dryerman *see Dryer*	
Drying man *see Dryer*	
Dubber (*textile mfr.*)	**814**
Duffer	**889**
Duler (wool)	**811**
Dumper-	
coal mine	**889**
mine, not coal	**887**
textile mfr.	**552**
Duplicator-	**490**
tape recordings	**999**
Dustman	**933**
Duster; colour	**591**
Duster-	
ceramics mfr.	**591**
coal mine	**869**
printing	**569**
Dye house operative (*textile mfr.*)	**552**
Dye house worker (*textile mfr.*)	**552**
Dye worker; natural	**820**
Dyer;	
beam	**552**
black (*textile mfr.*)	**552**
brush (*leather dressing*)	**810**
calico	**552**
carpet	**552**
Dyer; *continued*	
clothes	**552**
colour	**552**
cop	**552**
cord	**552**
fibre	**552**
fur	**810**
fustian	**552**
garment	**552**
glove	**810**
hair-	**552**
hairdressing	**660**
hank	**552**
hat	**552**
head	**F552**
jig	**552**
job	**552**
master	**F552**
operative	**552**
piece	**552**
skein	**552**
skin	**810**
technical	**219**
vat	**552**
vessel	**552**
warp	**552**
winch	**552**
yarn	**552**
Dyer-	
grass, straw, etc.	**552**
leather	**810**
plastics	**829**
textiles	**552**
artificial flowers mfr.	**552**
button mfr.	**869**
cable mfr.	**552**
dyeing and cleaning	**552**
fancy goods mfr.	**552**
hairdressing	**660**
leather goods mfr.	**810**
tannery	**810**
textile mfr.	**552**
Dyer and cleaner	**673**
Dyer's operative	**552**

Code number

E

E.A. (*Dept. of Emp. Job Centre*) ... **132**
E.D.H. ... **880**
E.N.G. ... **340**
E.O. (*government*) ... **132**
E.T.G.II ... **301**
Ebonite worker ... **824**
Ecclesiastic ... **292**
Ecologist ... **201**
Economist; ... **252**
  home ... **399**
Edgeman ... **821**
Edger; gilt ... **562**
Edger-
  bedding mfr. ... **554**
  ceramics mfr. ... **591**
  lens mfr. ... **591**
Editor; ... **M380**
  camera; video ... **386**
  dubbing ... **386**
  film ... **384**
  sales ... **M380**
  sound ... **386**
  sub ... **380**
  technical ... **M380**
Egger and washer ... **810**
Egyptologist ... **291**
Elasticator ... **553**
Electrician; ... **521**
  auto ... **543**
  automobile ... **543**
  chief- ... **F521**
    shipping ... **F880**
  maintenance-
    motor vehicle repair ... **543**
    office machinery-
      electrical ... **521**
  radio ... **525**
Electroformer ... **834**
Electrologist ... **661**
Electrolysist ... **661**
Electroplater ... **834**
Electrotyper ... **560**
Electro-brasser (screws) ... **834**
Electro-chemist ... **200**
Electro-encephalographer ... **346**
Electro-therapeutist ... **343**
Electro-therapist ... **343**
Elevator man (goods) ... **441**
Embalmer ... **699**
Embosser;
  cloth ... **552**
  hilt (sword) ... **518**
  leather (*bookbinding*) ... **562**
Embosser-
  glass mfr. ... **591**
  hat mfr. ... **569**
  jewellery, plate mfr. ... **518**
  leathercloth mfr. ... **552**
  leather dressing ... **810**
  metal trades ... **841**
  paper goods mfr. ... **569**
  plastics goods mfr. ... **825**
  printing ... **569**
  textile mfr. ... **552**
  wood products mfr. ... **579**
Embroiderer ... **553**
Embryologist ... **201**
Employee; bank ... **411**

Code number

Emptier;
  biscuit ... **889**
  press; electrical ... **590**
  press (*ceramics mfr.*) ... **590**
  rubbish (*steelworks*) ... **889**
  wagon (*coal mine*) ... **889**
  ware ... **889**
  wheel ... **919**
Emptier- ... **990**
  ceramics mfr. ... **889**
  charcoal mfr. ... **829**
Enamel man (*stove mfr.*) ... **869**
Enamel worker ... **869**
Enameller- ... **869**
  ceramics mfr. ... **591**
Ender-
  textile mfr.- ... **814**
    flax mfr. ... **811**
Endocrinologist ... **201**
Engineman;
  donkey-
    coal mine ... **886**
    shipping ... **880**
  haulage ... **886**
  hydraulic ... **893**
  malt ... **801**
  winding ... **886**
Engineman- ... **893**
  railways ... **882**
  shipping ... **880**
Engine room man (*shipping*) **880**
Engine worker ... **893**
Engineer; *see also notes*
  acoustical ... **529**
  administrative *see Engineer-prof.-*
  advisory *see Engineer-prof.-*
  aerial ... **850**
  aero ... **516**
  aeronautical ... **211**
  agricultural- ... **516**
    professional ... **219**
  aircraft- ... **516**
    maintenance ... **516**
  alarm ... **529**
  applications- *see Engineer-prof.-*
    industrial *see Engineer-prof.-*
  area- ... **516**
    technical ... **212**
    telecoms ... **110**
  armament ... **516**
  assembly (*vehicle mfr.*) ... **516**
  assessing (*insurance*) ... **361**
  assistant-
    mechanical ... **516**
    unit (*coal mine*) ... **516**
    broadcasting ... **302**
    coal mine- ... **110**
      H.Q. see Engineer-prof.-
    electricity board ... **212**
    gas board ... **301**
    government ... **301**
    local government ... **210**
    manufacturing- ... **301**
      professional *see Engineer-prof.-*
    shipping ... **332**
    telecoms ... **F523**
  assurance; quality ... **218**
  automobile- ... **540**

Code number

Engineer; *continued*
  automobile- *continued*
    professional ... **211**
  bakery ... **516**
  barge ... **516**
  battery ... **899**
  boiler ... **893**
  boilerhouse ... **893**
  bomb disposal-
    armed forces - U.K. ... **600**
  boring- ... **898**
    professional ... **210**
  borough ... **210**
  branch (*electricity board*) **212**
  brewer's ... **516**
  building ... **210**
  cable ... **529**
  cable and wireless ... **529**
  calibration ... **517**
  camera; video ... **386**
  capstan ... **510**
  carding ... **516**
  catering ... **516**
  ceramic ... **219**
  charge-
    coal mine ... **F521**
    electricity board ... **113**
  chartered *see Engineer-prof.-*
  chemical ... **215**
  chief; area (*coal mine*) ... **211**
  chief- *see also Engineer-prof.-*
    maintenance ... **110**
    boat, barge ... **880**
    electricity board ... **113**
    fishing ... **880**
    gas board ... **110**
    hovercraft ... **332**
    shipping ... **332**
  cinema ... **521**
  cinematograph ... **517**
  circuit (*cinema*) ... **521**
  city ... **210**
  civil ... **210**
  colliery ... **110**
  combustion ... **219**
  commercial ... **710**
  commissioning- ... **301**
    professional
      see Engineer-prof.-
  communication; ... **212**
    radio ... **213**
  computer- ... **526**
    design ... **216**
  conditioning; air ... **532**
  constructional- ... **535**
    professional ... **210**
  consultant *see Engineer-prof.-*
  consulting *see Engineer-prof.-*
  consumers (*electricity board*) **710**
  contract(s)- ... **301**
    professional
      see Engineer-prof.-
  contractor's ... **210**
  control;
    production ... **217**
    quality ... **218**
    strata ... **210**
    vision ... **386**
  control (*electricity board*) **113**
  co-ordinating *see Engineer-prof.-*

Code number

- Engineer; *continued*
  - county ... **210**
  - crane ... **516**
  - cryogenic ... **219**
  - customer (*office machinery mfr.*) ... **598**
  - cycle ... **516**
  - dairy ... **516**
  - dental ... **592**
  - depot (*transport*) ... **110**
  - design ... **216**
  - designing *see Engineer-prof.-*
  - development ... **216**
  - diesel- ... **516**
    - professional ... **211**
    - vehicle- ... **540**
      - *vehicle mfr.* ... **516**
  - distribution- ... **301**
    - *electricity board* ... **113**
  - district- ... **516**
    - *electricity board* ... **113**
    - *railways* ... **111**
  - dock(s) ... **210**
  - dockyard ... **516**
  - domestic ... **532**
  - drainage ... **210**
  - dredger ... **880**
  - drilling (*mining*) ... **210**
  - electrical;
    - area (*coal mine*) ... **212**
    - assistant ... **521**
    - auto ... **543**
    - charge; assistant (*electricity board*) ... **113**
    - chartered *see Engineer-prof.-*
    - chief ... **212**
    - colliery; assistant ... **F521**
    - group (*coal mine*) ... **212**
    - head ... **212**
    - maintenance ... **521**
    - n.o.s.- ... **522**
      - professional ... **212**
      - *coal mine* ... **521**
      - *shipping* ... **332**
      - *telecoms; cable ship* ... **332**
    - senior ... **212**
    - unit ... **521**
    - works ... **212**
  - electrical and mechanical- ... **521**
    - professional ... **212**
  - electro-mechanical ... **521**
  - electronic (maintenance) ... **529**
  - elevators; grain ... **516**
  - environmental ... **219**
  - equipment ... **212**
  - erection ... **516**
  - estate ... **516**
  - estimating ... **360**
  - excavator ... **516**
  - executive (*telecoms*) ... **302**
  - experimental ... **219**
  - explosive (*coal mine*) ... **215**
  - explosives (*demolition*) ... **896**
  - extrusion (*plastics goods mfr.*) ... **825**
  - fabrication ... **516**
  - field- ... **516**
    - computer servicing ... **526**
    - radio, television and video servicing ... **525**

Code number

- Engineer; *continued*
  - field- *continued*
    - *office machinery mfr.* ... **598**
  - film ... **521**
  - filter ... **516**
  - fire ... **611**
  - first- ... **332**
    - *fishing* ... **880**
  - fleet (vehicle) ... **540**
  - flight ... **331**
  - foundry ... **516**
  - fuel ... **219**
  - furnace ... **516**
  - garage ... **540**
  - gas; ... **219**
    - natural ... **210**
  - gas and water ... **532**
  - generating (*electricity board*) **212**
  - genetic ... **201**
  - geophysical ... **202**
  - glass ... **219**
  - grade I, II, III (*government*) *see Engineer-prof.-*
  - ground ... **516**
  - group *see Engineer-prof.-*
  - handling; materials *see Engineer-prof.-*
  - hardware (computer) ... **526**
  - heating; central ... **532**
  - heating- ... **532**
    - professional ... **219**
  - heat and domestic ... **532**
  - heating and lighting ... **532**
  - heating and plumbing ... **532**
  - heating and ventilating- ... **532**
    - professional ... **219**
  - heavy- ... **516**
    - professional ... **211**
  - helicopter ... **516**
  - highway(s) ... **210**
  - horological ... **517**
  - horticultural ... **219**
  - hosiery ... **516**
  - hospital ... **110**
  - house; ... **516**
    - assistant ... **516**
  - hovercraft ... **516**
  - hydraulic- ... **516**
    - professional ... **211**
    - *shipping* ... **332**
  - illuminating- ... **521**
    - professional ... **216**
  - industrial ... **218**
  - injection; fuel ... **516**
  - inspecting *see Engineer-prof.-*
  - inspection- ... **860**
    - professional ... **211**
    - *insurance* ... **313**
  - inspector ... **860**
  - installation- ... **516**
    - computer ... **526**
    - heating and ventilating ... **532**
    - radio, television and video **525**
    - telephones ... **523**
    - *electrical contracting* ... **521**
    - *electricity board* ... **302**
    - *telecoms* ... **523**
  - instrument; ... **517**
    - chief *see Engineer-prof.-*
  - insulating ... **896**
  - insulation ... **896**

Code number

- Engineer; *continued*
  - insurance ... **361**
  - investigating; technical ... **309**
  - investigation; defect ... **516**
  - irrigation ... **210**
  - lathe ... **510**
  - laundry ... **516**
  - liaison *see Engineer-prof.-*
  - lift ... **516**
  - light ... **516**
  - lighting (professional) ... **216**
  - line-
    - *oil refining* ... **516**
    - *telecoms* ... **524**
  - locomotive- ... **516**
    - professional ... **211**
  - lubrication ... **219**
  - machine- ... **516**
    - domestic electrical appliances ... **521**
    - office machines ... **598**
  - machinery ... **516**
  - mains; electrical ... **524**
  - mains-
    - *electricity board* ... **524**
    - *gas board* ... **532**
  - maintenance;
    - aircraft ... **516**
    - electrical ... **521**
    - plant ... **516**
    - tyre ... **861**
  - maintenance- ... **516**
    - aircraft ... **516**
    - buildings and other structures ... **111**
    - computer servicing ... **526**
    - electronics ... **529**
    - heating and ventilating ... **532**
    - instruments ... **517**
    - office machines ... **598**
    - radio, television and video **525**
    - vehicles ... **540**
    - *electricity board* ... **110**
    - *telecoms* ... **523**
  - making; tool ... **515**
  - manufacturing ... **899**
  - marine;
    - chief- ... **211**
      - *shipping* ... **332**
    - senior ... **211**
    - superintendent ... **110**
  - marine- ... **516**
    - professional ... **211**
    - *boat, barge* ... **880**
    - *shipping* ... **332**
  - materials *see Engineer-prof.-*
  - mechanical;
    - area (*coal mine*) ... **211**
    - chief ... **211**
    - colliery (assistant) ... **F516**
    - group (*coal mine*) ... **211**
    - n.o.s.- ... **840**
      - professional ... **211**
    - unit (*coal mine*) ... **110**
  - mechanical and electrical- **516**
    - professional ... **211**
    - *electricity board* ... **212**
  - mechanisation ... **211**
  - meter ... **517**
  - methods ... **364**
  - microwave ... **213**

	Code number
Engineer; *continued*	
mill-	516
professional	211
milling	513
mining	210
model	516
monotype	516
motor;	540
road (*railways*)	211
mud (*oil wells*)	210
municipal	210
n.o.s.-	840
professional *see also* Engineer-prof.-	
airline	331
boat, barge	880
broadcasting	529
coal mine (below ground)	516
fishing	880
shipping	332
telecoms	523
nuclear	219
oil	210
operations (*electricity board*)	211
optical	590
packaging	219
paper	516
patent	219
performance *see* Engineer-prof.-	
petroleum	210
photographic	517
physics; health	219
pipe	532
planer; steel	519
planing	519
planning	218
plant-	516
professional	110
plastics	215
plumbing	532
plumbing and heating	532
pneumatic	516
potter's	516
power	212
powerhouse	521
precision	517
press; rotary	516
prevention;	
crime	529
fire	301
pricing *see* Engineer-prof.-	
printer's	516
process	217
production	217
production and planning	217
programme *see* Engineer-prof.-	
progress	218
project	219
prototype	516
public health	210
pump	516
quarrying	210
quality	218
r & d	216
radar-	529
research	213
radio-	525
professional	213
radio and television	525

	Code number
Engineer; *continued*	
railway	516
reception (*garage*)	540
recording	386
refrigerating-	516
shipping	332
refrigeration-	516
professional	219
shipping	332
regional (*telecoms*)	212
relay	521
repair; motor	540
research *see* Engineer-prof.-	
resident-	111
electricity board	113
retort	516
rig; test	301
road	210
rolling stock	516
roofing	501
safety	396
sales	710
salvage; marine	211
sanitary-	532
professional	210
scientific	219
scribbling	516
sea-going	332
second-	332
boat, barge	880
fishing	880
textile mfr.	516
semi-skilled	899
senior *see* Engineer-prof.-	
service;	
computer	526
lift	516
sales	710
service-	516
aircraft	516
domestic electrical appliances	521
heating and ventilating	532
motor vehicles	540
office machinery-	529
electrical	521
mechanical	598
radio, television and video	525
telephone	523
cinema	521
electrical engineering	521
electricity board	521
engineering	516
heating engineers	532
oil company	516
servicing *see* Engineer; service-	
shafting	516
shift-	516
electricity board	113
ship's-	332
fishing	880
shop; machine	516
signal (*railways*)	110
site	111
software-	320
professional	214
sound	529
spares	441
staff-	
insurance	361

	Code number
Engineer; *continued*	
staff- *continued*	
telecoms	212
standards	364
station;	
power (*electricity board*)	212
pumping	516
station-	
Min. of Defence	111
oil refining	516
steam	893
stress	310
structural	210
study;	
method	364
time	364
work	364
subsidence	210
sub-area (*electricity board*)	113
sub-sea *see* Engineer-prof.-	
sub-station (*electricity board*)	212
superintendent	110
superintending *see* Engineer-prof.-	
supervising (*government*)	219
supply (*electricity board*) *see* Engineer-prof.-	
switchboard	520
switchgear-	520
professional	212
systems-	320
professional	214
technical-	219
telecoms	523
technician	301
telecommunications-	529
professional	212
radio; professional	213
telephone	523
telegraph	529
telephone-	523
professional	212
television-	525
professional	213
test-	860
technician	301
testing; cable;	212
assistant	302
textile-	516
professional	211
thermal-	532
professional	219
thermal and acoustic-	532
professional	219
third-	332
fishing	880
time and study	364
tool	515
tool; machine-	516
professional	211
tool room	515
traction; electric	212
traffic	219
transmission; power-	212
television	213
transmitter; radio	529
transport	540
trawler	880
treatment; heat	833
Trinity House	516
tug	880

	Code number
Engineer; *continued*	
turbine	**893**
turner	**510**
turner; lathe	**510**
typewriter	**598**
value	**364**
ventilating	**532**
ventilation-	**532**
coal mine	**F532**
video	**525**
water;	**210**
hot	**532**
welding-	**537**
professional	**211**
winding (*coal mine*)	**886**
wireless	**525**
wiring	**521**
work measurement	**364**
works;	
n.o.s.	**110**
public	**210**
sewage	**516**
water	**516**
workshop-	**516**
radio, television and video servicing	**525**
x-ray	**529**
Engineer-	
professional-	**211**
accoustics	**219**
aeronautical	**211**
agricultural	**219**
automobile	**211**
broadcasting	**213**
ceramic	**219**
chemical	**215**
civil	**210**
combustion	**219**
conditioning; air	**219**
constructional	**210**
corrosion	**219**
design	**216**
development	**216**
electrical	**212**
electronic	**213**
environmental	**219**
fuel	**219**
gas	**219**
glass	**219**
heating and ventilating	**219**
highway(s)	**210**
hydraulic	**211**
illuminating	**216**
locomotive	**211**
lubrication	**219**
marine	**211**
mechanical	**211**
mining	**210**
municipal	**210**
noise control	**219**
oil and natural gas	**210**
plastics	**215**
production	**217**
public health	**210**
quarrying	**210**
radar	**213**
radio	**213**
refrigeration	**219**
sanitary	**210**
structural	**210**
television	**213**
Engineer- *continued*	
professional- *continued*	
textile	**211**
water	**210**
Engineer and architect	**210**
Engineer and surveyor *see Engineer-prof.-*	
Engineer-designer *see Engineer-prof.-*	
Engineer-attendant	**516**
Engineer-draughtsman	**310**
Engineer-driller	**511**
Engineer-estimator	**360**
Engineer-examiner	**860**
Engineer-fitter	**516**
Engineer-in-charge (*electricity board*)	**113**
Engineering worker	**912**
Engineer-inspector	**860**
Engineer-machinist	**840**
Engineer-mechanic (*shipping*)	**880**
Engineer-surveyor-	
see also Engineer-prof.-	
insurance	**313**
Engineer-tool maker	**515**
Enginewright;	**516**
assistant	**516**
Engraver;	
bank-note	**569**
block; process	**560**
brass	**599**
chemical	**569**
copper	**569**
die	**569**
glass	**591**
gold	**599**
hand-	**599**
textile mfr.	**569**
heraldic	**569**
instrument	**599**
letter	**500**
line	**569**
machine-	**569**
instrument mfr.	**599**
jewellery, plate mfr.	**599**
map	**569**
mark; stamp	**569**
marquetry	**579**
metal	**599**
micrometer	**599**
monumental	**500**
music	**569**
pantograph (*roller engraving*)	**569**
parquetry	**579**
pattern; pottery	**591**
photo	**560**
photographic	**560**
photogravure	**569**
plate; copper	**569**
plate (precious metal)	**599**
portrait	**381**
potter's	**569**
pottery	**591**
process	**560**
punch	**569**
relief	**569**
roller	**569**
seal	**569**
silver	**599**
stone	**500**
transfer	**569**
Engraver-	
ceramics mfr.	**591**
glass mfr.	**591**
jewellery mfr.	**599**
metal trades	**599**
monumental masons	**500**
Ordnance Survey	**569**
printing	**569**
textile printing	**569**
Engraver-etcher	**599**
Enlarger (films)	**569**
Enrober (*sugar confectionery mfr.*)	**809**
Enterer (*textile mfr.*)	**552**
Entertainer	**384**
Entomologist	**201**
Enumerator;	
census	**420**
traffic	**430**
Erector;	
aerial; television	**899**
battery	**850**
beam (*shipbuilding*)	**534**
beam and frame	**534**
boiler	**534**
building; portable	**896**
ceiling	**896**
cell (*chemical mfr.*)	**850**
chassis	**516**
chimney; metal	**535**
concrete	**923**
conveyor-	**516**
coal mine	**899**
duct (work)	**899**
engine	**516**
engineer's	**516**
exhibition	**570**
fence	**929**
fencing	**929**
frame-	
shipbuilding	**534**
vehicle mfr.	**516**
furnace	**535**
garage	**896**
girder	**535**
greenhouse	**896**
hoarding	**570**
ironwork	**535**
lamp; gas	**532**
lift	**516**
light; street	**929**
locomotive	**516**
loom	**516**
machine	**516**
mains; gas	**532**
marquee	**699**
partitioning; office	**570**
pipe	**532**
plant	**516**
plate; steel	**535**
prefab	**896**
pump	**516**
roof	**501**
roofing; galvanized	**501**
scaffolding	**505**
sheeter	**501**
shuttering;	**570**
metal	**505**
sign	**896**
stage (*ship repairing*)	**505**
staircase; iron	**535**

Code number

Erector; *continued*
steel 535
steelwork 535
structural 535
switchgear 521
tent 699
tower 535
transformer 521
wicket (*ceramics mfr.*) 919
Erector-
machinery- 516
electrical 521
coal mine- 516
above ground 535
engineering- 516
structural engineering 535
Erector-fitter 516
Escort; bus; school 630
Escort-
social services 630
travel 630
Essence hand 809
Estate worker 990
Estimator; 360
carpet 506
chief 360
cost 360
print(ing) 360
technical 360
Estimator and buyer (*retail trade*) 700
Estimator and surveyor 262
Estimator-draughtsman 310
Estimator-engineer 360
Etcher;
black and white 381
block; process 569
colour 569
copper (*printing*) 569
cutlery 899
deep 569
fine 569
half tone 569
hand (glass) 591
line 569
machine 591
photogravure 569
roller 569
rough 569
Etcher-
integrated, printed circuits 599
aircraft mfr. 599
ceramics mfr. 591
cutlery mfr. 899
glass mfr. 591
jewellery, plate mfr. 599
printing 569
tool mfr. 899
Ethnologist 291
Ethnomusicologist 291
Etymologist 291
Evaluator; job 364
Evangelist 292
Evaporator man;
multiple (*glucose mfr.*) 809
Evaporator man-
chemical mfr. 820
food products mfr. 809
Eviscerator 582
Examiner;
ammunition 869

Code number

Examiner; *continued*
armaments 860
assistant (*government*) 132
audit (*D.O.E.*) 250
bag 861
bank-note 861
bankruptcy (*government*) 250
book (*printing*) 861
bottle (*brewery*) 863
boundary (*Ordnance Survey*) 310
brake (*railways*) 516
bridge (*railways*) 896
brush 869
bulb (*lamp mfr.*) 860
bullet 860
burr (*dental instrument mfr.*) 860
bus 860
car (*L.R.T.*) 860
carriage (*railways*) 516
carriage and wagon 516
chain 860
cheque 861
cigar 869
cloth; 861
leather 869
coach (*railways*) 516
cycle 860
decorator's (*ceramics mfr.*) 869
driving (*Dept. of Transport*) 395
engineering 860
file 860
film 869
final (*clothing mfr.*) 861
flight 395
fruit 861
gas (*Dept. of Energy*) 202
glass (*glass mfr.*) 869
heald 553
hosiery 861
impression (*Ordnance Survey*) 861
label 861
machine; cigarette 869
map (*Ordnance Survey*) 310
mechanical 860
meter (*Dept. of Industry*) 860
motor 860
pen 860
piece 861
plan (*Ordnance Survey*) 861
policy (*insurance*) 410
print(er's) 861
roller (*printing*) 861
scrap (*steelworks*) 863
shaft (*coal mine*) 899
shell 869
shoe 555
soundbox; gramophone 860
spring 860
steel (*steelworks*) 860
stem 869
stencil 861
thread 861
ticket-
entertainment 699
railways 631
road transport F870
timber 861
tool; edge 860
track 922
traffic (*Dept. of Transport*) 395

Code number

Examiner; *continued*
traffic and driving (*Dept. of Transport*) 395
trench 929
tyre 861
vehicle- 860
Dept. of Transport 869
wagon 516
wheel 860
wire 860
yarn 861
Examiner-
asbestos composition goods mfr. 869
Board of Trade 219
bookbinding 861
ceramics mfr. 869
chemical mfr. 869
clothing mfr. 861
coal mine F597
dyeing and cleaning 869
electrical, electronic equipment 860
electrical goods mfr. 860
examination board 239
fancy goods mfr. 869
food products mfr. 861
footwear mfr. 555
glass mfr. 869
incandescent mantle mfr. 869
Inland Revenue 361
laundry 869
leathercloth mfr. 869
leather dressing 863
legal services 430
match mfr. 869
metal trades 860
mica goods mfr. 869
Ministry of Defence 860
ordnance factory 860
paper mfr. 861
Patent Office 219
pencil, crayon mfr. 869
photographic film mfr. 869
plastics goods mfr. 861
printing 861
railways 860
Royal Mint 860
rubber goods mfr. 861
tannery 863
textile mfr. 861
textile goods mfr. 861
tobacco mfr. 869
toy mfr. 869
wallpaper mfr. 861
wood products mfr. 861
Examiner and finisher (net) 553
Examiner and mender (hosiery) 553
Excavator-
building and contracting 885
mine, not coal 898
steelworks 885
Executive; *see also Manager*
account (*advertising*) 123
advertising 123
chief-
large establishment 101
local government 102
commercial 121
editorial (*newspaper*) 380
legal M350

	Code number
F	
F.C.A.	**250**
F.C.I.S.	**127**
F.C.W.A.	**251**
F.R.C.O.	**385**
F.R.C.O.G.	**220**
F.R.C.P.	**220**
F.R.C.S.	**220**
F.S.A.A.	**250**
Fabric worker	**553**
Fabricator;	
steel	**535**
window and door	**516**
Fabricator-	
cast stone products mfr.	**599**
plastics mfr.	**825**
tube mfr.	**839**
Face worker (*coal mine*)	**597**
Facer; wood	**897**
Facer-	
coach painting	**869**
metal trades-	**510**
nut, bolt, rivet mfr.	**841**
stone dressing	**500**
Factor; *see also Dealer*	
estate (Scotland)	**170**
housing (Scotland)-	**170**
local government	**M371**
Factory hand *see Factory worker*	
Factory operative *see Factory worker*	
Factory worker-	**919**
packing	**862**
brewery	**801**
clothing mfr.	**559**
distillery	**801**
electrical goods mfr. (assembling, soldering)	**850**
engineering	**912**
food products mfr.	**809**
footwear mfr.	**555**
plastics goods mfr.	**825**
soft drinks mfr.	**809**
tobacco mfr.	**802**
Faience worker	**506**
Fan man; store; cold	**999**
Fan man-	
coal mine	**999**
lead mfr.	**830**
Fanner (*corset mfr.*)	**553**
Farm hand	**900**
Farm lad	**900**
Farm worker;	
fish	**903**
sewage	**892**
Farm worker-	**900**
self-employed	**160**
Farmer;	**160**
fish	**169**
Farmer's wife *see also notes*	**900**
Farrier	**530**
Fasher	**899**
Father; house	**370**
Father Christmas	**720**
Faultman (*electricity board*)	**521**
Faultsman (*telecoms*)	**523**
Feather worker	**814**
Feeder;	
auto *see Feeder-*	
bar	**899**
Feeder; *continued*	
belt	**919**
bin	**990**
biscuit	**800**
boiler	**893**
bowl	**811**
can	**862**
card	**811**
carder	**811**
clay	**829**
conveyor (*metal trades*)	**899**
cotton	**811**
crusher (*mine, not coal*)	**890**
drum (agricultural machinery)	**901**
engine (*textile mfr.*)	**811**
furnace	**830**
hopper-	
ceramics mfr.	**829**
cigarette mfr.	**802**
letterpress	**891**
line (*metal trades*)	**912**
machine *see Machinist*	
mill	**829**
pallet	**599**
pan	**829**
pass; skin (*steelworks*)	**839**
platen	**891**
printer's	**891**
roll(s) (*metal mfr.*)	**839**
scutcher	**811**
stenter	**552**
stock	**441**
tack	**841**
wool	**811**
woollen	**811**
Feeder-	
card and paste board mfr.	**821**
cement mfr.	**919**
felt hat mfr.	**814**
laundry	**673**
metal trades-	
bolt, nut, rivet mfr.	**841**
foundry	**839**
rolling mill	**839**
sheet metal working	**841**
tube mfr.	**839**
mine, not coal	**890**
printing	**891**
textile mfr.-	**811**
textile finishing	**552**
Feeder-in (*textile mfr.*)	**814**
Feeder-up (*tobacco mfr.*)	**802**
Feller;	
timber	**904**
tree	**904**
Feller-	
clothing mfr.	**553**
forestry	**904**
Feller hand	**553**
Felling hand	**553**
Fellmonger	**810**
Fellow;	
research-	**209**
polytechnic	**230**
university	**230**
Fellow (*university*)-	**230**
dentistry	**223**
medicine	**220**
surgery	**220**
Feltman-	
paper mfr.	**821**
Feltman- *continued*	
roofing felt mfr.	**814**
textile mfr.	**814**
Felt worker	**814**
Felter-	
printing rollers	**599**
building and contracting	**501**
plastics mfr.	**825**
shipbuilding	**912**
textile mfr.	**814**
Fencer	**929**
Fenter	**814**
Fermenter-	**801**
non-alcoholic drink	**809**
Fermenting man (*distillery*)	**801**
Ferrier	**898**
Ferryman-	**880**
railways	**882**
Festooner-	
linoleum mfr.	**829**
oilskin mfr.	**829**
Fetcher (*textile mfr.*)	**889**
Fettler;	
brass	**843**
card	**899**
castings	**843**
core	**843**
cupola	**500**
iron	**843**
machine	**899**
pipe; sanitary	**591**
shop; machine	**843**
tool	**515**
woollen	**899**
Fettler-	
cast concrete products mfr.	**599**
ceramics mfr.	**591**
metal trades-	**843**
puddling	**839**
textile mfr.	**899**
Fibre man (*asbestos-cement goods mfr.*)	**811**
Fibre worker-	
paper mfr.	**821**
rubber goods mfr.	**824**
Field worker;	**900**
brick	**591**
Fielder (*textile mfr.*)	**889**
Field(s)man-	**160**
professionally qualified	**201**
Fighter; iron	**535**
Filer;	
core	**531**
foundry	**843**
pattern	**843**
plastics	**825**
spoon and fork	**843**
tool	**899**
Filer-	
metal trades	**843**
plastics mfr.	**825**
tobacco pipe mfr.	**579**
Filler;	
ampoule	**862**
back	**552**
bag	**862**
bank (*textile mfr.*)	**552**
barrel	**862**
barrow	**912**
battery-	
accumulator mfr.	**899**

(Fi)

	Code number
Filler; *continued*	
battery- *continued*	
textile mfr.	**814**
bobbin	**814**
bottle	**862**
bottom (*boot mfr.*)	**555**
box-	**862**
blast furnace	**912**
textile mfr.	**814**
braid (silk)	**813**
brush	**599**
can-	
paint mfr.	**862**
petroleum distribution	**862**
cap (*lamp, valve mfr.*)	**850**
card	**811**
cartridge	**599**
chocolate	**809**
coal	**889**
coke	**889**
conveyor (*coal mine-below ground*)	**597**
cushion	**559**
cylinder	**862**
detonator	**599**
dresser's	**811**
drum (*oil refining*)	**862**
envelope	**420**
furnace (*blast furnace*)	**889**
hand-	
silk weaving	**814**
upholstery mfr.	**559**
hopper (*textile mfr.*)	**814**
kiln	**823**
machine-	
brush mfr.	**599**
textile mfr.	**814**
magazine (loom)	**814**
medical (*oxygen works*)	**862**
night-	
(*retail trade*)-	
shelf filling	**954**
oil	**862**
order	**441**
oven (*ceramics mfr.*)	**823**
oxygen	**862**
paint	**862**
pan (*steelworks*)	**830**
pickle	**862**
pie	**809**
plug	**830**
polish	**862**
pot (*steelworks*)	**912**
rag	**811**
rocket	**599**
salt	**919**
sausage	**809**
scribble	**811**
shelf (*retail trade*)	**954**
shop-	
(*retail trade*)-	
shelf filling	**954**
shuttle	**814**
silk	**814**
spare	**912**
sterile (C.S.S.D.)	**862**
stock	**441**
tin (*textile mfr.*)	**814**
tray	**919**
truck (*coal mine*)	**889**
tub (*coal mine*)	**889**

	Code number
Filler; *continued*	
varnish	**862**
wagon	**889**
weaver's	**814**
wire	**831**
wood	**869**
Filler-	
blast furnace	**912**
brewery	**862**
cast concrete products mfr.	**599**
cement mfr.	**862**
ceramics mfr.	**591**
coal mine	**889**
coke ovens	**887**
docks	**930**
explosive mfr.	**599**
firework mfr.	**599**
food products mfr.	**862**
match mfr.	**862**
mattress, etc. mfr.	**554**
mine, not coal	**889**
oil refining	**862**
ordnance factory	**599**
paint mfr.	**862**
pencil mfr.	**859**
petroleum distribution	**889**
textile mfr.	**814**
tobacco mfr.	**802**
Filler-in; polisher's	**869**
Filler-in-	
ceramics mfr.	**823**
furniture mfr.	**869**
paper mfr.	**821**
pencil mfr.	**859**
Filler-loader (*petroleum distribution*)	**889**
Filler-up (*card clothing mfr.*)	**899**
Filleter (fish)	**582**
Film worker; colour	**569**
Filmer; micro	**490**
Filter man-	
alcoholic drink mfr.	**801**
chemical mfr.	**820**
metal trades	**829**
sewage farm	**892**
vinegar mfr.	**801**
Filterer-	
alcoholic drink mfr.	**801**
chemical mfr.	**820**
food products mfr.	**809**
water works	**892**
Filtration hand-	
alcoholic drink mfr.	**801**
chemical mfr.	**820**
Filtration worker; red (*aluminium refining*)	**820**
Financier	**361**
Finder;	
fault	**860**
land	**719**
tool	**441**
worsted (*carpet mfr.*)	**814**
Finer;	
beer	**801**
super (*buckle mfr.*)	**899**
Finer (*jewellery mfr.*)	**899**
Finingsman	**801**
Finisher;	
armature	**520**
belt (*textile mfr.*)	**552**
blade	**899**

	Code number
Finisher; *continued*	
blanket	**552**
bleach (*textile mfr.*)	**552**
bobbin; brass	**840**
body (*vehicle mfr.*)	**541**
book (*printing*)	**562**
bottom	**555**
brass	**516**
brush;	**859**
wire	**851**
bush; axle	**510**
camera	**517**
can (*worsted mfr.*)	**811**
cap	**553**
car	**541**
card-	
card clothing mfr.	**899**
printing	**859**
carpet	**552**
case (jewel, etc. cases)	**859**
caustic	**820**
cellulose	**869**
chassis	**516**
chromium	**834**
cloth	**552**
coach	**541**
coat	**553**
coffin	**579**
coil	**850**
collar	**553**
combing	**811**
concrete	**599**
cord (telephone)	**599**
crucible (plumbago)	**591**
curtain	**553**
cycle	**516**
disc; wheel	**510**
dress	**553**
dyers	**552**
ebonite	**824**
fabric	**552**
faller	**899**
fork	**899**
frame (*cycle mfr.*)	**899**
fur	**810**
furniture	**869**
fuse; safety	**552**
glass	**591**
glove	**553**
gold	**562**
gown	**553**
hand-	
clothing mfr.	**553**
felt hat mfr.	**559**
knitted goods mfr.	**553**
hat	**559**
hook; spring	**899**
hosiery	**552**
jam	**862**
key	**899**
kilt	**553**
lace	**552**
leather	**810**
lens	**591**
metal	**533**
needle (*needle mfr.*)	**899**
paint	**869**
paper	**821**
peg; shuttle	**579**
pencil	**869**
photographic	**569**

	Code number
Finisher; *continued*	
piece	**552**
pipe-	
cast concrete products mfr.	**599**
ceramics mfr.	**591**
clay tobacco pipe mfr.	**591**
plastics	**825**
plate (*paper mfr.*)	**821**
plush	**552**
post (concrete)	**599**
print	**569**
printer's	**569**
propeller (*ships' propeller mfr.*)	**840**
quilt	**554**
racquet	**599**
reed	**599**
rod; fishing	**599**
rug	**552**
sanitary	**591**
satin (*metal trades*)	**842**
shirt	**553**
shoe	**555**
shop; machine	**899**
silk	**552**
silver	**518**
smith's	**843**
spade	**859**
spoon and fork	**518**
spray (*furniture mfr.*)	**596**
spring;	**833**
coach	**516**
motor car	**516**
stone (*cast concrete products mfr.*)	**599**
stove	**552**
surface (*aircraft mfr.*)	**869**
tailor's	**553**
taper's	**552**
tent	**559**
tool; edge	**899**
trouser	**553**
tube (*steelworks*)	**839**
tyre	**824**
umbrella	**553**
velvet	**552**
wood	**897**
woollen	**552**
wrench	**899**
Finisher-	
artificial teeth mfr.	**599**
asbestos-cement goods mfr.	**599**
bookbinding	**562**
briar pipe mfr.	**507**
broom, brush mfr.	**859**
canvas goods mfr.	**559**
cast concrete products mfr.	**599**
ceramics mfr.	**591**
christmas card, etc. mfr.	**859**
cigar mfr.	**802**
clothing mfr.	**553**
dyeing and cleaning	**673**
embroidery mfr.	**553**
firework mfr.	**859**
fishing rod mfr.	**599**
flour confectionery mfr.	**800**
footwear mfr.	**555**
fur goods mfr.	**553**
glass mfr.	**591**
hat mfr.	**559**
hosiery garment mfr.	**553**
Finisher- *continued*	
incandescent mantle mfr.	**599**
knitwear mfr.	**553**
leather dressing	**810**
leather goods mfr.	**555**
metal trades-	**899**
aircraft mfr.	**541**
brass foundry	**516**
coach building	**541**
coach trimming	**554**
cock founding	**516**
foundry	**843**
precious plate, metal mfr.	**518**
railway workshops	**541**
rolling mill	**839**
screw mfr.	**842**
spring mfr.	**833**
tube mfr.	**839**
vehicle mfr.	**541**
watch, clock mfr.	**851**
musical instrument mfr.	**593**
paper mfr.	**821**
paper products mfr.	**859**
pharmaceutical products mfr.	**862**
photographic film mfr.	**829**
piano mfr.	**593**
piano key mfr.	**593**
plaster castings	**591**
plastics goods mfr.	**825**
printing	**569**
process engraving	**569**
railway workshops	**541**
refractory goods mfr.	**591**
rubber goods mfr.	**824**
soft furnishings mfr.	**553**
soft toy mfr.	**553**
stencil paper mfr.	**821**
stick mfr.	**579**
sugar confectionery mfr.	**809**
textile mfr.-	**552**
flax, hemp mfr.	**811**
textile doubling	**812**
textile drawing	**811**
textile printing	**552**
toilet preparation mfr.	**862**
tooth brush mfr.	**599**
umbrella, parasol mfr.	**553**
Finisher and liner (*fur garment mfr.*)	**553**
Finner	**841**
Fire brigade man	**611**
Fireman;	
biscuit	**823**
boiler	**893**
engine-	**893**
locomotive	**882**
furnace-	
metal trades-	**830**
annealing	**833**
gas	**820**
industrial	**611**
kiln-	
ceramics mfr.	**823**
food products mfr.	**809**
glass mfr.	**823**
loco	**882**
locomotive	**882**
marine	**880**
oven; annealing	**833**
oven (*ceramics mfr.*)	**823**
Fireman; *continued*	
pot	**820**
private	**611**
retort-	**820**
charcoal	**821**
zinc	**830**
security	**611**
shed	**882**
soaker	**830**
stove	**830**
surface	**893**
works; n.o.s.	**611**
Fireman-	
boiler-	**893**
locomotive	**882**
abrasive mfr.	**829**
airport	**611**
bakery	**800**
ceramics mfr.	**823**
chemical mfr.	**820**
cinema	**611**
coal gas, coke ovens	**820**
coal mine-	
above ground	**893**
below ground	**F597**
composition die mfr.	**820**
electricity supply	**893**
fire service	**611**
fishing	**880**
food products mfr.	**809**
L.R.T.	**611**
malting	**801**
metal trades-	**830**
annealing	**833**
mine, not coal	**F898**
M.O.D.	**611**
oil refining	**820**
P.O.	**611**
pencil mfr.	**829**
railways	**882**
refuse disposal	**999**
salt mfr.	**820**
shipbuilding	**830**
shipping	**880**
theatre	**611**
Fireman and trimmer	**880**
Fireman-greaser (*shipping*)	**880**
Fire prevention man	**611**
Firer;	
boiler	**893**
foundry (*glass mfr.*)	**823**
kiln	**829**
shot-	
civil engineering	**599**
coal mine	**597**
mine, not coal	**898**
stove-	
blast furnace	**830**
ceramics mfr.	**823**
Firer-	
ceramics mfr.	**823**
chemical mfr.	**820**
malting	**801**
metal mfr.	**830**
First hand-	
bakery	**F580**
clothing mfr.	**556**
retail trade-	**720**
butchers	**581**
steelworks	**832**
First sales (drapery)	**720**

	Code number
Fish house worker	**582**
Fish worker-	
docks	**930**
food processing	**582**
Fisher (copper)	**830**
Fisherman	**903**
Fisherman-crofter	**169**
Fishmonger-	**582**
self-employed	**178**
Fitter;	
aerial; television	**899**
agricultural	**516**
aircraft-	**516**
maintenance	**516**
airframe	**516**
alteration	**556**
alternator	**520**
anchor	**516**
appliance;	
domestic	**521**
surgical	**346**
armament	**516**
asbestos	**501**
assembly	**516**
automobile	**540**
axle	**516**
bag;	
air	**859**
curing	**859**
balustrade	**899**
bank	**570**
bar; handle	**851**
bar (*hotel, etc. fitting*) ...	**570**
basket; work	**859**
battery	**599**
bead; tyre	**824**
beam	**516**
bearing; brass	**516**
bedstead	**516**
belt (*coal mine*)	**555**
belting	**555**
below ground (*coal mine*)	**516**
bench;	**516**
electrical	**520**
blade (turbines)	**516**
blind	**896**
body (vehicle)	**541**
boiler	**516**
bonnet (vehicle)	**851**
box;	
axle	**516**
cam	**516**
gear	**516**
iron	**516**
work	**859**
box-	
artists' colours mfr. ...	**862**
foundry	**899**
brake;	
vacuum	**516**
Westinghouse	**516**
brake-	**516**
cycle mfr.	**851**
brass	**516**
break-off	**516**
builder's	**929**
burner (*gas works*) ...	**532**
cabinet;	**571**
iron	**516**
cable	**524**
camera	**517**
Fitter; *continued*	
car-	**540**
vehicle mfr.	**516**
card (*textile mfr.*)	**811**
carpet	**506**
carriage	**516**
carriage and wagon ...	**516**
case;	
cabinet	**571**
piano	**571**
casement (metal)	**516**
chain	**516**
chassis	**516**
chock (*coal mine*)	**597**
clock	**517**
clothing (*retail trade*) ...	**556**
coach	**516**
coat	**556**
cock	**516**
colliery	**516**
component; cycle	**516**
constructional	**516**
controller	**520**
conveyor	**516**
cork	**862**
corset; surgical	**559**
corsetry	**559**
crane	**516**
curtain	**554**
cycle	**516**
dental	**592**
depositor's	**518**
detail	**516**
development	**516**
die	**515**
diesel-	**516**
vehicle-	**540**
vehicle mfr.	**516**
distribution-	
gas board	**532**
water works	**532**
district (*gas board*) ...	**532**
dock	**516**
door;	
car	**516**
steel	**516**
door (*gas stove works*) ...	**516**
dress	**556**
dynamo	**520**
electrical-	**520**
maintenance	**521**
electronic	**520**
engine;	**516**
aero-	**516**
maintenance	**516**
aircraft (maintenance) ...	**516**
diesel	**516**
engineering;	**516**
electrical	**520**
engineer's;	**516**
electrical	**520**
heating	**532**
sanitary	**532**
erection	**516**
excavator	**516**
exhaust-	
motor vehicle repair ...	**544**
vehicles	**544**
exhibition	**570**
experimental	**516**
fabrication	**516**
Fitter; *continued*	
fan	**520**
fire; gas	**532**
fireplace	**506**
fittings and furniture ...	**579**
frame;	
air	**516**
bag	**859**
door; metal	**516**
ring	**516**
frame-	
cycle mfr.	**516**
loco and rolling stock mfr.	**516**
picture frame mfr. ...	**579**
textile machinery mfr. ...	**516**
furnace	**516**
furnishing (soft)	**554**
furniture-	**571**
metal	**516**
garage	**540**
gas	**532**
gasholder	**534**
gate (iron)	**530**
gate and railings (iron) ...	**530**
gauge	**517**
gear	**516**
general	**516**
glass-	**503**
vehicle mfr.	**859**
watch mfr.	**859**
governor (*gas board*) ...	**516**
grate	**516**
grindstone	**516**
grip (tools)	**851**
gun	**516**
gymnastics	**579**
heating	**532**
heel	**859**
house;	
light	**516**
power	**516**
hydraulic	**516**
industrial	**516**
injection; fuel	**516**
inspector	**516**
installation-	**516**
telecoms	**523**
instrument;	**517**
aircraft	**529**
musical	**593**
telephone	**523**
instrument (aircraft) ...	**529**
insulating	**929**
interlocking	**529**
ironmonger's	**516**
ironmongery	**516**
ironwork	**516**
jig and tool	**515**
keg	**516**
kitchen	**570**
knife	**516**
laboratory	**516**
lamp; arc	**520**
last; bespoke	**555**
lift	**516**
light (electric)	**521**
limb	**346**
lining; brake	**540**
lino-	**506**
linotype machine ...	**516**
linoleum	**506**

	Code number
Fitter; *continued*	
linotype	516
locking (signals)	516
locomotive	516
loom	516
machine-	516
electrical machines	520
mains-	
electricity board	521
water board	895
maintenance;	
computer	526
electrical	521
tyre	544
maintenance-	516
aircraft engines	516
office machinery servicing	598
radio, television and video servicing	525
vehicle servicing	540
gas board-	532
gas works	516
telecoms	523
marine	516
mattress (wire)	516
mechanical-	516
vehicle-	540
vehicle mfr.	516
metal	516
meter	517
motor;	
gramophone	851
record player	851
motor-	540
electric	520
vehicle mfr.	516
mould;	839
bottle	516
mount; boiler	516
mouthpiece (pipes)	859
mule	516
net	814
nicker and turner's	516
n.o.s.	516
office	570
optical	517
ordnance	516
organ	593
oven	516
overmantel	571
paragon (umbrellas)	851
paste	859
pattern (*engineering*)	515
pen; fountain	859
piano	593
pillar	521
pipe;	532
boiler	516
briar	859
drain	895
plant	516
plate	534
potter's	516
precision-	516
instrument mfr.	517
printing	516
production (electrical, electronic)	520
pump	516
radar	529

	Code number
Fitter; *continued*	
radio	525
rail (bedstead)	516
range	516
rectification	516
repair; engine	516
research	516
retort	516
rheostat	520
room; tool	515
rope and belt	505
ropery; wire	505
rough	516
saddle (cycles)	851
safe	516
sanitary	532
scale	517
scissors	516
screen-	
coal mine	516
vehicle mfr.	859
scythe	899
semi-skilled	851
service-	516
aircraft-	516
electronic and related equipment	529
instruments	517
office machines	598
ship	516
shoe (*retail trade*)	720
shop; machine	516
shop-	570
metal trades	516
shop and office	570
sign-	896
electric signs	521
signal; railway	529
skilled	516
skip (*coal mine*)	516
soundbox	851
speed	516
speedometer	517
spring;	516
elastic	555
spring (*forging*)	530
sprinkler	532
stand-	
exhibition stand	570
sewing machine stand	516
starter; motor	520
steam	532
steam and hot water	532
steel	516
steelyard	516
stock-	
bedstead mfr.	516
footwear mfr.	863
stove-	
building and contracting	532
stove mfr.	851
structural	516
sun-blind	896
superintendent	F516
surface	516
switch	520
switchboard	520
switchgear	520
table; billiard	599
tailor's	556
tank	516

	Code number
Fitter; *continued*	
taximeter	517
telegraph;	529
ship's	517
telephone	523
television	525
tender	516
textile	516
tool;	515
edge	515
machine	516
press	515
torpedo	516
tractor	516
transformer	520
transport	540
tread; tyre	824
trolleybus	516
truck (electric)	520
try-out	516
tube-	532
boiler mfr.	534
locomotive mfr.	534
turbine	516
turning	516
tyre-	
motor vehicle repair	544
vehicles	544
umbrella	859
upholsterer's	554
valve-	
engineering	516
tyre mfr.	859
vehicles-	540
vehicle mfr.	516
ventilation	532
wagon (*railway workshops*)	516
water	532
weighbridge	516
wheel	516
window (metal)	516
windscreen	859
work; smith's	516
Fitter-	
machinery-	516
electrical machines	520
vehicles-	540
vehicle mfr.	516
bag frame mfr.	851
cabinet making	571
cardboard container mfr.	859
clothing mfr.	556
electricity board	521
fishing rod mfr.	599
footwear mfr.	555
garage	540
gas board-	532
gas works	516
heating contracting	532
leather goods mfr.	555
loose leaf book mfr.	851
metal trades-	516
instrument mfr.	517
jewellery, plate mfr.	518
mining	516
musical instrument mfr.	593
net mfr.	814
railways	516
shipbuilding	516
shop blind mfr.	896
tobacco pipe mfr.	859

	Code number
Fitter and assembler ...	**516**
Fitter and erector-	**516**
public lighting	**921**
constructional engineering	**535**
Fitter and examiner ...	**516**
Fitter and marker-off ...	**515**
Fitter and tester	**516**
Fitter and trimmer	**556**
Fitter and turner	**516**
Fitter-assembler	**516**
Fitter-driver	**516**
Fitter-engineer	**516**
Fitter-erector	**516**
Fitter-in-charge	**F516**
Fitter-inspector	**516**
Fitter-machinist	**516**
Fitter-mechanic-	**516**
garage	**540**
Fitter-operator;	
capstan	**516**
machine tool	**516**
Fitter-tester	**516**
Fitter-turner	**516**
Fitter-up; frame; picture ...	**859**
Fitter-up-	
clothing mfr.	**557**
footwear mfr.	**859**
foundry	**516**
musical instrument mfr.-	**593**
piano case mfr.	**571**
Fitter-welder; pipe	**532**
Fitter-welder-	**537**
heating and ventilating ...	**532**
Fixer;	
advertisement	**959**
appliances (*gas board*) ...	**532**
asbestos	**501**
blind	**896**
board; plaster	**896**
boiler	**500**
cap (lamp and valves) ...	**850**
carpet	**506**
ceiling	**896**
faience and mosaic ...	**506**
felt; roofing...	**501**
fibrous	**502**
fireplace	**506**
frame; metal	**896**
girder (*coal mine*)... ...	**597**
glazing; patent	**503**
grate	**506**
insulation	**929**
lath; metal	**921**
lens	**599**
light; lead	**503**
marble	**500**
mason's; stone	**500**
meter-	
electricity	**899**
gas	**532**
water	**532**
mosaic	**506**
motor-	**516**
electric	**520**
net	**814**
panel (vehicle)	**851**
pattern (lace machine) ...	**814**
price	**364**
range	**500**
rate	**364**
Fixer; *continued*	
reinforcement (*building and contracting*)	**536**
roof (*building and contracting*)	**570**
roofing	**501**
scaffolding	**505**
ship door and collar ...	**534**
sign-	**896**
electric	**521**
steel-	
re-inforced concrete ...	**536**
building and contracting	**536**
tape (*paper pattern mfr.*)	**822**
terra-cotta	**506**
tile	**506**
transfer (japanning) ...	**869**
trimmer	**557**
ventilator	**532**
vitrolite	**503**
window-	**896**
vehicles	**859**
Fixer-	
carpentry and joinery ...	**570**
clothing mfr.	**557**
net mfr.	**814**
railways	**516**
Fixer and bender; steel ...	**536**
Fixer-mason	**500**
Flagman	**883**
Flagger-	**924**
fibre preparation	**811**
Flaker-on (electric cable) ...	**839**
Flanger; beam	**516**
Flanger-	
hat mfr.	**559**
sheet metal working ...	**841**
tin box mfr.	**841**
Flasher	**590**
Flasher hand (*plastics mfr.*)	**825**
Flatman	**880**
Flattener;	
patent (galvanized sheet)...	**839**
sheet (metal)	**839**
Flattener-	
glass mfr.	**590**
metal trades-	**841**
wire mfr.	**899**
Flatter;	
cellulose	**869**
gold	**518**
paint	**869**
silver	**518**
Flatter-	
glass mfr.	**590**
vehicle mfr.	**869**
Flatter and polisher	**869**
Flautist	**385**
Flavouring man (cereals) ...	**809**
Flesher	**810**
Flight-Lieutenant-	
armed forces-	
foreign and Commonwealth	**M151**
U.K.	**M150**
Flight-Sergeant-	
armed forces- U.K. ...	**600**
Flipper; bead	**824**
Flitter (*coal mine*)	**899**
Floater; tube	**843**
Floater-	
metal trades-	**843**
blast furnace	**912**
Floor and kiln man (*malting*)	**801**
Floor hand (*printing*) ...	**891**
Floor man-	**990**
asphalt mfr.	**829**
malting	**801**
oil wells	**898**
Florist;	**791**
artificial	**791**
Fluffer-	**810**
L.R.T.	**990**
Flusher; starch	**809**
Flusher (tobacco pipe) ...	**897**
Flusher and cleanser; sewer	**892**
Fluter;	
drill	**840**
pot; tea	**518**
Fluter-	
ivory, bone, etc.	**599**
metal	**840**
silver, plate	**518**
Fly hand	**891**
Flyman	**999**
Foiler-	**862**
plasterboard mfr.	**829**
Folder;	
book	**562**
box-	
cardboard box mfr. ...	**859**
tin box mfr.	**841**
cloth	**814**
curtain	**862**
envelope	**569**
handkerchief	**862**
map	**569**
net	**862**
paper	**569**
pattern; paper	**859**
towel (*textile mfr.*) ...	**814**
Folder-	
bookbinding	**562**
clothing mfr.	**862**
drum, keg mfr.	**841**
footwear mfr.	**555**
laundry	**862**
printing	**562**
rag book mfr.	**562**
textile mfr.-	**814**
hosiery finishing	**862**
silk doubling	**812**
Folder-in (*glove mfr.*) ...	**859**
Folder-up (*textiles*)	**814**
Follower; crane	**932**
Food worker	**809**
Footman (*domestic service*)	**699**
Footballer	**387**
Footer (*hosiery mfr.*) ...	**551**
Forcer; rubber	**824**
Forcer-	
plastics goods mfr. ...	**825**
rubber goods mfr.... ...	**824**
Forecaster; economic ...	**252**
Forecaster (meteorological)	**202**
Forehand-	**830**
rope, twine mfr.	**814**
Foreman; *see also notes*	
abattoir	**F581**
assistant *see notes*	

	Code number
Foreman; *continued*	
bakery	F580
bank (*transport*)	F871
batch	F590
baths	F699
battery (*coke ovens*)	F820
belt (*mine, not coal*)	F889
blowing	F811
boiler	F893
bottling	F862
brewer	F801
bridge	F896
builder's	F896
building;	F896
coach	F541
cable	F524
calender (*paper mfr.*)	F821
capstan	F881
carbonising (*coal gas, coke ovens*)	F820
card	F811
carding	F811
cartage	F889
checking (*engineering*)	F860
chemical	F820
civilian (*government*)	F896
coal	F889
colour (*carpet mfr.*)	F552
comber	F811
combing	F811
concrete	F923
contractor's	F896
corporation *see Foreman-local government*	
cupola	F830
dairy-	F809
retail trade	F731
day *see Foreman-*	
delivery	F889
demolition	F896
departmental *see Foreman-*	
depot-	F441
coal merchants	F889
transport	F871
despatch	F441
destructor; dust	F990
distribution (*gas board*)	F895
district-	F896
retail trade	F720
sanitary services	F933
dock	F930
doubler	F812
drainage	F895
drawing (*textile mfr.*)	F811
dredging	F885
drill (*mine, not coal*)	F898
electrical	F521
electronics	F529
electroplating	F834
engineering;	F840
constructional	F535
estate(s)	F896
explosives (*mine, not coal*)	F898
export	F889
extrusion; metal	F839
factory- *see also Foreman-*	
telecoms	F521
farm	F900
field	F900
fittings (*gas board*)	F532
flat (*card clothing mfr.*)	F912
Foreman; *continued*	
forecourt	F722
forging	F530
foundry	F531
frame (carding)	F811
furnace; blast	F830
furnace-	
glass mfr.	F823
metal trades	F830
garage	F540
general- *see also notes*	F110
building and contracting	111
goods (*railways*)	F881
hatch	F930
haulage (*coal mine*)	F886
hearth; soak	F810
heat (*gas works*)	F820
highways	F923
house;	
boiler	F893
gas	F820
glass-	F595
glass mfr.	F590
power	F893
retort	F820
wash	F673
inspection-	F860
glass mfr.	F869
installation; electrical	F521
installation (*oil refining*)	F889
instrument	F517
jetty	F930
kiln-	
carbon goods mfr.	F820
ceramics mfr.	F823
laboratory	F864
labour (*agriculture*)	F900
landscape	F594
laundry	F673
length (*river board*)	F929
lighting	F699
lime-	F810
foundry	F531
line (*metal trades*)	F851
lines; overhead	F524
lock	F889
locomotive	F881
loom	F550
maintenance;	
electrical	F521
loco	F516
maintenance-	F896
electricity board	F521
gas board	F516
manufacturing	F516
telecoms	F523
transport	F540
mechanical	F840
milk (*dairy*)	F809
mill;	
blue	F820
rolling	F832
mill (*food products mfr.*)	F809
mule	F812
night *see Foreman-*	
outside (*mine, not coal*)	F898
oven	F820
overhauling; vehicle	F540
painting	F507
parcel(s) (*railways*)	F881
permanent way	F922
Foreman; *continued*	
physics; health	F300
piercing	F841
piling (*civil engineering*)	F885
pipe; main	F895
pit; clay	F898
plant;	
carbonisation	F820
coal (*electricity board*)	F893
crushing	F820
dry cleaning (*coal mine*)	F890
gas	F820
mixing (*asphalt mfr.*)	F829
reforming	F820
plant-	
bakery	F580
building and contracting	F885
platform (*railways*)	F631
polish	F820
press (*metal trades*)	F841
printing	F891
process-	F820
food products mfr.	F809
production *see Foreman-*	
progress	F420
purification (*gas board*)	F820
purifier; gas	F820
quality (*engineering*)	F860
quarry	F898
quay	F930
receiving	F441
refining; metal	F830
retort (*gas works*)	F820
ring	F812
road	F923
rock (*mine, not coal*)	F898
room;	
blowing	F811
card	F811
grey (*textile mfr.*)	F441
lamp (*coal mine*)	F441
machine-	
clothing mfr.	F553
printing	F891
mill (*fur dressing*)	F810
packing	F862
pattern (*textile mfr.*)	F441
sewing	F553
tool	F515
rounds	F731
running (*railways*)	F881
salle	F861
salvage	F990
screen(s)-	F890
gas works, coke ovens	F829
scribbling	F811
section *see Foreman-*	
senior *see also notes*	F110
sewer	F892
shed;	
press (*brick mfr.*)	F590
weaving	F550
shed-	
tannery	F810
transport-	
rail	F881
road	F871
shift *see Foreman-*	
shipping	F441
shop;	
auto	F519

(Fo)

	Code number
Foreman; *continued*	
shop; *continued*	
casting	**F531**
cutting (*glass mfr.*)	**F590**
enamelling	**F869**
erecting (*engineering*)	**F516**
machine	**F519**
melting	**F830**
paint	**F869**
panel	**F542**
pattern	**F573**
press-	
metal trades	**F841**
plastics goods mfr.	**F825**
steel	**F832**
trim	**F554**
shop-	
ceramics mfr.	**F590**
coal mine	**F519**
engineering	**F519**
paper mfr.	**F821**
retail trade	**F720**
site	**F896**
spinning-	**F812**
man-made fibre mfr.	**F826**
stable	**F902**
stage (*gas works*)	**F820**
staithes	**F930**
stamping	**F841**
station; pumping	**F999**
station-	
L.R.T.	**F631**
railways	**F631**
stock	**F441**
store(s)	**F441**
surface-	
coal mine	**F929**
mine, not coal	**F898**
tank (*glass mfr.*)	**F823**
technical *see Foreman-*	
test; motor	**F860**
textile	**F814**
timber-	**F897**
docks	**F930**
tool; press	**F515**
traffic-	**F871**
coal mine (below ground)	**F889**
train	**F881**
transport; internal	**F889**
transport-	
rail	**F881**
road	**F871**
road transport	**F871**
transporting	**F889**
treatment; heat	**F833**
turbine	**F893**
twisting	**F812**
warehouse	**F441**
weaving	**F550**
welding	**F537**
wharf	**F930**
winding	**F813**
woodwork	**F570**
wool	**F811**
working- *see also Foreman-*	
coal mine	**F910**
works *see also notes*	**F110**
workshop *see Foreman-*	
yard;	
brick	**F590**
Foreman; *continued*	
yard; *continued*	
coal	**F889**
scrap	**F889**
ship	**F534**
steel	**F441**
stock-	**F441**
coal mine	**F441**
tan	**F810**
timber	**F441**
yard-	**F990**
auctioneering	**F931**
builders' merchants	**F889**
building and contracting	**F889**
canal	**F889**
coal mine	**F929**
local government	**F889**
mine, not coal	**F898**
railways	**F881**
road transport	**F871**
of factory (*government*)	**F599**
of works	**F896**
Foreman-	
bottling	**F862**
bus service	**F871**
abrasive paper, etc. mfr.	**F821**
agricultural contracting	**F901**
agriculture	**F900**
asbestos mfr.	**F814**
asbestos-cement goods mfr.	**F899**
asphalt mfr.	**F829**
auctioneering	**F931**
bakery	**F580**
baths	**F699**
bedding mfr.	**F554**
blue and starch mfr.	**F820**
bookcloth mfr.	**F550**
brake linings mfr.	**F899**
brewery	**F801**
brush mfr.	**F599**
building and contracting	**F896**
calico printers	**F569**
canvas goods mfr.	**F559**
cardboard box mfr.	**F569**
cast concrete products mfr.	**F899**
catering	**F953**
cattle food mfr.	**F809**
cement mfr.	**F829**
cemetery	**F699**
ceramics mfr.	**F590**
chemical mfr.	**F820**
chocolate mfr.	**F809**
cigarette mfr.	**F802**
cinema	**F699**
civil engineering	**F896**
clothing mfr.	**F559**
coal merchants	**F871**
coke ovens	**F820**
construction	**F896**
cork mfr.	**F599**
cotton waste merchants	**F811**
D.O.E.	**F896**
dairy-	**F809**
retail trade	**F731**
denture mfr.	**F592**
docks	**F930**
dry cleaning	**F673**
dyeing and cleaning	**F673**
dyeworks	**F552**
Foreman- *continued*	
electrical contracting	**F521**
electricity board	**F521**
enamelling	**F869**
entertainment	**F699**
fancy goods mfr.	**F599**
flooring contracting	**F506**
flour confectionery mfr.	**F580**
food canning	**F862**
food products mfr.	**F809**
footwear mfr.	**F555**
forestry	**F904**
furniture mfr.	**F571**
garage	**F540**
gas board-	**F532**
by-product plant	**F820**
gas works	**F820**
gelatine mfr.	**F820**
glass mfr.	**F590**
grain milling	**F809**
grinding wheel mfr.	**F899**
heating engineering	**F532**
horticulture	**F595**
joinery mfr.	**F570**
lairage	**F902**
laundry	**F673**
leather cloth mfr.	**F814**
leather dressing	**F810**
leather goods mfr.	**F555**
linoleum mfr.	**F829**
local government-	**F896**
baths dept.	**F699**
cleansing dept.	**F933**
council depot	**F889**
engineer's dept.	**F896**
highways dept.	**F923**
housing dept.	**F896**
parks dept.	**F594**
public works	**F896**
refuse tip	**F990**
sanitary dept.	**F933**
sewage works	**F892**
surveyor's dept.	**F896**
transport dept.	**F871**
match mfr.	**F599**
metal trades-	
aero-engine mfr.	**F516**
annealing	**F833**
assembling	**F851**
blast furnace	**F830**
cable mfr.	**F899**
coach building	**F541**
constructional engineering	**F535**
cutlery mfr.	**F839**
electrical domestic appliance mfr.	**F850**
electrical lighting equipment mfr.	**F850**
electronic equipment mfr.	**F520**
electroplating	**F834**
forging	**F530**
foundry	**F531**
heat treatment	**F833**
hydraulic pump mfr.	**F516**
instrument mfr.	**F517**
internal combustion engine mfr.	**F516**
iron and steel mfr.	**F839**
jewellery mfr.	**F518**
lamp, valve mfr.	**F519**
machine shop	**F519**

	Code number
Foreman- *continued*	
metal trades- continued	
metal box mfr.	F533
metal extrusion	F839
metal pressing	F841
metal refining	F830
metal tube mfr.	F839
motor vehicle mfr.	F851
office machinery mfr.	F520
power tools mfr.	F529
press tool mfr.	F515
radio, television mfr.	F520
razor blade mfr.	F839
rolling mill	F832
sheet metal working	F533
shipbuilding	F534
signalling equipment	F520
small tools mfr.	F515
smallwares	F841
stamping and piercing	F841
steel drawing	F831
steel fabrication	F534
telecommunications equipment mfr.	F850
tinplate mfr.	F832
tool room	F515
transformers and switchgear mfr.	F520
welding	F537
wire mfr.	F831
mine, not coal	F898
mineral water mfr.	F809
nursery	F595
oil refining	F820
oil seed crushing	F809
opencast coal mining	F898
ordnance depot	F441
ordnance factory-	
explosive mfr.	F820
shell filling	F599
P.L.A.	F930
P.O. (post office railway)	F940
packing	F862
paint mfr.	F820
paper mfr.	F821
paper goods mfr.	F569
patent fuel mfr.	F820
pen mfr.	F599
pencil, crayon mfr.	F599
petrol station	F722
petroleum distribution	F889
plasterboard mfr.	F829
plastics goods mfr.	F825
power station	F893
printing	F891
provision merchants	F720
publishing	F891
railways-	F881
carriage and wagon dept.	F530
district engineer's dept.	F922
locomotive shop	F516
motive power dept.	F516
signal and telegraph dept.	F529
removal contracting	F931
repository	F441
retail trade	F720
river board	F929
road transport-	F871
bus service	F871
Foreman- *continued*	
rubber goods mfr.	F824
sawmilling	F897
scrap merchants	F889
security services	F615
sewage disposal	F892
slag wool mfr.	F820
soap mfr.	F820
spirit distilling	F820
sports goods mfr.	F599
sugar confectionery mfr.	F809
sugar refining	F809
surgical dressing mfr.	F814
tailoring	F556
tannery	F810
telecoms	F523
textile mfr.-	F814
combing dept.	F811
doubling, twisting dept.	F812
dyeing dept.	F552
finishing dept.	F552
hosiery mfr.	F551
man-made fibre mfr.	F826
opening, carding dept.	F811
printing dept.	F569
spinning dept.	F812
weaving dept.	F550
winding dept.	F813
timber merchants	F441
tobacco mfr.	F802
tobacco pipe mfr.	F579
toilet preparation mfr.	F820
toy mfr.	F599
typewriter ribbon mfr.	F814
upholstering	F554
wallpaper mfr.	F919
warehousing	F441
water works	F892
waterways	F929
woodware mfr.	F570
wreck raising	F990
zoo	F902
Foreman-ganger- *see also* Foreman-	
maintenance	F896
agriculture	F900
building and contracting	F896
cable laying	F895
docks	F930
electricity board	F895
gas board	F895
local government	F896
railways	F922
telecoms	F524
water works	F895
Forewoman; factory-	
telecoms	F850
Forewoman- *see also Foreman-*	
government	F958
P.O.	F569
Forest workman	904
Forest worker	904
Forester	F904
Forestry worker	904
Forge hand	839
Forgeman	839
Forge worker	839
Forger	530
Forker-	889
glass mfr.	829
wrought iron mfr.	830
Former;	
accumulator	899
battery	899
cable	850
cell (battery)	899
coil	850
copper (generators)	850
filament	899
glass	590
hat	814
lap	811
loom	850
plate; tungsten	899
rope	814
strand	814
tube	839
wire (*spring mfr.*)	899
Former-	
felt hat mfr.	814
plastics mfr.	825
tube mfr.	839
Fortune teller	699
Forwarder	562
Founder; type	839
Founder-	
glass mfr.	823
metal trades-	839
blast furnace	830
copper refining	830
type foundry	839
Foundry hand	911
Foundry man	839
Foundry worker	911
Fractionator (*chemical mfr.*)	820
Fraiser	843
Frame hand; mustard	809
Frame hand-	
hosiery mfr.	551
sugar confectionery mfr.	809
Frame man (*rope mfr.*)	814
Frame worker;	
hand	551
knitting	551
Frame worker (*rope mfr.*)	814
Framer;	
aluminium	516
bag	859
binocular	517
calico	559
picture	579
ring	812
rule	897
seat	571
Framer-	
chair mfr.	571
laundry	673
leather goods mfr.	859
shipbuilding	534
textile mfr.-	811
hosiery mfr.	552
wool spinning	812
Frazer-	
metal trades	843
tobacco pipe mfr.	897
Freeman (River Thames)	880
Freezer	809
Friar	292
Fridgeman (*ice cream mfr.*)	809
Frier *see Fryer*	
Friller	553
Fringer	551

	Code number
Fritter	**829**
Frogman	**599**
Front hand (*clothing mfr.*)	**559**
Froster-	
electric lamp mfr.	**591**
glass mfr.	**591**
Fruitman;	**595**
head	**F595**
Fruiterer-	**179**
market trading	**732**
Fryer; fish-	**620**
self-employed	**174**
Fryer-	
catering	**620**
food products mfr. ...	**809**
Fuelman (ship)	**880**
Fuller	**814**
Fumigator	**699**
Furnace hand; blast	**830**
Furnace hand-	
charcoal mfr.	**829**
metal mfr.	**830**
mine, not coal	**829**
Furnaceman;	
annealing	**833**
barium	**820**
blast	**830**
boiler	**893**
brass	**830**
calcining-	**820**
flint	**829**
chrome	**830**
cupola	**830**
electric	**830**
graphitising	**829**
hardening; case	**833**
hearth; open	**830**
spring; coach	**833**
treatment; heat	**833**
Furnaceman-	
ceramics mfr.	**823**
chemical mfr.	**820**
crematorium	**999**
electric bulb mfr.	**823**
gas works	**820**
glass mfr.	**823**
lead pencil mfr.	**829**
metal trades-	**830**
annealing	**833**
oil refining	**820**
red lead mfr.	**820**
Furnace worker; blast ...	**830**
Furnace worker (*metal trades*)	**830**
Furnisher;	
coffin	**579**
house	**179**
Furnisher (*retail trade*) ...	**179**
Furrier-	
fur products mfr.	**557**
retail trade	**179**
Fuser;	
bifocal	**823**
enamel	**829**
Fuser-	
glass mfr.	**829**
metal trades	**829**
textile products mfr. ...	**859**
Fuseroom worker (*chemical mfr.*)	**820**
Fusilier-	
armed forces-	
foreign and Commonwealth	**601**
U.K.	**600**

G

	Code number
G.I. *(armed forces-foreign)*	**601**
Gabler and corder (net)	**814**
Gaffer- *see also Foreman-*	
glass mfr.	**590**
Gaiter;	
beam	**552**
harness	**516**
loom	**F550**
warp	**552**
Gaiter-	
textile spinning	**813**
textile weaving	**516**
Galenical worker	**820**
Galley hand	**952**
Galvanizer	**834**
Gambler; professional	**699**
Gang man; shore *(ship-building)*	**912**
Gang man *(agriculture)*	**900**
Ganger;	
filtration *(water works)*	**F892**
highways	**F923**
navvy	**F923**
Ganger- *see also Foreman-*	
canal	**F929**
coal mine	**889**
docks	**F930**
electricity board	**F895**
gas board	**F895**
local government	**F896**
railways	**F922**
water works	**F895**
Gangwayman	**930**
Gantry man;	**886**
forge (steelworks)	**886**
Garage hand	**540**
Garage worker *(P.O.)*	**990**
Garde-manger	**F620**
Gardener;	
fruit-	**160**
employee	**595**
landscape	**594**
market-	**160**
employee	**595**
nursery-	**160**
employee	**595**
Gardener-	**594**
fruit growing-	**160**
employee	**595**
market gardening-	**160**
employee	**595**
nursery-	**160**
employee	**595**
Gardener-caretaker	**594**
Gardener-chauffeur	**874**
Gardener-groundsman	**594**
Gardener-handyman	**594**
Gardener's boy	**594**
Garnet worker	**811**
Garnetter	**811**
Garterer	**859**
Gas man; assistant *(iron and steelworks)*	**893**
Gasman-	
coal gas	**820**
water gas	**820**
blast furnace	**999**
cider mfr.	**801**
gas works	**820**
Gasman- *continued*	
railways	**889**
Gas worker;	
chlorine	**820**
maintenance	**532**
Gas worker-	**919**
industrial gas	**820**
Gasser	**552**
Gateman;	
bridge	**889**
dock	**889**
flood	**889**
lock	**889**
Gateman-	**615**
coal mine	**883**
docks	**889**
entertainment	**699**
railways	**883**
waterways	**889**
Gatekeeper-	**615**
coal mine	**883**
Gatekeeper and pointsman	**883**
Gatherer;	
mussel	**903**
rag *(woollen mfr.)*	**889**
seaweed	**903**
watercress	**902**
Gatherer-	
agricultural products	**902**
bookbinding	**562**
ceramics mfr.	**889**
glass mfr.	**590**
Gauger;	
bullet	**860**
cement	**863**
furnace	**830**
gut	**829**
mica	**829**
tank-	
oil refining	**863**
petroleum distribution	**863**
Gauger-	
cast stone products mfr.	**599**
glass mfr.	**590**
metal trades-	**860**
lamp, valve mfr.	**863**
oil refining	**863**
Gaulter	**898**
Gear man *(docks)*	**441**
Gelatine man *(explosives)*	**820**
Gelatine worker	**809**
Gemmologist	**202**
Genealogist	**291**
General-	
armed forces-	
foreign and Commonwealth	**M151**
U.K.	**M150**
General hand-	**990**
bacon curing	**809**
bakery	**800**
bookbinding	**562**
dressmaking	**556**
hotel	**958**
General operative *(textile mfr.)*	**919**
General worker-	**990**
coal mine	**910**
farming	**900**
Generator; acetylene	**820**
Generator man	**820**
Geneticist	**201**
Geochemist	**202**
Geographer	**291**
Geologist	**202**
Geomorphologist	**202**
Geophysicist	**202**
Geotechnologist	**202**
Geriatrician	**220**
Getter; clay	**898**
Getter-	
coal mine	**597**
mine, not coal	**898**
Ghillie	**699**
Gigger *(textile finishing)*	**552**
Gilder; composition	**869**
Gilder-	
bookbinding	**562**
ceramics mfr.	**591**
furniture mfr.	**869**
leather dressing	**810**
painting and decorating	**507**
printing	**569**
wallpaper mfr.	**569**
Gilder and plater	**834**
Giller-	
motor radiator mfr.	**851**
textile mfr.	**811**
Gillie	**699**
Gimper	**814**
Giver-out	**441**
Glassman	**952**
Glass worker;	
decorative	**503**
fibre	**590**
Glass worker-	
agriculture	**595**
glass mfr.	**590**
lamp, valve mfr.	**590**
Glasshouse worker	**595**
Glazer;	
assistant *(metal trades)*	**899**
button	**591**
cutlery	**842**
friction	**821**
lens	**591**
optical	**591**
patent	**503**
postcard	**821**
pottery	**591**
Glazer-	
ceramics mfr.	**591**
glass mfr.	**591**
leather dressing	**810**
metal trades	**842**
paper mfr.	**821**
sugar confectionery mfr.	**809**
textile mfr.	**552**
wallpaper mfr.	**821**
Glazier;	**503**
lens	**591**
optical	**591**
Glazier and decorator	**509**
Glosser; silk	**552**
Glosser *(footwear mfr.)*	**555**
Glove hand (knitted gloves)	**551**
Glove worker	**557**
Glover *(glove mfr.)*	**553**
Gluer-	
furniture mfr.	**859**
paper products mfr.	**859**
sports goods mfr.	**859**
Gluer-up (woodwork)	**859**

Code number

Glycerine worker ... 820
Gold worker ... 591
Goldsmith ... 518
Golf ball worker ... 824
Golf course man ... 594
Golfer ... 387
Goods worker;
leather ... 555
railways ... 631
rubber ... 824
Gouger ... 534
Governess; ... 239
nursery ... 650
Governor *(prison service)* ... 154
Governor man *(gas works)* 999
Grade I, II Technical Class
(government) ... 309
Grade 5 *(government)* ... 100
Grade 6, 7 *(government)* ... 103
Grade 9
(Foreign and Commonwealth Office) ... 132
Grade 10
(Foreign and Commonwealth Office) ... 400
Grader;
coke ... 829
egg ... 863
fat ... 863
fruit ... 863
hosiery ... 863
leather ... 863
meat ... 863
pattern-
clothing mfr. ... 559
footwear mfr. ... 822
pelt *(fellmongery)* ... 863
pig ... 902
poultry *(retail trade)* ... 863
rag ... 863
sack ... 863
skin ... 863
sole ... 863
stock; live ... 902
wool ... 863
Grader-
abrasive paper, etc. mfr. ... 569
ceramics mfr. ... 863
chemical mfr. ... 820
coal mine ... 890
food products mfr. ... 863
glass mfr. ... 869
metal trades ... 863
paper pattern mfr. ... 559
photographic processing ... 569
plasterboard mfr. ... 869
textile mfr. ... 863
tobacco pipe mfr. ... 863
wholesale fish trade ... 863
Graduator; thermometer ... 517
Grafter *(agriculture)* ... 595
Grailer *(celluloid goods mfr.)* 825
Grainer; plate ... 899
Grainer-
brewery ... 919
leather dressing ... 810
painting and decorating ... 507
printing ... 899
Grainer and marbler ... 507
Granary hand... ... 919
Granary man ... 441

Code number

Granulator; aluminium ... 839
Granulator *(chemical mfr.)* 820
Granulator man (sugar) ... 809
Graphologist ... 699
Grater *(steelworks)* ... 912
Gravel worker *(gravel extraction)* ... 898
Grease man ... 820
Greaser;
cold roll ... 894
donkey *(shipping)* ... 880
electric *(shipping)* ... 880
fan *(shipping)* ... 880
kiln ... 894
refrigerating *(shipping)* ... 880
sheave ... 894
tin *(bakery)* ... 800
Greaser- ... 894
motor vehicles ... 540
bakery ... 800
fishing ... 880
shipping ... 880
tin box mfr. ... 912
Greengrocer- ... 179
market trading ... 732
mobile shop ... 731
Greenhouse worker
(agriculture) ... 595
Greensman ... 594
Grey room hand ... 441
Grey room man ... 441
Griddler *(catering)* ... 620
Grieve ... 160
Grill hand ... 620
Grinder;
anvil ... 899
asbestos ... 811
assistant *(metal trades)* ... 899
axle ... 512
ball (ball bearing) ... 841
billet *(steelworks)* ... 899
bit *(coal mine)* ... 899
bits; drill ... 512
blade ... 899
bolster ... 512
bone ... 829
bow ... 899
burr ... 899
cam-bowl ... 512
camshaft ... 512
carbide ... 820
carbon *(crucible mfr.)* ... 829
card ... 899
card clothing ... 899
cardroom ... 899
castings ... 843
centreless ... 512
clay *(ceramics mfr.)* ... 829
coffee ... 809
colour ... 829
comb ... 899
compo *(metal mfr.)* ... 829
composition-
ceramics mfr. ... 829
metal mfr. ... 829
corn ... 809
crankshaft ... 512
cutlery ... 512
cutter-
cemented carbide goods mfr. ... 599

Code number

Grinder; *continued*
cutter- *continued*
metal trades ... 512
cylinder-
metal trades ... 512
textile mfr. ... 811
cylindrical ... 512
disc-
abrasive wheel mfr. ... 599
metal trades ... 512
drill ... 512
dry (metal) ... 899
dust ... 829
ebonite ... 824
edge-
abrasive wheel mfr. ... 599
gramophone record mfr. 825
emery *(steelworks)* ... 843
enamel ... 829
external ... 512
face ... 512
file ... 512
flat- ... 811
glass ... 591
flint *(ceramics mfr.)* ... 829
flock ... 811
ganister ... 890
gear ... 512
gelatine ... 820
glass ... 591
glaze *(ceramics mfr.)* ... 829
hob ... 512
ink ... 820
instrument ... 512
internal ... 512
jig ... 512
jobbing ... 899
jute ... 811
knife ... 512
lens ... 591
logwood ... 821
machine *(metal trades)* ... 512
mower; lawn ... 512
needle ... 899
optical ... 591
paint ... 829
paper ... 821
precision ... 512
profile; optical ... 512
race ... 512
rag ... 811
razor ... 512
resin ... 820
roll ... 512
roller ... 512
rough cast ... 843
rubber ... 829
sand ... 829
saw ... 512
scissors ... 899
segmental ... 512
shaft ... 512
shears ... 512
shoddy ... 811
silica ... 829
slab; optical ... 591
slag ... 829
snuff ... 802
soap; dry ... 820
spindle ... 512
spline ... 512

	Code number
Grinder; *continued*	
spring	**512**
steel	**899**
stone;	**500**
lime *(quarry)*	**890**
lithographic	**500**
wet	**899**
stopper; glass	**591**
straight	**899**
sugar	**809**
surface-	**512**
carbon goods mfr. ...	**899**
glass mfr.	**591**
sweep	**912**
swing	**899**
tool;	**512**
universal	**512**
tool and cutter	**512**
tool room	**512**
universal	**512**
valve	**512**
wet-	**899**
chemicals	**820**
wheel; emery-	**899**
glass mfr.	**591**
Grinder-	
abrasive paper, etc. mfr. ...	**899**
brake lining mfr.	**899**
carbon goods mfr. ...	**899**
cast concrete products mfr.	**599**
ceramics mfr.	**591**
chemical mfr.	**820**
food products mfr. ...	**809**
glass mfr.	**591**
metal trades-	**512**
foundry	**843**
precious metal, plate mfr.	**843**
mine, not coal	**890**
paper mfr.	**821**
patent fuel mfr.	**829**
plastics goods mfr. ...	**825**
printing	**569**
textile mfr.-	**811**
textile finishing	**552**
Grinder and finisher; spring	**512**
Grinder and polisher-	
metal trades	**899**
optical goods mfr.	**591**
Grinderman-	
grain milling	**809**
paper mfr.	**821**
Grinder-setter *(metal trades)*	**512**
Gristman *(brewery)*	**801**
Grocer-	**179**
travelling	**731**
Grommeter	**859**
Groom	**902**
Groom-gardener	**902**
Groomsman	**902**
Groover; pencil	**897**
Groover *(metal trades)* ...	**840**
Grosser *(textile making-up)*	**862**
Ground worker *(building and contracting)*	**929**
Grounder; fur	**869**
Grounder *(wallpaper printing)*	**869**
Groundsman-	**594**
market	**990**
Grouter; mould *(steelworks)*	**839**
Grower-	**160**
bulb-	**160**
Grower- *continued*	
bulb- *continued*	
employee	**595**
fruit-	**160**
employee	**595**
mushroom-	**160**
employee	**595**
osier	**904**
rose-	**160**
employee	**595**
tomato-	**160**
employee	**595**
watercress-	**160**
employee	**595**
willow	**904**
withy	**904**
wood	**904**
Guard;	
ballast...	**881**
bank	**615**
body	**615**
bus	**875**
coast	**619**
fire	**611**
forest	**904**
goods	**881**
life	**619**
loco	**881**
night	**615**
passenger	**881**
security	**615**
train-	**881**
ropes	**889**
van	**615**
water *(Customs and Excise)*	**613**
works	**615**
Guard-	
L.R.T.	**881**
manufacturing	**615**
railways	**881**
road goods transport ...	**615**
road passenger transport	**875**
Guarder *(net mfr.)*	**814**
Guardsman *(armed forces-U.K.)*	**600**
Guide;	**630**
coach	**630**
store	**699**
Guide man; coke	**889**
Guider-	
textile printing	**569**
tube mfr.	**839**
Guider-in	**814**
Guillotine hand-	
asbestos-cement products mfr.	**599**
metal trades	**899**
paper products mfr. ...	**822**
Guillotine man *see Guillotine hand-*	
Guillotine worker *see Guillotine hand-*	
Guitarist	**385**
Gulley man	**990**
Gummer-	
coal mine	**597**
paper products mfr. ...	**859**
Gunner;	
civilian *(Min. of Defence)*	**999**
Gunner-	
armed forces-	
foreign and Commonwealth	**601**
U.K.	**600**
Gunner- *continued*	
steelworks	**899**
Gunsmith	**516**
Gutman	**581**
Gutter; fish	**582**
Gymnast;	**387**
remedial	**347**
Gynaecologist	**220**

	Code number
H	
H.E.O. *(government)*	**103**
H.M.F.I.	**394**
H.M.I.S.	**232**
Haberdasher-	**179**
market trading	**732**
Hackler	**811**
Haematologist	**300**
Hafter	**899**
Hair hand *(brush, etc. mfr.)*	**863**
Hair worker	**811**
Hairdresser	**660**
Halsher (wool)	**813**
Hammer worker; power	**839**
Hammerman-	**530**
jute mfr.	**919**
L.R.T.	**516**
leather dressing	**810**
pile driving	**885**
precious metal, plate mfr.	**518**
tobacco mfr.	**899**
Hammerer; saw	**899**
Hammerer *(precious metal, plate mfr.)*	**518**
Hander; machine *see Machinist*	
Handicapper	**387**
Handler;	
aircraft	**889**
animal	**902**
bag; paper	**569**
baggage *(air transport)*	**931**
body *(vehicle mfr.)*	**889**
coal	**889**
dog	**902**
freight *(warehousing)*	**931**
material	**889**
red press mud	**820**
sheet (metal)	**889**
spade and shovel	**859**
stock -	
asbestos-cement goods mfr.	**889**
retail trade	**954**
stone *(brush, etc. mfr.)*	**811**
tool *(edge tool mfr.)*	**859**
traffic	**420**
Handler-	
brush, etc. mfr.	**859**
ceramics mfr.	**859**
edge tool mfr.	**859**
photographic mfr.	**569**
tannery	**810**
Handyman;	
bar	**959**
builder's	**509**
carpenter's	**920**
electrician's	**913**
engineer's	**913**
estate	**509**
farm	**900**
fitter's-	**913**
pipe	**913**
garage	**540**
gardener's	**594**
general-	**896**
building and contracting	**509**
maintenance-	**896**
building and contracting	**509**
n.o.s.-	**896**
residential buildings	**896**
building and contracting	**509**
Handyman; *continued*	
n.o.s.- *continued*	
coal mine	**910**
gas works	**899**
grist milling	**809**
water works	**899**
office	**990**
Handyman-driver	**874**
Handyman-gardener	**594**
Handyman-labourer	**990**
Hanger;	
bell (church bells)	**505**
door (coach body)	**851**
linoleum *(linoleum mfr.)*	**829**
paper	**507**
poster	**959**
Hanger *(leather cloth mfr.)*	**814**
Hanger-on-	**932**
coal mine	**889**
Hanker-	
textile mfr.	**814**
textile packing	**862**
Hardener;	
blade	**833**
case	**833**
die and mill	**833**
drill	**833**
felt	**814**
file	**833**
ring	**833**
saw	**833**
section	**833**
tool	**833**
wool (hats)	**814**
Hardener-	
hats	**814**
metal	**833**
Harpist	**385**
Harpooner	**903**
Harvester; crop	**902**
Hatchman	**930**
Hatcher; fish	**903**
Hatchery worker-	
agriculture	**902**
fishing	**903**
Hatchwayman	**930**
Hatter-	
hat mfr.	**559**
retail trade	**179**
Hat worker	**557**
Haulage hand-	
coal mine	**889**
haulage contractor	**872**
mine, not coal	**889**
Haulage man; face	**889**
Haulage man *(coal mine)*	**889**
Haulage worker *(coal mine)*	**889**
Hauler;	
coal *(retail trade)*	**872**
timber	**872**
Haulerman	**889**
Haulier;	
butt	**810**
general	**872**
shop *(tube mfr.)*	**839**
timber	**872**
Haulier-	**872**
coal mine	**889**
Hawker	**732**
Head;	
departmental *see Manager*	
Head; *continued*	
section-	
clerical	**F430**
chemical mfr.	**200**
of department-	
educational establishments-	
higher and further education-	**231**
polytechnic	**230**
university	**230**
schools-	
secondary	**233**
sixth form college	**233**
of section *see Manager*	
Head lad *(racing stable)*	**902**
Headman; gear *(coal mine)*	**597**
Headman- *see also Foreman*	
racing stable	**F902**
Header;	
bolt	**899**
cold (rivets)	**899**
fish	**582**
Header-	
bolts, etc. mfr.	**899**
coal mine	**597**
Header-up-	
bolts, etc. mfr.	**899**
cask mfr.	**572**
Heading man; hard	**597**
Heald man	**552**
Healder	**552**
Hearthman *(brewery)*	**801**
Heatman *(linoleum mfr.)*	**829**
Heat treatment worker (metal)	**833**
Heater;	
coke oven	**820**
ingot	**830**
iron *(foundry)*	**830**
mill *(rolling mill)*	**830**
pit; soaking	**830**
retort *(chemical mfr.)*	**820**
rivet	**899**
rubber *(tyre mfr.)*	**824**
smith's	**830**
tube; steel	**830**
Heater-	
coal gas, coke ovens	**820**
metal trades-	**830**
annealing	**833**
cycle mfr.	**833**
file mfr.	**833**
Heaterman *(patent fuel mfr.)*	**820**
Heaver; coal	**930**
Hedger;	**902**
stone	**500**
Hedger and ditcher	**902**
Heeler (footwear)	**555**
Helminthologist	**201**
Helmsman	**880**
Help;	
baker's	**800**
bar	**622**
canteen	**953**
daily	**958**
domestic	**958**
electrician's	**913**
farm	**900**
general *(bakery)*	**800**
home	**958**
kitchen	**952**
meals; school	**953**

	Code number
Help; *continued*	
mother's	659
moulder's	911
part-time *(retail trade)*	720
plater's	913
printer's	891
room; dining	953
teacher's (school meals)	659
ward	641
Help *(domestic service)*	958
Helper;	
ancilliary *(school)*	652
bakehouse	800
bar	622
bender's; frame	913
blacksmith's	839
bricklayer's	921
canteen	953
carpenter's	920
caster's	839
classroom	652
club; youth	699
collier('s)	597
cutter's	899
domestic	958
electrician's	913
erector's; steel	913
examiner's *(net mfr.)*	814
first-	
rolling mill	839
tinplate mfr.	839
fitter's	913
forge	839
frame	899
furnaceman's	830
infant	659
keeper's	830
ladle	932
maker's; boiler	913
mason's	921
meals; school	953
miner's *(mine, not coal)*	898
nursery	650
operator's; wireline	898
part-time *(retail trade)*	720
people's; old	644
pickler's *(metal trades)*	839
pit	839
pitman's	839
plater's	913
playgroup	659
playschool	659
potman's (nickel)	830
press	839
repairer's *(coal mine)*	899
roller's	839
room; dining	953
school	652
shearer's *(metal trades)*	913
smith's;	839
boiler	913
stable	902
stamper's	839
straightener's-	913
rolling mill	839
ward	641
weaver's	814
worker's; process	820
Helper-	
catering	952
metal trades-	913

	Code number
Helper- *continued*	
metal trades- continued	
blast furnace	830
copper refining	839
forging	839
rolling mill	839
tube mfr.	839
paper mfr.	821
salt mfr.	820
textile mfr.-	919
textile weaving	814
Helper-up	889
Helver (tools)	859
Hemmer	553
Hemstitcher	553
Herbalist	346
Herdsman	900
Herpetologist	201
Herring worker	582
Hewer *(coal mine)*	597
Highwayman	923
Hinger; last	579
Hirer;	
boat	880
site; caravan	173
Histologist	201
Histopathologist	201
Historian	291
Hitcher *(coal mine)*	889
Hoistman	886
Hoister; crane	886
Holder;	
copy	430
double *(rolling mill)*	839
small-	160
forestry	904
stall-	732
coal mine	597
entertainment	699
store	441
at drill *(rolling mill)*	912
Holder-on (riveter's)	913
Holder-up;	
boilermaker's	913
riveter's	913
Holder-up *(shipbuilding)*	913
Holdsman	930
Holer;	
button-	553
button mfr.	899
eyelet	555
flyer	840
Holer *(mine, not coal)*	898
Hollanderman	829
Homeopath-	346
medically qualified	220
Homogeniser	809
Honer	840
Hookman	919
Hooker-	
mine, not coal	889
rolling mill	839
textile mfr.	552
Hooper; wheel	530
Hopperman; dredge	889
Hopperman-	
bakery	800
cement mfr.	829
dredging contractors	889
iron and steel mfr.	889
Horologist	517

	Code number
Horseman-	902
timber haulage	889
canal	889
tannery	919
Horticultural worker	595
Horticulturist-	201
market gardening, etc.	160
Hoseman	898
Hosier;	179
elastic	551
surgical	551
Hosier and haberdasher	179
Hosiery hand	551
Hosiery operative	551
Hosiery worker	551
Hospital worker	641
Hostess;	
air	630
ground	630
Hostess *(aircraft)*	630
Hostler	902
Hotel worker	958
Hotelier	173
Houseman;	
boiler	893
cylinder	820
press *(coal mine)*	899
sand	821
school	958
slip	829
tun *(brewery)*	801
wash	673
Houseman-	
domestic service	958
institution	958
museum	619
Housemaster	
(local government- social services dept.)	370
Houseworker;	
power	893
retort *(coal gas, coke ovens)*	820
slaughter	581
slip	829
House worker *(domestic service)*	958
Housemaid	958
Hugger-off	919
Humper; coal	990
Humper-	
meat market	931
slaughterhouse	931
Hunter	902
Huntsman	902
Hwsmyn	160
Hydraulicman *(docks)*	999
Hydrapulper	821
Hydrator; lime	829
Hydro hand *(laundry)*	673
Hydro man *(textile mfr.)*	814
Hydrobiologist	201
Hydro-blaster	844
Hydro-extractor	814
Hydrographer	313
Hydrologist	202
Hygienist;	
dental	346
occupational	396
Hypnotherapist	347
Hypnotist *(entertainment)*	384
Hyster	887

I

	Code number
Icer	**809**
Ichthyologist	**201**
Icing room worker	**800**
Illuminator	**381**
Illuminiser	**834**
Illusionist	**384**
Illustrator;	
book	**381**
chief	**M381**
leading	**F381**
senior	**F381**
technical	**381**
Illustrator-	
self-employed	**381**
advertising	**381**
government	**381**
Imam	**292**
Immunologist	**201**
Importer	**702**
Imposition hand	**560**
Impregnator; armature	**829**
Impregnator-	
asbestos composition goods mfr.	**829**
cable mfr.	**599**
Impresario	**384**
Impressioner (engraver's)	**569**
Impressionist	**384**
Improver; *see also notes*	
cutter	**557**
green	**594**
millinery	**557**
Improver *(wool spinning)*	**812**
Incubationist *(agriculture)*	**902**
Incumbent	**292**
Indexer-	**420**
bookbinding	**562**
Inflator;	
bed; air	**861**
cushion; air	**861**
Infuser; water *(coal mine)*	**597**
Infusion man; water	**597**
Ingiver	**552**
Ingot man-	
non-ferrous metal mfr.	**830**
rolling mill	**441**
Injector;	
mould *(plastics goods mfr.)*	**825**
wax	**839**
Inker;	
edge	**869**
ribbon; typewriter	**814**
Inker *(footwear mfr.)*	**869**
Innkeeper	**175**
Inseminator; artificial	**902**
Inserter; coil	**850**
Inserter; ferrule *(water works)*	**532**
Inserter-	
clothing mfr.	**859**
lamp, valve mfr.	**850**
Inspector;	
A.I.D. *(Board of Trade)*	**860**
accounts	**410**
advertisement	**F959**
advertising	**F959**
aeronautical	**860**
aircraft	**860**
alkali	**395**
apparatus; photographic	**860**
Inspector; *continued*	
area (automatic machines)	**516**
armaments	**860**
assembly	**860**
assistant-	
government	**132**
P.O.	**F940**
ballast	**F922**
bank	**M399**
bank-note	**861**
bar *(rolling mill)*	**860**
beach	**F615**
belt *(coal mine)*	**889**
bench	**860**
bill *(advertising)*	**F959**
billet *(steelworks)*	**860**
boiler	**860**
box *(electricity board)*	**521**
bridge	**F896**
building	**311**
bus	**F870**
business; new *(insurance)*	**719**
cabinet	**861**
cable-	**524**
cable mfr.	**860**
canal	**F929**
car-	**860**
dining car	**F953**
cargo	**420**
carpet	**861**
carriage *(railways)*	**516**
carriage and wagon	**516**
cartage *(railways)*	**F881**
cell *(chemical mfr.)*	**869**
cellar	**801**
chair; deck	**F959**
chemical	**395**
chicken *(food processing)*	**861**
chief-	
banking	**M399**
engineering-	**F860**
professional-	**211**
electrical engineering	**212**
electronic engineering	**213**
quality control	**218**
insurance	**719**
local government-	**394**
transport dept.	**140**
police service	**M152**
railways	**140**
water board	**F892**
claims *(insurance)*	**361**
cleansing	**F933**
cloth	**861**
clothing	**861**
coal *(opencast coal mining)*	**395**
coil	**860**
coke *(coke ovens)*	**F820**
component(s) *(metal trades)*	**860**
control;	
building	**311**
pest	**699**
quality-	
bakery	**861**
coal mine	**516**
electrical, electronic equipment mfr.	**860**
food products mfr.	**861**
glass mfr.	**869**
metal trades	**860**
paper mfr.	**861**
Inspector; *continued*	
control; *continued*	
quality- *continued*	
plastics goods mfr.	**861**
river, water authority	**395**
rubber goods mfr.	**861**
sugar confectionery mfr.	**861**
textile goods mfr.	**861**
wood products mfr.	**861**
core	**860**
crane	**395**
cylinder	**860**
depot; chief *(transport)*	**140**
depot-	**F441**
transport	**F871**
despatch	**F441**
detective	**M152**
diesel *(railways)*	**F516**
district-	**F896**
gas board	**394**
government-	
Min. of A.F.F.	**395**
Min. of Defence	**219**
insurance	**719**
transport-	
rail	**F881**
road	**F870**
water board	**F892**
divisional-	
government-	
Min. of Defence	**219**
local government	**394**
police service	**M152**
transport	**140**
drain(age)	**F895**
drug	**395**
effluent	**395**
electrical-	**860**
coal mine	**395**
government	**395**
electrical and mechanical *(coal mine)*	**395**
electronics *(components mfr.)*	**860**
employment;	**102**
railway	**363**
enamel	**860**
engine	**860**
engineering; chief	**211**
engineering-	**860**
D.O.E.	**210**
D.S.S.	**211**
Dept. of Energy	**301**
telecoms	**F523**
excavating *(electricity board)*	**F895**
explosives	**395**
factory-	
clothing mfr.	**861**
metal trades	**860**
field *(telecoms)*	**F524**
film	**869**
fire-	**395**
fire service	**M153**
fishery *(Min. of A.F.F.)*	**395**
fitting(s)-	
gas board	**394**
water board	**394**
flight-	**516**
radio *(airport)*	**529**
floor *(engineering)*	**860**
food-	**348**

	Code number
Inspector; *continued*	
food- *continued*	
food products mfr.	861
fuel *(local government)*	394
furnace-	830
furnace mfr.	860
gaming *(gaming club)*	699
garage	F871
garment	861
gas	394
gauge	860
glass	869
goods *(railways)*	F881
government (small arms)	860
graphite	869
guards *(railways)*	F881
health;	
environmental	348
public	348
highways	F923
hosiery	861
hotel	399
houses; public	719
housing	350
housing and planning	350
industrial *(gas board)*	394
infestation	699
installation-	
electricity board	394
gas board	394
telecoms	F523
instrument	860
insulation	860
insurance;	719
national	395
inwards; goods	441
laboratory *(glass mfr.)*	300
lamp	860
layout	860
leaf	869
lens	869
life *(insurance)*	719
lift-	516
D.O.E.	313
lighting; public	699
line; pipe	F895
line-	
railways	922
vehicle mfr.	860
lining *(brake lining mfr.)*	869
livestock; area	395
loading *(transport)*	F871
locomotive *(railways)*	F516
machine-	860
office machines	598
weighing machines-	516
coal mine	F516
docks	395
railways	395
machinery	516
mains	F895
maintenance-	
electricity board	F521
gas board	394
local government (housing dept.)	F896
market(s) *(local government)*	394
material(s)	399
meat	348
mechanical	860
metal	860

	Code number
Inspector; *continued*	
meter	860
micrometer	860
mineral *(railways)*	F881
mines	395
mirror	869
motor	860
mould *(glass mfr.)*	869
N.A.A.F.I.	720
navigation *(river board)*	929
nylon	861
office;	
head *(railways)*	F881
n.o.s.	430
operating *(railways)*	F881
operations; flight	395
optical	869
ore	863
paint *(engineering)*	860
parcels *(railways)*	F881
park	615
patrol-	F615
metal trades	860
paving and extension	F924
plant;	
electrical	860
gas	516
mechanical	860
preparation *(coal mine)*	516
process-	516
construction	860
oil refining	516
plastics	861
plate *(steelworks)*	860
platform *(railways)*	F631
plumbing	394
police	M152
pollution; air	348
pollution *(river, water authority)*	395
postal	F940
potato crisp	861
practice; standard	364
process	860
production	860
quality-	
coal mine	F863
engineering	860
radio	860
rail	860
railway	F881
reader; meter	F430
receiving; goods	441
records; musical	869
reinstatement *(gas board)*	394
relay	860
rent	412
revenue *(water board)*	410
ring *(engineering)*	860
river-	929
river authority or board	395
roads; chief *(L.R.T.)*	140
road(s)-	923
L.R.T.	F870
transport	F870
rodent	F699
roller *(metal trades)*	860
room; standards	364
rope	869
round(s) *(wholesale and retail trades)*	F731

	Code number
Inspector; *continued*	
rubber	861
safety-	
coal mine	395
engineering	396
sanitary-	348
ceramics mfr.	869
railways	F896
section *(waterways)*	929
senior *(Customs and Excise)*	155
service *(gas board)*	394
sewer	F892
shell	869
shop;	
fitting	860
machine	860
shops *(local government)*	348
shunting	F884
signal *(railways)*	F529
signal and telegraph *(railways)*	F529
signalman's	F883
site-	
advertising	F959
construction	311
smoke *(local government)*	348
staff *(government)*	103
station *(railways)*	F631
steel *(coal mine)*	899
stock; rolling	F516
stores;	F441
chief	141
street *(electricity board)*	699
sub-station *(electricity board)*	893
system	860
telecommunications	199
telegraph *(railways)*	F529
telephones	F523
test	860
textile	861
ticket; chair	959
ticket-	
public transport	F870
railways	F631
timber	861
timing *(L.R.T.)*	F870
tool	860
tool room	860
town planning	350
traffic; chief-	
P.O.	140
telecoms	140
traffic-	
rail	F881
road	F870
train	F881
transport-	
road-	F871
public transport	F870
trench	F895
trimming; coach	869
tube	860
tunnel	F896
tyre	861
upholstery	861
V.A.T. *(Customs and Excise)*	613
vehicle	860
veneer	861
veterinary	224
wages	395

	Code number
Inspector; *continued*	
wagon	**516**
waste *(water board)*	**895**
water;	**895**
chief	**F895**
waterways	**929**
way; permanent	**F922**
welding	**860**
works;	
district *(railways)*	**F922**
new *(railways)*	**F922**
public *(local government)*	**F896**
works-	
railways	**F922**
vehicle mfr.	**860**
workshops *(coal mine)*	**516**
yard	**F881**
yarn	**861**
of accidents *(Board of Trade)*	**395**
of ancient monuments	**271**
of armaments *(government)*	**860**
of audits *(D.O.E.)*	**250**
of electrical fitters	**F520**
of electricians	**F521**
of factories *(government)*	**394**
of fighting vehicles	**211**
of fitters	**F516**
of mechanics	**F516**
of mines *(Dept. of Industry)*	**395**
of naval ordnance	**860**
of park keepers	**F615**
of postmen	**F940**
of postal services	**199**
of rates and rentals	**102**
of schools	**232**
of shipping	**140**
of shipwrights	**F534**
of special subjects	**394**
of storehousemen	**F441**
of taxes	**362**
of weights and measures	**394**
of works	**111**
Inspector-	
abrasive paper, etc. mfr.	**861**
asbestos-cement goods mfr.	**869**
asbestos goods mfr.	**869**
banking	**M399**
brewery	**395**
brush mfr.	**869**
canvas goods mfr.	**861**
carbon goods mfr.	**869**
cardboard mfr.	**861**
carpet and rug mfr.	**861**
cartridge mfr.	**869**
casino	**699**
catering	**F953**
ceramics mfr.	**869**
civil engineering	**111**
clothing mfr.	**861**
dyeing and cleaning	**869**
electrical goods mfr.	**860**
electricity board	**394**
fancy goods mfr.	**869**
food products mfr.	**861**
footwear mfr.	**869**
furniture mfr.	**861**
gas board	**394**
glass mfr.	**869**
Inspector- *continued*	
government-	
Board of Trade (accident investigation branch)	**395**
D.O.E-	**313**
inspectorate of alkali, etc. works	**395**
inspectorate of housing and planning	**350**
Dept. of Industry	**395**
Dept. of Transport-	
coastguard service	**395**
railway inspectorate	**395**
survey branch	**262**
Home Office -	
children's dept.	**M371**
probation division	**M371**
instrument mfr.	**860**
insurance	**719**
leather cloth mfr.	**869**
leather dressing	**863**
local government-	**394**
cleansing dept.	**F933**
education dept.	**232**
highways dept.	**F923**
surveyor's dept.	**262**
works dept.	**F896**
man-made fibre mfr.	**861**
match mfr.	**869**
metal trades	**860**
mica goods mfr.	**869**
mine, not coal	**395**
motoring organisation	**F871**
N.H.B.R.C.	**311**
N.S.P.C.C.	**371**
office cleaning services	**F958**
opencast coal mining	**395**
P.O.	**F940**
paper mfr.	**861**
paper products mfr.	**861**
plasterboard mfr.	**869**
plastics goods mfr.	**861**
police service	**M152**
printing	**861**
R.S.P.C.A.	**395**
rubber goods mfr.	**861**
stone dressing	**869**
surgical goods mfr.	**869**
telecoms-	
engineering dept.	**F523**
telephone dept.	**F523**
telegraph service	**F524**
textile mfr.-	**861**
wool sorting	**F863**
transport-	
rail	**F881**
road	**F870**
water board	**895**
window dressing	**791**
wood products mfr.	**861**
Inspector and packer (yarn)	**861**
Installation hand *(oil refinery)*	**820**
Installation worker *(oil refinery)*	**820**
Installer;	
circuit *(L.R.T.)*	**524**
equipment; x-ray	**529**
heating	**532**
permanent way	**922**
signal *(railways)*	**529**
Installer; *continued*	
signal and telecommunications *(railways)*	**529**
systems; computer	**526**
telecommunications	**529**
telegraph	**529**
telephone	**523**
television	**525**
wireless apparatus	**529**
Installer-	
electrical contracting	**521**
railways	**524**
telephone service	**523**
Instructor; *see also notes*	
apprentice	**391**
civil defence	**619**
civilian *(government)*	**391**
craftsman; apprentice *(coal mine)*	**391**
dance	**239**
driving-	**393**
goods transport vehicles	**391**
public service vehicles	**391**
flying	**331**
handicraft(s)	**239**
keep-fit	**239**
manual	**391**
riding	**387**
simulation; flight	**331**
supervising	**391**
technical	**391**
trainee	**391**
training;	**391**
physical-	**239**
educational establishments-	
secondary schools	**233**
woodwork-	
educational establishments-	
higher and further education	**231**
schools-	
secondary	**233**
sixth form college	**233**
Instructor-	
physical training-	
educational establishments-	**239**
secondary schools	**233**
sports	**387**
apprentice school	**391**
coal mine	**391**
driving school	**393**
educational establishments-	
higher and further education-	**231**
polytechnic	**230**
university	**230**
schools-	
nursery	**234**
primary	**234**
secondary	**233**
sixth form college	**233**
special	**235**
training centre	**391**
Instrumentalist	**385**
Insulation hand	**896**
Insulator;	
bitumen	**599**
building	**896**
cable	**899**
coil	**599**
electrical	**899**

	Code number
Insulator; *continued*	
loft	**929**
pipe	**929**
refrigerator	**929**
thermal-	**896**
electrical appliances mfr.	**899**
wall; cavity	**896**
Insulator-	
construction	**896**
electrical appliances mfr.	**599**
Intake man	**441**
Interlacer; shoe	**555**
Interlacer (hair and fibre)	**814**
Interleaver (paper)	**821**
Interpreter	**380**
Interviewer;	
commercial	**430**
employment agency	**420**
press	**380**
television	**380**
Interviewer *(market, etc. research)*	**430**
Inventor	**399**
Investigator;	
accident	**396**
accounts	**410**
claims	**361**
credit	**615**
hire purchase	**615**
o & m	**364**
private	**615**
research; market	**430**
security	**615**
study; work	**364**
Investigator-	
D.S.S.	**400**
Historical Monuments Commission	**271**
Invigilator	**430**
Invoicer	**410**
Iron and steelworker	**912**
Iron worker;	
art	**899**
ornamental	**530**
sheet	**533**
wrought	**530**
Iron worker-	
constructional engineering	**535**
iron and steelworks	**912**
Ironer;	
boot	**859**
glove	**673**
Ironer-	
clothing mfr.	**673**
footwear mfr.	**859**
hosiery mfr.	**673**
laundry	**673**
leather dressing	**810**
Ironmonger	**179**
Ironstone worker	**898**
Irrigator	**902**
Issuer;	**441**
basket *(retail trade)*	**990**
work *(engineering)*	**F912**
Ivory worker	**599**

J

	Code number
Jack;	
lumber	**904**
steeple	**505**
Jackman	**919**
Janitor	**672**
Japanner-	**869**
leather dressing	**810**
Jennier	**862**
Jet man	**999**
Jet worker	**518**
Jetty hand	**930**
Jettyman	**930**
Jetty operative	**930**
Jeweller; *see also notes*	**518**
fancy	**518**
imitation	**518**
jobbing	**518**
manufacturing	**518**
masonic	**518**
watch	**859**
Jeweller *(retail trade)*	**179**
Jeweller and watch repairer	**517**
Jeweller and watchmaker	**517**
Jigman-	
constructional engineering	**889**
mine, not coal	**890**
Jigger; spindle	**860**
Jigger-	
leather dressing	**810**
metal trades	**839**
textile dyeing	**552**
Jiggerman	**552**
Jiggerer *(ceramics mfr.)*	**590**
Jobber;	
agent's; estate	**509**
back	**516**
builder's	**509**
card	**F811**
carding	**F811**
comb	**516**
combing	**516**
doubling; ring	**516**
loom	**516**
printer's	**891**
property	**509**
ring	**516**
stock	**361**
stock and share	**361**
twisting	**516**
Jobber-	
building and contracting	**509**
jewellery mfr.	**518**
leather dressing	**810**
textile mfr.-	**516**
textile dyeing	**552**
Jobbing hand *(rope, twine mfr.)*	**814**
Jobbing man	**518**
Jockey;	**387**
car	**955**
disc	**384**
Jogger *(paper mfr.)*	**821**
Joggler	**899**
Joiner;	
aircraft	**570**
builder's	**570**
bulb *(valve mfr.)*	**850**
coach	**541**
film	**569**
Joiner; *continued*	
fitter's; shop	**570**
machine	**897**
pipe	**895**
rubber (cycle tubes)	**824**
ship's	**570**
textile	**812**
Joiner-	**570**
cabinet making	**571**
lamp, valve mfr.	**850**
rubber footwear mfr.	**859**
textile mfr.-	**812**
hosiery mfr.	**551**
Joiner-machinist	**897**
Jointer;	
cable	**524**
chain	**537**
conduit; electric	**524**
edge; veneer	**579**
electric	**524**
pipe; sprinkler	**532**
pipe-	**895**
stoneware pipe mfr.	**591**
stanford	**591**
tapeless	**579**
wire	**524**
Jointer-	
cable laying	**524**
ceramics mfr.	**590**
civil engineering	**895**
cutlery mfr.	**899**
electricity board	**524**
gas board	**895**
soft toy mfr.	**859**
stoneware pipe mfr.	**591**
telecoms	**524**
water board	**895**
Jointer-plumber	**524**
Jollier	**590**
Journalist	**380**
Journeyman *see notes*	
Judge-	
entertainment	**387**
legal service	**240**
Juggler	**384**
Juiceman	**809**
Jumper; show	**387**
Jumper (fibre)	**811**
Junction man	**889**

K

	Code number
Keeker	**F890**
Keeper;	
animal	**902**
bar-	
hotel, etc.	**622**
shipping	**622**
bee	**902**
boat	**880**
book;	**410**
chief	**F410**
bridge;	**889**
toll	**412**
weigh	**863**
cemetery	**672**
chapel	**672**
church	**672**
company	**990**
court	**672**
cow	**900**
crossing;	**883**
level	**883**
die	**441**
door-	**615**
synagogue	**672**
floor *(Bank of England)*	**619**
forest	**904**
furnace-	
glass mfr.	**823**
metal mfr.	**830**
game	**902**
gate;	
crossing *(railways)*	**883**
lock	**889**
pier	**412**
gate-	**615**
coal mine	**886**
railways	**883**
granary	**441**
grass	**594**
green	**594**
ground; burial	**672**
ground(s)	**594**
hall	**672**
head-	
park	**F615**
zoological gardens	**F902**
horse;	**902**
head	**F902**
hotel	**173**
house;	
boarding	**173**
bridge	**889**
daily	**670**
gate	**615**
head	**173**
light	**889**
resident (offices)	**672**
ware	**F441**
house-	**670**
offices	**672**
hotel	**F671**
institution	**F671**
property management	**672**
school	**F671**
inn	**175**
kennel	**902**
laundry	**179**
ledger	**410**
light	**889**

	Code number
Keeper; *continued*	
lighthouse	**889**
linen	**441**
lock	**889**
lodge	**615**
machine; weighing	**863**
magazine	**441**
menagerie	**902**
mortuary	**672**
museum	**271**
office	**672**
paper	**420**
park;	**615**
head	**F615**
pattern	**441**
pig	**160**
plan *(railways)*	**441**
poultry	**160**
repository; furniture	**441**
reservoir	**929**
river	**902**
school	**672**
ship	**615**
shop *see Shopkeeper*	
sluice	**889**
stable;	**902**
livery	**169**
stall;	**732**
book	**179**
coffee	**174**
stanch	**889**
stationery	**441**
stock-	**441**
agriculture	**900**
store;	**441**
chief	**141**
drug	**179**
general	**179**
head	**F441**
room; engine	**F880**
store and vault; bonded	**441**
swingbridge	**889**
switch	**884**
time	**410**
tool	**441**
vault	**441**
wardrobe	**699**
warehouse	**F441**
weir	**889**
wharf; canal	**929**
of the signet	**240**
Keeper-	
blast furnace	**830**
museum	**271**
Public Record Office	**271**
Trinity House	**889**
zoological gardens	**902**
Keeper and pointsman; gate	**883**
Keeper-clerk; store	**441**
Keeper-companion; house	**670**
Kennelman	**902**
Kerner *(typefounding)*	**899**
Kettleman	**830**
Keysmith	**899**
Kibbler *(food products mfr.)*	**809**
Kicker *(metal stamping)*	**841**
Killer	**581**
Killer and plucker	**582**
Kiln hand *(ceramics mfr.)*	**823**
Kiln man;	
carbon	**829**

	Code number
Kiln man; *continued*	
dry	**829**
enamel	**823**
frit	**823**
glost	**823**
gypsum	**829**
lime	**829**
Kiln man-	
abrasive wheel mfr.	**829**
asbestos composition goods mfr.	**829**
cement mfr.	**829**
ceramics mfr.	**823**
chemical mfr.-	**820**
colour mfr.	**829**
composition die mfr.	**820**
distillery	**801**
glass mfr.	**823**
Kiln worker-	
ceramics mfr.	**823**
furniture mfr.	**821**
lime burning	**829**
Kipperer	**809**
Kitchen boy	**952**
Kitchen girl	**952**
Kitchen hand-	**952**
food products mfr.	**809**
Kitchen man	**952**
Kitchen worker	**952**
Knacker	**581**
Kneader *(bakery)*	**800**
Knife hand *(metal trades)*	**899**
Knitter	**551**
Knocker;	
catch; staple pit	**889**
catch *(coal mine)*	**889**
Knocker *(ceramics mfr.)*	**591**
Knocker-off-	
foundry	**911**
glass mfr.	**590**
Knocker-out-	
chocolate mfr.	**809**
foundry	**911**
glass mfr.	**590**
Knocker-up-	**699**
printing	**822**
Knock-out man	**912**
Knotter;	
reel	**814**
warp	**552**
Knotter-	
textile mfr.-	**814**
examining dept.	**553**
wig mfr.	**599**
Kollerganger	**821**

L

	Code number
L.A.H.	**220**
L.R.C.P.	**220**
L.S.A.	**221**
Labeller;	**862**
colour (glassware)	**591**
Laboratory man	**864**
Laboratory worker	**864**
Labourer;	
agricultural	**900**
bricklayer's	**921**
bricksetter's	**921**
builder's;	**929**
boat	**920**
bulking-floor	**889**
carpenter's	**920**
cooper's	**920**
Crown	**904**
dock;	**930**
dry	**912**
dyer's	**814**
electric track	**929**
electrician's	**913**
engineering; civil	**929**
erector's	**913**
estate	**900**
factory	**990**
farm	**900**
feller's; timber	**904**
fish	**930**
fitter's;	**913**
shop	**990**
fixer's;	
felt	**921**
sheet	**921**
steel	**913**
forest	**904**
foundry	**911**
garden-	**594**
local authority	**990**
market gardening	**595**
garden and parks	**990**
gardener's-	**594**
market gardening	**595**
grab	**889**
jetty	**930**
joiner's	**920**
layer's;	
granolithic	**921**
terrazzo	**921**
maker's; cabinet	**920**
mason's;	
fixer	**921**
stone	**921**
mechanic's	**913**
millhouse *(textile mfr.)*	**919**
millwright's	**913**
miner's; tunnel	**898**
moulder's	**911**
parks	**990**
pitwood	**930**
plasterer's	**921**
platelayer's	**929**
plater's	**913**
plumber's	**913**
policy (Scotland)	**594**
pontoon	**930**
production	**919**
quay	**930**
quayside	**930**

	Code number
Labourer; *continued*	
rigger's	**913**
riverside	**930**
riveter's	**899**
ship	**930**
shipwright's	**913**
slater's	**921**
steeplejack's	**921**
stevedore's	**930**
storekeeper's	**931**
stores	**931**
warehouse	**931**
waterside	**930**
wharf	**930**
willow garth	**904**
wood	**904**
Labourer-	**990**
agriculture	**900**
building and contracting	**929**
coal mine	**910**
docks	**930**
engineering	**912**
forestry	**904**
steelworks	**912**
warehousing	**931**
Lace hand	**550**
Lace man	**550**
Lace worker	**550**
Lacer;	
card	**814**
corset	**859**
jacquard	**814**
shade; lamp	**859**
wheel	**851**
Lacer-	
corset mfr.	**859**
footwear mfr.	**555**
textile weaving	**814**
Lacer and driller; wheel *(cycle mfr.)*	**851**
Lacquerer;	**869**
spray	**596**
Ladle man; direct	**839**
Ladle man *(metal mfr.)*	**839**
Ladler-	
copper lead refining	**830**
glass mfr.	**590**
Lady superior	**292**
Lagger;	**929**
asbestos	**929**
boiler	**929**
drum	**990**
pipe	**929**
Lairman	**902**
Laminator;	
fibreglass	**825**
plastic	**825**
wood	**821**
Laminator-	
paper mfr.	**821**
plastics mfr.	**825**
safety glass mfr.	**590**
textile mfr.	**814**
Lampman; signal	**990**
Lampman-	
coal mine	**441**
mine, not coal	**441**
railways	**990**
Lamp worker *(glass mfr.)*	**590**

	Code number
Lance-Bombardier-	
armed forces-	
foreign and Common-wealth	**601**
U.K.	**600**
Lance-Corporal *(armed forces - U.K.)*	**600**
Lance-Sergeant-	
armed forces-	
foreign and Common-wealth	**601**
U.K.	**600**
Lancer; thermic	**537**
Land girl	**900**
Land worker	**900**
Lander;	
clay	**889**
fish	**930**
Lander *(mine, not coal)-*	
above ground	**889**
below ground	**886**
Landholder	**160**
Landlady *(public house)*	**175**
Landlord-	
boarding, lodging house	**173**
inn	**175**
property managing or owning	**170**
public house	**175**
Landsaler *(coal mine)*	**889**
Landworker	**900**
Lapman	**814**
Lapidary	**518**
Lapper;	
barrel (gun)	**840**
cotton	**814**
gear	**840**
jeweller's	**842**
paper	**899**
tape	**814**
Lapper-	
cable mfr.	**899**
metal trades-	**840**
precious metal, plate mfr.	**842**
tin box mfr.	**841**
tube mfr.	**839**
textile mfr.	**814**
Laryngologist	**220**
Lasher;	**552**
car	**930**
Laster	**555**
Latchman *see Latcher*	
Latcher;	
crane *(steelworks)*	**932**
locomotive	**884**
wagon *(steelworks)*	**884**
Latcher-	
coal mine	**889**
needle mfr.	**841**
railways	**884**
steelworks	**932**
Latexer	**824**
Lathe hand	**840**
Lathe man-	**840**
textile machinery roller covering	**555**
Lathe worker-	**840**
glass mfr.	**590**
Lather; metal	**921**
Lather *(ceramics mfr.)*	**590**
Launch hand	**880**
Launch man	**880**

	Code number
Launderer	**673**
Laundress	**673**
Laundry hand	**673**
Laundry maid	**673**
Laundry man	**673**
Laundry worker	**673**
Lawyer	**242**
Layman; mussel	**903**
Lay worker	**371**
Layer;	
asphalt	**923**
block-	
blast furnace	**500**
mine	**922**
bobbin	**814**
brick	**500**
cable	**895**
carpet	**506**
concrete	**923**
core	**839**
covering; floor	**506**
drain	**895**
drum	**813**
felt-	
flooring	**506**
roofing	**501**
floor;	
block	**579**
composition	**506**
concrete	**923**
decorative	**506**
granolithic	**506**
jointless	**506**
mosaic	**506**
n.o.s.	**506**
parquet	**579**
patent	**506**
plastic	**506**
rubber	**506**
stone	**500**
terrazzo	**506**
tile	**506**
wood	**579**
glass; plate	**919**
ground	**591**
hedge	**902**
kerb	**924**
lino	**506**
linoleum	**506**
macadam; tar	**923**
main(s)	**895**
mosaic	**506**
pipe-	**895**
coal mine	**532**
plate-	**922**
micanite mfr.	**829**
printing	**560**
printer's *(textile printing)*	**569**
rail	**922**
road	**922**
service	**895**
sole	**859**
stone	**924**
surface *(gas board)*	**923**
tar	**923**
terrazzo	**506**
tile	**506**
track-	**922**
pipe	**895**
tray	**919**
turf	**594**

	Code number
Layer; *continued*	
veneer	**821**
Layer-	
paper mfr.	**821**
rope mfr.	**814**
textile spinning	**812**
wire rope mfr.	**899**
Layer and fixer; patent flooring and roofing	**896**
Layer-down *(textile finishing)*	**559**
Layer-on; machine	**891**
Layer-on-	
cardboard box mfr.	**569**
file mfr.	**912**
textile mfr.	**814**
Layer-out;	
tobacco	**802**
yarn	**814**
Layer-out-	
glove mfr.	**559**
textile mfr.	**889**
Layer-up-	
cable mfr.	**899**
clothing mfr.	**557**
tannery	**810**
Lay-out man-	
advertising	**381**
printing	**560**
Lead worker; tea	**839**
Lead worker-	
stained glass	**503**
accumulator mfr.	**899**
Leader;	
band	**385**
club	**371**
coal	**872**
girder *(coal mine)*	**889**
group research *see Engineer-prof.-*	
keep-fit	**239**
orchestra	**385**
play	**651**
playgroup	**651**
project *(software design)*	**214**
red	**507**
section-	
clerical office	**F430**
drawing office	**F310**
production control	**218**
progress	**420**
senior	**F430**
ambulance service	**F642**
fire service	**F611**
retail trade	**F720**
shift; computer	**F490**
shift *(ambulance service)*	**F642**
Squadron-	
armed forces-	
foreign and Commonwealth	**M151**
U.K.	**M150**
timber-	**889**
coal mine	**597**
trek *(equestrian trekking centre)*	**902**
water	**889**
window	**503**
youth	**371**
Leader-	
abrasive wheel mfr.	**839**
children's home	**370**

	Code number
Leader- *continued*	
social work	**293**
Leading hand-*see also notes*	
building and contracting	**509**
food products mfr.	**809**
laundry	**673**
metal trades-	**899**
blast furnace	**839**
foundry	**839**
rubber goods mfr.	**824**
textile mfr.	**814**
warehousing	**441**
Leading man *(building and contracting)*	**896**
Leadsman	**889**
Learner *see notes*	
Leaser; machine spinning	**802**
Leaser *(textile mfr.)*	**552**
Leather worker;	
fancy	**555**
hydraulic and mechanical	**555**
orthopaedic	**555**
Leather worker-	
artificial limb mfr.	**555**
leather dressing	**810**
leather goods mfr.	**555**
railways	**554**
vehicle mfr.	**554**
Lecturer;	
college	**231**
guide	**239**
political	**399**
polytechnic	**230**
university	**230**
Lecturer-*see also notes*	
dentistry	**223**
medicine	**220**
surgery	**220**
educational establishments-	
higher and further education-	**231**
polytechnic	**230**
university	**230**
schools-	
secondary	**233**
sixth form college	**233**
special	**235**
Legger; flyer	**530**
Legger *(hosiery finishing)*	**552**
Lehr man	**823**
Lender; money	**719**
Lengthener	**552**
Lengthman; road	**923**
Lengthman-	
canal	**929**
highway authority	**923**
local government	**923**
railways	**922**
Lengthsman *see Lengthman*	
Lens worker	**590**
Lepidopterist	**201**
Letterer *(signwriting)*	**507**
Levelhand	**830**
Leveller;	
concrete	**923**
plate	**839**
roller *(steelworks)*	**839**
Leveller-	
asphalt spreading machine	**885**
coke ovens	**889**
footwear mfr.	**555**

	Code number
Leveller- *continued*	
lithography	**891**
Leverman *(iron and steelworks)*	**839**
Lexicographer	**380**
Librarian;	
assistant-	**390**
qualified	**270**
branch-	**390**
qualified	**270**
card (automatic data records)	**390**
chartered	**270**
disc (automatic data records)	**390**
film	**390**
hospital-	**390**
qualified	**270**
magazine	**390**
media	**390**
newspaper	**390**
picture	**390**
tape;	
computer	**390**
magnetic	**390**
technical-	**390**
qualified	**270**
visual; audio	**390**
Librarian-	**390**
qualified	**270**
Licensee-	**175**
off-licence	**179**
Lidder-	
boot polish mfr.	**862**
cardboard box mfr.	**859**
Lieutenant-	
armed forces-	
foreign and Commonwealth	**M151**
U.K.	**M150**
Lieutenant-Colonel-	
armed forces-	
foreign and Commonwealth	**M151**
U.K.	**M150**
Lieutenant-Commander-	
armed forces-	
foreign and Commonwealth	**M151**
U.K.	**M150**
Lieutenant-General-	
armed forces-	
foreign and Commonwealth	**M151**
U.K.	**M150**
Lifeboatman	**880**
Liftman;	
gantry	**886**
service	**955**
steam	**886**
Liftman-	**955**
iron and steelworks	**886**
Lift worker	**955**
Lifter;	
beam	**814**
bin	**990**
box	**911**
butt	**810**
carriage	**516**
coke	**889**
fork	**887**
freight	**931**
heavy	**505**
Lifter, *continued*	
wagon	**516**
Lifter-	
railway workshops	**516**
steelworks	**886**
textile mfr.	**814**
warehouse	**931**
Lifter-up-	
foundry	**911**
rolling mill	**839**
Ligger	**814**
Ligger-on (wool)	**814**
Lighter;	
fire	**990**
lamp (ships- *Trinity House)*	**880**
shot *(coal mine)*	**597**
Lighterman	**880**
Lighthouse man	**889**
Lightsman *(lightship)*	**880**
Lightship man	**880**
Lime man-	**810**
steelworks	**839**
Lime worker	**810**
Limer-	
blast furnace	**912**
fellmongering	**810**
Limnologist	**201**
Lineman;	**524**
power	**524**
pump	**532**
signal; power	**524**
traction	**524**
Liner;	
basket	**859**
box; work	**859**
brake-	**859**
asbestos mfr.	**859**
cabinet *(upholstery mfr.)*	**859**
case	**859**
cycle	**869**
dry	**896**
furnace	**500**
glove	**859**
gold-	
ceramics mfr.	**591**
cycle mfr.	**869**
ladle	**500**
machine	**869**
picture	**859**
pipe-	
rubber lining	**824**
building and contracting	**929**
plant (rubber lining)	**824**
pouch; leather	**859**
roof	**501**
table	**859**
tank-	
glass fibre	**825**
rubber lining	**824**
tin *(bakery)*	**800**
tube	**591**
Liner-	
lenses	**590**
rubber	**824**
cardboard box mfr.	**859**
ceramics mfr.	**591**
clothing mfr.	**553**
fur garment mfr.	**553**
hat mfr.	**553**
metal trades-	**869**
safe mfr.	**515**
Liner and finisher *(vehicle mfr.)*	**869**
Liner-off *(engineering)*	**515**
Liner-out *(engineering)*	**515**
Liner-up *(engineering)*	**515**
Linesman;	
diver's	**929**
electrical	**524**
gas	**532**
instrument *(railways)*	**524**
overhead	**524**
power	**524**
progress	**420**
pump	**532**
railway	**524**
signal	**524**
survey *(coal mine)*	**597**
surveyor's	**929**
telegraph	**524**
telephone	**524**
tramways	**524**
Linesman-	**524**
brewery	**862**
coal mine-	**597**
above ground	**524**
electrical engineering	**524**
electricity board	**524**
radio relay service	**524**
railways	**524**
telecoms	**524**
water works	**929**
Linesman-erector	**524**
Lineworker *(vehicle mfr.)*	**851**
Linger	**814**
Lingerie hand	**556**
Linguist	**380**
Linisher	**842**
Linker;	
chain	**518**
sausage	**809**
Linker-	
textile mfr.-	**814**
hosiery and knitwear mfr.	**553**
Linkman *(entertainment)*	**699**
Linoleum worker	**899**
Lipper; glass	**590**
Liquefier; butter	**809**
Liquidator; company	**250**
Liquor man-	
leather tanning	**829**
sugar refining	**809**
Liquorice hand	**809**
Lithographer; photo	**560**
Lithographer-	
ceramics mfr.	**591**
printing	**891**
Loader;	
aircraft	**931**
barge	**930**
boat	**930**
bulk *(petroleum distribution)*	**889**
cartridge	**599**
cassette; cartridge *(photographic film mfr.)*	**569**
coal	**889**
coke	**889**
conveyor-	**990**
coal mine	**889**
dockside	**930**
film	**569**
fish	**930**

	Code number
Loader; *continued*	
furnace *(metal trades)*	**889**
kiln	**823**
lehr	**823**
lorry	**931**
machine	**990**
mechanical *(mine, not coal)*	**889**
milk *(dairy)*	**889**
mould *(asbestos composition goods mfr.)*	**599**
paper	**990**
power *(coal mine)*	**597**
refuse *(local government-cleansing dept.)*	**933**
stone *(mine, not coal)*	**889**
timber-	
coal mine	**889**
docks	**930**
forestry	**990**
sawmilling	**889**
wagon	**889**
warehouse	**931**
Loader-	**931**
ammunition mfr.	**599**
ceramics mfr.	**823**
charcoal mfr.	**829**
coal mine	**889**
coke ovens	**889**
docks	**930**
lithography	**891**
mine, not coal	**889**
Loader and unloader	**931**
Loaderman;	
power *(coal mine)*	**597**
ship	**930**
Loader-checker	**931**
Loader-driver *(airport)*	**931**
Lobber *(card and paste board mfr.)*	**889**
Lobby man	**951**
Lock man	**889**
Locker; flat	**553**
Locker *(hat mfr.)*	**862**
Locksmith	**516**
Locomotive man *(coal mine)*	**882**
Lodge man	**615**
Lofter (salt)	**820**
Loftsman-	
engineering	**310**
shipbuilding	**570**
Loftsman and scriever	**570**
Logger;	
mud	**300**
well	**300**
Loggist	**430**
Lollipop man	**619**
Longshoreman	**930**
Looker;	
cloth	**861**
piece	**861**
yarn	**861**
Looker-out; book	**421**
Looker-out-	
ophthalmic lenses	**441**
pen nib mfr.	**860**
Looker-over; decorator's	**869**
Looker-over-	
ceramics mfr.	**869**
footwear mfr.	**555**
textile finishing	**861**
Looker-to-ware; thrower's	**869**
Looker-up (footwear)	**441**
Look-out and A.B.	**880**
Look-out man *(railways)*	**990**
Loom hand; warp	**551**
Loom hand *(loom furniture mfr.)*	**599**
Loom worker; hand	**550**
Loomer	**552**
Loomer and twister	**552**
Looper-	
hosiery mfr.	**553**
wool spinning	**812**
Lopper; tree	**904**
Lowerer; wagon	**889**
Lubricator-	**894**
gun mfr.	**912**
Lugger *(mine, not coal)*	**890**
Lumberjack	**904**
Lump man *(salt mfr.)*	**820**
Lumper; fish	**930**
Lumper *(docks)*	**930**
Lurer	**559**
Lurrier	**569**
Lustrer	**591**
Luter *(coke ovens)*	**919**

	Code number
M	
M.B.	**220**
M.D.	**220**
M.E.P	**100**
M.L.S.O.	**201**
M.P.S.	**221**
M.R.C.P.	**220**
M.R.C.S.	**220**
M.R.C.V.S.	**224**
M.S.	**220**
Macer	**619**
Machine boy *(printing)*	**891**
Machine hand *see Machinist*	
Machine man-*see also Machinist-*	
asbestos composition goods mfr.	**829**
coal mine	**597**
paper mfr.	**821**
Machine operative *see Machinist*	
Machine worker *see Machinist*	
Machiner *see Machinist*	
Machinery man; grain	**809**
Machinist;	
accounting	**490**
accounts	**490**
action	**840**
adding	**490**
addressing	**490**
ageing	**552**
agricultural	**901**
anocut	**840**
armouring	**899**
automatic-	**841**
sewing	**553**
bolt, nut, screw, etc. mfr.	**841**
backer (footwear)	**859**
bag;	
carrier	**569**
paper	**569**
bag-	
leather goods mfr.	**555**
plastics goods mfr.	**859**
sack mfr.	**553**
bagging	**555**
ball	**811**
balling-	
textile mfr.-	**813**
wool combing	**811**
banding	**802**
barking	**897**
barring *(clothing mfr.)*	**553**
bartack	**553**
basting	**553**
battery	**899**
beading	**555**
beaming *(textile weaving)*	**814**
bearing; ball	**841**
bedding	**553**
belt; conveyor	**553**
bending; press	**841**
bending-	
iron works	**839**
sheet metal working	**899**
bias *(rubber tyre mfr.)*	**824**
binding;	**553**
perfect	**562**
biscuit	**800**
blanket	**553**
blasting; vapour	**844**
blocking	**559**

	Code number
Machinist; *continued*	
blouse	**553**
blowing	**811**
bobbin	**813**
bolt	**899**
book-keeping	**490**
boot	**555**
boring-	
metal	**840**
wood	**897**
coal mine	**597**
bottle	**590**
bottling	**862**
box; axle	**840**
box *(paper goods mfr.)*	**569**
box and slide *(cardboard box mfr.)*	**569**
braid	**814**
braiding-	
asbestos rope mfr.	**814**
cable mfr.	**899**
brass	**840**
brazing	**537**
breadthening	**552**
brick	**590**
broaching	**840**
bronzing	**569**
brush	**555**
brushing; cross	**552**
brushing-	
leather dressing	**810**
paper mfr.	**821**
textile mfr.	**552**
buffing-	
leather cloth mfr.	**552**
leather dressing	**810**
metal trades	**842**
plastics goods mfr.	**825**
builder's	**897**
building; micanite	**829**
bullet	**899**
bullion	**814**
bumping	**814**
burnishing	**821**
butcher's	**581**
button-	**899**
clothing mfr.	**553**
buttonhole	**553**
buttoning *(clothing mfr.)*	**553**
cabinet	**897**
cable	**899**
cabling-	**899**
rope, twine mfr.	**814**
calculating	**490**
calender *(plastics goods mfr.)*	**825**
canvas	**553**
cap;	**553**
bottle	**841**
capping;	
bottle	**862**
lamp	**850**
capstan	**840**
capsule (metal)	**841**
carbon	**899**
carding-	**811**
fur dressing	**810**
carpet	**553**
casting;	
centrifugal (steel)	**839**
die	**531**
film	**829**

	Code number
Machinist; *continued*	
casting; *continued*	
monotype	**560**
pig	**839**
casting *(transparent cellulose wrappings mfr.)*	**829**
centering	**840**
centrifugal (sugar)	**809**
chipping	**885**
chopping (meat)	**581**
cigar	**802**
cigarette	**802**
cleaning *(seed merchants)*	**829**
closing-	
canned foods mfr.	**862**
footwear mfr.	**555**
rope mfr.	**814**
wire rope mfr.	**899**
clothing	**553**
coat	**553**
coating;	
glass *(bulb, valve mfr.)*	**590**
paper	**821**
coating-	
carbon paper	**821**
photographic films	**829**
carpet mfr.	**814**
plastics goods mfr.	**825**
textile mfr.	**814**
coiling *(metal tube mfr.)*	**839**
collar-	
clothing mfr.	**553**
laundry	**673**
collating	**490**
collotype	**569**
combing *(textile spinning)*	**811**
combining-	
paper mfr.	**821**
textile printing	**569**
compressing (tablets, pills)	**820**
condenser *(textile mfr.)*	**811**
constructional	**534**
cooper's	**897**
copying	**840**
cording *(paper goods mfr.)*	**569**
cork	**899**
cornel(l)y	**553**
corrugating	**821**
corset	**553**
covering; rubber	**824**
cropping	**552**
curing (rubber)	**829**
cutting;	
core	**899**
emery cloth	**822**
gear	**840**
glass	**590**
paper	**822**
plastics	**825**
plate *(shipbuilding)*	**899**
rotary (metal)	**899**
rubber	**824**
tube (cardboard)	**822**
wood	**897**
cutting-	
asbestos	**829**
cork	**599**
metal	**899**
paper	**822**
plastics	**825**

	Code number
Machinist; *continued*	
cutting- *continued*	
rubber	**824**
clothing mfr.	**557**
coal mine	**597**
metal trades	**899**
paper mfr.	**822**
paper goods mfr.-	**822**
paper pattern mfr.	**822**
soap mfr.	**829**
sugar confectionery mfr.	**809**
textile mfr.	**814**
tobacco mfr.	**802**
tyre mfr.	**824**
cutting and wrapping *(bakery)*	**800**
cuttling	**814**
cycle	**840**
cylinder *(printing)*	**891**
damping *(textile mfr.)*	**552**
darning *(textile goods)*	**553**
decollating	**490**
developing; film	**569**
dipping	**869**
doubling	**812**
dough	**800**
drawing; wire	**831**
drawing-	
textile mfr.-	**811**
textile warping	**552**
dress	**553**
dressing;	
fibre	**811**
pelt	**810**
surgical	**553**
dressing *(metal trades)*	**843**
dressmaker's	**553**
drilling-	
metal trades	**840**
mine, not coal	**898**
wood products mfr.	**897**
drying; cloth	**814**
drying-	
food products mfr.	**809**
textile mfr.	**814**
tobacco mfr.	**802**
duplicating;	**490**
offset	**569**
dyeline	**490**
elasticator	**553**
electrochemical	**840**
embossing-	**569**
floor and leather cloth mfr.	**829**
leather dressing	**810**
wood products mfr.	**897**
embroidery	**553**
engineer's	**840**
engraver's	**899**
enrobing	**809**
envelope	**569**
extruding-	
metal tube mfr.	**839**
plastics goods mfr.	**825**
rubber goods mfr.	**824**
eyelet	**899**
eyelet-hole	**559**
fabric; circular	**551**
facing	**510**
fancy	**553**
feather	**553**
felling	**553**

	Code number
Machinist; *continued*	
felt; needleloom	**814**
fettling *(metal trades)*	**843**
fibre; vulcanised	**821**
filling; skin (sausage)	**809**
filling-	
cosmetic mfr.	**862**
food canning	**862**
filling and capping	**862**
film; cellulose	**829**
filter (celluloid)	**829**
finisher *(textile mfr.)*	**811**
flag	**553**
flanging	**841**
flat; hand	**551**
flat-	
clothing mfr.	**553**
footwear mfr.	**555**
fleshing	**810**
flock	**811**
foam	**825**
folding-	
printing	**562**
textile mfr.	**814**
fondant	**809**
foot	**553**
forcing	**824**
forge	**839**
forging	**839**
forming *(twine mfr.)*	**814**
frizing *(tannery)*	**810**
frosting *(glass mfr.)*	**591**
fur	**553**
garnet	**811**
gilling	**811**
gimping (pattern cards)	**814**
glove-	
leather	**553**
woollen	**551**
gluing and winding; tube (cardboard)	**569**
gold	**834**
gown	**553**
grading-	
garment pattern	**899**
sugar	**809**
graphite	**829**
gravure *(printing)*	**891**
grinding; shaft	**840**
grinding-	
cement mfr.	**829**
glass mfr.	**591**
metal trades	**840**
paint mfr.	**829**
paper mfr.	**821**
guillotine-	
metal trades	**899**
paper goods mfr.	**822**
plastics goods mfr.	**825**
rubber goods mfr.	**824**
textile goods mfr.	**559**
gully	**990**
gumming-	
gum paper, etc.	**821**
paper goods mfr.	**859**
hair; horse	**811**
hand-	
clothing mfr.	**553**
metal trades	**841**
handle	**897**
hanking	**814**

	Code number
Machinist; *continued*	
hardening	**814**
heading *(bolt, etc. mfr.)*	**899**
healding	**552**
hemming	**553**
hemstitch	**553**
hide *(leather merchants)*	**810**
hobbing	**840**
honing	**840**
hopper	**811**
hosiery;	**551**
surgical	**553**
house *(twine mfr.)*	**814**
ice cream	**809**
impregnating-	
paper mfr.	**821**
plastics goods mfr.	**829**
insulating; paper	**821**
jacket	**553**
jacquard	**551**
jigger	**590**
jigging	**552**
joggling	**899**
joiner('s)	**897**
jolley	**590**
knicker	**553**
knitting	**551**
knotting; warp	**552**
knotting *(textile mfr.)*	**814**
labelling	**862**
lace-	
lace mfr.	**550**
textile goods mfr.	**553**
lap	**811**
lapping-	
metal trades	**840**
textile mfr.	**814**
lashing	**553**
lasting	**555**
laundry	**673**
leather	**555**
levelling;	**555**
rail	**885**
linen	**553**
lining-	
clothing mfr.	**553**
footwear mfr.	**859**
hat mfr.	**553**
paper mfr.	**821**
linotype	**560**
lithographic	**891**
loading; power	**597**
lock; flat	**553**
lockstitch	**553**
looming	**552**
maintenance	**840**
maker's; crate	**897**
making;	
bottle	**590**
box-	**897**
cardboard	**569**
brick	**590**
chain (cycle, etc., chains)	**841**
cigarette	**802**
sausage	**809**
screw	**899**
making-	
abrasive paper, etc. mfr.	**821**
plasterboard mfr.	**829**
measuring (piece goods)	**863**

	Code number
Machinist; *continued*	
medicating (surgical dressings)	**552**
metal;	**840**
shipyard	**534**
mica	**829**
milk; dried	**809**
mill;	
boring	**840**
moulding	**897**
saw	**897**
millinery	**553**
milling-	
cemented carbide goods mfr.	**899**
food products mfr. ...	**809**
metal trades	**840**
mincing (meat)	**581**
mixing-	
abrasive paper, etc. mfr.	**821**
bakery	**800**
food products mfr. ...	**809**
rubber mfr.	**824**
moulding-	
lead refining	**839**
plastics goods mfr. ...	**825**
rubber goods mfr. ...	**824**
wood products mfr. ...	**897**
nail	**899**
nailing	**859**
needle	**553**
net	**550**
nosing	**840**
office	**490**
oilskin	**553**
opening *(asbestos opening)*	**811**
outer-wear	**553**
overhead	**553**
overlock	**553**
overlocking	**553**
packing	**862**
padding *(clothing mfr.)* ...	**553**
paint *(paint mfr.)*	**829**
painting; slip	**591**
paper;	
carbon	**821**
crinkled	**821**
paper *(paper goods mfr.)*	**569**
pasteboard	**821**
pasting (pasteboard) ...	**821**
paving; concrete	**885**
perforating-	
footwear mfr.	**555**
paper goods mfr. ...	**569**
perpetual	**552**
photocopying	**490**
photogravure	**891**
pickering *(textile mfr.)* ...	**811**
pie	**800**
pin	**899**
pipe; sanitary	**590**
piping *(textile smallwares mfr.)*...	**814**
plain (shirts)	**553**
plaiting *(rope mfr.)* ...	**814**
planing; plate	**899**
planing-	
metal trades	**840**
wood products mfr. ...	**897**
plastic *(cable mfr.)* ...	**825**
plastics	**825**

	Code number
Machinist; *continued*	
plate-backing *(photographic plate mfr.)*	**560**
platen	**891**
plating; wire	**834**
plating *(metal trades)* ...	**834**
pleating;	**553**
paper	**821**
plug assembly	**802**
polishing-	
metal trades	**842**
velvet mfr.	**552**
post-	
clothing mfr.	**553**
footwear mfr.	**555**
powder; soap	**820**
preparing	**811**
press; letter	**891**
press-	
metal trades	**841**
plastics goods mfr. ...	**825**
printing	**891**
rubber goods mfr. ...	**824**
pressing; transfer	**869**
pressing *(textile mfr.)* ...	**552**
pressure	**555**
printer's	**891**
printing;	**891**
film	**569**
production *(vehicle mfr.)*...	**851**
profiling	**840**
pulling; rag	**811**
punching-	
metal trades	**841**
paper goods mfr. ...	**822**
quilting	**553**
ragging (cotton rag) ...	**811**
raising	**552**
randing	**814**
ratchet	**898**
reamering	**840**
repairer hand	**553**
ribbon; typewriter	**814**
ring	**812**
rivet	**899**
riveting-	
leather goods mfr. ...	**859**
metal trades	**851**
plastics goods mfr. ...	**859**
roll; toilet	**569**
roller-	
plastics goods mfr. ...	**825**
textile mfr.	**552**
rolling-	
metal trades-	**832**
sheet metal working ...	**899**
textile mfr.	**814**
room; tool	**840**
rope-	
textile	**814**
wire	**899**
rotary-	**891**
textile bleaching	**552**
router *(metal trades)* ...	**840**
rubbing *(food products mfr.)*	**809**
rug and blanket; horse ...	**553**
ruling	**569**
running-down	**811**
sack	**553**
sample	**553**

	Code number
Machinist; *continued*	
sanding-	
metal	**844**
micanite	**569**
wood	**897**
sandpapering	**897**
sawing *(metal trades)* ...	**899**
scouring *(textile mfr.)* ...	**814**
screen; silk	**563**
screw; automatic	**841**
screwer	**840**
screwing	**840**
scutcher	**811**
sealing; metal; automatic	**841**
seaming-	
canned foods mfr. ...	**862**
metal trades	**841**
seamless	**551**
setting *(leather dressing)*	**810**
sewing-	
bookbinding	**562**
clothing mfr.	**553**
footwear mfr.	**555**
hospital service	**553**
institution	**553**
laundry	**553**
leather goods mfr. ...	**555**
textile mfr.	**553**
shaking	**829**
shaper	**840**
shaping-	
metal trades	**840**
wood products mfr. ...	**897**
shearing-	
metal trades	**899**
textile mfr.	**552**
shirt-	**553**
laundry	**673**
shoe; canvas	**555**
shrinking;	**552**
felt hood	**814**
silk *(clothing mfr.)* ...	**553**
singeing	**552**
sinking; die	**840**
sizing *(textile mfr.)* ...	**552**
skiver	**555**
skiving *(footwear mfr.)* ...	**555**
sleeving	**553**
slicing; bread	**800**
slicing (celluloid)	**825**
slipper	**555**
slitting-	
adhesive tape mfr. ...	**822**
fabric mfr.	**559**
paper mfr.	**822**
paper products mfr. ...	**822**
slitting and cutting (photographic film) ...	**822**
slitting and winding- ...	**559**
textile mfr.	**814**
slotter	**840**
slotting	**840**
slugger	**859**
socket	**899**
soldering	**537**
souring	**552**
spanishing *(leather cloth mfr.)*	**552**
special *(clothing mfr.)* ...	**553**
spewing	**824**
spindle	**897**
spinning (textiles)	**812**

	Code number
Machinist; *continued*	
splitting; stone	**500**
splitting *(tannery)*	**810**
spooling (yarn)	**813**
spreader	**811**
spring;	**899**
coach	**530**
staking	**810**
stamping-	
metal trades	**841**
plastics goods mfr.	**825**
stapling-	
footwear mfr.	**555**
mattress mfr.	**851**
starch	**809**
stationary	**893**
stemming	**802**
stentering	**552**
stiffening	**552**
stitch	**553**
stitching; wire	**559**
stitching *(footwear mfr.)*	**555**
stocking *(hosiery mfr.)*	**551**
stone	**500**
stoving-	
metal goods	**829**
tobacco	**802**
stranding-	**899**
rope, twine mfr.	**814**
stretching	**552**
tableting (tablet, pill)	**820**
tailor's	**553**
tamping	**885**
tape *(hat mfr.)*	**553**
taping-	
cable mfr.	**899**
footwear mfr.	**555**
tapping-	**840**
ceramics mfr.	**591**
tempering (chocolate)	**809**
tent	**553**
tenterer	**552**
testing *(metal trades)*	**860**
textile-	**814**
clothing mfr.	**553**
textile machinery mfr.	**840**
thicknessing	**897**
threshing; tobacco	**802**
tie	**553**
tile	**590**
timber	**897**
tinplate	**891**
tobacco	**802**
toffee	**809**
tool	**840**
towel	**553**
toy; soft	**553**
tracklaying	**885**
trim *(motor vehicle mfr.)*	**899**
trimming (brushes)	**899**
trouser	**553**
tube; paper	**569**
tube *(silk mfr.)*	**813**
tucking	**553**
tufting-	
carpet mfr.	**814**
mattress mfr.	**559**
turning; wood	**897**
twisting-	
textile mfr.-	**812**
textile warping	**552**
Machinist; *continued*	
twisting- *continued*	
textile mfr.- continued	
twine mfr.	**814**
tying; warp	**552**
upholsterer's	**553**
upholstery	**553**
upsetting	**839**
up-taking	**821**
varnishing-	
lithography	**821**
metal trades	**869**
velvet	**552**
veneer	**897**
vest	**553**
warping	**552**
washing-	
bottle	**999**
food products mfr.	**809**
laundry	**673**
textile mfr.	**814**
transport	**999**
washing and mixing *(abrasive mfr.)*	**829**
waxing	**821**
weaving; wire	**841**
weighing	**863**
welding; plastics	**859**
welt-	**555**
clothing mfr.	**553**
welting (hosiery)	**553**
wheel	**551**
winding-	
oilskin mfr.	**829**
textile mfr.-	**814**
yarn winding	**813**
window; metal	**840**
wire	**831**
wiring *(rubber tyre mfr.)*	**824**
wood-	**897**
paper mfr.	**821**
woodcutting	**897**
woodworking	**897**
wrapping	**862**
zigzag-	**553**
footwear mfr.	**555**
Machinist-	
office machinery	**490**
adhesive tape mfr.	**821**
animal food mfr.	**809**
asbestos-cement goods mfr.	**899**
atomic energy plant	**840**
bakery	**800**
banking	**490**
basket mfr.	**899**
bedding mfr.	**553**
bookbinding	**562**
brake lining mfr.	**899**
brewery	**801**
brush mfr.	**599**
building and contracting	**885**
button mfr.	**899**
canvas goods mfr.	**553**
carbon goods mfr.	**899**
cast concrete products mfr.	**899**
ceramics mfr.	**590**
chemical mfr.	**820**
cider mfr.	**801**
clothing mfr.	**553**
coal gas, coke ovens	**889**
coal mine-	**597**
Machinist- *continued*	
coal mine- continued	
above ground	**840**
cold storage	**999**
cork stopper mfr.	**899**
dairy	**809**
distillery	**801**
dyeing and cleaning	**673**
electric blanket mfr.	**553**
fishing rod mfr.	**899**
flour confectionery mfr.	**800**
food products mfr.	**809**
footwear mfr.	**555**
furniture mfr.	**897**
garage	**840**
glass mfr.	**590**
grain milling	**809**
hat mfr.	**553**
hatters' fur mfr.	**814**
laundry	**673**
lead pencil mfr.	**897**
leather cloth mfr.	**814**
leather dressing	**810**
leather goods mfr.	**555**
linoleum mfr.	**829**
malting	**801**
match mfr.	**579**
metal trades-	**840**
battery, accumulator mfr.	**899**
cable mfr.	**899**
card clothing mfr.	**899**
lamp, valve mfr.	**899**
metal smallwares mfr.	**899**
metal stamping	**841**
nail, rivet, etc. mfr.	**899**
nut, bolt, etc. mfr.	**899**
reed mfr.	**599**
shipbuilding	**534**
steel pen mfr.	**841**
tin box mfr.	**841**
wire goods mfr.	**899**
wire rope mfr.	**899**
mine, not coal	**898**
musical instrument mfr.	**593**
opencast coal mining	**885**
optical goods mfr.	**590**
P.L.A.	**889**
paper mfr.	**821**
paper dress pattern mfr.	**822**
paper goods mfr.	**569**
photographic film mfr.	**829**
photographic film processing	**569**
piano action, hammer mfr.	**897**
plastics mfr.	**820**
plastics goods mfr.	**825**
printing	**891**
railways-	
civil engineer's dept.	**885**
railway workshops	**840**
relief stamping	**569**
rope mfr.	**814**
Royal Mint	**841**
rubber goods mfr.	**824**
salt mfr.	**820**
sanitary towel mfr.	**559**
sewage disposal	**892**
soap mfr.	**820**
soft drinks mfr.	**809**
soft furnishing mfr.	**553**
sugar confectionery mfr.	**809**
sugar refining	**809**

	Code number
Machinist- *continued*	
surgical dressing mfr.	**553**
surgical goods mfr.	**599**
synthetics mfr.	**820**
tannery	**810**
textile mfr.-	**814**
carpets, rugs mfr.	**553**
hosiery mfr.-	**551**
overlocking	**553**
sewing	**553**
man-made fibre mfr.	**826**
textile bleaching	**552**
textile combing	**811**
textile dyeing	**552**
textile finishing	**552**
textile opening	**811**
textile printing	**569**
textile weaving	**550**
textile goods mfr.	**553**
tobacco mfr.	**802**
toy mfr.	**899**
upholstering	**553**
vinery	**801**
wallpaper mfr.-	**821**
wallpaper printing	**569**
wood products mfr.	**897**
Magazine worker (explosives)	**820**
Magician	**384**
Magistrate (stipendiary)	**240**
Magneter	**890**
Maid;	**958**
bar	**622**
buffet	**953**
canteen (school)	**953**
chalet	**958**
chamber	**958**
coffee	**953**
dispense	**622**
farm; dairy	**900**
hall; dining	**953**
house	**958**
kennel	**902**
kitchen	**952**
lady's	**670**
laundry	**673**
linen	**441**
nurse	**659**
pantry	**952**
parlour	**958**
room;	
coffee	**953**
dining	**953**
mess	**953**
still	**953**
sewing	**553**
table	**953**
tea	**621**
ward	**958**
Maidservant	**958**
Maintenance hand;	
electrical	**899**
estate	**509**
machine-	**894**
textile mfr.	**516**
typewriter	**598**
Maintenance hand-	**990**
aircraft	**516**
boilers	**893**
machinery	**894**
vehicles	**540**
building and contracting	**509**
Maintenance hand- *continued*	
canals	**929**
coal mine	**899**
electricity board	**521**
mine, not coal	**899**
telecoms	**523**
transport-	**540**
railways	**922**
Maintenance man;	
battery	**599**
conveyor *(coal mine)*	**516**
electrical	**521**
mechanical appliances *(coal mine)*	**516**
track *(railways)*	**922**
Maintenance man-	**509**
aircraft	**516**
belt	**555**
boilers	**893**
machinery-	**516**
electrical machines	**521**
office machines	**598**
scientific instruments	**517**
vehicles	**540**
weighing machines	**516**
coal mine	**899**
electricity board	**521**
gas board	**516**
transport-	**540**
railways	**922**
water works	**929**
Maintenance worker *see Maintenance hand*	
Maitre d'hotel	**F621**
Major;	
blow	**F811**
blower	**F811**
room; blow	**F811**
Major-	
armed forces-	
foreign and Commonwealth	**M151**
U.K.	**M150**
Salvation Army	**292**
Major-General-	
armed forces-	
foreign and Commonwealth	**M151**
U.K.	**M150**
Maker;	
accoutrements	**553**
acetate	**820**
acid	**820**
action *(piano mfr.)*	**593**
ammonium chloride	**820**
ammunition	**820**
apparatus; photographic	**517**
appliance;	
orthopaedic	**599**
sanitary	**590**
surgical	**599**
apron *(perambulator mfr.)*	**559**
asphalt	**829**
bag;	
air	**824**
gun	**553**
hand	**555**
jute	**559**
lady's	**555**
nail	**559**
paper	**569**
Maker; *continued*	
bag; *continued*	
polythene	**859**
rod; fishing	**553**
sand	**553**
travelling	**555**
bag-	
canvas goods mfr.	**553**
leather goods mfr.	**555**
paper goods mfr.	**569**
bait	**599**
bakelite	**829**
balance *(scales mfr.)*	**517**
ball;	
billiard	**825**
cricket	**555**
foot	**555**
golf	**824**
ball-	
rubber goods mfr.	**824**
celluloid goods mfr.	**825**
glass mfr.	**590**
band *(textile smallwares mfr.)*	**550**
bandage	**559**
bar; steel *(textile machinery mfr.)*	**840**
barb (barbed wire)	**899**
barometer	**517**
barrel-	
gun mfr.	**516**
paper goods mfr.	**569**
barrel and cask	**572**
barrow	**579**
base *(custard powder mfr.)*	**809**
basin	**590**
basket;	
chip	**859**
ornamental (ceramic)	**590**
wire	**899**
basket-	**599**
wire goods mfr.	**899**
bat; cricket	**579**
bat (clay)	**590**
battery (electric)	**899**
beam *(textile machinery)*	**516**
bed; air	**824**
bed-	
bedding mfr.	**554**
furniture mfr.	**571**
school, university	**958**
bedstead	**516**
bell (cycle bells)	**851**
bellows (pipe organ)	**555**
belly (piano)	**579**
belt;	
conveyor-	
plastics goods mfr.	**825**
rubber goods mfr.	**824**
life	**599**
surgical	**599**
vee	**824**
belt-	**553**
leather	**555**
rubber	**824**
abrasive paper, etc. mfr.	**859**
belting-	
leather	**555**
rubber	**824**
besom	**599**
bicycle	**851**

	Code number
Maker; *continued*	
biscuit;	**800**
dog	**809**
blade; razor	**841**
blanket	**553**
blind	**599**
block;	
asphalt	**829**
brake	**824**
breeze	**899**
building	**899**
carbon	**899**
cement	**599**
clog	**579**
concrete	**599**
cork	**821**
cylinder	**839**
fuel (patent fuel)	**829**
hat	**579**
radiator	**839**
block-	
ceramics mfr.	**590**
printing	**560**
rubber goods mfr.	**824**
wood products mfr.	**579**
blouse	**556**
board; circuit; printed	**850**
board *(paper mfr.)*	**821**
boat	**570**
bobbin-	
cardboard	**569**
metal	**899**
wood	**579**
electric battery mfr.	**899**
body;	
carriage	**541**
coach	**541**
motor	**541**
body-	
vehicles	**541**
hat mfr.	**559**
motor vehicle mfr.	**541**
railways	**541**
safe mfr.	**516**
boiler	**534**
bolster (cutlery)	**530**
bolt-	**899**
forged	**530**
clock mfr.	**841**
bon-bon *(sugar confectionery mfr.)*	**809**
book;	
pattern	**562**
pocket	**562**
book-	
betting	**691**
bookbinding	**562**
boot; surgical	**555**
boot-	**555**
rubber	**859**
retail trade	**179**
boot and shoe	**555**
bottle-	**590**
rubber	**824**
stoneware	**590**
bow-	
clothing mfr.	**553**
musical instrument mfr.	**593**
sports goods mfr.	**579**
bowl-	
ceramics mfr.	**590**
Maker; *continued*	
bowl- *continued*	
sports goods mfr.	**579**
textile machinery mfr.	**579**
box;	
card	**569**
cardboard	**569**
cigar	**859**
match	**899**
ointment	**569**
paper	**569**
tin	**533**
wooden	**572**
box-	
cardboard	**569**
metal	**533**
n.o.s.-	
female	**569**
male	**572**
wood	**572**
match mfr.	**899**
bracelet	**518**
braces	**555**
brake; car	**851**
brayle	**814**
brick	**590**
bridge;	**841**
weigh	**516**
bridle	**555**
brine *(preserves mfr.)*	**809**
briquette	**829**
brooch	**518**
broom	**599**
brush; twisted-in	**899**
brush-	**599**
carbon, electric	**899**
bucket-	
metal	**533**
plastics	**825**
buffer	**555**
bulb *(electric lamp mfr.)*	**850**
bullet	**899**
bunch	**802**
bush	**516**
butter	**809**
button	**899**
cabinet-	**571**
metal	**516**
cable;	
chain	**530**
rope	**814**
wire	**899**
cable-	
electric cable mfr.	**899**
spring mfr.	**899**
cake;	
fish	**809**
pontefract	**809**
cake-	
flour confectionery mfr.	**580**
sugar confectionery mfr.	**809**
camera	**517**
can; fibre	**569**
can (metal)	**841**
candle	**599**
candlewick	**812**
canister	**533**
canopy	**553**
cap; butt (fishing rods)	**841**
cap-	
clothing mfr.	**557**
Maker; *continued*	
cap- *continued*	
electric lamp mfr.	**841**
capsule *(drug mfr.)*	**820**
caramel *(sugar refining)*	**809**
carbon *(carbon goods mfr.)*	**829**
carbon dioxide	**820**
card;	
pattern	**569**
shade	**859**
show	**569**
card *(paper mfr.)*	**821**
carmine	**820**
carriage;	
invalid	**851**
lace	**516**
cart	**579**
carton	**569**
cartridge	**599**
case;	
attache	**555**
battery	**825**
book	**571**
brush	**555**
cabinet	**571**
cardboard	**569**
cigarette (precious metal)	**518**
clock-	**510**
wood	**571**
cutlery	**571**
dressing	**555**
hat	**555**
instrument	**571**
jewel	**571**
leather-	**555**
bookbinding	**562**
metal	**533**
meter	**533**
packing	**572**
pattern	**859**
show	**571**
small	**555**
spectacle	**599**
spring (small arms)	**841**
suit	**555**
television	**571**
watch	**510**
case-	**572**
accumulator mfr.	**825**
firework mfr.	**859**
mattress mfr.	**554**
musical instrument mfr.	**571**
packing case mfr.	**572**
paper goods mfr.	**569**
safe mfr.	**516**
tyre mfr.	**824**
watch, clock mfr.	**510**
casement-	
metal	**516**
wood	**570**
cast; plaster	**590**
catheter (rubber)	**824**
cell *(accumulator, battery mfr.)*	**899**
cellulose	**829**
cement	**829**
chain-	
metal-	**899**
precious metal	**518**
metal trades-	**899**
forging	**530**

	Code number
Maker; *continued*	
chain- *continued*	
textile mfr.	**814**
chair-	**571**
cane	**599**
foundry	**531**
metal furniture mfr.	**851**
cheese	**809**
chemical(s); fine	**820**
chenille	**812**
chloroform	**820**
chocolate	**809**
chronometer	**517**
churn	**572**
cider	**801**
cigar	**802**
cigarette	**802**
clay	**829**
clip; wire	**841**
clock	**517**
clog	**555**
cloth; glass	**821**
club; golf	**579**
coach	**541**
coat-	**556**
knitted coats	**551**
coffin	**571**
coffin and casket	**571**
cog *(clock mfr.)*	**517**
coil (electric)	**850**
coin	**841**
collar; horse	**555**
collar *(clothing mfr.)*	**553**
colour-	**829**
flag mfr.	**559**
comb-	**825**
textile machinery mfr.	**516**
compass	**517**
components *(telephone mfr.)*	**520**
composition-	**820**
boiler covering	**929**
concrete	**599**
condenser (electric)	**850**
confectionery-	
flour confectionery	**580**
sugar confectionery	**809**
cord	**814**
core; cable	**899**
core-	
coal mine	**531**
metal trades	**531**
rope mfr.	**814**
corset	**559**
corticine	**820**
cosmetic	**820**
costume	**556**
coupling	**530**
cover;	
loose	**553**
mattress	**554**
waterproof	**824**
cover *(ceramics mfr.)*	**590**
cracker *(paper goods mfr.)*	**859**
crank	**590**
crate;	**572**
steel	**899**
crayon	**899**
cream-	**809**
cosmetic mfr.	**820**
crucible	**590**
crystal	**820**

	Code number
Maker; *continued*	
cue; billiard	**579**
cup;	**590**
cream *(paper products mfr.)*	**569**
curb *(cast concrete products mfr.)*	**599**
curtain	**553**
cushion;	**554**
air	**824**
table; billiard	**824**
cycle	**851**
desk	**571**
detonator	**599**
dial	**517**
die	**515**
dish	**590**
doctor	**899**
doll	**859**
dolly *(toy mfr.)*	**859**
door;	
fireproof	**599**
steel	**516**
door-	**570**
safe, strong room mfr.	**516**
dough *(flour confectionery mfr.)*	**800**
drawer (safes)	**533**
drawers	**571**
dress	**556**
dressing; surgical	**553**
drum; cable	**572**
drum-	
metal	**533**
wood	**572**
musical instrument mfr.	**593**
drum and keg	**533**
dust *(ceramics mfr.)*	**829**
dye	**820**
eiderdown	**554**
electrode (carbon)	**899**
element	**899**
embroidery	**553**
emulsion	**820**
enamel	**820**
envelope *(paper products mfr.)*	**569**
essence (food)	**809**
eye; artificial-	
glass	**590**
plastics	**825**
fabric; glove	**551**
fan *(electrical goods mfr.)*	**850**
feed *(fountain pen mfr.)*	**899**
felt-	**814**
piano mfr.	**593**
fence; timber	**579**
fender; ship's	**814**
ferrule-	**841**
boiler ferrules	**510**
fertilizer	**820**
fibre;	
man-made	**826**
synthetic	**826**
fichu	**553**
figure;	**590**
wax	**599**
filament;	**850**
continuous	**826**
file;	**530**
box	**569**
finings	**801**

	Code number
Maker; *continued*	
fire; electric	**850**
fireplace (tiled)	**506**
firework(s)	**599**
fittings; tube	**839**
fittings *(safe mfr.)*	**516**
flag-	
cast concrete products mfr.	**599**
paper products mfr.	**859**
flake	**802**
flange *(electric lamp mfr.)*	**590**
float *(sports goods mfr.)*	**579**
flow *(ceramics mfr.)*	**829**
flower; artificial-	**599**
plastics	**859**
flower *(ceramics mfr.)*	**590**
fly-	
sports goods mfr.	**599**
textile machinery mfr.	**516**
foot	**590**
football	**555**
footwear	**555**
form-	**579**
cable mfr.	**850**
ceramics mfr.	**590**
forme *(paper box mfr.)*	**515**
frame;	
bed	**570**
chair	**571**
cork	**859**
handbag	**899**
hood	**899**
mirror	**579**
optical	**825**
oxon	**579**
photo-	**579**
leather	**555**
picture	**579**
racquet	**579**
spectacle	**825**
umbrella	**851**
window-	
metal	**516**
wood	**570**
wire	**899**
frame-	
box spring mattress mfr.	**570**
concrete mfr.	**579**
cycle mfr.	**516**
furniture mfr.	**571**
watch mfr.	**517**
fringe; metallic	**550**
furniture;	**571**
bamboo	**599**
cane	**599**
garden	**579**
metal	**516**
wicker	**599**
fuse	**850**
galvanometer	**517**
garment	**556**
gas	**820**
gasket	**599**
gate	**579**
gauge;	
pressure	**517**
steam	**517**
gauge *(metal trades)*	**515**
gear; sighting; gun	**516**
gig	**516**
gimp	**814**

	Code number
Maker; *continued*	
glass;	**590**
field	**517**
opera	**517**
glaze *(ceramics mfr.)*	**829**
glockenspiel	**593**
glove-	**553**
boxing	**555**
cricket	**555**
rubber	**824**
surgical	**824**
glucose	**809**
glue	**820**
gong (clock)	**517**
goods;	
abrasive	**899**
canvas	**553**
fancy	**599**
leather	**555**
gown	**556**
grate; tile	**506**
gravestone	**500**
grease	**820**
grid *(wood products mfr.)*	**579**
grom(m)et-	**814**
wire rope mfr.	**505**
guard; fork	**841**
guard *(wire goods mfr.)*	**899**
gun	**516**
halter (rope)	**814**
hammer *(piano mfr.)*	**593**
handle-	
wood	**897**
ceramics mfr.	**590**
leather goods mfr.	**555**
precious metal mfr.	**518**
hanger; coat (wood)	**897**
harness;	**555**
electrical	**850**
harp	**593**
hassock	**554**
hat;	**559**
paper	**859**
heald;	**899**
yarn	**551**
heel-	**859**
rubber	**824**
wood	**579**
helmet	**559**
helve	**897**
hinge	**851**
hole; button	**553**
hollow-ware-	**533**
ceramics mfr.	**590**
precious metal mfr.	**518**
hone	**599**
hood *(perambulator mfr.)*	**559**
hood and apron *(perambulator mfr.)*	**559**
hose;	**824**
leather	**555**
hosiery	**551**
hurdle	**579**
hydrometer	**517**
ice cream	**809**
ink	**820**
instrument-	**517**
dental	**899**
musical instruments-	**593**
brass	**516**
precision	**517**

	Code number
Maker; *continued*	
instrument- *continued*	
surgical	**899**
insulator (ceramic)	**591**
jacquard	**516**
jam	**809**
jar (ceramic)	**590**
jelly	**809**
jewellery	**518**
jig	**515**
jig and gauge	**515**
keg-	
metal	**533**
wood	**572**
kerb	**500**
kerbstone *(cast concrete products mfr.)*	**599**
kettle	**533**
key-	**840**
clock mfr.	**841**
musical instrument mfr.	**593**
key and action (barrel organs)	**593**
kilt	**556**
knapsack	**553**
knife	**530**
label;	**569**
wood	**897**
lace;	**550**
boot-	
leather goods mfr.	**555**
textile smallwares mfr.	**550**
warp	**551**
lacquer	**820**
ladder	**579**
lamp;	
electric	**850**
glow	**850**
oil	**533**
lanyard	**814**
lard	**809**
last-	**579**
iron	**839**
lead;	
printer's	**830**
red	**820**
white	**820**
lead oxide	**820**
leather;	
comb	**899**
fancy	**555**
lens	**590**
letter (wood)	**579**
level; spirit	**517**
light;	
lead	**503**
leaded	**503**
lighter; fire	**899**
limb; artificial	**599**
lime	**820**
line;	**814**
clothes	**814**
lingo	**899**
lining-	
clothing mfr.	**553**
footwear mfr.	**555**
linoleum	**829**
lock	**516**
locket (precious metal)	**518**
loom	**516**
lozenge	**809**
machine; weighing	**516**

	Code number
Maker; *continued*	
machine (office machinery)	**516**
machinery; textile	**516**
magneto	**520**
malt	**801**
manhole	**597**
mantle;	**556**
fur	**557**
gas	**899**
incandescent	**899**
mantlet (rope)	**814**
map;	**891**
dissected	**859**
margarine	**809**
mark	**569**
marker-	**559**
footwear mfr.	**899**
marquee	**553**
marzipan	**809**
mash *(leather cloth mfr.)*	**829**
mask-	**599**
beautician	**661**
mast *(shipbuilding)*	**534**
mat;	**550**
rubber	**824**
sheepskin	**810**
sinnet	**599**
wool	**553**
match	**899**
matrix *(typefounding)*	**899**
mattress;	**554**
asbestos	**599**
interior; spring	**554**
link	**851**
rubber	**824**
spring	**899**
wire	**899**
meat; potted	**809**
medal	**569**
meter;	**517**
gas	**859**
micanite	**829**
micrometer	**517**
microscope	**517**
mirror	**591**
model;	
architectural	**570**
display	**599**
exhibition	**570**
jewellery	**518**
plaster	**590**
ship's	**570**
wood	**570**
model-	
ceramics mfr.	**590**
engineering	**573**
toy mfr.	**570**
mop	**599**
mould;	
plaster *(plumbago crucible mfr.)*	**590**
press tool	**515**
mould-	
asbestos-cement goods mfr.	**599**
cast concrete products mfr.	**579**
ceramics mfr.	**590**
foundry	**531**
glass mfr.	**516**
plastics goods mfr.	**515**
sugar confectionery mfr.	**809**
mount; wig	**559**

	Code number
Maker; *continued*	
movement-	**517**
barometer mfr.	**517**
nail;	**841**
cut	**899**
forged	**839**
frost	**839**
wrought	**839**
needle	**899**
net	**550**
nib; pen	**899**
nut	**841**
oar	**579**
odd-stuff	**590**
oil	**820**
ointment	**820**
packing; rubber	**824**
pad; stamping	**599**
pad-	
basket mfr.	**599**
upholstery mfr.	**554**
pail-	**533**
wood	**579**
paint	**820**
pallet	**572**
panel-	**533**
plaster	**829**
wood	**897**
pantile	**590**
paper;	**821**
abrasive	**821**
carbon	**821**
emery	**821**
fly	**821**
glass	**821**
laced	**569**
photographic	**821**
sand	**821**
parachute	**553**
part; commutator	**520**
part *(piano mfr.)*	**571**
paste-	
chemical mfr.	**820**
flour confectionery mfr.	**800**
food products mfr.	**809**
paper goods mfr.	**820**
pattern;	
engineer's	**573**
metal *(footwear mfr.)*	**533**
wood	**573**
pattern-	
artificial flower mfr.	**559**
cast concrete products mfr.	**579**
ceramics mfr.	**590**
clothing mfr.	**557**
coal mine	**573**
footwear mfr.	**555**
jacquard card cutting	**814**
metal trades-	**573**
jewellery mfr.	**518**
plastics goods mfr.	**570**
textile mfr.	**430**
pedometer	**517**
peg	**579**
pen	**899**
pencil	**899**
pepper	**809**
perambulator	**851**
perfumery	**820**
petroleum	**820**
piano	**593**

	Code number
Maker; *continued*	
pick	**530**
picker	**555**
pickle	**809**
pie	**800**
pill	**820**
pin *(ceramics mfr.)*	**590**
pinch	**850**
pipe;	
asbestos	**829**
clay	**590**
drain	**590**
flexible	**824**
lead	**839**
organ	**533**
sanitary	**590**
pipe-	
cast concrete goods mfr.	**899**
ceramics mfr.	**590**
foundry	**531**
rubber goods mfr.	**824**
tobacco pipe mfr.	**579**
zinc refining	**590**
plaque	**590**
plate;	
accumulator	**839**
lithographic	**560**
stencil	**533**
plate-	**560**
ceramics mfr.	**590**
precious metal mfr.	**518**
pleat	**556**
plug; sparking	**850**
plug *(tobacco mfr.)*	**802**
plywood	**821**
pocket *(tyre mfr.)*	**824**
pole	**897**
polish	**820**
poppy	**599**
post (concrete)	**599**
postcard	**859**
pot-	**590**
metal	**533**
glass mfr.	**590**
pottery	**590**
pouffe	**555**
powder-	
chemical	**820**
food	**809**
prism	**590**
pudding	**800**
puff;	
powder	**559**
toe	**859**
pulp *(paper mfr.)*	**821**
pump	**516**
punch	**839**
purse (leather)	**555**
putty	**829**
pyjama	**553**
racquet	**579**
radiant; fire; gas	**590**
reed-	
musical instrument mfr.	**593**
textile machinery mfr.	**599**
reel; fishing	**599**
reel-	**897**
cable mfr.	**572**
refrigerator	**516**
resin	**820**
rib; umbrella	**899**

	Code number
Maker; *continued*	
ribbon; typewriter	**814**
ridge	**590**
rifle	**516**
ring;	
asbestos	**824**
jump	**518**
wax	**599**
ring *(precious metal mfr.)*	**518**
rivet	**899**
road	**923**
robe	**556**
rocket	**599**
rod; fishing	**579**
roll; dandy	**899**
roller;	
printer's	**824**
printer's composition	**824**
rubber	**824**
roller-	
pianoforte mfr.	**593**
textile machinery mfr.	**840**
rope-	**814**
metal	**899**
rosette (leather)	**555**
rotor	**520**
rubber	**824**
rubber tread	**824**
rug	**550**
rule; mathematical	**517**
rule *(instrument mfr.)*	**517**
runner	**830**
sack and bag	**553**
saddle-	**555**
ceramics mfr.	**590**
saddletree (wood)	**579**
safe	**516**
saggar	**590**
sagger	**590**
sail	**559**
saline	**820**
salt	**820**
sample-	
paper products mfr.	**569**
textile mfr.	**430**
sandwich	**699**
sauce	**809**
saucer	**590**
sausage	**809**
saw	**899**
scabbard	**555**
scale;	**516**
wood (piano)	**573**
scale and balance	**516**
screen;	
malt	**841**
silk	**569**
wind	**590**
screen-	
wood	**579**
textile printing	**569**
screw;	**899**
balance	**517**
frost	**839**
watch	**899**
wooden	**897**
scull	**579**
scythe	**530**
seat;	**571**
cane	**599**
garden	**579**

	Code number
Maker; *continued*	
seat; *continued*	
spring	**899**
segment	**500**
sett	**500**
shade; lamp	**599**
sheet-	
vulcanised fibre	**821**
railways	**553**
shirt	**556**
shoe;	**555**
horse	**530**
shovel-	
steel	**530**
wood	**579**
shroud	**553**
shutter (wood)	**570**
shuttle	**579**
shuttlecock	**599**
sieve *(wire goods mfr.)*	**899**
sign-	
electric	**850**
metal	**533**
neon	**850**
perspex	**825**
wood	**570**
sink-	
ceramic	**590**
metal	**841**
plastics	**825**
sinker	**841**
size	**820**
skep	**599**
skewer (wood)	**579**
skin; sausage	**809**
skip	**599**
skirt	**556**
slab-	
cast concrete products mfr.	**599**
ceramics mfr.	**590**
mine, not coal	**500**
slate	**500**
sleeve *(clothing mfr.)*	**553**
sley	**579**
slip-	
ceramics mfr.	**829**
pencil, crayon mfr.	**829**
slipper;	**555**
rubber	**859**
snuff	**802**
soap	**820**
sock-	
boots and shoes	**859**
hosiery mfr.	**551**
solution-	
celluloid	**820**
rubber	**824**
soup	**809**
spade	**530**
spar-	
metal	**534**
wood	**579**
spectacle	**825**
speedometer	**517**
spindle-	**899**
textile machinery mfr.	**516**
spindle and flyer	**516**
spirit	**820**
spring;	
balance	**516**
carriage	**841**

	Code number
Maker; *continued*	
spring; *continued*	
flat	**841**
laminated	**530**
leaf	**530**
lock	**841**
railway	**530**
spring-	**899**
carriage, wagon mfr.	**530**
railway locomotive mfr.	**530**
staging *(shipbuilding)*	**579**
stamp;	**569**
bleacher's-	
metal	**841**
wood	**579**
endorsing-	
metal	**859**
rubber	**824**
rubber	**859**
starch-	**809**
textile mfr.	**829**
stave	**579**
steelyard	**516**
step	**570**
stick;	
hockey	**579**
walking	**579**
stock *(gun mfr.)*	**579**
stone;	
artificial	**599**
composition	**599**
concrete (precast)	**599**
grave	**500**
kerb-	
cast concrete products mfr.	**599**
mine, not coal	**500**
oil	**500**
patent	**599**
pulp	**500**
rubbing	**599**
stopper-	
glass mfr.	**590**
steelworks	**590**
stove	**516**
strap;	**555**
fork	**839**
string-	**814**
metal	**599**
gut mfr.	**599**
sugar	**809**
sulphate	**820**
surplice	**553**
suspender	**553**
sweet	**809**
switch	**850**
switchboard	**520**
switchgear	**520**
syrup	**809**
table; billiard	**599**
table *(furniture mfr.)*	**571**
tablet *(pharmaceutical mfr.)*	**820**
tack	**899**
tallow	**829**
tank;	**534**
slate	**500**
tape *(adhesive tape mfr.)*	**821**
taper	**899**
tarpaulin	**553**
tassel	**551**
taximeter	**517**

	Code number
Maker; *continued*	
tea	**953**
teapot	**590**
telescope	**517**
template; wooden	**570**
template-	**515**
wood	**570**
temple	**516**
tent	**559**
thermometer	**590**
thimble-	
ceramics mfr.	**590**
precious metal mfr.	**518**
shipbuilding	**530**
thread	**812**
ticket;	**569**
reel	**891**
tie	**553**
tile-	**590**
asbestos-cement	**599**
concrete	**599**
glass	**590**
plastics	**825**
rubber	**824**
tissue; carbon	**899**
tool;	**515**
chasing	**530**
diamond	**518**
edge	**530**
engineer's	**515**
hand	**530**
machine	**516**
press	**515**
small	**515**
top *(textile mfr.)*	**811**
towel	**559**
toy	**599**
transfer	**569**
transformer	**520**
tray-	
metal	**533**
paper	**569**
plastics	**825**
wicker	**599**
wood	**579**
trellis	**859**
trimming(s)-	
clothing mfr.	**553**
slipper mfr.	**555**
tinsel mfr.	**812**
trouser	**556**
trumpet *(steelworks)*	**500**
trunk-	
leather	**555**
metal	**533**
wood	**572**
truss-	
joinery mfr.	**570**
surgical goods mfr.	**599**
tube;	
flexible	**824**
metal	**839**
television	**850**
tube-	
glass	**590**
metal	**839**
paper	**569**
plastics	**825**
rubber	**824**
musical instrument mfr.	**831**

	Code number
Maker; *continued*	
tubing-	
glass	**590**
rubber	**824**
twine	**814**
typewriter	**516**
tyre	**824**
umbrella	**559**
valve *(radio valve mfr.)*	**850**
varnish;	**820**
head	**F820**
vat	**572**
vestment	**556**
wadding	**814**
wafer	**800**
wagon;	**541**
timber	**579**
waistcoat	**556**
wardrobe	**571**
washer-	
leather	**555**
micanite	**899**
rubber	**824**
watch	**517**
watch and clock	**517**
water;	
mineral	**809**
soda	**809**
waterproof	**559**
wattle	**579**
wedge	**530**
weight	**840**
welt	**555**
wheel-	
abrasive paper, etc. mfr.	**569**
clock mfr.	**517**
cycle mfr.	**851**
whip	**555**
white *(wallpaper mfr.)*	**820**
wick	**899**
wig	**599**
window;	
lead	**503**
stained glass	**503**
window *(metal window mfr.)*	**516**
wing (motor car)	**533**
wool; wood	**821**
wreath; artificial	**791**
Maker-	
cast concrete products mfr.	**599**
flour confectionery mfr.	**580**
musical instrument mfr.	**593**
sports goods mfr.	**599**
Maker and joiner; cabinet	**571**
Maker and repairer;	
body	**541**
shoe	**555**
Maker-up;	
cloth	**862**
hosiery	**553**
jeweller's	**518**
piece	**862**
smallware	**862**
spool	**862**
yarn	**862**
Maker-up-	
art needlework mfr.	**559**
handkerchief mfr.	**862**
knitwear mfr.	**553**
leather goods mfr.	**555**
metal trades-	**516**

	Code number
Maker-up- *continued*	
metal trades- continued	
silver and plate mfr.	**518**
small chain mfr.	**899**
paper mfr.	**861**
printing	**560**
textile mfr.	**814**
umbrella mfr.	**553**
Make-up hand	**560**
Malt man	**801**
Malt room man	**801**
Malter	**552**
Maltster;	
floorman	**801**
kilnman	**801**
Manager;	
abattoir	**110**
account *(advertising)*	**123**
accounts	**139**
administration; *see also*	
Manager-	**199**
sales	**139**
advertisement	**123**
advertising	**123**
agency; ticket	**139**
airport	**140**
alley; bowling	**176**
arcade *(amusement hall)*	**176**
area; telephone	**139**
area-	
pools promoters	**M719**
sales force	**M710**
construction	**111**
market research	**121**
public houses	**175**
retail trade	**179**
transport	**140**
assurance; quality	**218**
audit	**139**
bank	**131**
banqueting	**174**
bar;	**F622**
snack	**174**
barber's	**M172**
baths	**176**
bingo	**176**
boatel	**173**
booking	**139**
bookmaker's	**691**
boxer's	**384**
branch-	
radio, television and video hire	**199**
accommodation bureau	**139**
assurance company	**139**
banking	**131**
building society	**131**
electricity board	**179**
entertainment ticket agency	**139**
government	**103**
insurance	**139**
private employment agency	**139**
trade association	**M190**
transport	**140**
wholesale, retail trade-	**179**
butchers	**M178**
fishmongers	**M178**
brand	**121**
buffet	**174**
building	**111**
business *see Manager-*	

	Code number
Manager; *continued*	
butcher's	**M178**
butchery	**178**
cafe	**174**
camp; holiday	**173**
canteen	**174**
casino	**176**
catering	**174**
cellar-	
brewery	**142**
wine merchants	**142**
centre;	
arts	**176**
leisure	**176**
sports	**176**
cinema	**176**
circuit *(entertainment)*	**176**
circulation	**179**
circus	**176**
claims	**M361**
cleansing	**199**
club;	
clothing	**179**
refreshment	**174**
residential	**173**
social	**176**
club-	**176**
catering	**174**
football club	**M387**
collection(s)	**139**
colliery	**113**
commercial	**121**
communications; data	**126**
company; insurance	**139**
computer	**126**
concession	**179**
conference	**199**
construction	**111**
contracts-	**121**
purchasing	**122**
sales	**121**
building and contracting	**111**
manufacturing	**110**
control;	
credit	**130**
quality	**218**
stock	**141**
conveyancing	**M350**
copyright	**139**
cost(ing)	**139**
credit	**130**
dairy-	**179**
food products mfr.	**110**
demolition	**111**
department(al)-*see also*	
Manager-	
building society	**131**
insurance	**139**
depot-	**142**
transport	**140**
wholesale, retail trade	**179**
despatch	**142**
development; systems	**126**
dispatch	**142**
display	**M791**
distribution	**142**
district-	
assurance company	**M719**
catering	**174**
electricity board	**139**
friendly society	**139**

	Code number
Manager; *continued*	
district- *continued*	
gas board	139
insurance	**M719**
manufacturing	199
retail trade	179
transport	140
wholesale trade	179
divisional-	
insurance	139
manufacturing	110
petroleum distribution	142
transport	140
docks	140
drawing *(textile mfr.)*	**F811**
entertainment	176
estate	170
estimating	**M360**
exchange; foreign	120
exhibition	176
export-	121
export agency	702
facilities	199
factory	110
fairground	176
farm	160
field	**M710**
finance	120
financial	120
fishmonger's	**M178**
flats;	
holiday	173
service	173
fleet; transport	140
flight	140
floor *(entertainment)*	**M384**
florist	179
forecourt *(filling station)*	179
foundry	110
freight	142
fund; pension	361
furnishing	199
garage	171
gas	113
general-*see also Manager-*	
large establishment	101
theatrical productions	384
ground;	
cricket	176
football	176
guest house	173
hairdresser's	**M172**
hall;	
bingo	176
concert	176
dance	176
hire;	
equipment	199
plant	199
hotel	173
house;	
acceptance	361
boarding	173
licensed	175
lodging	173
public	175
house *(entertainment)*	176
housing-	199
housing association	**M102**
local government	**M102**
import-	139

	Code number
Manager; *continued*	
import- *continued*	
import agency	702
installation; computer	126
installations; offshore	113
investment	361
invoice	139
kennel	169
laboratory	200
launderette	179
laundry	179
library	270
lighting *(television)*	**M384**
machine;	
collotype	569
letterpress	891
lithographic	891
photogravure	891
printing	891
machine-	
paper goods mfr.	569
printing	891
maintenance-	110
buildings and other structures	111
marina	176
market	199
marketing	121
media	123
merchandise	121
mill	110
motel	173
network	126
nursery; forest	169
office;	139
betting	691
box	139
drawing	**M310**
insurance;	139
D.S.S.	103
post	131
printing *(P.O.)*	110
office (credit control)	130
operating *(transport)*	140
operations; computer	126
operations *(mining)*	113
organisation and efficiency	125
organisation and methods	125
packaging	142
parts	141
pensions	139
personal *(entertainment)*	384
personnel	124
pharmacist's	221
piggery	160
planning *(manufacturing)*	218
plant-	110
building and contracting	111
practice *(medical and dental practices)*	139
prescription *(glass mfr.)*	**F590**
processing; data	**M126**
procurement	122
produce *(retail trade)*	179
product	121
production-	110
advertising	123
building and contracting	111
film production	**M384**
programming	126
progress	110

	Code number
Manager; *continued*	
project *(computing)*	126
projects-	110
advertising	123
building and contracting	111
promotion; sales	121
promotions; sports	176
property	170
publications; technical	110
publicity	123
publisher's	179
purchase; hire	130
purchasing	122
quality	218
quarry	113
racecourse	176
radio, television and video hire	199
regional (sales force)	**M710**
relations;	
industrial	124
public	123
research;	
market	121
operational	125
research-	209
agricultural	201
biochemical	201
biological	201
botanical	201
chemical	200
engineering;	
electrical	212
electronic	213
mechanical	211
geological	202
historical	399
horticultural	201
medical	300
meteorological	202
physical science	202
zoological	201
broadcasting	399
government	399
journalism	399
printing and publishing	399
reservations	139
resource; community	102
restaurant	174
room;	
ball	176
composing	110
pattern	**F441**
print	110
stock	141
safety	**M102**
sales;	
area	**M710**
district	**M710**
field	**M710**
regional	**M710**
sales-	121
retail trade	179
sales and advertising	121
sales and commercial	121
sales and marketing	121
sales and service	121
sauna baths	176
school *(riding school)*	176
section *see Manager-*	
security	199

	Code number
Manager; *continued*	
service;	110
rental	199
services;	
domestic	199
legal	350
management	253
marketing	121
shift	110
shipping	139
shop;	
betting	691
butcher's	M178
fishmonger's	M178
mobile	M731
shop-	
dyeing and cleaning	179
hairdressing	M172
laundry receiving shop	179
metal trades	110
retail trade-	179
butchers	M178
fishmongers	M178
mobile shop	M731
pharmacists	221
showroom	179
site;	111
camping	173
caravan	173
skating rink	176
social services	102
society;	
building	131
friendly	139
solicitor's	M350
spares	141
sports	176
stable	169
stadium	176
staff	124
stage *(entertainment)*	M384
stall; book	179
stall *(retail trade)*	M732
stand *(entertainment)*	176
station; petrol	179
station-	
bus	140
coach	140
railway	140
airline	140
stock	141
stores; ship's	141
store(s)-	141
retail trade	179
studio-	M381
entertainment	M384
study; works	M125
supplies	122
systems	M126
tailor's	179
taxation *(accountancy)*	362
team (sports)	M387
technical-	110
lighting	M384
technology; information	126
telephone	139
terminal *(oil distribution)*	142
theatre	176
touring *(entertainment)*	M384
trade	179
traffic	140
Manager; *continued*	
training	M124
transport	140
travel	177
valuation	M360
wages	139
warehouse	142
works; sewage	199
works-	110
building and contracting	111
workshop(s)	110
yard;	142
boat	110
ship	110
of field trials *(N.I.A.B.)*	201
Manager-	
catering	174
radio, television and video hire	199
accountancy	139
accountancy services	120
advertising	123
agricultural contracting	160
agriculture	160
airbroker's	703
auctioneering	M719
average adjusting	M361
banking and finance-	131
merchant banking	120
beauty treatment	172
betting and gambling-	691
casino, gaming club	176
building and contracting	111
building society	131
cable television broadcasting	176
camping site	173
car hire	199
car park	199
caravan site	173
charitable organisation	190
cinema	176
circulating library	179
clam cultivation	169
coal mine (open cast)	111
coke ovens	110
commission agents	703
credit company	130
education-	191
driving school	M393
employment agency (private)	139
estate agency	170
export agency	702
fish hatchery	169
fishing company	169
football club	M387
forestry	169
fruit growing	160
fuel merchant	179
funeral directors	690
gardening, grounds keeping services	169
hairdressing	M172
holiday camp	173
horticulture	160
hostel	173
hotel, etc.	173
import agency	702
insurance	139
insurance brokers	361
Job Centre (Dept. of Emp.)	103
Manager- *continued*	
laundry, launderette, dry cleaners	179
livestock dealing	179
machinery hire	199
mail order establishment	179
manufacturing	110
market gardening	160
market research	121
mine (not opencast), quarry	113
mineral oil processing	110
money lending	130
mussel cultivation	169
N.A.A.F.I.-	
canteen	174
shop	179
night club	176
nuclear fuel production	110
nursing home	M340
off-licence	179
office services	199
oyster cultivation	169
park	176
pawn brokers	179
photographic studios	199
plant hire	199
postal services	131
private detective agency	199
professional association	190
property investment company	170
public baths	176
public house	175
public utilities	113
radio broadcasting	176
radio station	139
refuse disposal, sanitation, etc.	199
religious organisation	199
repairing-	
motor vehicles	110
consumer goods	199
residential club	173
retail trade-	179
butchers	M178
fishmongers	M178
florist	179
market stall	M732
mobile shop	M731
opticians	222
party plan sales	M730
pharmacists	221
safe deposit	199
services development	199
ship broker's	703
shipping and freight forwarding agency	139
snooker, billiards hall	176
Social Security Office	103
solid fuel mfr.	110
sports activities	176
stock jobbers	361
storage	142
telecommunications services	131
television-	
broadcasting	176
station	139
theatre	176
ticket agency	139
trade association	M190
trade union	M190

	Code number
Manager- *continued*	
trading stamp redemption office	179
training centre	124
transport-	140
loading, unloading	142
travel agency	177
tree felling services and related	169
typewriting agency	199
vocational training	124
warehousing	142
welfare services	M102
well drilling	113
wholesale trade-	179
butchers	M178
fishmongers	M178
wine bar	175
Manciple	701
Mangle hand *see Mangler-*	
Mangle man *see Mangler-*	
Mangler; plate	839
Mangler-	
steelworks	839
textile mfr.	552
Manicurist	661
Manipulator;	
glass	590
tub *(coal mine)*	889
tube-	
metal	899
rubber	824
Manipulator-	
metal mfr.	839
plastics goods mfr.	825
Mannequin	699
Manual worker	990
Manufacturer-	
badges	553
bags	555
basketry	599
bedding	554
brushes, brooms	599
buttons	899
canvas goods	559
cast concrete goods	599
ceramics	590
chemicals	820
clothing	559
fancy goods	599
firelighters	859
fireplaces	506
food products-	809
flour confectionery	580
sugar confectionery	809
footwear	555
furniture-	571
cane furniture	599
metal furniture	899
gas	820
glass	590
gloves	553
hats	559
instruments	517
jewellery, plate	518
joinery	570
leather	810
leather goods	555
machinery	516
metal goods-	899
sheet metal goods	533
Manufacturer- *continued*	
metals	830
models	570
musical instruments	593
packing cases	572
paper	821
paper goods	569
plastics goods	825
rope, twine	814
rubber goods	824
shop and office fittings	570
soft drinks	809
sports goods	599
surgical appliances	599
textile machinery accessories	599
textiles	814
tobacco	802
toys	599
umbrellas	559
vehicles	516
watches, clocks	517
wood products	579
Marble worker	500
Marbler; paper	562
Marbler-	
bookbinding	562
leather dressing	810
Margarine worker	809
Marine-	
armed forces-	
foreign and Commonwealth	601
U.K.	600
Mariner;	
master-	332
fishing	169
Mariner-	880
fishing	903
Marker;	
bale	569
billet *(steelworks)*	839
billiard	699
board *(bookmakers)*	699
box	569
button	559
buttonhole	559
cask	801
dial	869
hall *(Assay Office)*	839
ingot *(metal mfr.)*	839
lining	559
part	515
pattern (down quilt, etc.)	559
piece *(textile mfr.)*	559
plate *(rolling mill)*	839
plater's	913
road	923
size	569
stitch *(footwear mfr.)*	555
strip	555
sub-assembly line *(radio mfr.)*	850
timber	569
trade	569
upper *(footwear mfr.)*	569
valve	569
Marker-	
brewery	569
clothing mfr.	557
embroidery mfr.	559
footwear mfr.	555
hosiery mfr.	559
Marker- *continued*	
laundry	569
metal trades-	
boiler mfr.	534
clog iron mfr.	899
cutlery mfr.	841
engineering	515
file mfr.	599
fish hook mfr.	841
galvanized sheet mfr.	863
needle mfr.	841
pen nib mfr.	899
rolling mill	869
scales mfr.	516
sheet metal working	533
shipbuilding	534
steel sheet, strip mfr.	869
tinplate mfr.	869
sugar confectionery mfr.	809
textile mfr.	559
Marker-off; piano	579
Marker-off-	
boiler mfr.	534
engineering	515
foundry	839
shipbuilding	534
textile mfr.	559
tube mfr.	863
wood products mfr.	579
Marker-out-	
engineering	515
fustian mfr.	863
glass mfr.	591
wood products mfr.	579
Marker-up; lens	591
Marker-up *(clothing mfr.)*	557
Market man-	732
coal mine	597
Marsh man	929
Marshal; air-	
armed forces-	
foreign and Commonwealth	M151
U.K.	M150
Marshal; field-	
armed forces-	
foreign and Commonwealth	M151
U.K.	M150
Marshal of the Royal Air Force	M150
Marshall(er) *(transport)*	889
Marshaller; aircraft	889
Marzipan worker	809
Mashman	801
Mash room man	801
Masher; tea	953
Masker; paint	869
Masker (files)	844
Mason;	
banker	500
fireclay	590
fixer	500
monumental	500
quarry	500
stone-	500
coal mine	500
street	924
walling	500
ware; sanitary	590
Mason-	500

	Code number
Mason- *continued*	
coal mine	**500**
Mason hand	**500**
Masseur	**347**
Master;	
baggage	**441**
ballet	**239**
band	**385**
bridge	**889**
caddy	**699**
card	**F811**
choir	**384**
club	**176**
derrick	**F880**
dock	**140**
dredger	**F885**
dredging	**F885**
gang-	**F900**
drainage board	**F895**
harbour	**140**
head-	
educational establishments-	
schools-	
nursery	**234**
primary	**234**
secondary	**233**
sixth form college ...	**233**
special	**235**
hopper	**F889**
house-	
educational establishments-	
schools-	
nursery	**234**
primary	**234**
secondary	**233**
sixth form college ...	**233**
special	**235**
lock	**889**
pier	**140**
port	**140**
post;	**131**
sub-	**131**
self-employed	**179**
property	**699**
quarter-	**441**
shipping	**880**
quay	**140**
riding	**387**
school-	
educational establishments-	
schools-	
nursery	**234**
primary	**234**
secondary	**233**
sixth form college ...	**233**
special	**235**
ship	**332**
spinning	**F812**
station	**140**
sub-post-	**131**
self-employed	**179**
swingbridge	**889**
toast	**699**
tug	**332**
wardrobe	**699**
winding	**F813**
yacht	**332**
at Arms-	
armed forces-	
foreign and Common-wealth	**601**

	Code number
Master; *continued*	
at Arms- *continued*	
armed forces- continued	
U.K.	**600**
shipping	**F880**
of ceremonies *(entertainment)*	**699**
of lightship	**332**
of works	**112**
Master-	
educational establishments-	
schools-	
nursery	**234**
primary	**234**
secondary	**233**
sixth form college ...	**233**
special	**235**
fishing	**169**
high courts	**240**
institution	**M370**
metal mine	**F898**
shipping	**332**
Trinity House	**332**
Matcher;	
colour-	
leather cloth mfr. ...	**814**
linoleum mfr.	**829**
paint mfr.	**829**
plastics goods mfr. ...	**829**
printing	**829**
textile mfr.	**814**
hair	**599**
veneer	**579**
yarn	**814**
Matcher-	
clothing mfr.	**559**
hat mfr.	**559**
Mate;	
asphalter's	**921**
bender's (metal)	**913**
blacksmith's	**839**
boat; fishing	**F903**
boatswain's	**F880**
builder's	**921**
burner's	**913**
carpenter's	**920**
carpenter's and joiner's ...	**920**
chief	**332**
cook's	**952**
coverer's; boiler	**921**
craftsman's-...	**921**
wood products mfr. ...	**920**
driller's *(shipbuilding)* ...	**913**
driver's;	**934**
crane	**932**
dredger	**889**
excavator	**889**
lorry	**934**
electrician's	**913**
emptier's; gulley	**990**
engineer's	**913**
erector's	**913**
examiner's; cable *(railways)*	**990**
first	**332**
fitter's;	**913**
pipe	**913**
fixer's...	**921**
flagger's	**921**
forger's; drop	**839**
fourth	**332**
fuser's	**829**
glazier's	**921**

	Code number
Mate; *continued*	
grinder's (metal)	**912**
joiner's	**920**
jointer's;	
cable	**913**
pipe	**921**
lagger's	**921**
layer's;	
brick	**921**
granolithic...	**921**
main	**921**
plate	**929**
service	**921**
terrazzo	**921**
linesman's	**913**
liquorman's (sugar) ...	**809**
machinist's; wood	**920**
maker's; boiler	**913**
mason's	**921**
mechanic's	**913**
miller's (cement)	**829**
millwright's...	**913**
painter's	**869**
pavior's	**921**
plasterer's	**921**
plater's	**913**
plumber's	**913**
plumber and jointer's ...	**913**
polisher's; french	**869**
printer's	**891**
rigger's	**913**
riveter's	**913**
roofer's	**921**
sawyer's	**920**
scaffolder's	**921**
second	**332**
sheeter's	**921**
shipwright's...	**913**
slater's	**921**
smith's-	**839**
boiler	**913**
copper	**913**
splicer's; rope	**814**
stamper's	**841**
steeplejack's	**921**
stoker's	**893**
tester's (motor cars) ...	**912**
third	**332**
tiler's	**921**
timberman's	**921**
trawler	**F903**
tug	**332**
weaver's	**814**
welder's	**913**
wheelwright's	**920**
wireman's	**913**
on barge	**880**
Mate-	
barge, boat	**F880**
dockyard	**880**
fishing	**F903**
shipping	**332**
Mate-in-charge	**F880**
Material man	**441**
Mathematician	**202**
Matron;	
hostel	**173**
laundry	**F673**
school	**M340**
sewing	**553**

	Code number
Matron-	
institution	**M370**
medical services	**M340**
nursery	**M370**
prison service	**619**
Mattock man	**896**
Measurer;	
braid	**863**
cloth *(textile mfr.)*	**863**
piece	**863**
skin *(food products mfr.)*	**863**
steel	**860**
timber	**863**
wood	**863**
Measurer-	
cable mfr.	**863**
carpet mfr.	**863**
chemical mfr.	**863**
clothing mfr.	**556**
coal mine	**410**
docks	**420**
leather dressing	**863**
paper pattern mfr.	**569**
rolling mill	**860**
tape mfr.	**863**
Mechanic;	
agricultural	**516**
battery	**599**
builder's	**599**
camera	**517**
clock	**517**
colliery	**516**
compass	**517**
cycle; motor	**540**
dental	**592**
dentist's	**592**
electrical	**521**
electro;	**521**
chief	**F521**
district	**F521**
electronic	**529**
experimental	**516**
farm	**516**
garage	**540**
hosiery	**516**
instrument;	**517**
electronic	**529**
optical	**517**
laboratory	**516**
loom	**516**
machine;	
adding	**598**
calculating	**598**
hosiery	**516**
knitting	**516**
sewing	**516**
vending	**516**
weighing	**516**
machine-	**516**
office machinery	**598**
maintenance *see Mechanic-*	
meter *(electricity board)*	**517**
motor	**540**
mower	**516**
optical	**590**
orthopaedic	**599**
pen	**599**
plant	**516**
radar	**529**
radio	**525**
reception	**540**
Mechanic; *continued*	
refrigeration	**516**
research and experimental	**516**
roof	**501**
semi-skilled	**540**
senior *(shipping)*	**880**
service-	**516**
domestic electrical appliances	**521**
garage	**540**
instruments	**517**
office machinery-electrical	**598**
electrical	**521**
radio, television and video	**525**
surgical	**899**
technical	**516**
telecommunications	**529**
telephone; assistant *(telecoms)*	**521**
telephone-	**523**
telecoms	**521**
teleprinter	**529**
television	**525**
time recorder	**517**
totalisator	**598**
typewriter	**598**
umbrella	**899**
vehicle	**540**
wireless	**525**
Mechanic-	**516**
aircraft	**516**
auto-engines	**540**
instruments	**517**
musical instruments	**593**
office machinery	**598**
radio, television and video	**525**
telephone, telegraph apparatus	**523**
vehicles	**540**
shipping	**880**
Mechanic and driver; motor	**540**
Mechanical hand *(rubber goods mfr.)*	**824**
Mechanic of the mine	**516**
Mechanic-examiner	**516**
Mechanic-fitter; motor	**540**
Mechanician *see Mechanic*	
Mechanic-in-charge	**F516**
Medallist	**841**
Medium	**292**
Melter;	
bullion	**830**
electric	**830**
emulsion (photographic)	**829**
fat	**829**
gold	**830**
grease	**820**
lead	**830**
platinum	**830**
silver	**830**
steel	**830**
sugar	**809**
Melter-	
glass mfr.	**591**
Royal Mint	**830**
steelworks	**830**
sugar refining	**809**
zinc smelting	**830**
Melter man *(food products mfr.)*	**809**
Member;	
of European Parliament	**100**
Member; *continued*	
of Lloyds	**361**
of Parliament	**100**
of Religious Community	**292**
of the Inner Temple	**241**
of the Stock Exchange	**361**
Member (appeals tribunal, inquiry, etc.)	**350**
Mender;	
bag	**553**
belt	**555**
carpet	**553**
cloth *(textile mfr.)*	**553**
comb	**516**
crate	**572**
dress (hosiery)	**553**
embroidery	**553**
hosiery	**553**
invisible	**553**
net	**553**
piece	**553**
road	**923**
sack	**553**
shoe	**555**
strap	**555**
tank	**533**
tub *(coal mine)*	**899**
Mender-	
embroidery mfr.	**553**
hotels, catering, etc.	**553**
institution	**553**
laundry	**553**
textile mfr.	**553**
Mercer	**179**
Merceriser	**552**
Merchandiser;	**790**
sales	**790**
Merchant; *see also Agent*	
agricultural	**179**
builders'	**179**
coal	**179**
firewood	**732**
fish-	**178**
wholesale	**179**
log	**732**
metal; scrap	**733**
paper; waste	**733**
rag and bone	**733**
scrap	**733**
wine	**179**
Messman	**953**
Messenger;	**941**
chief	**F941**
head	**F941**
Queen's	**941**
Messenger at arms	**619**
Messenger-clerk	**430**
Messroom boy	**953**
Metal worker;	
architectural	**899**
art	899
ornamental	**899**
precious	**518**
sheet	**533**
white	**518**
Metal worker-	**912**
hospital service	**516**
linoleum mfr.	**599**
Metaler (glass)	**823**
Metaller;	**839**
bronzing	**569**

	Code number
Metalliser; spray	**834**
Metalliser *(lamp, valve mfr.)*	**834**
Metallographer	**219**
Metallurgist	**219**
Meteorologist	**202**
Meter hand	**517**
Methylator	**820**
Metrologist	**300**
Mica man *(mine, not coal)*	**898**
Mica worker	**829**
Micanite worker	**829**
Microbiologist	**201**
Microscopist; electron	**300**
Middler *(rolling mill)*	**839**
Midshipman-	
armed forces-	
foreign and Common-wealth	**M151**
U.K.	**M150**
shipping	**332**
Midwife;	**341**
superintendent	**F341**
Midwife-tutor	**F341**
Milkman-	
farming	**902**
milk retailing	**731**
Milker	**902**
Milkmaid	**902**
Mill hand;	
finishing	**820**
flour	**809**
grain	**809**
grinding	**820**
ink	**820**
nitrate	**919**
provender	**809**
roller (gramophone records)	**825**
rolling	**839**
rubber	**824**
saw	**897**
tints	**820**
wash (cement)	**829**
Mill hand-	**829**
cattle food mfr.	**809**
chemical mfr.	**820**
food processing	**809**
galvanized sheet mfr.	**839**
hair, fibre dressing	**811**
mine, not coal	**890**
rubber goods mfr.	**824**
textile mfr.	**814**
tinplate mfr.	**839**
Mill man;	
lead	**829**
malt	**801**
paint	**829**
potter's	**829**
pug	**829**
rubber	**824**
Mill man-	
carbon goods mfr.	**829**
ceramics mfr.	**829**
chemical mfr.	**820**
leather dressing	**810**
metal mfr.	**839**
mine, not coal	**890**
plastics goods mfr.	**829**
rubber goods mfr.	**824**
salt mfr.	**809**
textile finishing	**552**
whiting mfr.	**829**

	Code number
Mill operative	**919**
Mill worker;	
asbestos	**811**
corn	**919**
cotton	**919**
flour	**919**
grog	**829**
paper	**821**
rolling	**839**
rubber	**824**
saw	**897**
sheet	**839**
slate	**500**
woollen	**919**
Mill worker-	**919**
animal foods mfr.	**809**
metal mfr.	**839**
Miller;	
bayonet	**513**
blanket	**552**
broaching	**513**
c.n.c.	**513**
cement	**829**
cloth	**552**
coal *(cement mfr.)*	**829**
concave (needles)	**513**
corn	**809**
diamond *(jewellery mfr.)*	**518**
die	**513**
dry *(textile mfr.)*	**552**
dust *(ceramics mfr.)*	**829**
dyewood	**829**
engineer's	**513**
felt	**552**
flint *(ceramics mfr.)*	**829**
flour;	**809**
wood	**821**
glaze *(ceramics mfr.)*	**829**
grain	**809**
gypsum	**829**
horizontal	**513**
lime	**829**
logwood	**821**
machine;	**513**
knife	**513**
madder	**829**
malt	**801**
metal	**513**
mustard	**809**
n.c.	**513**
oil	**809**
optical	**590**
paint	**829**
profile	**513**
provender	**809**
rice	**809**
rubber	**824**
saw	**897**
soap	**820**
solvent	**552**
space band	**513**
spice	**809**
stone *(mine, not coal)*	**890**
tool	**513**
tool room	**513**
universal	**513**
vertical	**513**
wash *(cement mfr.)*	**829**
wet *(cement mfr.)*	**829**
woollen	**552**

	Code number
Miller-	
animal foods mfr.	**809**
brewery	**801**
cement mfr.	**829**
ceramics mfr.	**829**
chemical mfr.	**820**
grain milling	**809**
hair, fibre dressing	**811**
metal trades	**513**
mine, not coal	**890**
paper mfr.	**821**
plastics goods mfr.	**825**
sugar refining	**809**
textile mfr.	**552**
whisky distilling	**801**
Milliner; hosiery	**551**
Milliner-	**557**
retail trade	**179**
Milling hand *(soap mfr.)*	**820**
Millwright	**516**
Milner *(textile finishing)*	**552**
Mincer; sausage meat	**581**
Minder;	
back *(textile mfr.)*	**814**
backwash	**814**
belt *(coal mine)-*	**889**
above ground	**889**
block *(wire mfr.)*	**912**
boiler	**893**
bowl;	
scouring	**814**
wash *(textile mfr.)*	**814**
box *(textile mfr.)*	**811**
can	**811**
card	**811**
carding	**811**
cart	**934**
cell *(metal trades-galvanizing)*	**834**
chain	**889**
child	**659**
comb	**811**
condenser	**811**
copper (straw plait)	**814**
crossing; railway	**883**
crusher *(mine, not coal)*	**890**
engine	**893**
finisher (blowing room)	**811**
frame;	**811**
cheesing	**813**
copping	**813**
lap (silk)	**811**
roving (jute)	**811**
slubbing	**811**
front	**811**
hatch	**930**
head;	**812**
balling	**811**
jack	**811**
joiner	**812**
machine *see Machinist*	
motion	**814**
mule	**812**
oven *(bakery)*	**800**
platen *(printing)*	**891**
pump	**999**
punch	**811**
reducer *(wool drawing)*	**811**
retort *(food canning)*	**809**
rover	**811**
roving	**811**

Code number

Minder; *continued*
- scribbling ... **811**
- scutcher ... **811**
- side ... **812**
- stenter... **552**
- stove ... **830**
- swift (wire) ... **912**
- tool ... **441**
- turn *(coal mine)* ... **889**
- twister (wool) ... **812**

Mine worker-
- *coal mine-see also notes* **910**
  - face working ... **597**
- *mine, not coal* ... **898**

Miner;
- clay ... **898**
- coal-*see also notes* ... **910**
  - face working ... **597**
- tunnel ... **509**
- wall ... **500**

Miner-
- *coal mine-see also notes* **910**
  - face working ... **597**
- *mine, not coal* ... **898**

Mineralogist ... **202**

Minister-
- *government* ... **100**
- *religion* ... **292**

Missionary ... **292**

Missioner ... **292**

Mistress;
- doffing ... **F814**
- head-
  - *educational establishments-*
    - *schools-*
      - *nursery* ... **234**
      - *primary* ... **234**
      - *secondary* ... **233**
      - *sixth form college* ... **233**
      - *special* ... **235**
- house-
  - *educational establishments-*
    - *schools-*
      - *nursery* ... **234**
      - *primary* ... **234**
      - *secondary* ... **233**
      - *sixth form college* ... **233**
      - *special* ... **235**
- needle ... **553**
- room; work ... **553**
- school-
  - *educational establishments-*
    - *schools-*
      - *nursery* ... **234**
      - *primary* ... **234**
      - *secondary* ... **233**
      - *sixth form college* ... **233**
      - *special* ... **235**
- sewing ... **F553**
- shifting ... **F814**
- wardrobe ... **699**
- weaving ... **F550**

Mistress-
- *educational establishments-*
  - *schools-*
    - *nursery* ... **234**
    - *primary* ... **234**
    - *secondary* ... **233**
    - *sixth form college* ... **233**
    - *special* ... **235**

Code number

Mixer;
- acid ... **820**
- adhesive *(abrasive paper mfr.)* ... **821**
- asphalt- ... **829**
  - *building and contracting* **929**
- banbury ... **824**
- batch- ... **809**
  - *chemical mfr.* ... **820**
  - *glass mfr.* ... **829**
- bleach (paper) ... **820**
- bristle ... **811**
- cake ... **800**
- carbide; tungsten ... **829**
- carbon ... **820**
- cement *(building and contracting)* ... **829**
- chemical(s) *(textile mfr.)* **552**
- chocolate ... **809**
- clay-
  - *ceramics mfr.* ... **829**
  - *paper mfr.* ... **820**
- colour- ... **829**
  - *custard powder mfr.* ... **809**
  - *plastics goods mfr.* ... **829**
- compound- ... **820**
  - *animal foods mfr.* ... **809**
- concrete ... **829**
- cosmetic ... **820**
- cotton ... **811**
- cream; ice ... **809**
- depolariser ... **820**
- dope ... **820**
- dough-
  - *flour confectionery mfr.* **800**
  - *plastics goods mfr.* ... **829**
  - *rubber mfr.* ... **824**
- dry-
  - *plastics goods mfr.* ... **829**
  - *rubber goods mfr.* ... **824**
- dubbing ... **386**
- dust *(ceramics mfr.)* ... **829**
- dye ... **820**
- electrolyte *(electric battery mfr.)* ... **820**
- emulsion ... **829**
- enamel ... **829**
- explosives ... **820**
- fibre; fur ... **814**
- flour ... **809**
- fluid *(engineering)* ... **829**
- food ... **809**
- glass ... **829**
- glaze *(ceramics mfr.)* ... **829**
- glue ... **820**
- grog *(ceramics mfr.)* ... **829**
- ink ... **820**
- lacquer ... **829**
- latex ... **824**
- linoleum ... **829**
- macadam ... **829**
- marl ... **829**
- metal ... **830**
- oil ... **820**
- paint ... **829**
- paste; lead ... **829**
- paste *(paper goods mfr.)*... **820**
- plastic(s) ... **829**
- polish; furniture ... **829**
- powder; fluorescent ... **820**
- putty ... **829**

Code number

Mixer; *continued*
- recipe *(food products mfr.)* **809**
- resin ... **820**
- rubber... **824**
- sand *(metal mfr.)* ... **839**
- size-
  - *paper mfr.* ... **820**
  - *textile mfr.* ... **552**
- slurry *(cement mfr.)* ... **829**
- soap- ... **820**
  - *textile bleaching* ... **552**
- solution ... **820**
- sound ... **386**
- spice ... **809**
- sponge *(bakery)* ... **800**
- starch ... **552**
- sugar *(condensed milk mfr.)* **809**
- syrup *(mineral water mfr.)* **809**
- tar *(building and contracting)* **929**
- vision *(television)* ... **386**
- wool ... **811**

Mixer-
- *abrasive paper mfr.* ... **821**
- *accumulator, battery mfr.* **820**
- *animal foods mfr.* ... **809**
- *artificial teeth mfr.* ... **829**
- *asbestos composition goods mfr.* ... **811**
- *cast concrete products mfr.* **829**
- *cement mfr.* ... **829**
- *cemented carbide goods mfr.* **829**
- *ceramics mfr.* ... **829**
- *chemical mfr.* ... **820**
- *composition die mfr.* ... **829**
- *felt hood mfr.* ... **811**
- *film production* ... **386**
- *flour confectionery mfr.* ... **800**
- *food products mfr.* ... **809**
- *glass mfr.* ... **829**
- *paper mfr.* ... **821**
- *pencil, crayon mfr.* ... **829**
- *plastics goods mfr.* ... **829**
- *rubber mfr.* ... **824**
- *soft drink mfr.* ... **809**
- *steelworks* ... **830**
- *tar macadam mfr.* ... **829**
- *textile mfr.-* ... **811**
  - *textile proofing* ... **552**
- *tobacco mfr.* ... **802**

Mixer man;
- asphalt- ... **829**
  - *building and contracting* **929**
- slag; tar ... **820**

Mixer man-
- *animal foods mfr.* ... **809**
- *building and contracting* ... **829**
- *steel mfr.* ... **830**
- *textile mfr.* ... **552**

Model ... **699**

Modeller;
- architectural... **570**
- artistic ... **381**
- clay ... **590**
- glass ... **590**
- pattern; paper ... **559**
- plaster... **590**
- styling (motor vehicles) ... **599**
- wax ... **599**

Modeller- ... **559**
- *art metal work mfr.* ... **899**
- *ceramics mfr.* ... **590**

Code number

Moderator-
examination board 239
Presbyterian Church ... 292
Monitor;
industrial *(atomic energy establishment)* 300
physics; health 300
radiation 300
Monitor-
atomic energy establishment 300
broadcasting 380
Monk 292
Mooring man... 889
Mopper *(metal trades)* ... 842
Mortician 699
Mosaic worker 506
Mother;
foster 370
house 370
Mother superior 292
Motor man;
belt 889
haulage 886
screen... 886
Motor man- 893
L.R.T. 882
railways 882
shipping 880
Mottler *(ceramics mfr.)* ... 591
Mould man-
cast concrete products mfr. 599
paper mfr. 821
steelworks 531
Moulder;
abrasive 599
aloe (plastics) 825
aluminium 531
bakelite 825
battery 839
bench 531
bottle 590
brass 531
brick 590
carbon 899
carborundum 599
chocolate 809
cigar 802
clay 590
compo. 829
compression *(plastics goods mfr.)* 825
concrete 599
connection 531
copper 531
core 531
cylinder 531
ebonite 824
faience 590
fibreglass 825
fireclay 590
floor 531
fork (digging, hay, etc.) ... 839
furnace 590
grate; stove 531
gutter 531
hand-
asbestos goods mfr. ... 599
ceramics mfr. 590
metal trades 531
plumbago crucible mfr. 590

Code number

Moulder; *continued*
injection-
footwear mfr. 555
plastics goods mfr. ... 825
rubber goods mfr. ... 824
insole 555
iron 531
lead *(battery mfr.)*... ... 839
leather 555
lens 590
loam 531
machine- 531
chocolate 809
marzipan 809
metal; gun 531
mica 829
micanite 829
pattern 531
pipe;
clay 590
iron 531
pipe-
asbestos-cement 829
cast concrete 899
metal 531
pipe founder's 531
plaster 590
plastic 825
plate (metal) 531
ploughshare... 531
press-
plastics 825
rubber 824
roll 531
rubber (moulds) 824
sand 531
shell 531
sole 555
spindle-
plastics 825
wood 897
spray 531
stamp 824
steel 531
stiffener 555
stone; patent 599
stove 531
tile; hand (ceramic) ... 590
tooth 599
tube; 825
rubber 824
tyre 824
wax 560
wheel; abrasive 599
wheel-
abrasive wheel mfr. ... 599
metal trades 531
wood 897
Moulder-
abrasives mfr. 599
asbestos-cement goods mfr. 599
bakery 800
bottle cap mfr. 824
brake lining mfr. 599
candle mfr. 599
cast concrete products mfr. 599
ceramics mfr. 590
chemical mfr. 531
coal mine 531
cork goods mfr. 899
felt lining mfr. 814

Code number

Moulder- *continued*
footwear mfr. 555
glass mfr. 590
lead pencil, chalk, crayon mfr. 599
metal trades 531
plastics goods mfr. ... 825
printing 560
rubber goods mfr.... ... 824
sugar confectionery mfr. ... 809
tobacco mfr. 802
Moulder and coremaker *(foundry)* 531
Moulds man *(metal mfr.)* ... 839
Mounter;
barometer 517
body 851
boiler 516
card; 859
pattern 814
show 859
diamond 518
drawing 859
engine 516
feather 859
filament 850
gold 518
handle; umbrella 859
lens 859
map 859
metal 518
photographer's 569
picture 599
print (lithographer's) ... 859
process 569
silver 518
stick; walking 859
thermometer 517
wheel 517
wheel and axle 516
wing (coach body) ... 851
Mounter-
instrument mfr. 517
jewellery mfr. 518
net mfr. 814
precious metal, plate mfr. 518
printing 569
textile weaving 550
vehicle building 851
Mover; conveyor *(coal mine)* 899
Mower; lawn 594
Muffle man-
annealing 833
foundry 830
glass mfr. 590
steel mfr. 830
Muffle worker; foundry ... 830
Muffle worker *(annealing)* 833
Mule man 812
Muller 810
Municipal worker 990
Munitions worker 912
Musician 385
Musseler 903
Mycologist 201

Code number

N

Nailer; card ... **899**
Nailer-
box mfr. ... **859**
footwear mfr. ... **859**
fur goods mfr. ... **557**
tannery ... **810**
Nannie ... **659**
Nanny ... **659**
Naturalist ... **201**
Naturopath ... **346**
Navigator-
hovercraft ... **332**
airline ... **331**
shipping ... **332**
Navvy; slurry pond- ... **929**
cement mfr. ... **919**
Navvy- ... **929**
mine, not coal ... **990**
Navvy man ... **885**
Necker; ... **913**
fly ... **530**
flyer ... **530**
Needle hand; latch ... **551**
Needle woman- ... **553**
hospital service ... **553**
institution ... **553**
laundry ... **553**
Needle worker ... **553**
Needler (*textile making-up*) **814**
Needlework hand ... **553**
Negotiator;
property ... **719**
sales (*building and contracting*) ... **719**
Negotiator-
auctioneering ... **719**
estate agency ... **719**
insurance ... **719**
Nematologist ... **201**
Net hand; braiding ... **814**
Netter (*net mfr.*) ... **814**
Neurologist ... **220**
Neutraliser-
chemical mfr. ... **820**
textile mfr. ... **814**
Newsboy (*bookstall*) ... **720**
News hand ... **891**
Newsagent ... **179**
Newscaster (*broadcasting*) ... **384**
Newsreader ... **384**
Nibber (*cocoa mfr.*) ... **809**
Nickel worker (*electro-plating*) ... **834**
Nipper (*paper mfr.*) ... **821**
Nitrider ... **833**
Nobber; fish ... **582**
Normaliser ... **833**
Norseller (net) ... **814**
Nosseller (net) ... **814**
Notary ... **350**
Notcher-
glassware ... **590**
tin box mfr. ... **841**
Novelist ... **380**
Numberer;
parts ... **569**
piece ... **441**
Numberer-
bookbinding ... **562**

Code number

Numberer- *continued*
printing ... **569**
Numismatist ... **179**
Nun ... **292**
Nurse;
animal ... **349**
assistant ... **640**
auxiliary ... **640**
canine ... **349**
charge ... **F340**
chief male ... **F340**
children's- ... **650**
domestic service ... **659**
dental ... **643**
nursery ... **650**
orderly ... **641**
staff ... **340**
surgery; dental ... **643**
veterinary ... **349**
Nurse- ... **340**
grade A, B ... **640**
Nurse-companion ... **340**
Nursemaid ... **659**
Nurse-receptionist; dental ... **643**
Nurse-tutor ... **F340**
Nursery hand ... **595**
Nurseryman- ... **160**
employee ... **595**
Nursery worker ... **595**
Nut room worker ... **809**
Nutritionist;
agricultural ... **201**
animal ... **201**
research ... **201**
Nutter-up ... **851**
Nylon worker (*nylon mfr.*) **826**

O

	Code number
O.S. (*shipping*)	880
Oboist	385
Observer;	
radar (marine)	463
teeming	F531
Obstetrician	220
Oceanographer	202
Odd job man-	990
agriculture	900
coal mine	910
Oddman;	
bank	919
biscuit	823
glost	823
kiln	823
oven	823
Oddman (*ceramics mfr.*)	919
Odd worker-	
coal mine	910
engineering	899
Office boy	430
Office girl	430
Office junior	430
Office worker; post	940
Office worker-	430
government	400
Officer;	
accommodations	371
accounts-	410
government	120
acquisition (*forestry*)	169
administration; staff	363
administrative-	199
government	400
local government	102
admission (*hospital*)	420
advisory;	
careers	392
district	201
advisory-	
poultry	201
Min. of A.F.F.	201
agricultural-	
county	103
district;	201
assistant	400
aids; visual	386
allocation	420
ambulance;	642
chief	199
appliance	346
appointments (*government*)	103
area-	
government	103
local government	102
assessment	400
assistance; national	400
attendance; school	371
authorised (*local government*)	401
bank	411
board; national assistance	400
borstal	612
budget	410
building	111
carbonisation (*coal mine*)	219
care; child	293
careers	392
cargo	420
catering-	174
Officer; *continued*	
catering- *continued*	
shipping	F630
certifying (*Dept. of Transport*)	211
chief-	
fire service	M153
local government-	102
weights and measures dept.	394
prison service	154
railways	140
shipping	332
church	430
Church Army	292
claims	361
clerical;	
higher-	430
government	132
local government	102
clerical-	430
bank	411
building society	411
government	400
health authority	401
local government	401
police service	401
prison service	400
collecting; authorised	412
commanding-	
armed forces-	
foreign and Commonwealth	M151
U.K.	M150
commercial (*railways*)	121
communications-	F463
Home Office	219
community	371
company (*fire service*)	M153
compensation (*coal mine*)	410
complaints	430
conciliation	363
conservation;	
assistant (*government*)	400
chief (*government*)	103
senior (*government*)	103
conservation (*government*)	132
consular	103
consultation (*coal mine*)	363
contracts; sales	121
contract(s)-	
building and contracting	111
government	701
manufacturing	110
control;	
air traffic	330
budget	410
building	311
development	261
dust (*coal mine*)	396
fire;	
principal (*fire service*)	153
materials (*coal mine*)	F441
pest	699
production	420
reservations (*air transport*)	420
rodent	699
roof (*coal mine*)	F597
senior (*Inland Revenue*)	132
smoke (*local government*)	348
space (*airport*)	330
Officer; *continued*	
control; *continued*	
stock (*coal mine*)	141
traffic	140
control-	
ambulance service	199
fire service	463
controlling (*P.O.*)	F940
costs; technical	360
Council; British	190
customs	613
Customs and Excise	613
cypher (*Foreign Office*)	400
deck-	332
dredging contractors	F885
defence;	
civil-	619
local government	102
dental	223
design; air traffic control	301
development;	
career	363
cost (*coal mine*)	251
curriculum	232
economic	252
tourist	123
discipline (borstal)	612
disinfecting	699
disposal; refuse	933
disposals (*government*)	132
distribution-	420
coal mine	420
gas board	113
district-	
coastguard service	F619
Forestry Commission	169
Min. of A.F.F.	399
river board	395
salvage corps	M153
division (*Ordnance Survey*)	103
divisional-	
fire service	M153
Forestry Commission	169
local government	102
duty (*airport*)	140
education-	232
museum	271
effluent (*water board, sewage works*)	395
electrical (*shipping*)	332
electronics (*shipping*)	332
employment;	
senior (*Dept. of Emp.*)	103
youth	392
employment-	363
Dept. of Emp. Job Centre	400
enforcement (*local government*)	303
engineer-	
hovercraft	332
airline	331
shipping	332
engineering-	
government	211
shipping	332
enquiry;	430
school	371
equipment (*local government*)	102
establishment-	363
government	103

Code number

- Officer; *continued*
  - estate-
    - *forestry* ... **169**
    - *local government* ... **401**
  - evaluation; job ... **364**
  - excise (*Customs and Excise*) **613**
  - executive;
    - chief-
      - *government* ... **103**
      - *P.O.* ... **131**
    - higher-
      - *government* ... **103**
      - *P.O.* ... **131**
    - senior-
      - *government* ... **103**
      - *P.O.* ... **131**
  - executive- *see also Manager*
    - *government* ... **132**
    - *insurance* ... **F410**
    - *local government* ... **102**
    - *P.L.A.* ... **140**
    - *P.O.* ... **F430**
  - expenditure (*coal mine*) ... **251**
  - experimental; ... **300**
    - chief- ... **209**
      - biologist ... **201**
      - chemist ... **200**
    - senior- ... **209**
      - biologist ... **201**
      - chemist ... **200**
  - fatstock (*Min. of A.F.F.*) **201**
  - field-
    - advisory ... **201**
    - professional ... **201**
    - *food products mfr.* ... **861**
    - *Min. of A.F.F.* ... **399**
  - finance;
    - deputy ... **410**
    - regional- ... **103**
      - *P.O.* ... **139**
  - finance- ... **410**
    - *coal mine* ... **139**
    - *hospital service* ... **139**
    - *local government* ... **102**
    - *P.O.* ... **139**
    - *telecoms* ... **139**
  - financial (*local government*) **102**
  - fingerprint; ... **610**
    - civilian ... **420**
  - fire;
    - chief ... **M153**
    - divisional ... **M153**
    - leading ... **611**
  - fire- ... **M153**
    - *coal mine* ... **611**
  - fire brigade ... **M153**
  - first-
    - hovercraft ... **332**
    - *airline* ... **331**
    - *fire service* ... **M153**
    - *shipping* ... **332**
  - fishery- ... **395**
    - *Min. of A.F.F.* ... **399**
  - flag (*armed forces-U.K.*) ... **150**
  - forestry ... **169**
  - freight (*air transport*) ... **420**
  - fuel ... **441**
  - government;
    - local; n.o.s. ... **401**
    - n.o.s. ... **400**
  - grade I-IV (*Dept. of Emp.*) **103**

Code number

- Officer; *continued*
  - grade V (*Dept. of Emp.*) **132**
  - grade VI (*Dept. of Emp.*) **400**
  - graphics ... **381**
  - group (*Min. of Defence*); **400**
    - chief ... **103**
    - senior ... **103**
  - health;
    - environmental ... **348**
    - mental ... **293**
    - public ... **348**
  - horticultural ... **201**
  - hospital (*prison service*) ... **641**
  - House; Trinity ... **332**
  - housing ... **M371**
  - hydrographic ... **313**
  - hygiene ... **340**
  - immigration; ... **613**
    - chief ... **155**
  - information; research ... **390**
  - information- ... **390**
    - public relations ... **123**
  - Inland Revenue ... **400**
  - inspecting (*Dept. of Transport*) ... **395**
  - inspection (*Dept. of Energy*) **211**
  - instructional ... **391**
  - insurance ... **410**
  - intelligence;
    - grade II (*Min. of Defence*) **390**
    - trade ... **252**
  - intelligence (*government*) **390**
  - investigating (*Dept. of Transport*) ... **395**
  - investigation;
    - chief (*Customs and Excise*) **155**
    - veterinary ... **224**
  - investigation-
    - *D.S.S.* ... **400**
    - *local government* ... **371**
  - labour ... **363**
  - land and minerals (*coal mine*) **262**
  - legal ... **240**
  - lettings (*local government*) **401**
  - liaison;
    - customer ... **179**
    - labour ... **363**
    - medical ... **710**
    - press ... **123**
    - sales ... **179**
    - technical ... **309**
  - liaison- ... **430**
    - *government* ... **103**
    - *manufacturing* ... **399**
    - *railways* ... **123**
  - licensing (*local government*) **102**
  - local I (*D.S.S.*) ... **132**
  - local II (*D.S.S.*) ... **400**
  - local authority ... **401**
  - magisterial ... **420**
  - maintenance- ... **896**
    - *local government* ... **F896**
    - *printing* ... **516**
    - *telecoms* ... **523**
  - management;
    - labour ... **363**
    - time ... **364**
  - manpower (*coal mine*) ... **363**
  - marketing ... **121**
  - markets (*Min. of A.F.F.*) ... **395**
  - measurement; work ... **364**

Code number

- Officer; *continued*
  - mechanisation ... **301**
  - medical- ... **220**
    - *armed forces-*
      - *foreign and Commonwealth* ... **M151**
      - *U.K.* ... **M150**
  - merchant navy ... **332**
  - meteorological ... **202**
  - methods ... **364**
  - mining ... **113**
  - navigating-
    - *airline* ... **331**
    - *shipping* ... **332**
  - non-commissioned-
    - *armed forces-*
      - *foreign and Commonwealth* ... **601**
      - *U.K.* ... **600**
  - nursery ... **650**
  - nursing ... **M340**
  - o & m- ... **364**
    - *government* ... **364**
    - *local government* ... **364**
  - occupational ... **347**
  - occupations ... **347**
  - operations; ... **199**
    - flight ... **330**
  - organisation (*government*) **364**
  - outdoor ... **941**
  - passenger (hovercraft) ... **F630**
  - patent(s) (*government*) ... **219**
  - patrol; ... **615**
    - security ... **615**
  - pensions ... **410**
  - personnel ... **363**
  - pest ... **699**
  - petty- ... **332**
    - *armed forces-*
      - *foreign and Commonwealth* ... **601**
      - *U.K.* ... **600**
  - placement ... **392**
  - planning-
    - *building and contracting-*
      - *local government* ... **261**
    - *manufacturing* ... **218**
  - police- ... **610**
    - non-statutory ... **615**
  - pollution (*waterboard*) ... **395**
  - port ... **140**
  - postal (*P.O.*) ... **411**
  - postal and telegraph ... **411**
  - press ... **380**
  - press and information ... **380**
  - prevention;
    - accident ... **396**
    - fire- ... **611**
      - *fire service* ... **611**
      - *hospital service* ... **611**
  - preventive; ... **613**
    - chief ... **155**
  - pricing ... **410**
  - principal-
    - *children's home* ... **370**
    - *government* ... **103**
    - *local government* ... **102**
    - *old people's home* ... **370**
    - *prison service* ... **154**
  - prison; ... **612**
    - chief ... **154**

	Code number
Officer; *continued*	
probation	**293**
procurement;	
facilities (T.V., etc.)	**701**
livestock; assistant	**701**
production;	
milk	**201**
technical	**399**
productivity and costs (*coal mine*)	**217**
professional and technological (*government*)-	
grade I, II *see Engineer-prof.-*	
grade III, IV	**301**
progress	**420**
promotion; sales	**121**
protection;	
consumer	**394**
fire	**M153**
publicity	**123**
purchasing	**701**
R.S.P.C.A.	**395**
radio-	**332**
aircraft	**463**
government	**199**
telecommunications	**463**
rates	**401**
rates and charges (*transport*)	**360**
rating	**360**
rating and valuation	**360**
rebate (*local government*)	**102**
reception	**460**
records; medical	**139**
recovery (debt)	**410**
recruiting-	
P.O.	**363**
telecoms	**363**
recruitment	**363**
refrigeration (*shipping*)	**332**
regional-	
public boards	**199**
government	**103**
R.S.P.C.A.	**395**
railways	**140**
registration	**430**
rehabilitation	**293**
relations;	
customer	**123**
industrial	**363**
labour	**363**
public	**123**
relieving-	**M371**
shipping	**332**
rent	**360**
repeater (*telecoms*)	**523**
research;	
medical	**300**
operational	**364**
political	**390**
veterinary	**224**
research-	**209**
agricultural	**201**
biochemical	**201**
biological	**201**
botanical	**201**
chemical	**200**
engineering-	
electrical	**212**
electronic	**213**
mechanical	**211**

	Code number
Officer; *continued*	
research- *continued*	
geological	**202**
government	**399**
historical	**399**
horticultural	**201**
meteorological	**202**
physical science	**202**
zoological	**201**
broadcasting	**399**
journalism	**399**
printing and publishing	**399**
university	**230**
reservations (*air transport*)	**420**
revenue	**410**
rodent	**699**
running and maintenance	**110**
safety;	**396**
fire	**611**
road	**396**
safety and training-	
coal mine-	**396**
above ground	**391**
salaries	**410**
sales	**121**
salvage;	
fire	**M153**
marine	**332**
salvage-	
coal mine	**597**
manufacturing	**919**
salvage corps	**M153**
salvage corps	**M153**
Salvation Army	**292**
sampling; milk	**200**
sanitary	**348**
schools	**371**
scientific;	
assistant	**300**
laboratory;	**300**
medical;	**201**
junior	**300**
scientific-	**209**
agricultural	**201**
biochemical	**201**
biological	**201**
botanical	**201**
chemical	**200**
engineering;	
electrical	**212**
electronic	**213**
mechanical	**211**
geological	**202**
horticultural	**201**
medical	**300**
meteorological	**202**
physical science	**202**
zoological	**201**
search	**420**
second-	
hovercraft	**332**
airline	**331**
banking	**411**
fire service	**M153**
shipping	**332**
section	**430**
securities-	
banking	**411**
government	**103**
security;	**615**
chief	**F615**

	Code number
Officer; *continued*	
security; *continued*	
fire	**611**
service;	
colonial	**400**
fire-	
fire service	**M153**
government	**M153**
foreign-	**400**
grade A1-A8; B1-B4	**103**
grade B5	**132**
health	**430**
training	**391**
services;	
cabin (*airline*)	**630**
management	**253**
productivity (*gas board*)	**364**
settlement	**430**
sheriff	**619**
shipping (*coal mine*)	**420**
ship's	**332**
signals (*Min. of Defence*)	**302**
staff;	
general-	
armed forces-	
foreign and Commonwealth	**M151**
U.K.	**M150**
staff-	
gas board	**363**
government	**103**
local government	**363**
railways	**363**
stamping	**410**
standards; trading	**394**
station-	
airport	**420**
ambulance service	**199**
coastguard service	**619**
fire service	**M153**
salvage corps	**M153**
statistical;	
grade D (*Min. of Defence*)	**400**
statistical-	
coal mine	**252**
electricity board	**420**
gas board	**420**
government	**252**
stock; live	**201**
store (*Min. of Defence*);	**141**
assistant	**F441**
stores;	
grade I (*Min. of Defence*)	**141**
stores-	**141**
Min. of Defence	**F441**
study;	**364**
work	**364**
substitution (*Min. of Defence*);	**132**
grade I	**103**
superannuation	**410**
supervising (*P.O.*)	**F940**
supplies;	**420**
chief	**122**
supply;	
armament	**701**
assistant (*Min. of Defence*)	**132**
chart (*Min. of Defence*)	**132**
fuel	**420**
supply-	
chemical mfr.	**420**
engineering	**420**

Code number

Officer; *continued*
supply- *continued*
Min. of Defence **701**
suppression; dust (*coal mine*) **396**
survey; social;
assistant (*government*) ... **132**
principal (*government*) ... **103**
senior (*government*) ... **103**
survey; social (*government*) **103**
survey-
government **262**
telecoms **523**
tax; **400**
higher grade **132**
taxation (*Inland Revenue*); **400**
higher grade **132**
technical;
assistant (*chemical mfr.*) **300**
carbonisation (*coal mine*) **219**
principal **211**
scientific (*coal mine*) ... **309**
telecommunications (*Civil Aviation Authority*) ... **529**
technical- **309**
work study **364**
chemical mfr. **200**
civil engineering **304**
gas board **301**
government- **309**
Min. of A.F.F. **201**
National Institute of Agricultural Botany ... **300**
telecoms **523**
telecommunications ... **463**
telegraph **463**
third-
fire service **M153**
shipping **332**
traffic;
telecommunications ... **F462**
traffic-
airline **140**
port authority **140**
road haulage **140**
telecoms **F462**
training; **391**
colliery **391**
sales **M391**
training and education ... **M391**
transport;
mechanical; **301**
chief **211**
motor-
P.O. **140**
telecoms **140**
transport- **140**
Dept. of Transport ... **301**
Trinity House **332**
trust **120**
vacancy (*Dept. of Emp.*) ... **400**
valuation **360**
ventilation (*coal mine*) ... **396**
veterinary **224**
visiting (*D.S.S.*) **400**
wages; assistant **410**
wages and control (*coal mine*) **F410**
warrant-
armed forces-
foreign and Commonwealth **601**

Code number

Officer; *continued*
warrant- *continued*
armed forces- continued
U.K. **600**
county court **619**
police service **F610**
wayleave **719**
welfare;
chief **371**
education **371**
welfare- **371**
P.O. **M371**
telecoms **371**
works **210**
workshops (*Min. of Defence*) **399**
youth **371**
Officer-
hovercraft **332**
airline **331**
armed forces-
foreign and Commonwealth **M151**
U.K. **M150**
fire service **M153**
insurance **410**
shipping **332**
W.R.N.S. **M150**
Officer-in-charge-
local government-
social services dept. ... **370**
Official;
airline **420**
bank **411**
brewery **430**
claims; marine **361**
court **420**
government **400**
insurance **719**
local government **401**
N.A.A.F.I. **953**
racecourse **387**
sports **387**
tax (*Inland Revenue*) ... **400**
Official-
charitable organisation ... **190**
coal mine **597**
dock board **430**
employers' association ... **190**
P.O. **430**
professional organisation **190**
trade union **190**
Off-licensee **179**
Oil rig worker-
oil rig construction ... **534**
well drilling **898**
Oilman; engine **820**
Oilman-
coal mine **894**
shipping **880**
Oiler;
frame (*textile mfr.*) ... **894**
loom **894**
machine; printing **894**
machine (*textile mfr.*) ... **894**
mould (asbestos) **829**
silk **552**
skin (leather) **810**
tube (*tube mfr.*) **839**
wool **814**
Oiler- **894**
canvas goods mfr. ... **552**

Code number

Oiler- *continued*
leather dressing **810**
varnish mfr. **829**
Oiler and bander (*textile mfr.*) **894**
Oiler and beltman **894**
Oiler and cleaner- **894**
textile mfr. **814**
Oiler and greaser- **894**
motor vehicles **540**
Oncost man (*mine, not coal*) **990**
Onsetter; **886**
staple pit (*coal mine*) ... **886**
Opener;
asbestos **811**
bale- **990**
textile mfr. (*opening dept.*) **811**
fibre **811**
hot (*steel mfr.*) **839**
piece-
glass mfr. **590**
textile mfr. **814**
plate (tinplate) **839**
Opener-
foundry **911**
textile mfr.- **813**
fibre opening **811**
tinplate mfr. **839**
Operative; pit **898**
Operator;
acidifier **809**
addressograph **490**
assembly *see Assembler*
audio-visual aids **386**
auto **841**
autoclave-
asbestos composition goods mfr. **829**
chemical mfr. **820**
food products mfr. ... **809**
glass mfr. **829**
banbury (*rubber mfr.*) ... **824**
banda **490**
bath; salt (*metal goods*) ... **833**
bay (*garage*) **540**
belt (conveyor) **889**
bench; draw **831**
benzole **820**
bingo **699**
blending (*custard powder mfr.*)... ... ... **809**
block; bull **831**
board; test **529**
boiler; **893**
sugar **809**
boom (*film production*) ... **386**
boot **555**
booth; toll **412**
brake-
bakery **800**
steelworks **899**
bridge; weigh **863**
bridge- **889**
coal mine **886**
building **509**
bullard **840**
bulldozer **885**
burner; kiln (*carbon goods mfr.*) **829**
burster **490**
button **889**
cable- **463**

	Code number
Operator; *continued*	
cable- *continued*	
cable mfr.	**899**
calender-	
laundry	**673**
paper mfr.	**821**
plastics mfr.	**825**
rubber mfr.	**824**
textile mfr.	**552**
camera; video	**386**
camera-	
photocopying	**490**
film production	**386**
printing	**386**
process engraving	**386**
television service	**386**
capstan-	**840**
railways	**889**
capsulation	**820**
car; ingot	**889**
card;	
cotton	**811**
punch	**490**
cash and wrap	**721**
caster; monotype	**560**
castings-	
metal mfr.	**839**
rubber goods mfr.	**824**
caterpillar	**885**
cathedral	**590**
centrifugal (starch)	**809**
centrifuge (chemicals)	**820**
charger (*rolling mill*)	**887**
check-out	**721**
chemical	**820**
cinema	**386**
cinematograph	**386**
circuit; printed	**850**
clipper; veneer	**897**
coach	**873**
coal (*power station*)	**893**
coatings; plastic (*plastics goods mfr.*)	**834**
coil; steel	**839**
colorado beetle	**699**
column (*oxygen mfr.*)	**820**
combine	**899**
communications	**463**
composer; IBM	**560**
compressor-	**893**
paper, leather board mfr.	**821**
comptometer	**490**
computer	**490**
consol	**555**
control;	
fire *(fire service)*	**463**
pest	**699**
sound	**386**
control-	
railways	**893**
steelworks	**839**
control room (electric)	**893**
conveyor	**889**
cooker-	
canned foods	**809**
dry batteries	**899**
cooler; brine (milk)	**809**
crane	**886**
cropper	**899**
crusher *(mine)*	**890**
cuber	**809**
Operator; *continued*	
cutter; coal	**597**
degrease(r)	**839**
densification (chemicals)	**820**
depiler (*metal mfr.*)	**839**
deseaming (steel)	**537**
detector (*engineering*)	**860**
dictaphone	**452**
die cast	**531**
dip (*metal trades*)	**834**
disc (*coal mine*)	**597**
disintegrator (chemicals)	**820**
display; visual	**490**
disposal; refuse	**999**
drawtwist	**811**
dredger	**885**
drier (plasterboard)	**829**
drier's; grain (milk foods)	**809**
drill;	**840**
pneumatic	**885**
drott	**885**
drum room	**810**
dry cleaner-	
coal mine	**890**
laundry	**673**
drying room	**829**
duplicator	**490**
dyeline	**490**
edit; tape	**490**
electrical (*rolling mill*)	**889**
elevator	**886**
embosser (*engineering*)	**841**
engine;	**893**
winding	**886**
evaporator-	
chemical mfr.	**820**
food products mfr.	**809**
excavator	**885**
extruder-	
chemical mfr.	**820**
metal trades	**839**
plastics mfr.	**825**
rubber goods mfr.	**824**
fan (*coal mine*)	**999**
film; micro	**490**
filter; drum; rotary (*chemical mfr.*)	**820**
filter (*whisky distilling*)	**801**
flexowriter	**490**
flotation; froth (*coal mine*)	**890**
forge	**839**
frame; spinning	**812**
freezer (*fruit, vegetable preserving, ice cream making*)	**809**
froster (*fruit, vegetable preserving, ice cream making*)	**809**
furnace;	
annealing	**833**
carburising	**833**
electric (*enamelling*)	**829**
electrical (*metal mfr.*)	**830**
glass	**823**
pusher slab	**839**
treatment; heat	**833**
furnace-	
ceramics mfr.	**823**
glass mfr.	**823**
metal mfr.	**830**
garnett	**811**
Operator; *continued*	
gas	**820**
gauger (cartridges)	**860**
gearhead	**893**
glass; fibre	**590**
glazing (explosives)	**820**
gravure (printer's)	**891**
grinder	**840**
grinder and roller (*cheese processing*)	**809**
guide	**820**
guillotine-	
coach trimming	**559**
coal mine	**899**
metal trades	**899**
paper goods mfr.	**822**
plastics goods mfr.	**825**
pressed woollen felt mfr.	**814**
printing	**822**
gun; cement	**929**
hammer	**839**
heat treatment-	
carbon	**820**
carbon goods	**829**
metal	**833**
heel bar	**555**
hoist	**886**
homogeniser (ice cream)	**809**
hot	**839**
house;	
power	**893**
tin (tinplate)	**834**
hydrate	**829**
hydraulic	**999**
hydro-	**673**
laundry	**673**
textile finishing	**814**
hydro-extractor-	**814**
chemical mfr.	**820**
laundry	**673**
tannery	**810**
IBM	**490**
ICL	**490**
incinerator	**999**
intertype	**560**
J.C.B.	**885**
jetty	**930**
jig (*textile mfr.*)	**814**
jointer	**579**
kardex	**490**
kettle (*chemical mfr.*)	**820**
keyboard (typesetting)	**560**
key; punch	**490**
key-punch	**490**
key-to-disc	**490**
kiln-	**829**
ceramics mfr.	**823**
wood products mfr.	**821**
knife; band (*textile mfr.*)	**814**
lamp (*electric lamp mfr.*)	**860**
last; seat	**555**
lathe-	
carbon goods mfr.	**899**
coal mine	**510**
industrial felt mfr.	**814**
metal trades	**840**
wood products mfr.	**897**
laundry	**673**
lift;	**955**
fork	**887**
limelight	**386**

	Code number
Operator; *continued*	
line;	
assembly (*vehicle mfr.*)	**851**
drag	**885**
dye	**490**
paint	**869**
pickle (*steel mfr.*) ...	**839**
trim (*motor vehicle mfr.*)	**851**
line-	**569**
electrical	**850**
engineering	**851**
linotype	**560**
litho; offset	**569**
loader; power	**597**
loom	**552**
ludlow	**560**
machine *see Machinist*	
machine tool	**840**
mangle;	**839**
bleaching	**552**
manifold	**820**
manipulator (*steel mfr.*) ...	**839**
mill;	
ball-	
ceramics mfr.	**829**
chemical mfr.	**820**
boring	**840**
foil (aluminium)	**832**
hot (*metal trades*) ...	**832**
mortar	**829**
plano	**840**
pug (chemicals)	**820**
rolling	**832**
sand (*steelworks*) ...	**899**
saw	**897**
sheeting (chemicals) ...	**820**
tube	**839**
mill-	
grain milling	**809**
plastics goods mfr. ...	**825**
rolling mill	**832**
rubber goods mfr. ...	**824**
steel foundry	**840**
milling-	
metal trades	**840**
soap mfr.	**820**
mixer-	
cast concrete products mfr.	**829**
sugar confectionery mfr.	**809**
mixing	**820**
monotype	**560**
moulder (chocolate) ...	**809**
Multilith	**569**
multi-roller (hats)	**814**
N.C.R.	**490**
night (*telephone service*) ...	**462**
offset	**569**
oil (*metal trades*)	**912**
oven;	
coke	**820**
vacuum (*food products mfr.*)	**809**
pan; vacuum-	
chemical mfr.	**820**
food products mfr. ...	**809**
pan (*food products mfr.*) ...	**809**
panel (*steel mfr.*)	**889**
pantograph	**899**
photo (*lithography*) ...	**386**
photographic	**386**
Operator; *continued*	
photogravure studio ...	**386**
photo-litho	**386**
photometer	**860**
pilger	**839**
pipe; blow (quartz) ...	**590**
plant;	
bakery	**800**
benzole	**820**
brick	**823**
builder's	**885**
chemical	**820**
chlorination	**820**
concrete	**829**
constructional	**885**
cracker (*oil refining*) ...	**820**
degreasing	**839**
dehydration (*fruit, vegetable preserving*) ...	**809**
distillation (chemicals) ...	**820**
drying-	**999**
food products mfr. ...	**809**
flotation	**890**
gas	**820**
mobile (*steel mfr.*) ...	**889**
oxygen	**820**
painting; electrophoretic	**869**
power	**893**
sedimentation (*chemical mfr.*)	**820**
sinter	**839**
spray (*milk processing*)	**809**
sterilising (surgical dressings)	**552**
sulphur	**820**
vacuum (metallisation) ...	**834**
water softener	**892**
water treatment	**892**
plant-	
bakery	**800**
building and contracting	**885**
chemical mfr.	**820**
coal gas, coke ovens ...	**820**
electricity board ...	**893**
nuclear power station ...	**893**
oil refining	**820**
paper mfr.	**821**
plastics goods mfr. ...	**825**
quarry	**898**
rubber goods mfr. ...	**824**
sewage works	**892**
water works	**892**
plastic(s)	**825**
plating	**834**
point; transfer	**889**
points (*railways*)	**884**
pot (*aluminium mfr.*) ...	**830**
preparation; data	**490**
preserving (fruit pulp) ...	**809**
press *see Presser*	
presser; steam	**673**
print; photo	**490**
print room	**490**
printer's	**891**
process; chemical	**820**
process-	
aircraft component mfr.	**899**
chemical mfr.	**820**
clay extraction	**890**
man-made fibre mfr. ...	**826**
oil refining	**820**
Operator; *continued*	
process- *continued*	
plastics goods mfr. ...	**825**
plastics mfr.	**820**
printing	**569**
processor; word	**452**
producer; gas	**820**
production *see Process worker-*	
profile	**840**
pullover (*footwear mfr.*) ...	**555**
pulpit (*steel mfr.*)	**832**
pump	**999**
pumphouse; vacuum (*oil refining*)	**820**
punch; key	**490**
punch-	**490**
paper goods mfr. ...	**822**
pusher-	
coke ovens	**889**
metal mfr.	**839**
radio	**463**
recorder;	
film	**386**
videotape	**386**
refinery	**820**
refrigerator	**999**
reproduction (*atomic energy establishment*)	**820**
research (*oil refining*) ...	**300**
retort-	
coal gas production ...	**820**
food products mfr. ...	**809**
ring	**812**
rodent	**699**
rolls; calender (*plastics goods mfr.*)	**825**
room;	
closing (*footwear mfr.*) ...	**555**
control-	
electrical	**893**
ambulance service ...	**463**
fire service	**463**
tool	**840**
ropeway	**889**
rotaprint	**490**
rotary (*printing*)	**891**
router	**840**
sales; telephone	**792**
sand blast	**844**
saw;	
band-	
wood	**897**
asbestos goods mfr. ...	**829**
metal trades	**899**
circular (meat)	**581**
saw-	
metal trades	**899**
sawmilling	**897**
scanner (*printing*)	**386**
scoreboard	**699**
screen;	**890**
silk	**563**
separator; magnetic ...	**890**
separator (*food processing*)	**809**
shear(s);	**899**
flying	**839**
sheathing (explosives) ...	**599**
shoe	**555**
shop; paint (*vehicle mfr.*)	**596**
shot blast	**844**
sieve; rotex (*tobacco mfr.*)	**802**

Code number

Operator; *continued*
sieve (*food products mfr.*) **809**
sifting room **809**
signal (*railways*) **883**
silo (*tobacco mfr.*) **441**
sinter **839**
slitter (*metal mfr.*) **899**
slusher (*coal mine*) **889**
softener; water **892**
spectroscope **300**
spray; mechanical **596**
steel (*metal mfr.*) **839**
stenter **552**
sterilizer;
milk **809**
telephone **958**
sterilizer (*hospital service*) **641**
still **820**
stretcher (*metal mfr.*) **899**
submersible **599**
supermarket- **179**
employee **441**
swaging **839**
switch (*coal mine*) **889**
switchboard-
telephone **462**
power station **893**
tabulator **490**
take-down (abrasive sheet) **821**
tandem (chocolate) **809**
tank;
asphalt **929**
glass **590**
telecine **386**
telecommunications **463**
telegraph **463**
telephone; **462**
radio **463**
teleprinter **463**
teletype **463**
telex **463**
till (*retail trade*) **721**
tilter (steel) **830**
tippler **889**
tool; machine **840**
totalisator **411**
tow; ski **699**
transfer (*metal mfr.*) **839**
transport **872**
traverser; wagon **889**
treater (*petroleum refining*) **820**
treatment;
heat-
carbon **820**
carbon goods **829**
metal **833**
water **892**
trimming; bullet **899**
triples **809**
tube-
lamp, valve mfr. **850**
plastics goods mfr. **825**
tumbler-
ceramics mfr. **591**
laundry **673**
tunnel (gelatine, glue, size) **820**
turbine **893**
turntable **889**
turret **840**
twisting **812**
typographical **560**

Code number

Operator; *continued*
unit- **893**
dry cleaning **673**
textile finishing **552**
v.d.u. **490**
vat (*metal mfr.*) **834**
vessel; reaction (chemicals) **820**
viscoliser (ice cream) **809**
votator **809**
washery **890**
wheelabrator **844**
willey (wool) **811**
winch **886**
winder; fibreglass **814**
winder (*paper mfr.*) **821**
wireless **463**
wireline **898**
works; sewage **892**
xerox **490**
x-ray **342**
Operator-
agricultural machinery **901**
construction machinery **885**
office machinery- **490**
word processor **452**
oil refining **820**
radio relay service **463**
Royal Mint **841**
Ophthalmologist **220**
Optical worker **590**
Optician; **222**
dispensing **345**
manufacturing **590**
ophthalmic **222**
Optologist **222**
Optometrist **222**
Orchestrator **385**
Order lad **941**
Order man **441**
Order room hand **441**
Orderly;
civilian **670**
domestic (*hospital service*) **958**
hospital **641**
kitchen **952**
market **990**
medical **641**
mess **953**
nursing **641**
road **957**
room; dining **953**
sanitary **990**
street **957**
ward **641**
Orderly-
office **941**
hospital service **641**
institution **644**
Organiser;
appeals **123**
catering **174**
defence; civil **102**
district (*community services*) **293**
drama **176**
exhibition **176**
help; home **371**
meals; school **174**
music **176**
national (*charitable organisation*) **190**
playgroup **651**

Code number

Organiser; *continued*
programme (*broadcasting*) **384**
publicity **123**
safety; road **396**
sales **121**
welfare **371**
youth **371**
Organiser-
vocational training **391**
political party **190**
trade union **190**
welfare services **371**
Organist **385**
Originator (*printing*) **560**
Ornament worker; black **518**
Ornamenter-
ceramics mfr. **590**
japanned ware mfr. **869**
Ornithologist **201**
Orseller (net) **814**
Orthodontist **223**
Orthoptist **347**
Orthotist **346**
Osseller (net) **814**
Osteopath **347**
Ostler **902**
Otologist **220**
Otorhinolaryngologist **220**
Outfitter (*retail trade*) **179**
Oven hand-
bakery **800**
ceramics mfr. **823**
micanite mfr. **829**
Ovenman;
biscuit **823**
coke **820**
glost **823**
malleable iron **833**
Ovenman-
abrasive coated paper cloth mfr. **821**
bakery **800**
brake lining mfr. **829**
ceramics mfr. **823**
food products mfr. **809**
japanning, enamelling **829**
Oven worker; coke **820**
Ovensman (*bakery*) **800**
Overman; **113**
deputy *(coal mine)* **F597**
Overhauler-
vehicles **540**
rag sorting **811**
tramways **873**
Overlocker **553**
Overlooker;
cloth **861**
frame (maintenance) **516**
greenhouse **869**
loom-
maintenance- **516**
textile mfr.-
textile weaving **550**
weaving (maintenance) **516**
wire **599**
Overlooker- *see also Foreman*
maintenance (*textile mfr.*) **516**
clothing mfr. **861**
hat mfr. **861**
lace examining **861**
warping **F552**

Code number

P

P.C. ... **610**
P.O. n.o.s. (*local government*) **102**
P. and T.O. (*government*)-
  grade I, II *see Engineer- prof.*-
  grade III, IV ... **301**
Packman (*woollen carding*) **919**
Packer;
  asbestos ... **929**
  cable ... **862**
  chlorine ... **862**
  cop ... **862**
  drum; furnace ... **863**
  flock (*bedding mfr.*) ... **554**
  gland ... **894**
  kiln ... **823**
  oven (*foundry*) ... **839**
  potter's ... **823**
  sagger ... **829**
  shelf (*retail trade*) ... **954**
  shoddy ... **811**
  wheel ... **899**
  wool ... **862**
Packer- ... **862**
  coal mine ... **597**
  furniture mfr. ... **862**
  mine, not coal ... **889**
  shipbuilding ... **534**
  steel mfr. ... **862**
Packer and sorter (*laundry*) **862**
Packer and stacker ... **862**
Packer-driver ... **872**
Packer-hooper ... **862**
Packer-labourer ... **862**
Padder; colour ... **869**
Padder-
  clothing mfr. ... **553**
  leather dressing ... **810**
  textile mfr. ... **552**
Paediatrician ... **220**
Page (*hotel*) ... **951**
Page boy ... **951**
Pager-
  bookbinding ... **562**
  printing ... **569**
  type foundry ... **862**
Paint hand ... **869**
Paint worker-
  paint mfr. ... **820**
  vehicle mfr. ... **596**
Painter;
  aircraft ... **596**
  bottom ... **869**
  car ... **596**
  coach ... **596**
  design ... **310**
  enamel ... **591**
  engraver's (*textile printing*) **599**
  flower ... **591**
  freehand ... **591**
  glaze ... **591**
  hide (*tannery*) ... **810**
  house ... **507**
  landscape ... **381**
  marine ... **381**
  miniature ... **381**
  portrait ... **381**
  pottery ... **591**
  roller (*textile printing*) ... **599**
  rough (*glass mfr.*) ... **591**

Painter; *continued*
  scenic ... **507**
  skin (*fellmongering*) ... **810**
  slip ... **591**
  spray- ... **596**
    ceramics mfr. ... **591**
    painting and decorating **507**
  tin ... **596**
  toy ... **869**
  underglaze ... **591**
  wagon ... **596**
Painter- ... **507**
  artificial flower mfr. ... **869**
  ceramics mfr. ... **591**
  garage ... **596**
  glass etching ... **591**
  roller engraving ... **599**
  tannery ... **810**
  textile designing ... **430**
  vehicle mfr. ... **596**
Painter and decorator ... **507**
Painter and glazier ... **507**
Painter hand ... **869**
Painter-decorator ... **507**
Pairer-
  corset mfr. ... **859**
  hosiery mfr. ... **862**
Palaeographist ... **291**
Palaeontologist ... **202**
Palm and needle hand ... **553**
Palmist ... **699**
Pan hand (*brush mfr.*) ... **599**
Pan man;
  acid ... **820**
  boiling (foods) ... **809**
  vacuum (*food products mfr.*) **809**
Pan man-
  catering, hotels, etc. ... **952**
  ceramics mfr. ... **829**
  chemical mfr. ... **820**
  coal mine ... **597**
  food products mfr. ... **809**
  paper mfr. ... **821**
  sugar refining ... **809**
Pan worker; revolving (*sugar confectionery mfr.*) ... **809**
Panelman (*oil refining*) ... **820**
Panner-
  coal mine ... **597**
  tobacco mfr. ... **802**
Panner-out ... **919**
Pansman (*sugar refining*) ... **809**
Pantographer-
  embroidery mfr. ... **553**
  glassware mfr. ... **591**
  lace mfr. ... **559**
  roller engraving ... **569**
Pantry man ... **952**
Paper boy (*newsagents*) ... **941**
Paper girl (*newsagents*) ... **941**
Paper hand (piano hammers) **897**
Paper man (*plasterboard mfr.*) **829**
Paper worker-
  paper mfr. ... **821**
  printing ... **919**
Paperer;
  chair ... **869**
  sand- ... **869**
    mask mfr. ... **599**
  tin (*bakery*) ... **800**

Paperer-
  ceramics mfr. ... **862**
  lace mfr. ... **862**
  tobacco pipe mfr. ... **897**
Paperer-on (whips) ... **859**
Paperhanger ... **507**
Paperkeeper ... **420**
Paraflow man (brewing) ... **801**
Parasitologist ... **201**
Paratrooper-
  armed forces-
    foreign and Commonwealth ... **601**
    U.K. ... **600**
Parceller ... **862**
Parchmentiser ... **821**
Parent;
  foster ... **370**
  house ... **370**
Parer; sheet (*steelworks*) ... **899**
Parer-
  clothing mfr. ... **559**
  footwear mfr. ... **555**
  leather dressing ... **810**
  rolling mill ... **899**
  saw mfr. ... **899**
Parish worker ... **371**
Parlourman ... **958**
Parlourmaid ... **958**
Parochial worker ... **371**
Partner; *see also Owner-*
  dancing ... **239**
Partsman ... **441**
Passer;
  cigar ... **869**
  cloth ... **861**
  final (*tailoring*) ... **861**
  finished (*textile mfr.*) ... **861**
  garment ... **861**
  glove; finished ... **861**
  machine (*clothing mfr.*) ... **861**
  piece ... **861**
  proof (*lithography*) ... **569**
  sample ... **F830**
Passer-
  brush mfr. ... **869**
  canned food mfr. ... **861**
  cardboard box mfr. ... **861**
  clothing mfr. ... **861**
  footwear mfr. ... **869**
  fur goods mfr. ... **861**
  glove mfr. ... **861**
  metal trades- ... **860**
    rolling mill ... **839**
  textile goods mfr. ... **861**
  textile mfr. ... **861**
Paster;
  battery ... **899**
  biscuit ... **800**
  lead ... **899**
  sock ... **859**
Paster-
  accumulator mfr. ... **899**
  biscuit mfr. ... **800**
  footwear mfr. ... **859**
  leather dressing ... **810**
  leather goods mfr. ... **859**
  paper goods mfr. ... **859**
Pasteuriser- ... **809**
  brewery ... **801**
  milk processing ... **809**

	Code number
Pastor	**292**
Pastry hand	**580**
Pastrycook-	**620**
bakery	**580**
Patcher;	
cupola (*steelworks*)	**500**
oven	**500**
vessel	**500**
wool	**559**
Patcher (*lithography*)	**569**
Patenter; wire	**833**
Pathologist;	**201**
plant	**201**
veterinary	**201**
Patrolman;	
belt	**889**
crossing; school	**619**
road (*motoring organisation*)	**540**
Patrolman-	**615**
coal mine	**889**
motor vehicle mfr.	**860**
motoring organisation	**540**
railways	**922**
Pattern hand (*lace mfr.*)	**430**
Pattern man (*textile mfr.*)	**441**
Pattern room hand	**441**
Pattern room man	**441**
Pattern room worker (*wallpaper mfr.*)	**569**
Pavior;	**924**
tar	**923**
tile	**506**
Pawnbroker	**179**
Pearler	**820**
Peat worker	**902**
Pedicurist	**661**
Pedlar	**732**
Peeler;	
lemon	**809**
orange	**809**
Peeler (*food processing*)	**809**
Pegger;	
barrel (*textile mfr.*)	**814**
bobbin	**814**
card	**814**
dobby	**814**
Pegger-	
footwear mfr.	**555**
textile weaving	**814**
Penciller-	
clothing mfr.	**559**
textile mfr.	**814**
Percher (*textile mfr.*)	**861**
Perforator;	
card-	
jacquard card cutting	**814**
stationery mfr.	**569**
jacquard	**814**
pattern (*paper dress pattern mfr.*)	**569**
stamp	**569**
Perforator-	
bookbinding	**569**
embroidery mfr.	**559**
footwear mfr.	**555**
glove mfr.	**559**
jacquard card cutting	**814**
metal trades	**841**
Perfumer	**820**
Perfusionist (*hospital service*)	**346**
Periodontist	**223**
Permanent way man	**922**
Perryman	**801**
Peter; steeple	**505**
Pewterer-	**533**
brewery	**532**
Pharmaceutical worker	**820**
Pharmaceutist	**221**
Pharmacist	**221**
Pharmacologist	**221**
Philatelist	**179**
Philologist	**291**
Phlebotomist	**641**
Phosphater	**834**
Photocopier	**490**
Photographer	**386**
Photogravure worker	**560**
Phrenologist	**699**
Physician	**220**
Physicist	**202**
Physiologist	**201**
Physiotherapist;	**343**
superintendent	**F343**
Pianist	**385**
Picker;	
bobbin (*textile mfr.*)	**889**
bone (*ceramics mfr.*)	**829**
bowl	**863**
carpet	**553**
cloth	**553**
coal (*railways*)	**990**
confectionery	**861**
cotton	**863**
flint	**890**
flock	**863**
flower	**902**
fruit-	
farming	**902**
food processing	**809**
hop	**902**
lime	**863**
metal (*mine, not coal*)	**890**
mushroom	**902**
nut	**860**
order (*retail trade*)	**862**
pea-	
farming	**902**
food processing	**863**
potato	**902**
prawn	**863**
roller	**814**
silk	**811**
slate	**930**
stilt	**869**
stone-	
coal mine	**890**
stone dressing	**863**
thimble	**869**
yarn	**553**
Picker-	
building and contracting	**863**
ceramics mfr.	**829**
clothing mfr.	**557**
coal mine	**890**
engineering	**441**
food processing	**809**
hat mfr.	**810**
mine, not coal	**890**
paper mfr.	**861**
stone dressing	**863**
textile mfr.-	**553**
flock mfr.	**863**
Picker- *continued*	
textile mfr.- continued	
silk throwing	**811**
wool sorting	**863**
Picker-out (*galvanized sheet mfr.*)	**860**
Picker-packer (*vehicle mfr.*)	**863**
Picker-up-	
galvanized sheet mfr.	**889**
textile mfr.	**814**
tobacco mfr.	**802**
Pickle worker	**809**
Pickler;	
aluminium	**839**
beef	**809**
cloth	**552**
iron	**839**
sleeper	**821**
steel; strip	**839**
tube	**839**
underhand	**839**
wire	**839**
Pickler-	
fellmongering	**810**
food products mfr.	**809**
metal trades	**839**
tannery	**810**
textile mfr.	**552**
Pickman (*coal mine*)	**441**
Piece worker (*coal mine*)	**597**
Piecener	**812**
Piecer;	
belt	**555**
cotton	**812**
cross	**812**
mule	**812**
ring	**812**
side	**812**
silk	**812**
sole	**859**
twiner	**812**
waste	**811**
Piecer-	
leather dressing	**810**
textile mfr.	**812**
Piecer-out (*flax mfr.*)	**812**
Piecer-up (*clothing mfr.*)	**553**
Pier head man	**889**
Pierman	**889**
Pierce worker	**518**
Piercer;	
saw	**518**
strap	**555**
Piercer-	
ceramics mfr.	**591**
jewellery and plate mfr.	**518**
pen nib mfr.	**841**
tube mfr.	**839**
Pigman	**900**
Piggeryman	**900**
Piler;	**889**
bobbin	**814**
hot	**889**
roving	**811**
Pilot;	
canal	**332**
dock	**332**
helicopter	**331**
hovercraft	**M332**
river	**332**
submersible	**599**

	Code number
Pilot; *continued*	
test	**331**
Pilot-	
airline	**331**
shipping	**332**
Pinner; woollen comb	**851**
Pinner-	
ceramics mfr.	**590**
lamp, valve mfr.	**850**
metal trades	**851**
textile mfr.-	**552**
textile making-up	**814**
Pinner-on (*textile mfr.*)	**814**
Pipe man; brine	**532**
Pipe man (*coal mine*)	**532**
Piper; sugar	**809**
Piper (*sugar confectionery mfr.*)	**809**
Pisciculturist	**903**
Pit hand (*tube mfr.*)	**830**
Pit man-	
coal mine-	**597**
above ground	**910**
mine, not coal	**898**
steelworks-	**839**
soaking pit	**830**
Pit worker (*coal mine*)	**910**
Pitch man	**919**
Pitcher;	
flour	**919**
stone	**896**
Pitcher-	
building and contracting	**896**
ceramics mfr.	**829**
meat market	**931**
Pitcher and malletter	**590**
Placer;	
biscuit	**823**
glost	**823**
kiln	**823**
sanitary ware	**823**
tile	**823**
Placer (*ceramics mfr.*)	**823**
Plaiter-	
cordage	**814**
textile mfr.	**814**
Planer;	
die	**513**
edge; plate	**899**
slate	**500**
stone	**500**
Planer-	
metal	**513**
plastics	**825**
stereotypes	**560**
wood	**897**
coal mine	**513**
metal trades	**513**
Planer and slotter; wall	**513**
Planisher; iron	**533**
Planisher (*sheet metal goods mfr.*)	**533**
Planker	**814**
Planner;	
carpet	**506**
clothier's	**559**
die (*footwear mfr.*)	**555**
flight	**330**
footwear	**382**
gravure	**560**
group (*coal mine*)	**218**
Planner; *continued*	
kitchen	**381**
linoleum	**506**
lithographic	**560**
load	**889**
materials	**399**
media	**123**
mine (*coal mine*)	**218**
process	**218**
production	**218**
progress	**420**
sales	**121**
town	**261**
traffic;	**420**
air	**330**
transport	**420**
work	**420**
Planner-	
clothing mfr.	**559**
engineering	**218**
printing	**560**
Planner-estimator	**360**
Plant hand;	
acid	**820**
bakery	**800**
Plant man;	
benzole	**820**
dehydration (*food products mfr.*)	**809**
Plant man (*chemical mfr.*)	**820**
Plant worker;	
gas	**820**
hydrating; lime	**890**
screening	**890**
sinter	**839**
Plant worker-	
bakery	**800**
chemical mfr.	**820**
coke ovens	**820**
Planter;	
coffee	**160**
rubber	**160**
tea	**160**
tobacco	**160**
tree	**904**
Plasterer; fibrous	**502**
Plasterer-	**502**
cast concrete products mfr.	**599**
coke ovens	**919**
plaster cast mfr.	**590**
Plasterer and decorator	**509**
Plastics worker	**825**
Plate hand-	
printing	**560**
rope mfr.	**814**
Plate man-	
asphalt spreading	**885**
hotel, etc.	**952**
Plate worker;	
iron	**534**
metal	**534**
tin-	**533**
tinplate mfr.-	
female	**912**
male	**839**
zinc	**533**
Plater;	
barrel	**834**
boiler	**534**
brass	**834**
bridge	**534**
Plater; *continued*	
cadmium	**834**
chrome	**834**
chromium	**834**
constructional	**534**
copper	**834**
dip	**834**
electro	**834**
engineer's; gas	**534**
framing	**534**
gold	**834**
hand	**834**
heavy	**534**
hoe	**530**
hot	**552**
iron	**534**
last	**533**
light	**534**
lock	**834**
metal;	**834**
white	**834**
needle	**834**
nickel	**834**
roof	**534**
shell	**534**
ship('s)	**534**
shovel	**530**
silver	**834**
steel	**534**
stem	**534**
structural	**534**
tank	**534**
tin-	
tinplate mfr.	**834**
tinplate printing	**891**
tool; edge-	**530**
surgical instrument mfr.	**834**
wire	**834**
Plater-	
bookbinding	**562**
chemical mfr.	**534**
coal mine	**534**
construction	**534**
fertiliser mfr.	**820**
gas board	**534**
leather dressing	**810**
metal trades-	**534**
boiler mfr.	**534**
boot last mfr.	**533**
constructional engineering	**534**
cutlery mfr.	**530**
edge tool mfr.	**530**
electroplating	**834**
iron tank mfr.	**534**
railway locomotive shop	**534**
shipbuilding	**534**
steelworks	**534**
paper mfr.	**821**
textile mfr.	**552**
Plater and gilder	**834**
Plater-down (*textile making-up*)	**814**
Plater-welder	**534**
Platform man (*steelworks*)	**839**
Player-	
musical instruments	**385**
sports	**387**
Playwright	**380**
Pleater;	
accordion	**814**
cloth	**814**

	Code number
Pleater-	
clothing mfr.	556
incandescent mantle mfr.	599
textile mfr.	552
Plier; needle (*hosiery and knit-wear mfr.*)	551
Plough man	901
Plucker; chicken	582
Plucker (*poultry dressing*)	582
Plugger; rod; fishing	859
Plugger (*stoneware pipe mfr.*)	599
Plumber	532
Plumber and decorator	532
Plumber and gasfitter	532
Plumber and jointer	524
Plumber-jointer	524
Plumber-welder	532
Pocket hand	556
Podiatrist	344
Poet	380
Pointer;	
bar	899
brick	500
hook; fish	841
machine	553
rod (*wire mfr.*)	899
Pointer-	
bolt mfr.	899
building and contracting	500
pin, needle mfr.	841
screw mfr.	899
wire mfr.	899
Pointsman-	884
L.R.T.	889
road transport	889
Poker-in (*coke ovens*)	919
Policeman-	
non-statutory	615
airport	610
docks	610
government	610
Ministry of Defence	610
police force	610
railways	610
Polisher;	
bakelite	825
barrel (gun)	842
bobbin;	842
wood	579
boot	555
brass	842
brush	810
button	899
car; motor (*garage*)	958
celluloid	825
cellulose	869
cutlery	842
cycle	842
diamond	518
die	842
edge	591
emery	842
enamel	591
fibre	552
fine (glass)	591
floor-	958
building and contracting	896
frame;	842
spectacle	825
french	507
furniture	507
Polisher; *continued*	
glass	591
glost	591
gold-	842
ceramics mfr.	591
granite	500
hame	842
hand (*glass mfr.*)	591
hat	559
heald	579
ivory	599
jewellery	842
key (*piano mfr.*)	593
lathe-	
metal trades	842
stone dressing	500
lens	591
lime	842
marble	500
metal	842
mirror (*cutlery mfr.*)	842
mould (metal)	842
pen; fountain	899
piano	507
pipe (wood)	579
plate (*precious metal mfr.*)	842
plater's	842
racquet; tennis	596
roll (*tinplate mfr.*)	842
roller	842
sand	842
silver-	842
hotels, catering, etc.	952
slab; optical	591
slate	500
spoon and fork	842
spray	596
steel; stainless	842
stick	869
stone-	500
lithography	899
terrazzo	506
tile-	
asbestos-cement goods mfr.	599
ceramics mfr.	591
tin	842
tube	899
twine	552
wire	899
wood	507
yarn	552
Polisher-	
brass musical instruments mfr.	842
ceramics mfr.	591
clog mfr.	555
footwear mfr.	555
furniture mfr.	507
glass mfr.	591
hat mfr.	559
leather dressing	810
metal trades	842
plastics goods mfr.	825
stone dressing	500
straw hat mfr.	552
terrazzo floor laying	506
textile mfr.	552
Pontoon man	889
Popper	898
Port worker	930
Porter;	
coal	931
despatch	931
dock	930
domestic (*hospital service*)	950
furniture	931
gate	615
general	931
goods-	931
canal	930
railways	631
hall-	951
hospital service	950
head-	
residential buildings	F951
hospital service	F950
hotel	F951
hospital	950
hotel	951
house-	951
L.R.T.	931
kitchen	952
laundry	931
lodge	615
lodging	951
mail	631
motor	934
night-	951
market	931
hospital service	950
parcel(s) (*railways*)	631
resident	951
store(s)	931
timber-	930
furniture mfr.	889
timber yard	889
van	934
ward	950
warehouse	931
Porter-	931
food-	931
docks	930
market	931
office	931
residential buildings	951
timber-	930
timber yard	889
auctioneering	931
catering	952
club	951
educational establishment-	
college	672
entertainment	699
government	931
hospital service	950
hostel	951
hotel	951
institution	950
local government	931
manufacturing	889
retail trade	931
schools	672
transport-	931
railways	631
Porter and liftman	951
Porter-caretaker	672
Porter-cleaner	958
Porter-driver	872
Porter-guard	631
Porter-handyman	929
Porter-messenger	889

	Code number
Porter-packer	**931**
Porter-signalman	**631**
Porter-storeman	**931**
Possession man	**619**
Post boy (*glass mfr.*)	**590**
Postman;	
head	**F940**
higher grade	**940**
works	**941**
Postman-	**940**
glass mfr.	**590**
Postman-driver	**940**
Postwoman	**940**
Post office worker	**940**
Postal worker	**940**
Poster; bill	**959**
Poster hand	**560**
Posticheur	**599**
Potman; asphalt	**929**
Potman-	
building and contracting	**929**
cable mfr.	**839**
catering, hotel, etc.	**959**
metal mfr.-	**830**
die casting	**531**
Potcherman	**821**
Potter;	
clay	**590**
furnace; blast	**830**
shrimp	**862**
Potter-	
celluloid mfr.	**820**
ceramics mfr.	**590**
lead smelting	**830**
zinc refining	**590**
Pottery worker	**590**
Poulterer-	**178**
farming	**900**
Poultry hand (*food processing*)	**582**
Poultry man	**900**
Poultry worker	**900**
Pouncer	**559**
Pounder	**555**
Pourer (*foundry*)	**839**
Powder man;	**441**
bleaching	**919**
Power house man	**893**
Practitioner;	
Christian Science	**292**
dental	**223**
general	**220**
homeopathic-	**346**
medically qualified	**220**
hydropathic	**347**
medical;	**220**
general	**220**
registered	**220**
study; works	**364**
veterinary	**224**
Prebendary	**292**
Pre-boarder (*hosiery mfr.*)	**552**
Precipitator	**820**
Pre-former	**825**
Premixer (chemicals)	**820**
Pre-packer *see Packer*	
Preparer;	
case	**555**
colour (*ceramics mfr.*)	**829**
cylinder	**999**
design; textiles	**430**
dough (artificial teeth)	**829**

	Code number
Preparer; *continued*	
fish	**582**
food	**620**
fruit; preserved	**809**
gelatine	**809**
glaze (*ceramics mfr.*)	**829**
hair-	**811**
wig mfr.	**599**
jute	**811**
litho (*ceramics mfr.*)	**869**
lithographic (*printing*)	**560**
paper	**569**
plate; lithographic	**899**
raw ingredient (*flour confectionery mfr.*)	**800**
starch	**552**
veneer	**579**
warp	**552**
yarn	**812**
for dyeing	**814**
Preparer-	
ceramics mfr.	**591**
clothing mfr.	**557**
embroidery mfr.	**559**
food preserving	**809**
footwear mfr.	**555**
glass mfr.	**590**
laundry	**673**
leather goods mfr.	**555**
lithography	**560**
metal trades	**899**
textile mfr.-	**811**
cotton doubling	**552**
Preparer and sealer (*cable mfr.*)	**899**
Preserver; timber	**821**
Preserver (*food products mfr.*)	**809**
President (college)	**230**
Press hand *see Presser-*	
Press man *see Presser-*	
Press operator *see Presser-*	
Press worker *see Presser-*	
Press worker (*metal trades*)	**841**
Presser;	
belt	**829**
bending	**839**
blanking	**555**
block (*plastics goods mfr.*)	**825**
blouse	**673**
brick	**590**
brush; carbon	**829**
cap	**673**
carbon	**829**
clicking	**555**
clipping	**839**
cloth	**552**
clothes	**673**
cocoa	**809**
coil	**850**
coining	**841**
collar	**673**
component	**841**
contact lens (plastics)	**825**
die	**590**
draw	**841**
dust (*ceramics mfr.*)	**590**
extruding (*metal trades*)	**839**
filter-	
coal mine	**890**
food products mfr.	**809**
fitter's	**839**

	Code number
Presser; *continued*	
flat-	
ceramics mfr.	**590**
pressed woollen felt mfr.	**552**
fly-	
cutlery mfr.	**841**
forging	**530**
forge	**530**
fusing	**859**
garment	**673**
general	**673**
glass	**590**
hand-	
metal trades	**841**
sports goods mfr.	**599**
tailoring	**673**
textile finishing	**673**
heel-	
footwear mfr.	**859**
rubber goods mfr.	**824**
Hoffman	**673**
hollow-ware	**590**
hop	**801**
hosiery	**552**
hot-	
cemented carbide goods mfr.	**829**
ceramics mfr.	**590**
metal trades	**530**
paper mfr.	**821**
printing	**821**
rubber goods mfr.	**824**
textile finishing	**552**
hydraulic-	
metal trades-	**841**
forging	**530**
packing	**862**
paper merchants	**862**
plastics goods mfr.	**825**
textile mfr.	**552**
jobbing	**829**
lead (*cable mfr.*)	**839**
lining; brake	**829**
lining-	**673**
footwear mfr.	**859**
machine-	
clothing mfr.	**673**
metal trades	**841**
textile mfr.	**552**
mica	**829**
oil (*oil seed crushing*)	**809**
paper	**862**
pipe	**839**
plastics	**825**
polishing	**825**
pottery	**590**
powder (*chemical mfr.*)	**820**
power-	
carbon goods mfr.	**899**
metal trades	**841**
record; gramophone	**825**
ring	**841**
rotary-	
printing	**891**
textile mfr.	**552**
rubber	**824**
sagger	**590**
scale (*knife handle mfr.*)	**899**
seam	**673**
shirt	**673**
shoe	**859**
sleeve	**673**

(Pr)

	Code number
Presser; *continued*	
stamping	**841**
steam-	
clothing	**673**
metal	**841**
rubber	**824**
steel	**530**
stone; artificial	**599**
stuff	**552**
tailor's	**673**
tile (*ceramics mfr.*)	**590**
tool	**841**
top	**673**
trouser	**673**
tube	**841**
veneer	**821**
washer	**829**
yarn	**552**
yeast	**801**
Presser-	
asbestos-cement goods mfr.	**899**
bookbinding	**562**
cable mfr.	**899**
cast concrete products mfr.	**899**
cemented carbide goods mfr.	**829**
ceramics mfr.	**590**
chemical mfr.	**820**
cider mfr.	**801**
clothing mfr.	**673**
crayon, pencil mfr.	**829**
distillery	**801**
food products mfr.	**809**
footwear mfr.	**859**
glass mfr.	**590**
gramophone record mfr.	**825**
laundry	**673**
leather dressing	**810**
leather goods mfr.	**859**
metal trades-	**841**
electric battery mfr.	**899**
forging	**530**
rolling mill	**530**
tube mfr.	**839**
mica, micanite goods mfr.	**829**
mine, not coal	**890**
oil seed crushing	**809**
paper mfr.	**821**
patent fuel mfr.	**829**
plastics goods mfr.	**825**
plywood mfr.	**821**
printing	**891**
rubber goods mfr.	**824**
textile mfr.-	**552**
textile packing	**862**
tobacco mfr.	**802**
waste merchants	**862**
wood pulp mfr.	**821**
Presser and threader	**814**
Presser-out (*textile machinery mfr.*)	**841**
Press-pate man	**821**
Pressureman (*gas board*)	**430**
Pricer; prescription	**430**
Pricker (*leather goods mfr.*)	**555**
Pricker-up	**555**
Priest	**292**
Primer; cap	**599**
Primer-	
brewery	**801**
cartridge mfr.	**599**
Principal;	
school-	
dancing (private)	**239**
music (private)	**239**
Principal-	
banking	**120**
dancing school	**239**
educational establishments-	**239**
higher and further	
education-	**231**
polytechnic	**230**
university	**230**
schools-	
primary	**234**
secondary	**233**
sixth form college	**233**
special	**235**
evening institute	**239**
government	**103**
training establishment	**239**
Printer;	
arc light	**490**
block	**563**
blue	**490**
bromide	**569**
bronze letter	**569**
calico	**569**
carbon	**560**
cloth	**569**
colour	**569**
contact	**569**
copy	**490**
dial	**569**
dyeline	**490**
embroidery	**569**
film	**569**
general	**561**
glass	**563**
gold	**569**
gravure	**891**
hand	**569**
hat	**569**
label (hat labels)	**569**
letterpress	**891**
litho; offset	**569**
lithographic	**891**
map	**891**
master	**561**
mat	**596**
metal (*process engraving*)	**560**
Multilith	**569**
n.o.s.-	**561**
photocopying	**490**
ceramics mfr.	**569**
film processing	**569**
leather dressing	**810**
screen printing	**563**
office; drawing	**490**
offset	**569**
p.o.p.	**569**
photo	**490**
photographic	**569**
photostat	**490**
phototype	**490**
plan	**490**
plate (*ceramics mfr.*)	**569**
press	**891**
process	**569**
rota	**490**
sack	**569**
screen;	**563**
Printer; *continued*	
screen; *continued*	
silk	**563**
silver	**569**
spray	**596**
textile	**569**
ticket;	**891**
metal leaf	**569**
title (*film processing*)	**569**
transfer	**569**
wallpaper	**569**
wax (*textile mfr.*)	**552**
Printer and stationer	**561**
Printer-compositor	**560**
Printer-down	**560**
Printer's devil	**919**
Printer's operative	**891**
Printer-to-metal	**560**
Prior	**292**
Prism hand	**590**
Prism worker	**590**
Private-	
armed forces-	
foreign and Commonwealth	**601**
U.K.	**600**
Probationer (*railways*)	**524**
Process hand *see Process worker-*	
Processman *see Process worker-*	
Process worker-	
abrasives mfr.	**599**
adhesive and sealants mfr.	**820**
animal foods mfr.	**809**
asbestos mfr.	**811**
asbestos-cement goods mfr.	**829**
Atomic Energy Authority	**820**
bakery	**800**
brewery	**801**
cable mfr.	**899**
cast concrete products mfr.	**599**
cellulose film mfr.	**820**
cement mfr.	**820**
cemented carbide goods mfr.	**599**
ceramics mfr.	**590**
chemical mfr.	**820**
chocolate mfr.	**809**
clay extraction	**890**
coal gas, coke ovens	**820**
dairy	**809**
distillery	**801**
dry cleaning	**673**
electrical engineering	**899**
explosives mfr.	**820**
fat recovery	**829**
felt mfr.	**814**
fibre glass mfr.	**590**
film processing	**569**
flour confectionery mfr.	**800**
food products mfr.	**809**
glass mfr.	**590**
jewellery mfr.	**899**
lamp, valve mfr.	**850**
leather mfr.	**810**
leather cloth mfr.	**899**
linoleum mfr.	**899**
lubricating oil mfr.	**820**
meat products mfr.	**809**
metal trades-	**899**
steelworks	**839**
vehicle mfr.	**851**
mica, micanite mfr.	**829**

	Code number
Process worker- *continued*	
nickel mfr.	830
nuclear fuel production	820
oil refining	820
ordnance factory	820
organic oil and fat processing	809
paint mfr.	820
paper and board products mfr.	569
paper mfr.	821
patent fuel mfr.	820
pharmaceutical mfr.	820
photographic film mfr.	569
plastics goods mfr.	825
plastics mfr.	820
polish mfr.	820
printing	569
printing ink mfr.	820
rubber goods mfr.	824
rubber reclamation	829
slaughterhouse	581
soap and detergent mfr.	820
soft drinks mfr.	809
starch mfr.	809
sugar and sugar confectionery mfr.	809
tannery	810
textile mfr.-	814
fibre preparing	811
man-made fibre mfr.	826
textile finishing	552
textile printing	569
tobacco mfr.	802
toilet preparations mfr.	820
vinery	801
wood products mfr.	821
yeast mfr.	801
Processor;	
data	490
film	569
milk	809
pharmaceutical	820
photographic	569
poultry	582
word	452
Processor *see Process worker-*	
Proctologist	220
Procurator fiscal	240
Producer;	
egg	160
gas	820
film	M384
Producer (*entertainment*)	M384
Production worker *see Process worker-*	
Products worker; medicinal	820
Professional (sport)	387
Professor; university	230
Professor-	
dentistry	223
medicine	220
surgery	220
educational establishments-	
higher and further education-	231
polytechnic	230
university	230
Profiler (metal)	840
Programme boy	720
Programmer;	320

	Code number
Programmer; *continued*	
applications	320
computer	320
control; numerical	320
n.c.	320
systems	320
Programmer-analyst	320
Progress hand	420
Progress man	420
Progress worker	420
Progressor	420
Projectionist	386
Promoter (*sport*)	176
Prompter	384
Pronger (*fork mfr.*)	841
Proofer;	
dry	552
moisture (*transparent paper mfr.*)	821
rot	552
rust	834
water-	
building and contracting	929
clothing mfr.	552
rubber goods mfr.	814
textile mfr.	552
yarn	552
Proofer-	
clothing mfr.	552
lithography	891
rubber goods mfr.	814
textile mfr.	552
Propagator	595
Property man	699
Propman-	
coal mine-	597
above ground	929
Propper-	
coal mine-	597
above ground	929
Proprietor *see Owner-*	
Prosthetist	346
Prover;	
colour (*printing*)	569
die	860
file	860
gun	860
meter	860
process (*printing*)	569
stove (*gas board*)	860
Prover-	
lithography	569
Ordnance Survey	569
tube mfr.	860
Prover and tester (*metal trades*)	860
Provision hand	720
Provost-	
educational establishments-	
higher and further education-	231
polytechnic	230
university	230
Pruner; tree-	
forestry	904
fruit growing	595
local government	594
Pruner-	
fruit growing	595
nursery	595
park	594
Psychiatrist	220

	Code number
Psycho-analyst	220
Psychologist	290
Psychometrist-	290
entertainment	384
Psychotherapist	347
Publican	175
Publicist	380
Publisher	179
Pudding worker	809
Puddler (metal)	830
Puffer (*footwear mfr.*)	859
Pug man	829
Pugger-	829
ceramics mfr.	829
enamel mfr.	829
Puller;	
base (*clothing mfr.*)	559
baste	559
conveyor (*coal mine*)	899
pallet	599
pea	902
proof	569
rag	811
silk	811
stamp	841
tack	555
waste (*textile mfr.*)	811
wool-	811
fellmongering	810
Puller-	
coal mine	899
fellmongering	810
fur dressing	810
textile mfr.	811
Puller-back (*meat market*)	931
Puller-down	889
Puller-off-	
metal trades	912
sawmilling	920
Puller-on (*footwear mfr.*)	555
Puller-out (*metal mfr.*)	830
Puller-over (*footwear mfr.*)	555
Puller-up-	919
coal mine	899
Pulleyman (*coal mine*)	894
Pulpman (*paper mfr.*)	821
Pulper-	
food products mfr.	809
paper mfr.	821
Pulperman (*paper mfr.*)	821
Pulveriser	820
Pumicer-	
horn, etc.	599
precious metal, plate	842
tobacco pipes	579
wood	579
Pump hand	999
Pumpman; still (*vinegar mfr.*)	999
Pumpman-	999
fishing	880
petrol filling station	722
shale oil refining	820
shipping	F880
Pumpman-dipper	999
Pumper; syphon (*gas board*)	999
Pumper-	
lamp, valve mfr.	899
mining	999
Pumpsman	999
Pumpwright	516

	Code number
Puncher;	
card-	**569**
jacquard card cutting	**814**
textile mfr.	**814**
eye (needles)	**841**
fishplate	**841**
jacquard	**814**
label	**569**
lamp shade	**599**
paper	**569**
pattern (*paper pattern mfr.*)	**569**
piano (*jacquard card cutting*)	**814**
rail	**841**
shoe tip	**841**
steel bar	**841**
Puncher-	
footwear mfr.	**555**
glove mfr.	**557**
metal trades-	**841**
boiler mfr.	**534**
shipbuilding	**534**
zinc smelting	**590**
paper goods mfr.	**569**
wool combing	**811**
Puncher and shearer	**841**
Puppeteer	**384**
Purchaser-	
manufacturing	**420**
retail trade	**700**
wholesale trade	**701**
Purification man	**820**
Purifier-	**820**
flock merchants	**811**
food products mfr.	**809**
Purifier man-	**820**
food products mfr.	**809**
Purler	**553**
Purser-	**173**
pier	**412**
Purserette (hovercraft)	**630**
Purveyor *see Shopkeeper*	
Pusher;	
tool	**113**
truck	**889**
Pusher (*coal gas, coke ovens*)	**889**
Pusher-out	**889**
Putter; pony	**889**
Putter (*coal mine*)	**889**
Putter-in (*textile mfr.*)	**814**
Putter-on;	
band	**814**
tape (*silk spinning*)	**814**
Putter-on-	
clog mfr.	**555**
glue mfr.	**820**
photographic plate mfr.	**829**
textile printing	**430**
textile spinning	**812**
Putter-together; scissors	**516**
Putter-together (*cutlery mfr.*)	**516**
Putter-up-	
textile mfr.-	**862**
textile weaving	**550**
Pyrotechnist	**699**

Q

	Code number
Q.C.	**241**
Q.M. (*shipping*)	**880**
Quarrier	**898**
Quarry man	**898**
Quarry worker	**898**
Quartermaster-	**441**
shipping	**880**
Quartermaster-Corporal-	
armed forces-	
foreign and Commonwealth	**601**
Quartermaster-General-	
armed forces-	
foreign and Commonwealth	**M151**
U.K.	**M150**
Quartermaster-Sergeant-	
armed forces-	
foreign and Commonwealth	**601**
Quartz crystal worker	**518**
Quayman	**930**
Queen's counsel	**241**
Quencher man (*coal gas, coke ovens*)	**919**
Quiller; comb	**825**
Quiller (*textile mfr.*)	**813**
Quilter (*textile goods mfr.*)	**553**

	Code number
R	
R.G.N.	**340**
Rabbi	**292**
Rackman (*metal mfr.*)	**839**
Racker-	**441**
alcoholic drink mfr.	**801**
laundry, dry cleaning	**863**
lithography	**891**
textile finishing	**552**
tinplate goods mfr.	**889**
vinegar mfr.	**801**
whiting mfr.	**889**
Radiator man (vehicle)	**533**
Radiodiagnostician	**220**
Radiographer;	
superintendent	**F342**
Radiographer-	**342**
industrial	**301**
Radiologist	**220**
Radiotherapist	**220**
Rafter	**930**
Rag and bone man	**733**
Rag house worker	**821**
Rag man	**733**
Railman-	
coal mine	**922**
docks	**930**
L.R.T.	**631**
railways-	**631**
shunting	**884**
Railer (*bedstead mfr.*)	**516**
Railway employee-	**631**
shunting	**884**
Railwayman-	**631**
shunting	**884**
Railway worker-	**631**
shunting	**884**
Raiser;	
blanket	**552**
cloth	**552**
flannelette	**552**
fund	**123**
steam	**893**
Raiser-	
printing	**560**
textile finishing	**552**
Raiser and finisher (*embroidery mfr.*)	**553**
Raker; asphalt	**923**
Raker-out (*asbestos mfr.*)	**919**
Ram man	**889**
Rammer;	
chair	**531**
plug	**830**
Rammer-	
foundry	**531**
metal mfr.	**830**
Rammerman	**929**
Rammer-up	**531**
Rander (*twine mfr.*)	**813**
Range worker	**990**
Ranger;	
estate	**615**
forest	**904**
national park	**615**
park	**615**
wood	**904**
Ranger-	**615**
footwear mfr.	**555**
glass mfr.	**869**
Ransacker (*fishing net mfr.*)	**861**
Rasper (remould tyres)	**824**
Rating;	
engine-room (*shipping*)	**880**
Rating-	
armed forces-	
foreign and Commonwealth	**601**
U.K.	**600**
Ratliner	**814**
Rayon worker	**826**
Reacher (*textile mfr.*)	**552**
Reacher-in (*textile mfr.*)	**552**
Reader;	
lay	**292**
literary	**380**
meter	**412**
news (*broadcasting*)	**384**
newspaper	**430**
proof	**430**
publisher's	**380**
Reader-	
dentistry	**223**
medicine	**220**
surgery	**220**
lace mfr.	**814**
press cutting agency	**421**
printing	**430**
university	**230**
Reader-compositor	**560**
Reader-in	**552**
Reader-off	**814**
Reamer (metal)	**840**
Reamerer; barrel	**840**
Reamerer (*metal trades*)	**840**
Rearer; poultry	**160**
Re-beamer	**552**
Recaster	**839**
Receiver; official	**250**
Receiver-	**441**
Board of Trade	**250**
docks	**420**
laundry	**720**
leather cloth mfr.	**552**
rolling mill	**839**
tobacco mfr.	**869**
Receptionist;	
beet	**441**
dental	**460**
doctor's	**460**
door	**699**
medical	**460**
vehicle (*garage*)	**540**
Receptionist-	**460**
radio, television and video hire	**412**
cinema, theatre	**699**
garage	**540**
Receptionist-telephonist	**461**
Reckoner (*tinplate mfr.*)	**863**
Reclaimer (rubber)	**829**
Reconditioner;	
girder	**899**
machine	**516**
Recorder;	
milk	**420**
progress	**420**
stock	**440**
temperature	**430**
time	**410**
wagon	**430**
Recorder-	
laboratory	**864**
H.M. dockyard	**430**
legal services	**240**
milk marketing board	**420**
sound recording	**386**
steelworks	**430**
Recorder of work	**420**
Recordist;	
electroencephalographic	**346**
sound	**386**
Recoverer;	
acetone	**820**
solvent	**820**
zinc	**830**
Recoverer-	
paper mfr.	**821**
rubber reclamation	**829**
Recovery hand *see Recoverer-*	
Recovery man *see Recoverer-*	
Recovery worker *see Recoverer-*	
Rectifier;	
cycle; motor	**899**
paint (*vehicle mfr.*)	**869**
tube	**839**
Rectifier-	**820**
footwear mfr.	**555**
metal trades	**516**
textile mfr.	**553**
Rectifying man-	**820**
metal trades	**516**
Rector-	
church	**292**
college	**230**
educational establishments-	
secondary education	**233**
Red coat (*holiday camp*)	**699**
Re-drawer (silk)	**813**
Reducer; data; geophysical	**202**
Reducer-	
textile printing	**552**
wool drawing	**811**
Re-dyer	**552**
Reeder	**552**
Reel hand	**891**
Reelman	**821**
Reeler;	
bar	**839**
bobbin	**813**
cop	**813**
rope	**814**
twine	**813**
twist	**813**
yarn	**813**
Reeler-	
paper mfr.	**821**
photographic film mfr.	**569**
plastics goods mfr.	**825**
printing	**891**
rolling mill	**839**
textile mfr.-	**813**
textile bleaching	**552**
wallpaper mfr.	**821**
wire rope, cable mfr.	**899**
Reeler and lacer	**813**
Reelerman-	
paper mfr.	**821**
rolling mill	**839**
roofing felt mfr.	**814**
Referee; official (*legal services*)	**240**

	Code number
Referee-	**387**
medical (*government*)	**220**
Refiner;	
bullion	**830**
clay; china	**890**
dripping	**809**
fat	**809**
gold	**830**
lard	**809**
nickel	**830**
oil; cotton	**809**
paint	**820**
silver	**830**
Refiner-	
candle mfr.	**820**
chemical mfr.	**820**
chocolate mfr.	**809**
food products mfr.	**809**
metal mfr.	**830**
oil refining	**820**
oil seed refining	**809**
paper mfr.	**821**
rubber reclamation	**829**
sugar refining	**809**
Refiner hand *see Refiner-*	
Refiner man *see Refiner-*	
Refinery worker; oil	**820**
Refinisher	**596**
Refractory worker	**919**
Refrigerator man (*brewery*)	**801**
Refueller; aircraft	**889**
Refueller-	
vehicles	**722**
airport	**889**
Regenerator; oil (*coal gas*)	**820**
Registrar;	
additional	**102**
cemetery	**199**
company	**127**
county court	**240**
land	**350**
probate	**240**
superintendent	**102**
of births, deaths and marriages	**102**
of deeds	**102**
of marriages	**102**
of stock	**127**
of stocks and bonds	**127**
Registrar-	**127**
educational services	**191**
government	**103**
hospital service	**220**
legal services	**240**
local government	**102**
Post Office	**199**
Regulator;	
gas (*coal gas, coke ovens*)	**999**
steam	**893**
traffic	**F870**
Regulator-	
piano, organ mfr.	**593**
transport	**F870**
Reheater	**830**
Re-laster	**555**
Relayer (*railways*)	**922**
Reliner;	
bearing	**839**
brake	**859**
Reliner (*steelworks*)	**500**
Remoistener (dextrin)	**809**
Remoulder-	
glass mfr.	**591**
rubber goods mfr.	**824**
Removal hand (*road transport*)	**931**
Removalman (*road transport*)	**931**
Remover;	
belt (*coal mine*)	**899**
cattle	**872**
conveyor (*coal mine*)	**899**
furniture	**931**
refuse	**933**
scrap	**889**
Renderer; lard	**809**
Renewer; tread	**824**
Renovator;	
antiques	**571**
car	**542**
Renovator-	
clothing	**553**
furniture	**571**
Renter; film	**719**
Repairman *see Repairer-*	
Repair worker (*coal mine*)-	**597**
above ground	**534**
Repairer;	
airway-	
coal mine	**597**
mine, not coal	**898**
antiques	**571**
appliance; domestic	**521**
bag (hand bags)	**555**
bank (canal)	**929**
barge	**534**
battery	**599**
beam (*textile mfr.*)	**516**
belt	**555**
belting	**555**
blanket; electric	**521**
blind	**599**
boat	**570**
bobbin	**516**
body (vehicle)	**542**
boiler	**534**
book	**562**
box;	**572**
horse	**541**
brake	**516**
bridge	**896**
builder's	**509**
building	**509**
cable (electric)	**524**
camera	**517**
carpet	**553**
carriage	**516**
case-	
watch	**518**
wood	**572**
cask	**572**
chain	**530**
chair-	**571**
cane furniture	**599**
chimney	**500**
china	**591**
chronometer	**517**
clock	**517**
clockwork	**517**
coach-	**541**
railways	**516**
coil	**850**
container; freight	**533**
controller	**521**
Repairer; *continued*	
conveyor	**516**
cord (telephones)	**523**
crate	**572**
cupola	**500**
cycle-	**516**
motor	**540**
die	**515**
farm implements	**516**
film	**599**
furnace	**500**
furniture	**571**
glass	**590**
hosiery	**553**
house	**509**
hydraulic	**516**
instrument-	**517**
dental and surgical instruments	**899**
musical instruments	**593**
precision	**517**
jewellery and plate	**518**
kiln	**500**
lamp	**516**
machine-	**516**
office machinery	**598**
magneto	**521**
mangle	**516**
meter	**517**
motor	**540**
net	**553**
oven	**500**
paint-work (*vehicle mfr.*)	**596**
pen; fountain	**599**
pipe (tobacco pipes)	**579**
plate (*printing*)	**560**
propeller	**530**
property	**509**
radiator (vehicle)	**533**
railway	**922**
recorder; time	**517**
reed	**599**
revolver	**516**
road-	**923**
coal mine	**597**
mine, not coal	**922**
roof	**501**
sack	**553**
saw	**899**
scale	**517**
sheet	**553**
ship	**534**
shoe	**555**
spring	**530**
stove (gas stoves)	**516**
syphon	**516**
tarpaulin	**553**
tent	**553**
tool	**515**
toy	**599**
tractor	**516**
tub	**899**
tube-	
boiler mfr.	**534**
carpet mfr.	**516**
typewriter	**598**
tyre	**824**
umbrella	**559**
van	**542**
vehicle body (metal)	**542**
wagon	**516**

	Code number
Ringer; bell	**385**
Rinser;	
bottle	**999**
file	**912**
Ripener; banana	**441**
Ripper;	
muslin	**811**
rag	**811**
Ripper-	
coal mine	**597**
shoddy mfr.	**811**
Ripperman (*paper mfr.*)	**821**
Riser;	
mill	**839**
steam	**893**
Riser (*metal rolling*)	**839**
River (*mine, not coal*)	**500**
Riverman	**929**
River worker	**929**
Riveter-	**534**
bag frames	**851**
china	**591**
corsets	**851**
curry combs	**851**
footwear	**859**
glass	**590**
glove fastenings	**859**
leather goods	**859**
plastics goods	**859**
umbrella ribs	**851**
soft toy mfr.	**859**
Road man-	
building and contracting	**923**
local government	**923**
mining	**922**
Road worker	**923**
Roadsman-	
canal	**880**
mining	**922**
Roaster;	
barley	**801**
malt	**801**
Roaster-	
food products	**809**
minerals, etc.	**829**
Rock hand-	
mine, not coal	**898**
sugar confectionery mfr.	**809**
Rockman (*mine, not coal*)	**898**
Rodder-	
fish curing	**809**
tube mfr.	**899**
Rodent operative	**699**
Rodsman	**919**
Roll hand (*steel mfr.*)	**839**
Roller;	
bacon	**581**
ball	**809**
bandage	**814**
bar; puddled	**832**
belly	**810**
bend (*tannery*)	**810**
cogging	**832**
cold-	**832**
paper mfr.	**821**
cross	**518**
finishing	**839**
forge	**832**
head	**832**
hot-	**821**
steel mfr.	**832**
Roller; *continued*	
leather	**810**
mill;	
blooming	**832**
roughing	**839**
sheet	**832**
mill (*iron and steel tube mfr.*)	**832**
pastry	**800**
piece	**811**
plate	**832**
rod	**832**
roughing	**839**
section	**839**
side	**839**
slab	**809**
strip	**832**
thread (screws)	**841**
tube-	
metal	**839**
micanite	**829**
paper	**569**
plastics	**825**
rubber	**824**
tyre (steel)	**832**
under	**832**
wire	**832**
Roller-	
bookbinding	**562**
cigar mfr.	**802**
coal mine	**894**
flour confectionery mfr.	**800**
flour milling	**809**
food products mfr.	**809**
leather dressing	**810**
metal trades-	**832**
fork, hoe mfr.	**839**
precious metal mfr.	**839**
oil seed crushing	**809**
paper mfr.	**821**
paper tube mfr.	**569**
rubber goods mfr.	**824**
sugar confectionery mfr.	**809**
textile mfr.-	**814**
flax, hemp mfr.	**811**
Roller lad (*metal trades*)	**912**
Rollerman *see Roller-*	
Roller-up-	
textile mfr.	**814**
wallpaper mfr.	**821**
Rollsman (*copper rolling*)	**832**
Roofman	**990**
Roofer;	**501**
felt	**501**
Room hand (*footwear mfr.*)	**555**
Room worker;	
grey (*textile mfr.*)	**441**
pattern	**441**
still	**953**
stock	**441**
Ropeman (*mining*)	**505**
Rope worker (*rope mfr.*)	**814**
Roper	**862**
Rope-way man; aerial	**889**
Rougher;	
outsole	**555**
upper (*footwear mfr.*)	**555**
Rougher-	
foundry	**843**
glass mfr.	**591**
rolling mill	**839**
Rougher and borer (*wood-wind instrument mfr.*)	**897**
Roughneck	**898**
Rounder-	
footwear mfr.	**555**
hat mfr.	**559**
tube mfr.	**839**
Rounder-off	**559**
Roundsman	**731**
Rouser	**809**
Roustabout	**990**
Router-	
plastics	**825**
printing plates	**899**
wood	**897**
Router and mounter	**899**
Rover;	
asbestos	**811**
cone	**813**
dandy (wool)	**811**
Rover (*textile mfr.*)	**811**
Rubber-	
textile finishing	**552**
vehicle mfr.	**869**
Rubber and flatter (*coach building*)	**869**
Rubber and polisher (*vehicle mfr.*)	**869**
Rubber goods worker	**824**
Rubber worker	**824**
Rubber-down-	**869**
footwear mfr.	**555**
jewellery, plate mfr.	**843**
Rubberer; tyre	**824**
Rubberiser (carpets)	**814**
Rubber-off-	
footwear mfr.	**555**
foundry	**843**
Rucker (*blast furnace*)	**912**
Ruler; printer's	**569**
Ruler-	
printing	**569**
textile printing	**569**
Ruller (*mine, not coal*)	**889**
Rullyman	**872**
Rumbler-	
ceramics	**591**
metal	**842**
Runner;	
belt (*coal mine*)	**889**
bobbin	**889**
clay	**889**
deal (*timber merchants*)	**931**
metal (white)	**839**
mould (*ceramics mfr.*)	**591**
rope	**889**
wagon-	**889**
coal mine	**889**
water	**889**
wool	**889**
wort	**801**
Runner-	
ceramics mfr.	**889**
docks	**930**
shipping	**880**
steelworks	**886**
textile mfr.	**889**
Runner man (*steelworks*)	**886**
Runner-off (*hosiery mfr.*)	**551**
Runner-on (*hosiery mfr.*)	**551**

Code number

S

S.E.N. ... 340
S.E.O. (*government*) ... 103
S.O. n.o.s. (*local government*) 102
S.R.N. ... 340
Sackhand (*sack mfr.*) ... 559
Sacristan ... 672
Saddle worker ... 555
Saddler ... 555
Safe man (*sugar refining*) ... 809
Safety man-
  coal mine ... 899
  steel mfr. ... 396
Safety worker (*U.K.A.E.A.*) 396
Sailor-
  armed forces-
    foreign and Commonwealth ... 601
    U.K. ... 600
  shipbuilding ... 913
  shipping ... 880
Sailorman ... 913
Sales; first ... 720
Salesman;
  advertising ... 719
  bread-
    retail trade- ... 720
      delivery round ... 731
  butcher's ... 720
  car ... 720
  cattle ... 710
  commercial ... 710
  commission ... 710
  counter ... 720
  credit ... 730
  delivery ... 710
  drinks; soft ... 731
  export ... 710
  fish- ... 720
    self-employed ... 178
    wholesale trade ... 710
  fish and fruit ... 720
  fish and poultry ... 720
  fishmonger's ... 720
  forecourt (*garage*) ... 722
  ice cream ... 731
  indoor ... 720
  insurance ... 719
  land (*estate agents*) ... 719
  market- ... 732
    wholesale trade ... 720
  meat- ... 720
    wholesale trade ... 710
  milk-
    retail trade- ... 720
      delivery round ... 731
  mineral water ... 710
  motor ... 720
  outside ... 710
  parts (*motor vehicle repair*) 720
  petrol (*garage*) ... 722
  powder (*mining*) ... 441
  property ... 719
  retail ... 720
  shop- ... 720
    mobile shop ... 731
  showroom ... 720
  space; advertising ... 719
  tea ... 710
  technical ... 710

Code number

Salesman; *continued*
  telephone ... 792
  travelling- ... 710
    retail trade ... 730
  tyre ... 710
  van- ... 731
    manufacturing ... 710
    wholesale trade ... 710
  warehouse ... 720
  wool (*scrap merchant*) ... 710
Salesman-
  hawking ... 732
  ice cream ... 731
  self-employed ... 710
  services ... 719
  building and contracting ... 720
  mail order house ... 730
  manufacturers' agents ... 710
  manufacturing ... 710
  retail trade- ... 720
    credit trade ... 730
    door to door sales ... 730
    mobile shop ... 731
    party plan sales ... 730
  wholesale trade ... 710
Salesman-buyer ... 700
Salesman-collector ... 730
Salesman-driver ... 731
Salesman-mechanic ... 710
Salle worker ... 861
Saloon boy ... 621
Salt cake man ... 820
Salt man ... 919
Salt worker ... 820
Salter;
  dry ... 809
  fish ... 809
Salter-
  bacon, meat curing ... 809
  tannery ... 810
Salvage corps man ... 611
Salvage hand- ... 990
  coal mine ... 597
  mooring and wreck raising service ... 880
Salvage man (*coal mine*) ... 597
Salvage worker- ... 990
  coal mine ... 597
Sample hand-
  clothing mfr. ... 553
  footwear mfr. ... 555
Sample man ... 441
Sampler;
  grain (*grain milling*) ... 861
  milk ... 861
  tea ... 861
Sampler- ... 869
  food processing ... 861
  sugar refining ... 861
Sandman- ... 990
  abrasive paper, etc. mfr. ... 821
Sander;
  hand (*furniture mfr.*) ... 869
  wet (*motor body mfr.*) ... 869
Sander-
  metal trades ... 843
  wood products mfr. ... 897
Sandwichman ... 699
Sand worker (*quarry*) ... 898
Sanforizer ... 552

Code number

Sapper-
  armed forces-
    foreign and Commonwealth ... 601
    U.K. ... 600
Sausage room worker ... 809
Saw man-
  metal ... 899
  stone ... 500
Saw worker; hot ... 899
Sawduster ... 810
Sawer *see* Sawyer
Sawyer;
  back- ... 897
    metal ... 899
  band- ... 897
    metal ... 899
  circular ... 897
  cross cut ... 897
  diamond ... 518
  hot ... 899
  ivory ... 599
  mill ... 897
  rack ... 897
  rail ... 899
  roller ... 899
  slate ... 500
  whip ... 897
  wood pulp ... 897
Sawyer-
  bone, ivory, etc. ... 599
  meat ... 581
  metal ... 899
  plastics ... 825
  stone ... 500
  wood ... 897
  asbestos-cement goods mfr. 599
  coal mine ... 897
  converting mill ... 897
  steel tube mfr. ... 899
Scabbler (stone) ... 500
Scaffolder ... 505
Scalder (*tripe dressing*) ... 809
Scaleman- ... 863
  rolling mill ... 912
Scaler;
  boiler ... 899
  metal ... 912
  ship('s) boiler ... 899
Scaler-
  boiler scaling ... 899
  rolling mill ... 839
  shipbuilding ... 912
  slaughterhouse ... 863
  steel mfr. ... 839
  vehicle mfr. ... 869
Scalesman ... 863
Scalloper-
  coal mine ... 597
  textile mfr. ... 552
Scapler ... 500
Scappler ... 500
Scarfer (*steel mfr.*) ... 537
Scavenger ... 933
Scene hand ... 999
Scheduler; ... 420
  materials ... 399
Scientist;
  agricultural ... 201
  behavioural ... 291
  horticultural ... 201

	Code number
Scientist; *continued*	
information	**390**
laboratory; medical	**201**
political	**291**
research; operational	**125**
research-	**209**
agricultural	**201**
biochemical	**201**
biological	**201**
botanical	**201**
chemical	**200**
geological	**202**
horticultural	**201**
medical	**300**
meteorological	**202**
physical science	**202**
zoological	**201**
social	**291**
Scientist-	**209**
agricultural	**201**
biochemical	**201**
biological	**201**
botanical	**201**
chemical	**200**
geological	**202**
horticultural	**201**
medical	**300**
meteorological	**202**
physical science	**202**
zoological	**201**
Scolloper-	
ceramics mfr.	**591**
lace mfr.	**552**
Scorer; cricket	**420**
Scotcher	**889**
Scourer;	
cloth	**814**
grease	**810**
piece	**814**
pin	**899**
wool	**814**
Scourer-	
ceramics mfr.	**591**
footwear mfr.	**555**
foundry	**842**
leather dressing	**810**
needle mfr.	**899**
textile mfr.	**814**
tinplate mfr.	**839**
wire mfr.	**839**
Scout; football	**387**
Scout-	
college	**958**
motoring organisation	**540**
Scraper;	
boiler	**899**
gut	**829**
heel (*footwear mfr.*)	**555**
metal	**843**
Scraper-	
coal mine	**597**
shipbuilding	**912**
Scrap man	**912**
Scrap shop worker (celluloid)	**919**
Scrapper-	
metal mfr.	**912**
textile mfr.	**814**
Scratcher-	
linoleum mfr.	**829**
metal trades	**842**
Screeder	**923**
Screen hand-	
coal gas, coke ovens	**820**
coal mine	**890**
Screen man (*coal mine*)	**890**
Screener;	
coal	**890**
coke (*coke ovens*)	**829**
cytology	**300**
paint	**820**
seed	**809**
silk	**563**
Screener-	
chemical mfr.	**820**
coal mine	**890**
grain milling	**809**
iron shot and grit mfr.	**829**
mine, not coal	**890**
sewage disposal	**892**
textile mfr.-	**811**
linen mfr.	**814**
Screensman; seed	**809**
Screensman *see Screener-*	
Screenworker (*coal mine*)	**890**
Screwman-	
asphalt spreading	**885**
metal mfr.	**832**
Screwer;	
button (*bolt, nut mfr.*)	**899**
tube	**840**
Screwer-	
metal trades-	**840**
nut, bolt mfr.	**899**
rolling mill	**832**
small arms mfr.	**840**
Screwer-down (*rolling mill*)	**832**
Scribbler	**811**
Scriber	**515**
Scriever	**570**
Scriever-in	**570**
Scrubber; chair	**843**
Scrubberman (*coke ovens*)	**820**
Scudder	**810**
Sculptor	**381**
Scurfer;	
boiler	**899**
retort	**919**
Scurfer (*aircraft mfr.*)	**912**
Scutcher-	
textile mfr.-	**811**
textile bleaching, finishing	**814**
Seafarer	**880**
Sealer;	
box	**862**
car	**851**
Sealer-	
double glazing	**590**
lamp, valve mfr.	**850**
meat market	**809**
Sealer-in	**859**
Seaman;	
landing stage	**889**
merchant	**880**
Seaman-	
armed forces-	
foreign and Commonwealth	**601**
U.K.	**600**
fishing	**903**
shipping	**880**
Seamer;	
can	**862**
Seamer; *continued*	
corset	**553**
cup (*knitwear mfr.*)	**553**
hollow ware	**841**
Seamer-	
carpet, rug mfr.	**553**
clothing mfr.	**553**
hosiery mfr.	**553**
metal trades	**841**
Seamer-round	**553**
Seamless hand	**551**
Seamstress-	**553**
hospital service	**553**
institution	**553**
laundry	**553**
Searcher-	
manufacturing-	**619**
woollen mfr.	**861**
Seasonal worker (*agriculture, market gardening*)	**902**
Seasoner (*paper mfr.*)	**821**
Seater;	
chair	**599**
key	**840**
Seater (*catering*)	**621**
Second hand; roller's	**832**
Second hand-	
clothing mfr.	**556**
fishing	**F903**
metal rolling	**832**
steelworks	**832**
Second man on lorry	**934**
Secondman (*railways*)	**882**
Secretary;	
appeals; hospital	**190**
area-	
charitable organisation	**190**
coal mine	**127**
professional organisation	**190**
trade association	**190**
trade union	**190**
assistant-	**127**
charitable organisation	**M190**
government	**100**
hospital service	**M127**
local government	**102**
professional association	**M190**
trade association	**M190**
trade union	**M190**
association	**M190**
branch-	
building society	**131**
insurance	**139**
trade union	**M190**
chartered	**127**
club-	**176**
burial club	**719**
youth club	**M371**
commercial	**459**
committee	**399**
company	**127**
confidential	**459**
corporation	**127**
county (youth clubs)	**M371**
deputy (*government*)	**100**
district (*insurance*)	**139**
farm	**459**
financial	**127**
first	**100**
fund	**190**

	Code number
Secretary; *continued*	
general-	
charitable organisation	M190
professional association	M190
trade association	M190
trade union	M190
welfare services	M371
group-	
hospital service	M127
trade union	M190
hospital	M127
legal	451
managing-	
co-operative society	179
welfare services	M371
medical	450
national (*trade union*)	M190
organising-	
charitable organisation	M190
professional association	M190
trade association	M190
trade union	M190
welfare services	M371
parliamentary	100
permanent (*government*)	100
personal	459
political	190
press	380
private;	459
parliamentary	100
principal	103
resident	127
school	420
second	100
sports	176
third	103
under (*government*)	100
of charitable organisation	190
of political association	190
of professional association	190
of state	100
of trade association	190
of trade union	190
Secretary-	459
school	420
chamber of commerce	190
health authority or board	M127
joint industrial council	190
research association	190
welfare services	M371
Secretary and company director	127
Secretary and legal adviser	127
Secretary-accountant	127
Secretary-director	127
Secretary-manager *see Manager*	
Secretary-typist	459
Securer	898
Security man	615
Sediment worker (*whisky distilling*)	801
Seed man	441
Seed worker	595
Seedsman (*wholesale, retail trade*)	179
Seismologist	202
Selector;	
biscuit (*ceramics mfr.*)	863
glass	591
gut	829
sack	863
skin;	863
Selector; *continued*	
skin; *continued*	
sausage	809
spares (*vehicle mfr.*)	441
stores	441
Selector-	
canvas goods mfr.	863
ceramics mfr.	863
flax mfr.	863
government	441
mine, not coal	863
plastics mfr.	863
Selector and classifier (mica)	863
Seller;	
book-	179
H.M.S.O.	720
car	179
fish and chips-	174
employee	720
map	179
newspaper	732
paper	732
programme	720
space (*advertising*)	719
ticket	411
Seller-	
bingo hall	699
totalisator	411
Sempstress	553
Sensitiser; film	829
Separator;	
metal and oil	829
milk	809
ore	890
plate (car battery)	850
skin; sausage	809
stitch	555
Separator (*textile mfr.*)	814
Sergeant;	
detective	F610
town	619
Sergeant-	
non-statutory police	F615
airport police	F610
armed forces-	
foreign and Commonwealth	601
U.K.	600
dock police	F610
government police	F610
Min. of Defence	F610
police service	F610
railway police	F610
Royal parks	F610
Sergeant-Major-	
armed forces-	
foreign and Commonwealth	601
U.K.	600
Serpentine worker	500
Serrator (knives)	899
Servant;	958
civil; n.o.s.-	400
industrial	919
college	958
daily	958
domestic	958
hunt	902
Server;	
canteen	953
dinner	953
Server; *continued*	
meals	953
Server-	
confectionery mfr.	809
school meals	953
silk mfr.	889
take-away food shop	720
textile mfr.-	811
hair weaving	814
Servery hand	953
Service hand-	
catering	953
garage	540
Service man;	
carriage-	990
railways	958
ground	516
sales-	
domestic appliances-	521
gas appliances	516
office machinery	598
radio, television and video	525
Service man-	
automatic vending machines	516
domestic appliances-	521
gas appliances	516
office machinery-	529
electrical	521
mechanical	598
radio, television and video	525
chemical mfr.	889
chocolate mfr.	809
garage	540
gas board	516
metal trades	516
radio relay service	529
Service room hand	953
Service worker-	
school meals	953
textile mfr.	889
Servicer; machinery	894
Servicer-	
motor mfr.	540
textile printing	569
Servitor (*glass mfr.*)	590
Set hand	810
Setter;	
auto (*metal trades*)	519
axle	530
barrel	899
beam	814
block	500
bobbin	814
brick-	500
brick mfr.	823
capstan	510
card-	
textile mfr.	811
textile accessories mfr.	516
carpet	552
chain	814
circle (*textile mfr.*)	899
clamp (*ceramics mfr.*)	823
core	839
crepe (*textile mfr.*)	552
diamond	518
die-	514
wire mfr.	831
door (*vehicle mfr.*)	851
drill	511
driller	511

	Code number
Setter; *continued*	
engineer's	**519**
file	**899**
film (*textile mfr.*)	**569**
fixture	**500**
flame	**850**
forme (*paper box mfr.*)	**569**
frame	**899**
fuse; damper	**899**
gauge	**515**
gem	**518**
guide (*steel mfr.*)	**839**
handle (*textile mfr.*)	**516**
jewel-	**518**
watch mfr.	**851**
jig	**519**
kerb	**924**
kiln	**823**
lathe;	
capstan	**510**
centre	**510**
turret	**510**
lathe (*metal trades*)	**510**
leather	**810**
lens	**591**
loom	**516**
machine;	
automatic	**519**
board	**569**
coiling	**519**
electrode	**599**
grid	**599**
heading (bolts, rivets)	**519**
metalising	**599**
moulding (rubber)	**824**
optical	**F590**
sealing	**599**
woodcutting	**897**
machine-	
brush mfr.	**599**
button mfr.	**599**
man-made fibre mfr.	**516**
metal trades	**519**
paper goods mfr.	**569**
plastics goods mfr.	**825**
printing	**891**
tannery	**810**
milling	**513**
mosaic	**506**
mould (*steelworks*)	**839**
needle (*textile mfr.*)	**899**
oven (*ceramics mfr.*)	**823**
pattern	**516**
pin	**899**
pipe	**823**
press;	
c.n.c.	**514**
n.c.	**514**
power	**514**
press-	
metal trades	**514**
textile finishing	**552**
press tool	**514**
prop (*coal mine*)	**597**
rate	**364**
reed	**599**
retort	**500**
road	**922**
roll (*steelworks*)	**516**
saw	**899**
spindle	**516**

	Code number
Setter; *continued*	
spool	**552**
spring	**833**
steel (*corset mfr.*)	**859**
stone (jewellery)	**518**
teasel	**552**
teazle	**552**
thermostat	**850**
tile-	**823**
building and contracting	**506**
timber	**898**
tool;	**519**
edge	**899**
machine	**519**
tray (hospital sterile supplies)	**641**
tube (*textile mfr.*)	**814**
type	**560**
van (*railways*)	**872**
yarn	**552**
Setter-	
arc welding electrode mfr.	**599**
brush, broom mfr.	**599**
carpet mfr.	**552**
ceramics mfr.	**823**
glass mfr.	**591**
metal trades-	**519**
boring	**511**
die stamping	**514**
drilling	**511**
grinding	**512**
milling	**513**
press stamping	**514**
cutlery mfr.	**530**
jewellery mfr.	**518**
typefounding	**839**
watch, clock mfr.	**517**
plastics goods mfr.	**825**
sugar confectionery mfr.	**809**
tannery	**810**
textile mfr.	**552**
Setter and drawer (*ceramics mfr.*)	**823**
Setter and turner; lathe	**510**
Setter-in (*ceramics mfr.*)	**823**
Setter-operator;	
capstan	**510**
drill	**511**
engraving; pantograph	**599**
lathe;	**510**
capstan	**510**
centre	**510**
turning; roll	**510**
turret	**510**
machine;	
c.n.c.	**519**
die sinking	**514**
n.c.	**519**
paper	**569**
machine-	
metal trades-	**519**
boring	**511**
die stamping	**514**
drilling	**511**
grinding	**512**
milling	**513**
press stamping	**514**
press; brake	**514**
press (*metal trades*)	**514**
tool;	**519**
machine	**519**

	Code number
Setter-operator; *continued*	
tool; *continued*	
press	**514**
turret	**510**
Setter-operator-	
metal trades-	**519**
boring	**511**
die stamping	**514**
drilling	**511**
grinding	**512**
milling	**513**
press stamping	**514**
Setter-out;	
lead light	**503**
mill (*sawmilling*)	**899**
Setter-out-	
engineering	**515**
technical drawings	**381**
metal trades	**515**
wood products mfr.	**F897**
Setter-up-	
metal trades-	**519**
diamond polishing	**518**
typefounding	**899**
spectacle mfr.	**825**
Settlement worker	**371**
Settler; claims; insurance	**361**
Settler-	
betting	**410**
fish hook mfr.	**841**
hat mfr.	**814**
Sewage worker	**892**
Sewer;	
bag	**553**
belting	**555**
button	**553**
carpet	**553**
cloth	**553**
felt	**553**
fur	**553**
glove	**553**
hand	**553**
harness (*wool weaving*)	**814**
hat	**553**
piece	**553**
rug; skin	**555**
seam	**553**
sole	**555**
spangle	**553**
tape (*textile spinning*)	**894**
tent	**553**
vellum	**562**
welt	**555**
wire	**555**
Sewer-	
bookbinding	**562**
canvas goods mfr.	**553**
carpet, rug mfr.	**553**
cloth mending	**553**
clothing mfr.	**553**
footwear mfr.	**555**
glove mfr.	**553**
hat mfr.	**553**
leather goods mfr.	**555**
powder puff mfr.	**559**
rubber footwear mfr.	**555**
textile goods mfr.	**553**
Sewerage man (*local government*)	**892**
Sewerman	**892**
Sewing hand	**553**

	Code number
Sexer; chick	**902**
Sexton	**672**
Shackler	**889**
Shader-	
artificial flower mfr.	**869**
ceramics mfr.	**829**
textile mfr.	**814**
Shaftman (*coal mine*)	**899**
Shaker;	
bag	**919**
rag	**811**
waste	**811**
Shaker (*textile mfr.*)	**811**
Shampooer	**661**
Shanker (*footwear mfr.*)	**859**
Shaper;	
blades; airscrew (metal)	**840**
brim	**559**
collar	**557**
die	**840**
filament	**899**
tool; machine	**519**
tool room	**519**
Shaper-	
clothing mfr.	**557**
glass mfr.	**590**
hosiery mfr.	**552**
incandescent mantle mfr.	**599**
metal trades-	**840**
clog iron mfr.	**530**
steel pen mfr.	**899**
millinery mfr.	**559**
wood products mfr.	**897**
Sharpener;	
gear (*mining*)	**530**
pick	**840**
pit prop	**897**
saw	**899**
tool	**840**
Sharpener (*edge tool mfr.*)	**899**
Sherper *see Sharpener*	
Shaver;	
gear	**840**
hood	**559**
Shaver-	
hat mfr.	**559**
leather dressing	**810**
Shearman-	
clothing mfr.	**559**
metal trades	**899**
Shearer;	
billet (*rolling mill*)	**899**
bloom	**899**
cloth	**552**
coil (*metal trades*)	**899**
mat	**552**
rotary	**899**
sheep	**902**
Shearer-	
carpet, rug mfr.	**552**
coal mine-	**899**
below ground	**597**
glove mfr.	**559**
leather dressing	**810**
metal trades	**899**
textile finishing	**552**
Shearsman; scrap (*metal trades*)	**899**
Sheather; cable	**839**
Sheavesman (*coal mine*)	**894**
Shecheta	**581**
Shedman-	
docks	**930**
leather dressing	**810**
transport	**990**
Shed worker-	
railways	**990**
tannery	**810**
Sheerer (metal)	**534**
Sheet worker (metal)	**533**
Sheeter;	
asbestos-	
asbestos-cement goods mfr.	**599**
building and contracting	**501**
n.o.s.	**501**
cement; asbestos	**501**
constructional	**501**
iron; corrugated	**501**
roof	**501**
wagon	**631**
Sheeter-	
building and contracting	**501**
chemical mfr.	**501**
docks	**930**
paper mfr.	**821**
plastics goods mfr.	**825**
railways	**631**
rubber goods mfr.	**824**
steel mfr.	**534**
Shellerman	**809**
Shepherd	**900**
Sherardizer	**830**
Sheriff (*Scottish Courts*)	**240**
Sheriff-substitute (*Scottish Courts*)	**240**
Shifthand (*coal mine*)	**910**
Shiftman (*mine, not coal*)	**898**
Shift worker (*coal mine*)	**910**
Shifter;	
conveyor (*coal mine*)	**899**
iron	**889**
scene	**999**
Shifter-	
coal mine	**597**
jute spinning	**812**
rolling mill	**889**
Shingler (*iron works*)	**839**
Ship worker	**930**
Shipper-	
docks	**930**
patent fuel mfr.	**889**
tinplate mfr.	**889**
wholesale trade	**702**
Shipsmith	**530**
Shipwright	**534**
Shipwright-liner	**534**
Shocket	**581**
Shoddy man	**811**
Shoe hand	**555**
Shoe operative	**555**
Shoer; horse	**530**
Shoeroom worker	**555**
Shooter; trouble	**301**
Shooter (*gun mfr.*)	**860**
Shop girl; tailor's	**941**
Shop worker;	
core (*metal trades*)	**531**
paint-	**990**
vehicle mfr.	**596**
Shop worker-	
fried fish	**720**
retail trade	**720**
Shop worker- *continued*	
take-away food shop	**720**
Shopkeeper;	
chip potato	**174**
cook	**174**
fish	**178**
fish and chip	**174**
fried fish	**174**
Shopkeeper-	**179**
butchers	**178**
fishmongers	**178**
laundry, launderette, dry cleaners	**179**
mobile shop	**731**
Shopman;	
bottle (*iron, steel tube mfr.*)	**839**
butcher's	**581**
meat	**581**
Shopman (*railway workshops*)	**912**
Shopman-cutter (butcher's)	**581**
Shotman (*mine, not coal*)	**898**
Shotsman (*coal mine*)	**597**
Show girl	**384**
Showman	**176**
Shredder-	
chemical mfr.	**820**
food products mfr.	**809**
Shrimper	**903**
Shrinker; London	**552**
Shrinker-	
rubber goods mfr.	**824**
textile mfr.	**552**
Shuntman (*mine, not coal*)	**889**
Shunter-	**884**
road transport	**873**
Shutter; door (*coke ovens*)	**919**
Shutterer (*building and contracting*)	**570**
Shuttler	**559**
Side man (*brewery*)	**801**
Sider (*glass mfr.*)	**591**
Sidesman; copper (*brewery*)	**801**
Siever-	
abrasive paper, etc. mfr.	**821**
chemical mfr.	**820**
food products mfr.	**809**
Sifter;	
dust (*ceramics mfr.*)	**829**
flour	**809**
Sifter-	
ceramics mfr.	**829**
chemical mfr.	**820**
food products mfr.	**809**
Sighter; bottle (*brewery*)	**862**
Signalman;	
civilian (*Min. of Defence*)	**463**
diver's	**929**
Lloyd's	**889**
marine	**463**
port	**463**
relief	**883**
Signalman-	
mining	**886**
railways	**883**
steelworks	**932**
yacht club	**387**
Signaller (*mine, not coal*)	**886**
Silk worker-	**919**
greeting card mfr.	**553**
Silker (*textile mfr.*)	**553**
Silksman	**809**

	Code number
Siloman (*seed crushing*)	**809**
Silo worker	**441**
Silverman	**952**
Silver worker	**518**
Silverer-	
electroplating	**834**
glass mfr.	**834**
Silviculturist-	**904**
professionally qualified	**201**
Singer-	
entertainment	**384**
textile mfr.	**552**
Sinker;	
counter	**840**
die-	
metal trades	**515**
printing	**569**
pit	**509**
seat	**555**
shaft	**509**
well	**509**
Sinker-	
coal mine	**597**
mine sinking	**509**
Sinterer-	
metal mfr.	**839**
mine, not coal	**839**
Sister;	
home (nurses home)	**173**
housekeeping (hospital)	**173**
midwifery	**341**
Sister-	**F340**
religion	**292**
Sister-tutor	**F340**
Sitter; baby	**659**
Sizeman-	**810**
paper mill	**821**
Sizer;	
bobbin	**897**
engine (*paper mfr.*)	**821**
warp	**552**
yarn	**552**
Sizer-	
paper mfr.	**821**
textile mfr.-	**552**
rope, twine mfr.	**552**
Sizer and dryer; back	**552**
Skater; ice	**384**
Skeiner (*textile mfr.*)	**813**
Sketcher; design	**430**
Skewerer (*textile dyeing*)	**814**
Skilled workman (*telecoms*)	**523**
Skimmer-	
glass mfr.	**829**
metal mfr.	**830**
food products mfr.	**581**
slaughterhouse	**581**
tannery	**810**
Skipman	**863**
Skipper; yacht	**332**
Skipper-	
barge, boat	**332**
building and contracting	**F896**
fishing	**169**
shipping	**332**
Skirt hand	**556**
Skiver; belt (*abrasive paper, etc. mfr.*)	**899**
Skiver-	
footwear mfr.	**555**
leather dressing	**810**
Slab hand	**809**
Slab man	**500**
Slabber;	
tile	**506**
toffee	**809**
Slabber-	
builder's merchant	**506**
fireplace mfr.	**506**
textile mfr.	**814**
Slagman (*blast furnace*)	**830**
Slagger-	
blast furnace	**830**
steel casting	**839**
Slaker (*ceramics mfr.*)	**829**
Slaker man	**829**
Slate worker; enamelled	**500**
Slater	**501**
Slater and tiler	**501**
Slaughterman	**581**
Slaughterer	**581**
Sleever-	
cable mfr.	**899**
clothing mfr.	**553**
electrical goods mfr.	**841**
gramophone record mfr.	**862**
radio valve mfr.	**850**
Slicer; veneer	**897**
Slicer-	
bakery	**800**
celluloid sheet mfr.	**825**
Slicker (*leather dressing*)	**810**
Slider (*metal trades*)	**510**
Slimer (*gut cleaning*)	**829**
Slinger-	**932**
textile mfr.	**814**
Sliphouse hand	**829**
Slipper;	
cushion	**553**
last	**555**
shoe	**555**
tie	**553**
Slipper-	
asbestos-cement mfr.	**829**
furniture mfr.	**553**
Slipper operative	**555**
Slipper worker	**555**
Slitter;	
fabrics	**559**
foil; tin	**899**
metal	**899**
optical glass	**591**
paper	**822**
steel	**899**
Slitter-	
abrasive paper mfr.	**822**
paper and printing	**822**
pen nib mfr.	**899**
photographic film mfr.	**822**
plastics goods mfr.	**825**
steelworks	**899**
tobacco mfr.	**802**
transparent cellulose wrapping mfr.	**822**
Slitterman (*paper mfr.*)	**822**
Sliverer	**811**
Slotter; frame	**840**
Slotter-	
metal trades	**840**
needle mfr.	**841**
paper products mfr.	**569**
Slubber (*textile mfr.*)	**811**
Slugger; paste	**829**
Slugger (*footwear mfr.*)	**859**
Sluice man	**889**
Slurryman	**820**
Slurry worker (*coal mine*)	**890**
Smallholder-	**160**
forestry	**904**
Smash hand	**550**
Smearer (*waterproof garment mfr.*)	**559**
Smeller; cask	**869**
Smelter;	
lead	**830**
steel	**830**
Smelter-	
glass mfr.	**823**
metal mfr.	**830**
Smith;	**530**
boiler	**534**
bright	**518**
chain	**839**
coach	**530**
coil-	
spring mfr.	**530**
tube mfr.	**839**
cold	**899**
copper	**533**
engineering	**530**
gold	**518**
gun	**516**
iron; sheet	**533**
key	**899**
lock	**516**
metal; britannia	**518**
metal (*gas meter mfr.*)	**533**
padlock	**516**
pan;	
copper	**533**
salt	**530**
pan (*salt mfr.*)	**530**
plate	**534**
platinum	**518**
rope (*coal mine*)	**505**
saw	**899**
silver	**518**
tin	**533**
tool	**530**
white	**533**
Smither	**530**
Smocker	**553**
Smoker (*food products mfr.*)	**809**
Smoother-	
clothing mfr.	**673**
lens mfr.	**591**
Smudger	**889**
Snagger	**533**
Sniffer	**861**
Snipper	**811**
Soaker;	
lime	**810**
silk	**552**
Soaker (*leather dressing*)	**810**
Soap worker	**820**
Soaper; rope	**814**
Soapstoner (*roofing felt mfr.*)	**814**
Social worker	**293**
Sociologist	**291**
Socker	**859**
Softener;	
lead	**830**
water	**892**

	Code number
Softener-	
flax, hemp mfr.	**811**
leather dressing	**810**
Solderer-	**537**
radio and television mfr.	**850**
Solderer and jointer; case	**537**
Soldier-	
armed forces-	
foreign and Commonwealth	**601**
U.K.	**600**
Solicitor	**242**
Solutioner-	
footwear mfr.	**859**
rubber goods mfr.	**859**
Solutionist (*rubber goods mfr.*)	**859**
Sorter;	
biscuit	**863**
bobbin	**863**
bottle	**863**
breakage (*food products mfr.*)	**863**
bulb (*electric lamp mfr.*)	**863**
card; playing	**861**
clip	**863**
cloth	**863**
coal (*coal mine*)	**890**
cocoa bean	**809**
cork	**863**
diamond	**863**
dyehouse (*textile mfr.*)	**863**
egg	**863**
feather	**863**
fent	**863**
fibre	**863**
flock	**863**
foil; tin	**863**
fruit	**863**
fur	**863**
gelatine	**863**
glass	**869**
glove	**861**
gum	**863**
hair	**863**
head-	
galvanized sheet mfr.	**863**
P.O.	**940**
hide	**863**
hosiery	**863**
iron (*shipbuilding*)	**912**
label	**861**
last	**863**
leaf	**863**
leather	**863**
letter	**940**
lime	**863**
linen (*hospital service*)	**863**
machine (*ceramics mfr.*)	**863**
mail	**940**
meat	**863**
metal; sheet	**863**
metal-	**863**
scrap metal dealer	**863**
mica	**863**
mohair	**863**
newspaper	**863**
note (*paper products mfr.*)	**861**
order (*mail order*)	**420**
paper-	
paper mfr.	**861**
paper products mfr.	**861**
wallpaper mfr.	**861**
Sorter; *continued*	
paper- *continued*	
waste paper merchants	**863**
parcel-	**941**
P.O.	**940**
pipe; ceramic	**863**
post	**940**
printer's	**861**
rag	**863**
rag and metal	**863**
refuse	**863**
rubber	**863**
sack	**863**
salvage	**863**
scrap	**863**
seed-	**863**
mustard	**809**
sheet (*printing*)	**861**
shuttle	**863**
skin	**863**
slag	**863**
sole	**863**
spool	**863**
stocking	**863**
stores	**863**
tape	**863**
tile; roofing	**863**
timber	**863**
tin	**863**
tube (*textile spinning*)	**814**
warehouse; biscuit	
(*ceramics mfr.*)	**863**
waste-	**863**
textile mfr.	**863**
weft	**814**
wood	**863**
wool-	**863**
fellmongering	**863**
woollen	**863**
yarn	**863**
Sorter-	
broom, brush mfr.	**863**
button mfr.	**863**
ceramics mfr.-	**863**
roofing tile mfr.	**863**
cigar mfr.	**863**
clothing mfr.	**863**
cutlery handle mfr.	**863**
dyeing and cleaning	**863**
food products mfr.	**863**
footwear mfr.	**863**
fur dressing	**863**
glass mfr.-	**869**
glass bottle mfr.	**863**
incandescent mantle mfr.	**863**
laundry	**863**
metal trades-	**863**
galvanized sheet mfr.	**863**
mine, not coal	**863**
P.O.	**940**
paper mfr.	**861**
paper goods mfr.	**861**
printing	**861**
seed merchants	**863**
stick mfr.	**863**
sugar confectionery mfr.	**863**
tannery	**863**
textile mfr.-	**863**
flax, hemp mfr.	**863**
hair, bass, fibre dressing	**863**
waste merchants	**863**
Sorter- *continued*	
wholesale fish trade	**863**
Sorter and grader	
(*canvas goods mfr.*)	**863**
Sorter and packer	**863**
Sounder; survey	**889**
Spare hand-	
fishing	**903**
rolling mill	**839**
Specialist;	
beauty	**661**
ceiling	**507**
computer (sales)	**710**
ear, nose and throat	**220**
flooring	**506**
organisation and methods	**364**
software-	**320**
professional	**214**
systems	**320**
taxation	**362**
woodworm	**699**
Spectrographer	**300**
Speeder; braiding machine	**814**
Speeter (*fish curing*)	**809**
Spiderman	**535**
Spiler (*textile mfr.*)	**553**
Spillager (*coal mine*)	**886**
Spindle hand	**897**
Spindler; ribbon	**813**
Spinner;	
acetate	**826**
asbestos	**812**
cap	**812**
concrete	**599**
cord	**814**
crimp	**812**
doffer; self	**812**
fibreglass	**812**
fly	**812**
frame	**812**
fuse; safety	**814**
gill	**812**
gimp	**550**
gut	**829**
mule	**812**
nylon	**826**
paper (*cellulose film mfr.*)	**812**
pipe-	
cast concrete products mfr.	**599**
iron, steel tube mfr.	**839**
polyester	**826**
pot (*carborundum mfr.*)	**829**
rayon	**826**
ring	**812**
rope	**814**
silk;	**812**
artificial	**826**
glass	**590**
sugar	**809**
thread (metal)	**812**
twine	**814**
viscose	**826**
wire	**899**
Spinner-	
metal	**519**
textiles	**812**
electric cable mfr.	**899**
gut processing	**829**
mining, safety fuse mfr.	**814**
paper twine mfr.	**812**
sugar, glucose mfr.	**809**

	Code number
Spinner- *continued*	
textile mfr.-	**812**
man-made fibre mfr.	**826**
tobacco mfr.	**802**
wire rope mfr.	**899**
Spiraller; filament	**899**
Splicer;	
film	**569**
rope-	**814**
coal mine	**505**
steel mfr.	**505**
veneer	**579**
wire	**505**
yarn	**814**
Splicer-	
rope-	**814**
wire	**505**
textile cords, etc.	**814**
coal mine	**505**
textile mfr.	**814**
tyre mfr.	**824**
Splitter;	
bale (*rubber goods mfr.*)	**919**
cloth	**814**
fish	**582**
fork (*digging, etc. fork mfr.*)	**530**
gut	**829**
hide	**810**
mica	**829**
skin	**810**
slate	**500**
Splitter-	
gut dressing	**829**
leather dressing	**810**
mine, not coal-	
above ground	**500**
below ground	**898**
rubber reclamation	**829**
textile mfr.	**814**
tobacco mfr.	**802**
Sponger of clayware	**590**
Sponger (*ceramics mfr.*)	**590**
Spooler; wire	**899**
Spooler-	
paper products	**569**
photographic film mfr.	**569**
textile mfr.-	**813**
Axminster carpet mfr.	**552**
lace mfr.	**814**
Spoon and fork worker	**841**
Sportsman; professional	**387**
Spotter-	
artificial flower mfr.	**869**
dry cleaning	**673**
film processing	**569**
footwear mfr.	**555**
lace mfr.	**814**
laundry	**673**
printing	**569**
textile finishing	**861**
Spragger (*coal mine*)	**889**
Sprayer;	
aerograph (ceramics)	**591**
agricultural	**901**
asbestos	**599**
cellulose-	**596**
ceramics mfr.	**591**
colour-	
ceramics mfr.	**591**
glass mfr.	**596**
copper	**839**
Sprayer; *continued*	
crop	**160**
enamel (*ceramics mfr.*)	**591**
glaze	**591**
insulation	**896**
leather	**596**
lime (*iron and steel mfr.*)	**839**
machine	**596**
metal	**834**
paint	**596**
steam	**552**
tar	**885**
Sprayer-	**596**
agricultural contracting	**901**
ceramics mfr.	**591**
insulation contracting	**896**
lamp, valve mfr.	**590**
textile finishing	**552**
wood preservation service	**699**
Spreader;	
asphalt;	**923**
mastic	**506**
cold lay	**506**
glue (*abrasive paper, etc. mfr.*)	**821**
plaster	**814**
rubber-	**824**
textile mfr.	**814**
tar	**923**
Spreader-	
building and contracting	**929**
food products mfr.	**809**
laminated plastics mfr.	**829**
leathercloth mfr.	**814**
linoleum mfr.	**829**
rubber mfr.	**824**
surgical dressing mfr.	**814**
textile mfr.-	**814**
flax mfr.	**811**
tobacco mfr.	**802**
Springer;	
carriage	**516**
heald	**552**
umbrella	**851**
Springer-	
needle mfr.	**899**
textile mfr.	**552**
tube mfr.	**839**
Springer-in (spectacles)	**859**
Spring worker	**899**
Squarer-up	**555**
Squeezer (*textile dyeing*)	**552**
Squirter; lead (*cartridge mfr.*)	**839**
Stable boy	**902**
Stable girl	**902**
Stable hand	**902**
Stable lad	**902**
Stableman	**902**
Stacker;	**889**
shelf (*retail trade*)	**954**
Stacker and packer	**441**
Stacker-driver	**887**
Stage hand-	
docks	**889**
entertainment	**999**
Stageman; landing	**889**
Stager (*shipbuilding*)	**505**
Stainer;	
boot	**869**
edge (*footwear mfr.*)	**869**
leather	**869**
Stainer; *continued*	
paper	**821**
shoe	**869**
wood	**507**
Stainer-	
furniture mfr.	**507**
glass mfr.	**591**
leather goods mfr.	**869**
tobacco pipe mfr.	**507**
Staithman	**930**
Staker (*leather dressing*)	**810**
Stamper;	
box	**569**
brass;	**841**
hot	**530**
brush	**569**
bulb; electric	**569**
card (*textile mfr.*)	**814**
cloth	**569**
cold	**841**
collar	**569**
die-	**841**
printing	**569**
drop; hot	**530**
drop-	
forging	**530**
sheet metal goods mfr.	**841**
gold-	
ceramics mfr.	**569**
footwear mfr.	**569**
hat mfr.	**569**
jewellery mfr.	**841**
hammer	**530**
hollow-ware	**841**
hot	**530**
ingot	**839**
metal; hot	**530**
metal-	**841**
forging	**530**
pattern-	
ceramics mfr.	**569**
paper pattern mfr.	**569**
printer's	**569**
relief	**569**
rubber (*rubber goods mfr.*)	**824**
silver	**841**
size	**569**
soap	**569**
sock	**569**
tool; edge	**530**
Stamper-	
Assay Office	**839**
ceramics mfr.	**569**
footwear mfr.	**569**
Inland Revenue	**400**
metal trades-	**841**
forging	**530**
galvanized sheet mfr.	**530**
rolling mill	**530**
tube fittings mfr.	**530**
mine, not coal	**890**
P.O.	**940**
paper goods mfr.	**569**
tannery	**569**
textile mfr.	**569**
Stapler;	
box (*cardboard box mfr.*)	**859**
slipper	**859**
wool (*textile mfr.*)	**552**
Stapler-	
bedding mfr.	**851**

	Code number
Stapler- *continued*	
footwear mfr.	**859**
leather goods mfr.	**859**
Starch room worker	**809**
Starcher-	
laundry	**673**
textile finishing	**552**
Starrer	**559**
Stationman; railway	**631**
Stationman (*L.R.T.*)	**631**
Stationer-	**179**
paper goods mfr.	**569**
printing warehouse (Scotland)	**F569**
Stationer and printer	**561**
Stationmaster	**140**
Statistician	**252**
Staver (*tube mfr.*)	**839**
Stayer (*cardboard box mfr.*)	**569**
Steam hand (*catering*)	**953**
Steamer;	
hat	**559**
silk	**552**
spun pipe	**829**
Steamer-	
dyeing and cleaning	**673**
felt hat mfr.	**559**
straw hat mfr.	**552**
textile finishing	**552**
Steel man (*coal mine*)	**899**
Steelworker-	**912**
shipbuilding	**534**
structural engineering	**535**
Steephouseman (*starch mfr.*)	**809**
Steeple jack	**505**
Steeple peter	**505**
Steepsman (*starch mfr.*)	**809**
Steerer (*barge, boat*)	**880**
Steersman;	**880**
bridge	**889**
Stemmer; leaf	**802**
Stemmer-	
coal mine	**597**
tobacco mfr.	**802**
Stemmer and waxer (*battery carbon mfr.*)	**859**
Stencil worker	**569**
Stenciller;	
aerographing (*ceramics mfr.*)	**591**
box	**869**
Stenciller-	**869**
art needlework mfr.	**559**
Stenographer	**452**
Stenter	**552**
Stenter hand	**552**
Stenter man	**552**
Stenterer	**552**
Stereographer	**560**
Stereotyper	**560**
Steriliser; milk	**809**
Steriliser-	
canned food mfr.	**809**
hospital service	**641**
surgical dressing mfr.	**552**
telephone sterilising service	**958**
textile mfr.	**552**
Stevedore;	**930**
superintendent	**142**
Steward;	
air	**630**
bar	**622**
Steward; *continued*	
cabin	**630**
canteen	**621**
catering	**621**
chief-	**F621**
aircraft, shipping	**F630**
club	**175**
railways	**F621**
club	**175**
college	**173**
dining car	**621**
dwellings	**672**
estate	**160**
farm	**160**
flats	**672**
flight	**630**
ground	**630**
hostel	**173**
house	**958**
kitchen	**F953**
laboratory	**990**
mess	**621**
messroom	**621**
officer's	**630**
pantry	**952**
room; billiard	**959**
saloon (*shipping*)	**630**
shore	**441**
wine	**621**
Steward-	
aircraft	**630**
canteen	**621**
club	**175**
institution	**173**
naval shore establishment	**621**
race course	**387**
railways	**621**
service flats	**672**
shipping-	**630**
catering	**621**
university-	**990**
catering	**621**
working men's institute	**175**
Sticker;	
bill	**959**
cloth (*needle mfr.*)	**862**
feather	**859**
junction (*ceramics mfr.*)	**591**
label	**862**
leaf (*artificial flower mfr.*)	**859**
pattern (*paper pattern mfr.*)	**859**
poultry	**582**
punty	**590**
sole	**555**
Sticker-	
clothing mfr.	**559**
footwear mfr.	**555**
needle mfr.	**862**
slaughterhouse	**581**
Sticker-up (*ceramics mfr.*)	**859**
Stiffener; hat; straw	**552**
Stiffener (*footwear mfr.*)	**859**
Still man-	**820**
hotel, catering, etc.	**953**
metal smelting	**830**
Stillhouse man (*distillery*)	**820**
Stillroom man-	
distillery	**820**
hotel, catering, etc.	**953**
Stitcher;	
bale	**862**
Stitcher; *continued*	
box	**859**
boxing glove	**555**
carton	**859**
collar	**555**
cricket ball	**555**
football	**555**
hem	**553**
leather	**555**
lock-	**553**
slipper mfr.	**555**
mattress	**554**
rapid	**555**
tennis ball	**553**
wire-	
leather goods mfr.	**555**
paper and paper goods mfr.	**859**
Stitcher-	**553**
bookbinding	**562**
footwear mfr.	**555**
hosiery mfr.	**553**
leather goods mfr.	**555**
paper and paper goods mfr.	**859**
printing	**562**
wire goods mfr.	**899**
Stock hand *see Stockman-*	
Stockman-	
farming	**900**
manufacturing-	**441**
blast furnace	**889**
leather dressing	**810**
rolling mill	**889**
Stockroom man	**441**
Stocker; whip	**555**
Stocker-	
gun mfr.	**579**
steel mfr.	**912**
tinplate mfr.	**441**
Stocker-up	**889**
Stockinger	**551**
Stocksman-	**810**
farming	**900**
Stocktaker; chief (*steelworks*)	**F440**
Stocktaker-	**410**
rolling mill	**441**
steel smelting	**F441**
Stoker;	
boiler	**893**
destructor	**999**
drifter	**880**
engine-	**893**
barge, boat	**880**
railways	**882**
shipping	**880**
furnace-	**893**
ceramics mfr.	**823**
metal mfr.	**830**
gas	**820**
gas plant	**820**
high pressure	**893**
kiln;	**820**
brick	**823**
lime	**829**
leading	**F893**
retort (*coal gas*)	**820**
Stoker-	**893**
coal gas, coke ovens	**820**
fishing	**880**
glass mfr.	**823**

(St)

	Code number
Stoker- *continued*	
metal mfr.	830
shipbuilding	830
shipping	880
Stoker-cleaner	893
Stoker-engineer	893
Stoker-mechanic-	893
shipping	880
Stoker-porter	893
Stone hand	560
Stoneman-	
coal mine	597
stone dressing	500
Stone worker;	
artificial	599
precious	518
Stone worker-	
cast concrete products mfr.	599
coal mine	597
mine, not coal	898
Stopper; glaze	591
Stopper (*ceramics mfr.*)	591
Stopper man (*coal gas, coke ovens*)	919
Storage hand; cold	931
Storehand	931
Store holder	441
Storeman;	441
chief	F441
head	F441
Storeman-clerk	441
Storeman-driver	441
Storewoman; superintendent (*P.O.*)	F441
Storehouseman	441
Storer	441
Storeroom man	441
Storesman	441
Stove hand *see Stover-*	
Stoveman *see Stover-*	
Stover; seasoning	829
Stover-	829
bacon, ham curing	809
blast furnace	830
food products mfr.	809
hat mfr.	552
iron foundry	839
leather dressing	810
starch mfr.	809
textile mfr.	552
tobacco mfr.	802
Stower;	
cake	889
cement	889
coal	889
power	597
ship	930
Stower-	
coal mine	597
grain milling	889
railways	631
Straightener;	
axle	530
bar	839
barrel	899
carriage (*textile machinery mfr.*)	516
comb	899
drill	839
hard (*needle mfr.*)	899
iron	839
Straightener; *continued*	
plate;	839
iron	899
saw	899
prop (*coal mine*)	899
rail	839
rod mills	839
roller	839
section	839
shaft; crank	839
steel-	839
coal mine	899
tube	839
wire	899
yarn	861
Straightener-	
coal mine	899
metal mfr.	839
needle mfr.	899
sheet metal working	533
textile mfr.-	861
flax mfr.	811
hosiery mfr.	552
textile machinery mfr.	516
vehicle mfr.	533
wire mfr.	899
Strainer-	
chemical mfr.	820
paint, etc. mfr.	829
tannery	810
textile printing	829
Strainerman (*paper mfr.*)	821
Strander; wire	899
Strander-	
cable mfr.	899
rope mfr.	814
wire rope mfr.	899
Strap man	555
Strapper-	
corset mfr.	553
textile mfr.	889
Stratigrapher	202
Straw worker (*hat mfr.*)	559
Stretcher;	
clip (*textile mfr.*)	552
dry (*textile mfr.*)	552
tube	839
yarn	552
Stretcher-	
metal mfr.	839
tannery	810
textile mfr.	552
Stretcher hand (*aluminium mfr.*)	839
Striker;	
anvil	839
catch (*coal mine*)	889
chain	839
colour	829
forge	839
forger's	839
iron	839
smith's	839
wheel	839
Striker-	
metal trades	839
railways	839
Striker-out	810
Stringer;	
bag; paper	859
bead	859
Stringer; *continued*	
pearl	859
racquet	599
Stringer-	
footwear mfr.	555
piano mfr.	593
plastics goods mfr.	825
printing	859
sports goods mfr.	599
Strip worker; copper	839
Striper (*fur dressing*)	810
Stripper;	
biscuit	800
bobbin	814
boiler; locomotive	516
brake	516
cable	869
car	540
card	899
cardboard	569
carriage and wagon	516
carton	569
cloth	811
cop	814
dog	902
engine	516
file	899
film	569
frame	919
gold	839
ingot	839
leaf	802
leather lace	555
liquorice	809
locomotive	516
motor	540
paint; vehicle (*vehicle mfr.*)	869
paper	569
pirn	814
polish	869
rag	811
rubber	824
silver	839
spring	516
tin (*biscuit mfr.*)	800
tyre	824
wool	814
yarn	814
Stripper-	
candle mfr.	919
cast stone products mfr.	591
ceramics mfr.	919
coal mine	597
metal trades-	843
electroplating	834
gold refining	830
wire drawing	831
mine, not coal	898
paper products mfr.	569
process engraving	560
railway workshop	516
textile mfr.	814
tobacco mfr.	802
Stripper and buncher	814
Stripper and grinder	899
Stripper and setter (*soap mfr.*)	820
Stripper-assembler (*cast concrete products mfr.*)	919
Stripping hand (*hosiery mfr.*)	559
Stubber	899
Studder (*clothing mfr.*)	859

	Code number
Student *see notes*	
Studhand	**902**
Stuffer;	
chair	**559**
cushion	**559**
Stuffer-	
mattress, upholstery mfr.	**559**
textile dyeing	**863**
toy mfr.	**559**
Stumper	**814**
Stunner	**581**
Stunt man	**384**
Stylist; hair	**660**
Stylist-	
hairdressing	**660**
vehicle mfr.	**382**
Sub-agent (*building and construction*)	**111**
Sub-contractor *see Contractor*	
Sub-editor	**380**
Sub-foreman *see Foreman-*	
Sub-ganger *see Ganger-*	
Sub-inspector- *see also Inspector-*	
Min. of Defence	**M152**
railway-	**F881**
engineering	**922**
Sub-Lieutenant-	
armed forces-	
foreign and Commonwealth	**M151**
U.K.	**M150**
Sub-officer (*fire service*)	**F611**
Sub-postmaster-	**131**
self-employed	**179**
Sueder	**810**
Sugar worker	**809**
Sulphitation man	**809**
Sulphonator man	**820**
Sumper	**597**
Superintendent;	
administrative (*insurance*)	**F410**
airport	**140**
ambulance room	**199**
assistant- *see also Superintendent-*	
cemetery, crematorium	**699**
bath(s)-	**176**
coal mine	**F699**
branch (*insurance*)	**M719**
building	**672**
cargo	**142**
chief (*police service*)	**M152**
claims	**M361**
cleansing (*local government*)	**199**
club	**174**
departmental *see Manager-*	
depot-	**142**
transport	**140**
distribution-	
gas board	**113**
water works	**113**
district-	
clothing club	**730**
gas board	**113**
insurance	**M719**
transport	**140**
divisional (*railways*)	**140**
drilling	**113**
electrical-	**110**
electricity board	**113**
Superintendent; *continued*	
electrical- *continued*	
Min. of Defence	**212**
engineering	**110**
estate (*local government*)	**111**
factory	**110**
fire-	**M153**
insurance	**M719**
flight	**140**
floor (*department store*)	**F720**
general (*L.R.T.*)	**140**
grain (*Min. of A.F.F.*)	**103**
house;	
boiler	**F893**
n.o.s.	**672**
turbine (*electricity board*)	**113**
insurance	**M719**
kitchen (*hospital service*)	**F620**
laundry (*hospital service*)	**F673**
mains	**113**
maintenance	**F896**
marine-	**140**
docks	**313**
market	**199**
marketing	**121**
medical	**220**
mess	**174**
meter (*electricity board*)	**212**
motor (*insurance*)	**M719**
night-	
hospital service	**F340**
manufacturing	**110**
office	**139**
operating	**199**
operations (*transport*)	**140**
park	**176**
pilot	**332**
plant (*refinery*)	**110**
platform (*coal tar distillers*)	**F820**
power	**113**
principal (telegraphs)	**139**
process	**110**
production-	**110**
Min. of Defence	**217**
progress	**F420**
radio (*P.O.*)	**139**
range	**699**
refinery	**110**
rents (*local government*)	**F401**
repairs	**F896**
rescue (*coal mine*)	**F619**
reservoir	**929**
sales-	**121**
telecoms	**M710**
sanitary	**199**
shift	**110**
shipping	**140**
shop-	
manufacturing	**110**
retail trade	**F720**
staff	**363**
station;	
assistant	**F610**
power	**113**
rescue	**F619**
station-	**199**
airline	**140**
store(s)	**141**
supplies (*P.O.*);	**F441**
chief	**141**
technical	**110**
Superintendent; *continued*	
telecommunications	**139**
telegraph; overseas	**139**
town hall	**F672**
traffic;	**140**
telecommunications	**139**
transport	**140**
warehouse	**142**
welfare	**M371**
works;	
gas	**113**
water	**113**
works-	**110**
building and contracting	**111**
local government	**111**
public utilities	**113**
workshop	**110**
of bill distributors	**F941**
of canvassers	**730**
of pilots	**332**
of Stamping (1st Class)	**132**
of typists	**F452**
of works	**111**
Superintendent-	
apprenticeship	**391**
laboratory	**F300**
residential buildings	**672**
sales force	**M710**
ambulance service	**199**
bakery	**110**
banking	**131**
baths	**176**
biscuit mfr.	**110**
building and contracting	**111**
catering	**174**
cemetery	**199**
children's home	**M370**
clothing club	**730**
crematorium	**199**
Customs and Excise	**155**
D.O.E.	**111**
docks	**140**
domestic services	**173**
engineering-	**110**
civil engineering	**111**
structural engineering	**111**
flour confectionery mfr.	**110**
garage	**171**
hospital service	**199**
institution	**M370**
insurance	**M719**
Land Registry	**103**
library	**270**
local government-	**102**
highways department	**111**
metal trades	**110**
Min. of Defence (Air) designs office	**260**
motoring association	**199**
National Physical Laboratory	**202**
nursing association	**M340**
old people's home	**M370**
P.O.	**131**
park	**176**
passenger transport	**140**
police service	**M152**
prison service	**154**
public utilities	**113**
R.S.P.C.A.	**395**
railways	**140**
retail trade	**F720**

Code number

Superintendent- *continued*
- *Royal Mint* ... **110**
- *salvage corps* ... **M153**
- *storage* ... **142**
- *W.R.N.S.* ... **M150**
- *waterguard* ... **155**

Supervisor;
- account (*advertising*) ... **123**
- apprenticeship ... **391**
- area- ... **M710**
  - *building and contracting* **F896**
  - *gas board* ... **F532**
  - *railway signalling* ... **F883**
- banking ... **F411**
- building ... **F896**
- canteen ... **F953**
- catering ... **F953**
- centre; service (*electricity board*) ... **F720**
- chief-
  - *P.O.* ... **462**
  - *telecoms* ... **462**
- chief; senior-
  - *P.O.* ... **199**
  - *telecoms* ... **199**
- children's ... **659**
- claims ... **F411**
- clerical ... **F430**
- commercial ... **F410**
- communications (*air transport*) ... **F463**
- contract(s)- ... **211**
  - *building and contracting* **111**
- cotton ... **F553**
- craft (*oil refining*) ... **F840**
- credit ... **F410**
- display ... **791**
- distribution- ... **F441**
  - *water board* ... **F895**
- domestic- ... **F670**
  - *hospital service* ... **F641**
- erection (*building and contracting*) ... **F896**
- field; playing ... **699**
- field (*market research*) ... **F420**
- higher grade (*telecoms*) ... **F462**
- hostel ... **173**
- laundry ... **673**
- loading (aircraft) ... **F931**
- mail ... **940**
- market ... **619**
- meals (schools) ... **659**
- meat (*abattoir*) ... **F581**
- movements (*railways*) ... **881**
- nursery- ... **F340**
  - horticulture ... **595**
- office ... **F430**
- order ... **F441**
- park ... **F615**
- payroll ... **F410**
- planning; production ... **F420**
- playground ... **659**
- playgroup ... **651**
- pool; swimming ... **F699**
- pools; football ... **F430**
- postal ... **F940**
- pricing ... **F410**
- process-
  - *explosives mfr.* ... **F820**
  - *oil refining* ... **F820**
- processing; data ... **F490**

Supervisor; *continued*
- progress ... **F420**
- ramp (*air transport*) ... **F990**
- research; market ... **121**
- reservations (*air transport*) **F420**
- room;
  - dining (*hospital service*) **F953**
  - print ... **F490**
  - show ... **F720**
- rope; trot ... **889**
- round(s) (*retail trade-delivery round*) ... **731**
- safety ... **396**
- sales- ... **M710**
  - *retail trade-* ... **F720**
    - *delivery round* ... **F731**
- service-
  - instruments ... **F517**
  - *electrical engineering* ... **F521**
  - *gas board* ... **F516**
- signalling (*railways*) ... **F883**
- station ... **631**
- steel (*coal mine*) ... **899**
- stock ... **F441**
- store- ... **F441**
  - *retail trade* ... **F720**
- switchboard ... **462**
- tool ... **441**
- trade (*retail trade*) ... **F720**
- trainee (*coal mine*) ... **391**
- training ... **391**
- transport-
  - *rail* ... **F881**
  - *road-* ... **F871**
    - *public transport* ... **F870**
- typing ... **F452**
- unit; poultry ... **F900**
- wages ... **F410**
- warehouse ... **F441**
- welfare ... **371**
- of sorting assistants (*P.O.*) **F940**

Supervisor- *see also Foreman-*
- accountancy ... **F410**
- institutions ... **370**
- office machines ... **F490**
- training ... **391**
- *ambulance service* ... **F642**
- *betting* ... **F411**
- *Dept. of Emp.* ... **132**
- *gas board* ... **532**
- *insurance* ... **719**
- *local government* ... **F401**
- *mail order house* ... **F440**
- *oil refining* ... **110**
- *P.O.-*
  - *sorting office* ... **F940**
  - *telegraph service* ... **F463**
  - *telephone service* ... **F462**
- *school meals service* ... **659**
- *Stationery Office* ... **F889**
- *telecoms* ... **462**

Supervisor-instructor (*government*) ... **391**

Supplier;
- leaf ... **802**
- timber (*coal mine*) ... **889**

Supply man (*coal mine*) ... **889**

Supply worker (*retail trade*) **441**

Supporter (*lamp, valve mfr.*) **899**

Suppressor; dust (*coal mine*) **597**

Surface hand-
- *coal mine* ... **910**
- *mine, not coal* ... **990**

Surface man-
- *civil engineering* ... **923**
- *coal mine* ... **910**
- *railways* ... **990**

Surface worker; road ... **923**

Surface worker-
- *coal mine* ... **910**
- *mine, not coal* ... **990**

Surfacer;
- lens; optical ... **591**
- optical ... **591**
- road ... **923**
- steel shot ... **599**

Surgeon; ... **220**
- dental ... **223**
- tree ... **169**
- veterinary ... **224**

Surgical hand (*rubber goods mfr.*) ... **824**

Surveyor;
- agricultural ... **170**
- aircraft ... **211**
- boiler and engine (*insurance*) ... **313**
- bonus ... **312**
- borough ... **210**
- building ... **262**
- cartographic ... **262**
- chartered ... **262**
- city ... **210**
- colliery ... **262**
- control; pest ... **F699**
- county ... **210**
- design (*Air Registration Board*) ... **211**
- district ... **210**
- divisional; county ... **210**
- electrical ... **212**
- estate ... **170**
- fire ... **313**
- group (*coal mine*) ... **262**
- hydrographic ... **313**
- infestation; timber ... **699**
- insurance ... **313**
- land ... **262**
- Lloyd's ... **395**
- marine ... **313**
- measuring ... **312**
- mineral ... **262**
- mining ... **262**
- nautical ... **313**
- naval ... **313**
- photographic ... **262**
- quantity ... **312**
- rating ... **360**
- river ... **313**
- ship ... **395**
- topographic ... **262**
- valuation ... **360**
- of Customs and Excise ... **155**

Surveyor- ... **262**
- *Customs and Excise* ... **155**
- *insurance* ... **313**
- *pest control* ... **F699**
- *river authority* ... **313**

Surveyor and estimator ... **262**

Surveyor and valuer ... **360**

Surveyor and water engineer **262**

	Code number
Surveyor-engineer	**262**
Suspender; butt	**810**
Suspender hand	**553**
Suspender man	**810**
Swabber	**559**
Swager (*cutlery mfr.*) ...	**899**
Swarfer (*tube mfr.*)	**899**
Sweater-	
hat mfr.	**559**
metal trades	**537**
Sweep (chimney)	**957**
Sweeper;	**958**
chimney	**957**
cotton (*textile mfr.*) ...	**919**
loom	**814**
road;	**957**
mechanical	**874**
tube	**958**
Sweeper-up	**958**
Swiftman	**839**
Swiller-	
bedstead mfr.	**912**
enamelling	**869**
tinplate mfr.	**912**
Swingbridge man	**889**
Swinger...	**814**
Switch hand	**893**
Switchman-	
coal mine	**889**
electricity board	**893**
Switchboard hand	**893**
Synchroniser (*film production*)	**569**
Syphon man	**999**
Systematist	**201**

	Code number
T	
T.1 (*telecoms*)	**523**
T.2A (*telecoms*)	**523**
T.2B (*telecoms*)	**524**
T.T.O.-	
Civil Aviation Authority	**529**
telecoms	**F462**
Tabber-	
corset mfr.	**553**
glove mfr.	**862**
hosiery mfr.	**862**
laundry	**569**
Table hand *see Table man-*	
Table man; surface	**515**
Table man-	
bakery	**580**
bookbinding	**562**
box mfr.	**569**
clothing mfr.	**559**
food products mfr.	**809**
footwear mfr.	**869**
leather dressing	**810**
printing	**569**
rubber goods mfr.	**824**
Table worker-	
cigar mfr.	**802**
printing	**569**
Tacker; board	**896**
Tacker-	
corset mfr.	**559**
footwear mfr.	**555**
hosiery mfr.	**553**
tack mfr.	**841**
tailoring	**556**
Tackleman-	
docks	**930**
steelworks	**505**
Tackle worker; fishing	**859**
Tackler;	
braid machine	**516**
dobby	**516**
jacquard	**516**
loom	**516**
Tackler-	
wire weaving	**519**
paper goods mfr.	**569**
textile weaving	**516**
Tagger; label	**859**
Tagger-	
lace mfr.	**859**
steel mfr.	**839**
tube mfr.	**839**
Tailer (beret)	**551**
Tailor;	**556**
merchant	**179**
Tailor and outfitter	**556**
Tailoress	**556**
Taker;	
care-	**672**
cemetery	**672**
reservoir	**929**
woodlands	**904**
copy (*publishing*)	**941**
impression (*printing*)	**569**
number	**441**
stock; chief (*steelworks*)	**F440**
stock-	**410**
rolling mill	**441**
steel smelting	**F441**
Taker; *continued*	
stock- *continued*	
valuers	**410**
temperature	**830**
weight	**863**
work	**F912**
Taker-in; piece (*textile mfr.*)	**441**
Taker-in-	
glass mfr.	**823**
textile weaving	**552**
Taker-off;	
bobbin	**814**
dipper's	**869**
machine (*printing*)	**891**
paper bag	**569**
Taker-off-	
cast concrete products mfr.	**599**
ceramics mfr.	**869**
ceramic transfer mfr.	**569**
clothing mfr.	**559**
glass mfr.	**590**
metal trades	**889**
plasterboard mfr.	**829**
quantity surveying	**312**
textile mfr.-	**814**
lace finishing	**673**
wool sorting	**863**
Taker-out; can (*textile mfr.*)	**811**
Taker-out-	**990**
ceramics mfr.	**889**
Tallyman; timber	**441**
Tallyman-	**412**
self-employed	**730**
Tambourer (*textile making-up*)	**553**
Tamer (animal)	**384**
Tamperman	**923**
Tankhand (vulcanised fibre)	**821**
Tankman;	
seed (yeast)	**809**
storage	**999**
Tankman-	
glass mfr.	**823**
non-ferrous metal mfr.	**830**
Tank worker; wax (*cardboard box mfr.*)	**821**
Tanker (*galvanized sheet mfr.*)	**834**
Tankerman (*whisky distilling*)	**801**
Tanner-	**810**
net, rope mfr.	**552**
Tannery worker	**810**
Taper; coil	**599**
Taper-	
cable mfr.	**899**
cardboard box mfr.	**569**
electrical goods mfr.	**899**
footwear mfr.	**555**
plasterboard mfr.	**502**
textile mfr.	**552**
Taper girl	**599**
Taperer (*metal trades*)	**840**
Tapestry worker	**553**
Tapper;	
nut and socket (*tube fittings mfr.*)	**841**
stay	**534**
wheel (*railways*)	**860**
Tapper-	
bolt mfr.	**841**
carbide mfr.	**820**
footwear mfr.	**555**
iron, steelworks	**830**
Tapper- *continued*	
railways	**860**
Tapper-out	**830**
Tar man-	
building and contracting	**923**
coal gas by-products mfr.	**820**
Tare man (*textile mfr.*)	**862**
Targer (*flax mfr.*)	**811**
Tarmac man (*airport*)	**889**
Tarmac worker	**923**
Tarrer;	
bag	**552**
sack	**552**
Task worker (*coal mine*)	**910**
Tassel hand	**859**
Taster;	
coffee	**863**
tea	**863**
wine	**863**
Taster (*food products mfr.*)	**863**
Tatter (waste)	**990**
Tattooist	**381**
Taxidermist	**699**
Taxonomist	**201**
Tea boy	**953**
Tea lady	**953**
Teacher; *see also notes*	
dancing (private)	**239**
head-	
educational establishments-	
schools-	
nursery	**234**
primary	**234**
secondary	**233**
sixth form college	**233**
special	**235**
music (private)	**239**
sales	**391**
singing (private)	**239**
swimming	**387**
Teacher-	
physical training-	
educational establishments-	
secondary schools	**233**
educational establishments-	
higher and further education-	**231**
polytechnic	**230**
university	**230**
schools-	
nursery	**234**
primary	**234**
secondary	**233**
sixth form college	**233**
special	**235**
kindergarten	**234**
Teamer (*tobacco mfr.*)	**802**
Teamsman (*farming*)	**902**
Teamster-	**889**
farming	**902**
Teaser *see Teazer*	
Teaserman *see Teazer*	
Teazer; shoddy	**811**
Teazer-	
glass mfr.	**823**
metal trades	**830**
textile mfr.	**811**
Teazerman *see Teazer*	
Teazler	**552**
Technical class, Grade I, II (*government*)	**309**

	Code number
Technical grade (*government*)	**309**
Technician;	
I, IIA (*telecoms*)	**523**
IIB (*telecoms*)	**524**
aids; visual	**386**
analytical	**300**
anatomy	**300**
animal (*hospital service*)	**349**
architectural	**303**
assistant (*railway signalling*)	**529**
botanical	**300**
building	**304**
camera;	**517**
video	**386**
cardiological	**346**
cephalographic	**346**
cine	**386**
control; quality	**300**
cytological	**300**
darkroom	**569**
dental	**592**
development	**309**
dispensing	**346**
electrical-	**302**
telecoms	**523**
electronic	**302**
engineering;	**301**
civil	**304**
mechanical	**301**
structural	**304**
factory (*tele-communications*)	**520**
film	**386**
histological	**300**
hospital-	**300**
audiology	**346**
cardiography	**346**
encephalography	**346**
laboratory	**300**
pathology	**300**
hospital theatre	**346**
insemination; artificial	**902**
installation-	**301**
electrical, electronics	**529**
instrument-	**517**
steelworks	**301**
laboratory;	**300**
animal care	**349**
medical	**300**
lens; contact	**591**
lighting; stage	**521**
maxillo-facial	**599**
medical	**346**
mortuary	**699**
motor	**301**
optical	**517**
orthodontic	**599**
orthopaedic	**599**
pharmacy	**346**
photographic	**386**
physics (*hospital service*)	**300**
piano	**593**
planning; town	**303**
plumbing	**532**
process	**309**
psychology	**347**
radar	**529**
radio	**525**
research	**309**
room; control (*gas board*)	**820**
rubber	**300**

	Code number
Technician; *continued*	
scientific	**300**
service; computer	**526**
service-	**309**
office machines	**598**
signal (*railways*)	**529**
sound	**386**
surgical	**346**
telecommunications-	**529**
telecoms	**523**
television	**525**
test	**309**
town planning	**303**
vehicle;	**301**
motor	**540**
video	**525**
wall; cavity	**896**
wireless	**525**
workshop-	**309**
education services	**300**
Technician-	**309**
electrical equipment	**521**
electronic equipment-	**520**
maintenance	**529**
engineering;	**301**
civil	**304**
mechanical	**301**
structural	**304**
flight test	**301**
instrument (*steelworks*)	**301**
laboratory;	**300**
animal care	**349**
motor vehicles	**540**
plastics	**309**
radio, television and video equipment	**525**
surgical, dental appliances	**599**
telegraph, telephone equipment	**523**
textile	**300**
wind tunnel	**301**
accountancy	**399**
armed forces-	
foreign and Commonwealth	**601**
U.K.	**600**
film studio	**386**
hospital service	**300**
telecoms-	**523**
IIB	**524**
Technologist;	**219**
laboratory; medical	**300**
medical	**300**
scientific (*coal mine*)	**219**
Teemer;	
coal-	**930**
above ground (coal mine)	**889**
ladle	**839**
Teemer-	
coke ovens	**889**
steelworks	**839**
Teerer (*textile printing*)	**569**
Tele-ad girl	**792**
Telegraphist	**463**
Telephone worker (male)	**524**
Telephonist;	**462**
shorthand	**459**
Telephonist-clerk	**430**
Telephonist-receptionist	**461**
Telephonist-typist	**452**
Teller; fortune	**699**

	Code number
Teller-	
banking	**411**
printing	**863**
Temperer; wire	**833**
Temperer-	
ceramics mfr.	**829**
metal trades-	**833**
blast furnace	**829**
Templater	**515**
Tenant; house; public	**175**
Tender;	
back *see Tenter; back*	
bar	**622**
diver's	**929**
engine	**893**
furnace (*metal trades*)	**830**
lock	**889**
loom	**550**
Tenon hand	**897**
Tension hand	**891**
Tenter;	
back;	
frame (*textile mfr.*)	**811**
machine; linen	**821**
roving	**811**
back-	
paper mfr.	**821**
paper staining	**821**
textile mfr.-	**552**
textile printing	**569**
wallpaper printing	**569**
boiler	**893**
box-	**811**
silk mfr.	**814**
braid (*silk mfr.*)	**814**
can	**811**
card	**811**
comb	**811**
comber	**811**
conant	**516**
condenser	**811**
cotton	**811**
crane	**886**
cupola	**830**
derby	**811**
devil	**811**
diver's	**929**
double	**811**
draw	**811**
drawing	**811**
engine;	
blowing (*metal mfr.*)	**893**
engine-	**893**
textile mfr.	**811**
engine head	**F811**
fly	**811**
frame;	**811**
cheesing	**813**
clearing	**812**
copping	**813**
doubling	**812**
draw	**811**
flyer	**812**
jacquard	**516**
ring	**812**
twisting	**812**
front	**811**
furnace	**830**
gill	**811**
hard waste	**811**

Code number

	Code number
Tier; *continued*	
battery	**899**
hook;	**859**
cork	**862**
knot (*textile mfr.*)	**553**
ream	**862**
ring	**859**
sausage	**809**
smash	**550**
tackle (fishing tackle)	**859**
warp	**552**
Tierer	**569**
Tier-in (*textile mfr.*)	**814**
Tier-on; warp	**552**
Tier-on-	
fishhook mfr.	**859**
textile mfr.	**814**
Tier-up (*cloth hat mfr.*)	**859**
Tile worker-	
cast concrete products mfr.	**599**
ceramics mfr.	**590**
plastics goods mfr.	**825**
Tiler;	**501**
cork	**506**
floor	**506**
glaze	**506**
range	**506**
roof	**501**
wall	**506**
Tiler and plasterer	**506**
Tilter	**830**
Tilterman	**830**
Timber hand *see Timber man-*	
Timber man-	
building and contracting-	**929**
tunnelling contracting	**898**
coal mine-	**597**
above ground	**929**
electricity board	**929**
forestry	**904**
local government	**929**
mine, not coal	**898**
railways	**929**
timber merchants	**889**
vehicle mfr.	**541**
water board	**929**
Timber worker	**889**
Timberer (*coal mine*)	**597**
Timekeeper	**410**
Timer	**517**
Tin can operative	**841**
Tin man-	
sheet metal working	**533**
tin plate mfr.	**834**
Tin worker; fancy	**841**
Tin worker (*sheet metal working*)	**533**
Tindal; first (*shipping*)	**F880**
Tinker	**533**
Tinner;	
coil	**834**
copper	**834**
fruit	**862**
grease	**834**
wire	**834**
Tinner-	
food canning	**862**
metal trades	**834**
Tinplate worker (*tinplate mfr.*)-	
female	**912**
male	**839**
Tinplater (*tinplate mfr.*)	**834**
Tinsman; drying (*textile mfr.*)	**552**
Tinsmith	**533**
Tinter;	
enamel (*enamel mfr.*)	**829**
paint	**829**
Tinter-	
chemical mfr.	**829**
film processing	**569**
textile mfr.	**552**
Tipman; refuse	**990**
Tipman (*mine, not coal*)	**889**
Tipper;	
ballast	**930**
coal-	
docks	**930**
patent fuel mfr.	**889**
steelworks	**889**
metal	**841**
ore (*steelworks*)	**889**
scrap	**889**
shale	**889**
slag	**889**
umbrella	**553**
Tipper-	
coal mine	**889**
docks	**930**
enamelling	**869**
mine, not coal	**889**
Tippler-	
flax mfr.	**814**
steelworks	**889**
Tipplerman (*coal mine*)	**889**
Tipster	**699**
Tirrer	**990**
Tobacco operative	**802**
Tobacco worker	**802**
Tobacconist	**179**
Toffee man	**809**
Toggler (*leather dressing*)	**810**
Tonger (wire)	**839**
Tongsman; back	**839**
Tongsman-	
rolling mill	**839**
steel hoop mill	**839**
wrought iron mfr.	**839**
Tonguer	**839**
Tool man-	**889**
fustian, velvet mfr.	**552**
Tool worker; edge	**899**
Tooler;	
glass	**590**
stone	**500**
Tooler (*fustian, velvet mfr.*)	**552**
Toother (*saw mfr.*)	**899**
Topman; battery (*coke ovens*)	**919**
Topman-	
bacon curing	**809**
coal mine	**910**
coal gas, coke ovens	**919**
demolition	**896**
pile driving	**885**
Topographer	**262**
Topper;	
beet (*sugar mfr.*)	**809**
jam	**862**
Topper-	
boot polish mfr.	**862**
clothing mfr.	**553**
cord mfr.	**814**
fur dyeing	**869**
Topper- *continued*	
hosiery mfr.	**551**
Topper and tailer	**551**
Totter	**733**
Toucher-up-	
ceramics decorating	**591**
vehicle mfr.	**869**
Toughener (glass)	**823**
Tower (*ceramics mfr.*)	**591**
Towerman-	**820**
paper mfr.	**999**
Townsman	**719**
Toxicologist	**221**
Tracer-	**491**
chocolate mfr.	**809**
embroidery mfr.	**559**
footwear mfr.	**555**
printing	**430**
Tracker-	
ball bearing mfr.	**841**
coal mine	**597**
Trackman-	
mine, not coal	**922**
railways	**922**
tramways	**922**
Trackworker (*vehicle mfr.*)	**851**
Trader;	
credit	**730**
market	**732**
motor	**179**
street	**732**
Trader-	**179**
mobile shop	**731**
Traffic man (*coal mine*)	**889**
Trailer-down (*rolling mill*)	**839**
Trainee *see notes*	
Trainer;	
animal (performing animals)	**384**
dog	**169**
greyhound	**169**
horse	**169**
industrial	**391**
pony	**169**
technology; information	**391**
Trainer (sports)	**387**
Trammer	**889**
Transcriber;	
communications (*government*)	**400**
music	**385**
Transferer;	
hosiery	**551**
lithograph-	
ceramics mfr.	**591**
printing	**560**
Transferer-	**869**
ceramics mfr.	**591**
glass mfr.	**590**
japanning	**869**
tinplate mfr.	**891**
Transformer hand	**850**
Transit worker (*coal mine*)	**889**
Translator; tailor's	**556**
Translator-	**380**
clothing mfr.	**556**
footwear mfr.	**555**
umbrella mfr.	**553**
Transport man (*docks*)	**930**
Transport worker-	**889**
docks	**930**
waterways	**930**

(Tr-Tu)

	Code number
Transporter;	
cable (*coal mine*)	**889**
cattle	**872**
livestock	**872**
supplies (*coal mine*) ...	**889**
Trapper;	
rabbit	**902**
wool	**811**
Trapper-	
forestry	**902**
textile mfr.	**811**
Traveller;	
advertisement	**719**
advertising	**719**
commercial-	**710**
drapers; credit	**730**
services	**719**
drapers; credit	**730**
grocers	**731**
insurance	**719**
van	**731**
Traveller-	**710**
retail trade-	**730**
credit trade	**730**
Traveller-salesman (*credit trade*)	**730**
Trawler hand	**903**
Trawler man	**903**
Treasurer;	
company	**120**
county	**120**
Treasurer-	
educational establishment	**120**
hospital services	**120**
local government	**120**
Treater;	
heat	**833**
timber	**821**
Treatment worker;	
heat (*metal trades*) ...	**833**
water	**892**
Treer	**555**
Trenchman	**929**
Trichologist	**346**
Trimmer;	
asbestos	**829**
bakelite	**825**
ballast	**930**
barge	**930**
blade (*aircraft mfr.*) ...	**843**
block (*rubber goods mfr.*)	**824**
boat	**930**
body; car	**554**
boiler	**990**
boot	**555**
box (*steelworks*)	**843**
bristle	**811**
bullet	**899**
cable	**899**
cake	**800**
car	**554**
card	**822**
carriage	**554**
cloth	**552**
coach	**554**
coal-	**990**
coal mine	**889**
docks	**930**
shipping	**880**
coffin	**559**
disposal; refuse	**990**
Trimmer; *continued*	
face (*coal mine*)	**597**
fancy (*brush mfr.*)... ...	**811**
fibre	**811**
floor board (*coach trimming*)	**554**
heel	**555**
hosiery (*textile finishing*)	**552**
house; boiler	**990**
ice	**990**
lamp (*shipping*)	**880**
leather (*vehicle mfr.*) ...	**554**
lime	**890**
meat	**581**
motor	**554**
needle	**841**
pad; heel	**824**
paper (*printing*)	**822**
plastic(s)	**825**
plate (*metal trades*) ...	**899**
print; photographic	**822**
rubber	**824**
seat; car	**554**
sheet (*paper goods mfr.*)...	**822**
soap	**599**
sponge	**829**
steel	**843**
tooth	**599**
tyre; solid	**824**
upholsterer's	**554**
vegetable	**809**
veneer	**897**
wagon	**889**
wallpaper	**822**
window	**791**
Trimmer-	
artificial teeth mfr. ...	**599**
boiler house	**990**
bookbinding	**562**
broom, brush mfr.... ...	**599**
cement mfr....	**599**
clothing mfr.	**553**
coal gas, coke ovens ...	**919**
coal mine	**889**
docks	**930**
electricity board	**990**
embroidery mfr.	**559**
fishing	**880**
footwear mfr.	**555**
furniture mfr.	**554**
glass and ceramics mfr. ...	**590**
glove mfr.	**559**
hat mfr.	**553**
knitwear mfr.	**559**
leather dressing	**810**
leather goods mfr. ...	**555**
manure mfr.	**919**
metal trades-	**843**
aircraft mfr.	**554**
bolt, nut mfr.	**841**
gold, silver wire mfr. ...	**899**
needle mfr.	**841**
tin box mfr.	**841**
vehicle mfr.	**554**
vehicle body building ...	**554**
mine, not coal	**500**
plastics mfr.	**825**
powder puff mfr.	**599**
power station	**990**
railway workshop	**554**
rubber mfr....	**824**
shipping	**880**
Trimmer- *continued*	
textile mfr.-	**552**
carpet mfr.	**814**
hosiery finishing	**552**
Trimmer and finisher (*hosiery mfr.*)...	**552**
Trolley boy-	
catering	**953**
street trading	**732**
Trolleyman;	**889**
refreshments	**953**
Trombonist	**385**
Trouncer-	**934**
metal trades	**899**
Trouser hand	**556**
Trowel hand (*cement mfr.*)	**820**
Trowel worker	**500**
Truckman-	
blast furnace	**889**
coal mine	**889**
road transport	**872**
Trucker	**887**
Truer; wheel (*cycle mfr.*) ...	**899**
Truer-up; wheel (*cycle mfr.*)	**899**
Trumpet man	**500**
Trusser; fowl	**582**
Trusser (*farming*)	**902**
Tryer (*metal and electrical goods mfr.*)	**860**
Tub hand (*foundry*)	**531**
Tubber (*leather dressing*) ...	**810**
Tube hand	**824**
Tube worker-	
paper	**569**
steel	**839**
Tuber;	
engine (*railways*)	**534**
mule	**812**
wire (*wire mfr.*)	**833**
Tuber-	
boiler mfr.	**534**
locomotive mfr.	**534**
rope mfr.	**814**
textile mfr.	**814**
wire mfr.	**833**
Tucker-	
blanket mfr.	**552**
clothing mfr.	**553**
textile mfr.	**814**
Tufter-	
carpet mfr.	**814**
mattress mfr.	**559**
soft furnishings mfr. ...	**559**
Tug hand	**880**
Tugman	**880**
Tugboatman	**880**
Tumbler (*metal trades*) ...	**842**
Tun room man	**801**
Tuner; head	**F516**
Tuner-	
looms	**516**
musical instruments ...	**593**
television	**525**
vehicles	**540**
textile mfr.	**516**
Tunnel man (ice cream) ...	**809**
Tunnel oven operative ...	**823**
Tunneller-	**509**
coal mine	**597**
Tupper-	
building and contracting...	**929**

	Code number
Tupper- *continued*	
steel mfr.	**839**
Turf worker	**594**
Turn man; bye (*steelworks*)	**912**
Turncock	**892**
Turner;	
asbestos	**599**
axle	**510**
belt (*coal mine*)	**899**
billiard ball	**825**
biscuit	**800**
block; wood	**897**
bobbin-	**897**
metal	**510**
bowl (*tobacco pipe mfr.*)	**897**
brass	**840**
bush; axle	**510**
button	**899**
capstan	**510**
centre boss	**510**
collar	**559**
commutator	**510**
conveyor (*coal mine*)	**899**
copper band	**510**
core	**839**
cork	**599**
counter	**897**
crank	**510**
crankshaft	**510**
cutter	**510**
die	**510**
ebonite	**824**
engine; rose	**518**
engine-	**510**
jewellery mfr.	**518**
engraver's	**510**
frame (*shipbuilding*)	**899**
general	**510**
glove	**559**
graphite	**899**
gun	**510**
hand (*metal trades*)	**510**
handle	**897**
heel (wood heels)	**897**
ivory	**599**
lathe;	
capstan	**510**
centre	**510**
c.n.c.	**510**
n.c.	**510**
turret	**510**
lathe (*metal trades*)	**510**
locomotive	**510**
loom	**510**
machine; pottery	**590**
maintenance	**510**
marine	**510**
mould; fringe	**897**
mould (*glass mfr.*)	**510**
optical	**840**
pipe-	**532**
tobacco pipe mfr.	**897**
pirn	**897**
porcelain; electric	**590**
ring	**510**
rod (fishing rods)	**897**
roll	**510**
roller-	
metal	**510**
rubber	**824**
wood	**897**
Turner; *continued*	
roller- *continued*	
textile machinery mfr.	**510**
rough	**510**
rubber	**824**
sheet-	
galvanized sheet mfr.	**912**
rolling mill	**869**
shell	**840**
shive	**897**
slipper	**555**
spiral	**897**
spool	**897**
textile	**510**
tool	**510**
tool room	**510**
tube; steel	**510**
tyre (metal)	**510**
valve	**510**
vulcanite	**824**
wheel-	
abrasive mfr.	**599**
ceramics mfr.	**919**
metal trades	**510**
wire	**899**
wood	**897**
Turner-	
metal	**510**
plastics	**825**
rubber	**824**
stone	**500**
wood	**897**
asbestos-cement goods mfr.	**599**
brewery	**801**
canvas goods mfr.	**559**
cemented carbide goods mfr.	**899**
ceramics mfr.	**590**
clothing mfr.	**559**
coal mine	**510**
footwear mfr.	**555**
hosiery mfr.	**559**
leather dressing	**810**
metal trades-	**510**
precious metal, plate mfr.	**518**
plastics goods mfr.	**825**
process engraving	**560**
rubber goods mfr.	**824**
stone dressing	**500**
wood products mfr.	**897**
wood-wind instrument mfr.	**897**
Turner and fitter	**516**
Turner-down (*glove mfr.*)	**559**
Turner-engineer	**510**
Turner-fitter	**516**
Turner-in (*steel mfr.*)	**869**
Turner-out (*glass mfr.*)	**590**
Turner-over (*rolling mill*)	**869**
Turner-up (*rolling mill*)	**869**
Turnover man (*coal mine*)	**899**
Turnstile man	**615**
Turret hand	**840**
Tutor;	
midwife	**341**
private	**239**
Tutor-*see also notes*	
educational establishments-	
higher and further	
education-	**231**
polytechnic	**230**
university	**230**
hospital service	**F340**
Twinder	**813**
Twiner (*textile mfr.*)	**812**
Twiner-joiner-minder	**812**
Twist hand;	**550**
plain net	**550**
Twister;	
barley sugar	**809**
cap (*textile mfr.*)	**812**
cop	**812**
cotton	**812**
doubling	**812**
false	**812**
fly	**812**
gut	**829**
hat wire	**841**
machine	**814**
patent-	**812**
textile warping	**552**
ring	**812**
silk	**812**
single	**812**
spinning	**812**
sprig	**812**
tube	**825**
twine	**814**
warp	**552**
wool	**812**
worsted	**812**
yarn	**812**
Twister-	
brush mfr.	**899**
textile mfr.-	**812**
rope, twine mfr.	**814**
Twister and drawer	**552**
Twister-in (*textile mfr.*)	**552**
Twister-on (*textile mfr.*)	**552**
Twister-up (*textile mfr.*)	**552**
Tyer *see Tier*	
Tyer-on *see Tier-on*	
Tyer-up *see Tier-up*	
Tympanist	**385**
Typer (*textile mfr.*)	**569**
Typist;	**452**
copy	**452**
shorthand	**452**
superintendent	**F452**
vari	**560**
Typist-clerk-	**430**
college	**420**
school	**420**
university	**420**
Typographer	**560**
Tyreman (*railways*)	**530**
Tyre worker; rubber (*perambulator mfr.*)	**824**

Code number

W

- W.P.C. ... **610**
- Wadder ... **823**
- Wageman (*coal mine*) ... **910**
- Wagoner-
  - *coal mine-* ... **886**
    - *above ground* ... **889**
  - *farming* ... **902**
- Wagonwayman ... **922**
- Wagonwright ... **541**
- Waistcoat hand ... **556**
- Waiter;
  - commis ... **621**
  - head ... **F621**
  - service; silver ... **621**
  - wine ... **621**
- Waiter- ... **621**
  - *stock exchange* ... **941**
- Waitress ... **621**
- Walker;
  - floor ... **F720**
  - shop ... **F720**
- Waller; dry ... **500**
- Waller- ... **500**
  - *salt mfr.* ... **820**
- Warden;
  - barrack ... **672**
  - camp ... **672**
  - castle ... **672**
  - civil defence ... **619**
  - club; youth ... **371**
  - community centre ... **293**
  - crossing (school) ... **619**
  - dinner (school) ... **659**
  - dog ... **699**
  - game ... **902**
  - garage ... **619**
  - national park ... **615**
  - range ... **699**
  - security ... **615**
  - station ... **672**
  - traffic ... **614**
  - wood ... **F904**
- Warden-
  - detention centre ... **154**
  - sheltered housing ... **293**
  - *caravan site* ... **672**
  - *day nursery* ... **650**
  - *forestry* ... **F904**
  - *government* ... **672**
  - *hostel* ... **173**
  - *institution* ... **M370**
  - *L.R.T.* ... **619**
  - *local government-*
    - *sheltered housing* ... **293**
  - *lodging house* ... **173**
  - *manufacturing* ... **619**
  - *museum, etc.* ... **619**
  - *nurse's home* ... **173**
  - *old people's dwellings* ... **293**
  - *old people's home* ... **M370**
  - *police service* ... **173**
  - *school* ... **619**
  - *social settlement* ... **293**
  - *youth club* ... **371**
- Warder;
  - chief ... **154**
  - river ... **902**
  - yeoman ... **619**

Code number

- Warder-
  - *museum, etc.* ... **619**
  - *prison service* ... **612**
- Wardrobe woman (*theatre*) **699**
- Ware room worker ... **889**
- Warehouse hand; lace ... **889**
- Warehouse hand- ... **441**
  - loading, unloading ... **931**
- Warehouseman;
  - biscuit (*ceramics mfr.*) ... **F591**
  - black ... **823**
  - chief ... **F441**
  - glost (*ceramics mfr.*) ... **F591**
- Warehouseman- ... **441**
  - loading, unloading ... **931**
- Warehouseman-clerk ... **441**
- Warehouseman-packer ... **441**
- Warehouse worker- ... **441**
  - loading, unloading ... **931**
- Warehouser- ... **441**
  - loading, unloading ... **931**
- Warmer; rivet ... **899**
- Warp hand ... **551**
- Warper ... **552**
- Washman (*laundry*) ... **673**
- Washer;
  - back (*textile mfr.*) ... **814**
  - barrel ... **999**
  - basket (*docks*) ... **990**
  - benzol ... **820**
  - blanket (*blanket mfr.*) ... **814**
  - board ... **919**
  - body (*hat mfr.*) ... **814**
  - boiler ... **899**
  - bottle ... **999**
  - box ... **999**
  - brush ... **814**
  - bulb (*lamp mfr.*) ... **999**
  - cab ... **958**
  - cake (*man-made fibre mfr.*) **829**
  - car ... **958**
  - carriage ... **999**
  - cask ... **999**
  - cloth (*textile mfr.*) ... **814**
  - coal (*coal mine*) ... **890**
  - coke ... **829**
  - cullet ... **863**
  - dish (*hotels, catering, etc.*) **952**
  - drum ... **999**
  - feather ... **814**
  - felt ... **814**
  - fruit ... **809**
  - glass- ... **919**
    - *hotels, catering, etc.* ... **952**
  - grit ... **890**
  - hair; horse ... **814**
  - hand (*coal mine*) ... **890**
  - jar ... **999**
  - keg ... **999**
  - lime ... **890**
  - lorry ... **958**
  - meat ... **809**
  - metal ... **919**
  - plate ... **952**
  - pot ... **990**
  - rag (*textile mfr.*) ... **814**
  - rubber ... **829**
  - silk ... **814**
  - skin (*fellmongery*) ... **810**
  - stencil ... **919**
  - sugar beet ... **809**

Code number

- Washer; *continued*
  - tin; biscuit ... **919**
  - van ... **958**
  - wool ... **814**
  - yarn ... **814**
- Washer-
  - *ceramics mfr.* ... **591**
  - *chemical mfr.* ... **820**
  - *fellmongery* ... **810**
  - *fish curing* ... **809**
  - *flour confectionery mfr.* ... **919**
  - *grain milling* ... **809**
  - *hat mfr.* ... **814**
  - *laundry* ... **673**
  - *metal trades* ... **839**
  - *mine, not coal* ... **890**
  - *paper mfr.* ... **821**
  - *photographic processing* ... **569**
  - *tannery* ... **810**
  - *textile mfr.* ... **814**
  - *transport* ... **999**
- Washerman-
  - *grain milling* ... **809**
  - *laundry* ... **673**
  - *paper mfr.* ... **821**
  - *textile mfr.* ... **814**
- Washerwoman ... **673**
- Washer-up (*hotels, catering, etc.*) ... **952**
- Washery hand (*coal mine*) **890**
- Washhouse hand *see Washhouseman-*
- Washhouseman; wool ... **814**
- Washhouseman-
  - *baths* ... **699**
  - *laundry* ... **673**
  - *raw silk processing* ... **814**
- Waste house hand (*textile mfr.*) ... **919**
- Wasteman;
  - assistant (*coal mine*) ... **597**
  - wool ... **919**
- Waste man-
  - *coal mine* ... **597**
  - *textile mfr.* ... **919**
- Waste worker (*coal mine*) ... **597**
- Watchman- ... **615**
  - barge ... **880**
- Watchman-operator (*petroleum distribution*) **889**
- Watcher;
  - calciner ... **829**
  - customs ... **400**
  - furnace ... **830**
  - night ... **615**
  - river ... **902**
  - ship ... **615**
- Watcher-
  - *Customs and Excise* ... **400**
  - *metal mfr.* ... **830**
- Watchmaker and jeweller ... **517**
- Waterman;
  - dock ... **930**
  - furnace; blast ... **999**
- Waterman-
  - *coal gas, coke ovens* ... **919**
  - *coal mine* ... **910**
  - *local government* ... **892**
  - *paper mfr.* ... **821**
  - *sewage disposal* ... **999**
  - *steel mfr.* ... **999**

Occupation	Code number
Waterman- *continued*	
textile mfr.	**552**
water transport	**880**
water works	**892**
Watercress worker	**595**
Waterguard (*Customs and Excise*)	**613**
Wax man	**810**
Waxer;	
block; thread	**824**
cord	**552**
stencil paper	**821**
Waxer-	
battery mfr.	**899**
leather dressing	**810**
paper mfr.	**821**
Weaver;	
asbestos	**550**
cane	**599**
carpet	**550**
cloth; wire	**841**
contour	**550**
hair (*wig mfr.*)	**599**
lace	**550**
loom; pattern	**550**
spring	**899**
withy	**599**
Weaver-	**550**
basketry mfr.	**599**
wig mfr.	**599**
wire goods mfr.	**841**
Weaving operative	**550**
Webber	**557**
Wedger; clay	**590**
Weeder	**902**
Weft man	**441**
Weft room man	**441**
Weighman;	**863**
charge (*foundry*)	**889**
check	**863**
wagon (*coal mine*)	**863**
Weighbridgeman	**863**
Weigher;	
check	**863**
chemical (*rubber goods mfr.*)	**863**
coiler	**814**
colour-	
linoleum mfr.	**863**
textile dyeing	**863**
drug (*rubber goods mfr.*)	**863**
heat	**863**
ingredient (*flour confectionery mfr.*)	**863**
powder (*plastics goods mfr.*)	**863**
pulp	**863**
tobacco	**863**
traffic (*coal mine*)	**863**
weft	**863**
wool (*woollen mfr.*)	**863**
Weigher-	**863**
abrasive wheel mfr.	**863**
carbon goods mfr.	**863**
cemented carbide goods mfr.	**863**
coal mine	**863**
felt hood mfr.	**863**
flour confectionery mfr.	**863**
food products mfr.	**863**
mine, not coal	**863**
textile finishing	**863**
Weigher- *continued*	
wool blending	**863**
Weigher and finisher; coil (*asbestos rope mfr.*)	**814**
Weigher and mixer; colour	**863**
Weigher and mixer (*sugar confectionery mfr.*)	**809**
Weigherman (*card, paste board mfr.*)	**441**
Weighter (golf club heads)	**579**
Weightsman	**310**
Welder;	
arc	**537**
CO_2	**537**
chain	**537**
electric	**537**
fabricator	**537**
maintenance	**537**
plastic	**859**
spot (metal)	**537**
Welder-	**537**
double glazing units	**590**
footwear mfr.	**859**
plastics goods mfr.	**859**
Welder and cutter	**537**
Welfare worker-	**371**
school	**652**
Welter-	
footwear mfr.	**555**
hosiery, knitwear mfr.	**553**
Wetter (*footwear mfr.*)	**555**
Whaler; hosiery	**551**
Wharf man	**930**
Wharfinger	**F930**
Wheelabrator	**844**
Wheelman-	
coal mine	**894**
copper refining	**839**
Wheeler;	
frit	**889**
metal (*metal mfr.*)	**889**
pick (*mine, not coal*)-	
above ground	**889**
below ground	**889**
welt	**555**
wet (*leather dressing*)	**810**
Wheeler-	**889**
footwear mfr.	**555**
leather dressing	**810**
railway rolling stock mfr.	**516**
sheet metal working	**533**
silver and plate mfr.	**899**
vitreous enamelling	**869**
wheelwrights	**579**
Wheeler-in	**889**
Wheelwright	**579**
Wherryman	**880**
Whetter (cutlery)	**899**
Whimseyer	**811**
Whip (*hunting*)	**902**
Whipper; blanket	**553**
Whipper-in (*hunting*)	**902**
White room man	**862**
Whitesmith	**533**
Whiting worker	**820**
Whizzerman (*chemical mfr.*)	**820**
Wholesaler	**179**
Wicker	**859**
Willeyer	**811**
Willier	**811**
Willow worker	**599**
Willower-	
paper mfr.	**811**
textile mfr.	**811**
Willowyer	**811**
Willyer	**811**
Winchman-	**886**
shipping	**F880**
textile mfr.	**552**
Winder;	
armature	**850**
ball; golf	**824**
ball (*textile mfr.*)	**813**
beam	**552**
belt; rubber	**824**
bit (*textile mfr.*)	**813**
bobbin;	
brass	**813**
ring	**813**
bobbin-	
electrical goods mfr.	**850**
textile mfr.	**813**
wire mfr.	**899**
cable	**899**
cage (*coal mine*)	**886**
card	**813**
cheese	**813**
clear	**813**
clock	**699**
cloth (*oil cloth mfr.*)	**814**
coil	**850**
coloured	**813**
cone	**813**
cop	**813**
copper (*cable mfr.*)	**899**
core-	
cable mfr.	**899**
golf ball mfr.	**824**
cotton	**813**
disc; armature	**850**
double (*textile mfr.*)	**813**
doubler (*textile mfr.*)	**813**
doubling	**813**
drum	**813**
dynamo	**850**
electrical	**850**
element	**850**
engine-	
mining	**886**
textile mfr.	**813**
filament	**899**
gas	**552**
hank	**813**
incline	**886**
insulating (*electrical engineering*)	**899**
jute	**813**
machine (*surgical dressing mfr.*)	**814**
mesh	**850**
mohair	**813**
motor; induction	**850**
pin	**813**
pirn	**813**
pit; staple	**886**
rayon	**813**
reel	**813**
ribbon	**814**
ring	**813**
rope; wire	**899**
rotor	**850**
rubber	**813**

	Code number
Winder; *continued*	
silk; raw	**813**
skip (*coal mine*)	**886**
slip	**813**
spiral (*paper tube mfr.*) ...	**569**
spool-	
electrical goods mfr. ...	**850**
textile mfr.	**813**
stator	**850**
tape (*electrical engineering*)	**814**
thread (*textile mfr.*) ...	**813**
towel (*laundry*)	**673**
transformer	**850**
tube-	
paper tube mfr.	**569**
textile mfr.	**813**
turbo	**850**
twist	**813**
wallpaper	**821**
warp	**813**
weft	**813**
weight	**813**
wheel (*lace mfr.*)	**813**
wire	**899**
wool	**813**
yarn	**813**
Winder-	
cable mfr.	**899**
electrical goods mfr. ...	**850**
mining	**886**
paper mfr.	**821**
textile mfr.-	**813**
textile smallwares mfr. ...	**814**
typewriter ribbon mfr. ...	**814**
wallpaper mfr.	**821**
wire goods mfr.	**899**
Winderman-	
coal mine	**886**
paper mfr.	**821**
Wiper;	
bobbin	**814**
cutlery (*cutlery mfr.*) ...	**912**
knife; table (*cutlery mfr.*)	**912**
scissors	**912**
Wiper (*glass mfr.*)	**919**
Wire boy	**590**
Wire hand (*cable mfr.*) ...	**899**
Wireman;	
electrical	**521**
electronic	**850**
indoor	**850**
instrument	**850**
overhead	**524**
radar	**850**
telegraph	**524**
telephone	**524**
Wireman-	**850**
cycle mfr.	**851**
railways	**524**
rediffusion service	**524**
telecoms	**524**
Wireman-assembler	**850**
Wire worker; tungsten ...	**839**
Wire worker-	**899**
cable mfr.	**899**
hop growing	**900**
silver, plate mfr.	**518**
Wirer;	
box	**841**
card (*carpet mfr.*)	**814**
electrical	**521**
Wirer; *continued*	
panel	**850**
tyre	**824**
Wirer-	
artificial flower mfr. ...	**599**
metal trades-	**913**
electrical engineering ...	**521**
electronic apparatus mfr.	**850**
telephone, telegraph apparatus mfr.	**521**
Wirer and paperer	**859**
Wirer and solderer (*radio and television mfr.*) ...	**850**
Wirer-up (*electroplating*) ...	**839**
Wiring hand	**859**
Woodman-	**904**
mine, not coal	**898**
Woodworker-	**579**
aircraft	**570**
Woodsman	**904**
Woolleyer	**811**
Work study man	**364**
Worker;	
line; *see Assembler*	
assembly *see Assembler*	
production *see Assembler*	
piece *see Assembler*	
production *see Assembler*	
Worker-off (*sugar confectionery mfr.*)	**809**
Worker-round (*iron, steelworks*)	**912**
Worker-up (quantity surveying)	**312**
Worksetter	**899**
Wrapper;	
bead (*tyre mfr.*)	**824**
cable	**899**
tube (*rubber goods mfr.*)	**824**
Wrapper-	**862**
cardboard box mfr. ...	**569**
inner tube mfr.	**824**
Wrapper-up	**862**
Wren (*armed forces-U.K.*) ...	**600**
Wrestler	**387**
Wringman	**552**
Wringer (*gun cotton mfr.*) ...	**814**
Wringer-out (*hat mfr.*) ...	**559**
Writer;	
advertisement	**380**
advertisement drop curtain	**507**
card	**507**
copy (*advertising*)	**380**
dial	**869**
glass	**507**
leader	**380**
letter (*sign writing*) ...	**507**
lyric	**380**
news	**380**
poster	**507**
publicity	**380**
reports; senior (*broadcasting*)	**380**
scenario	**380**
script	**380**
shorthand	**452**
sign	**507**
specialist	**380**
technical-	**380**
patents	**399**
ticket	**507**
to the signet	**240**
Writer; *continued*	
to the trade	**507**
Writer-	
self-employed	**380**
authorship	**380**
coach building	**507**
journalism	**380**
Min. of Defence	**400**
newspaper publishing ...	**380**
sign writing	**507**

X

Y

	Code number
Yachtsman	**880**
Yard man; metal (*steelworks*)	**912**
Yard man-	**990**
coal mine	**863**
farming	**900**
livery stable	**902**
vulcanised fibre board mfr.	**889**
Yard worker;	**990**
lime	**810**
tan	**810**
Yardage hand	**569**
Yardsman-	
blast furnace	**884**
dairy	**919**
farming	**900**
Yarn man	**814**
Yeast man	**809**
Youth worker	**371**

Z

	Code number
Zinc worker	**533**
Zoologist	**201**

Printed in the United Kingdom for HMSO
Dd 292632, C110, 3/90.